THE CAMBRIDGE COMPANION TO
CARNAP

Rudolf Carnap (1891–1970) is increasingly regarded as one of the most important philosophers of the twentieth century. He was one of the leading figures of the logical empiricist movement associated with the Vienna Circle and a central figure in the analytic tradition more generally. He made major contributions to philosophy of science and philosophy of logic, and, perhaps most importantly, to our understanding of the nature of philosophy as a discipline. In this volume a team of contributors explores the major themes of his philosophy and discusses his relationship with the Vienna Circle and with philosophers such as Frege, Husserl, Russell, and Quine. New readers will find this the most convenient and accessible guide to Carnap currently available. Advanced students and specialists will find a conspectus of recent developments in the interpretation of Carnap.

MICHAEL FRIEDMAN is Frederick P. Rehmus Family Professor of Humanities in the Department of Philosophy, Stanford University. He is editor and translator of *Kant: Metaphysical Foundations of Natural Science* (2004).

RICHARD CREATH is a Professor in the Department of Philosophy and also in the School of Life Sciences, Arizona State University. He is co-editor with Jane Maienschein of *Biology and Epistemology* (2000).

HEIDEGGER 2nd edition *Edited by* CHARLES GUIGNON
HOBBES *Edited by* TOM SORELL
HUME *Edited by* DAVID FATE NORTON
HUSSERL *Edited by* BARRY SMITH *and* DAVID
  WOODRUFF SMITH
WILLIAM JAMES *Edited by* RUTH ANNA PUTNAM
KANT *Edited by* PAUL GUYER
KANT AND MODERN PHILOSOPHY *Edited by*
  PAUL GUYER
KEYNES ROGER E. BACKHOUSE *and* BRADLEY W. BATEMAN
KIERKEGAARD *Edited by* ALASTAIR HANNAY *and*
  GORDON MARINO
LEIBNIZ *Edited by* NICHOLAS JOLLEY
LEVINAS *Edited by* SIMON CRITCHLEY *and* ROBERT
  BERNASCONI
LOCKE *Edited by* VERE CHAPPELL
MAIMONIDES *Edited by* KENNETH SEESKIN
MALEBRANCHE *Edited by* STEVEN NADLER
MARX *Edited by* TERRELL CARVER
MEDIEVAL JEWISH PHILOSOPHY *Edited by*
  DANIEL H. FRANK *and* OLIVER LEAMAN
MEDIEVAL PHILOSOPHY *Edited by* A. S. MCGRADE
MERLEAU-PONTY *Edited by* TAYLOR CARMAN *and*
  MARK B. N. HANSEN
MILL *Edited by* JOHN SKORUPSKI
MONTAIGNE *Edited by* ULLRICH LANGER
NEWTON *Edited by* I. BERNARD COHEN *and* GEORGE E.
  SMITH
NIETZSCHE *Edited by* BERND MAGNUS *and* KATHLEEN
  HIGGINS
OCKHAM *Edited by* PAUL VINCENT SPADE
PASCAL *Edited by* NICHOLAS HAMMOND
PEIRCE *Edited by* CHERYL MISAK
PLATO *Edited by* RICHARD KRAUT
PLOTINUS *Edited by* LLOYD P. GERSON
QUINE *Edited by* ROGER F. GIBSON
RAWLS *Edited by* SAMUEL FREEMAN
THOMAS REID *Edited by* TERENCE CUNEO *and* RENÉ
  VAN WOUDENBERG

The Cambridge Companion to
CARNAP

Edited by

Michael Friedman
Stanford University

and

Richard Creath
Arizona State University

CAMBRIDGE
UNIVERSITY PRESS

CAMBRIDGE UNIVERSITY PRESS
Cambridge, New York, Melbourne, Madrid, Cape Town, Singapore, São Paulo, Delhi

Cambridge University Press
The Edinburgh Building, Cambridge CB2 8RU, UK

Published in the United States of America by Cambridge University Press, New York

www.cambridge.org
Information on this title: www.cambridge.org/9780521549455

First published 2007

Printed in the United Kingdom at the University Press, Cambridge

A catalogue record for this publication is available from the British Library

ISBN 978-0-521-84015-6 hardback
ISBN 978-0-521-54945-5 paperback

CONTENTS

CONTRIBUTORS

STEVE AWODEY is Associate Professor in the Department of Philosophy, Carnegie-Mellon University. His research interests include category theory and the history of logic and analytic philosophy, and he recently co-edited (with E. Reck) *Frege's Lectures on Logic* and (with C. Klein) *Carnap Brought Home*.

ANDRE W. CARUS is the author of numerous papers on Carnap as well as the forthcoming book *Carnap in Twentieth-Century Thought: Explication as Enlightenment* (Cambridge University Press).

RICHARD CREATH is Professor in the Department of Philosophy and in the School of Life Sciences and Director, Program in the History and Philosophy of Science, at Arizona State University. He is the author of numerous articles on Carnap and Quine and the editor of *Dera Carnap, Dear Van* as well as general editor of the forthcoming *Collected Works of Rudolf Carnap*.

WILLIAM DEMOPOULOS is Professor in the Department of Logic and Philosophy of Science, University of California at Irvine. His research interests center on the connection between developments in logic on one hand and general philosophy and philosophy of science on the other.

MICHAEL FRIEDMAN is Frederick P. Rehmus Family Professor of Humanities and Professor of Philosophy at Stanford University. His books include volumes on space-time physics, Kant, logical positivism, and most recently *Dynamics of Reason*.

GOTTFRIED GABRIEL is Professor in the Institüt für Philosophie at the Friedrich-Schiller-Universität, Jena. He is the author of many

ix

works on Frege, Carnap, and in logic, philosophy of science and aesthetics.

THOMAS MORMANN is Professor in the Department of Logic and Philosophy of Science at the University of the Basque Country, Donostia-San Sebastian, Spain. His many publicatioins include books on Carnap and structural invariance in science.

CHRISTOPHER PINCOCK is Assistant Professor of Philosophy at Purdue University. He is the author of numerous papers on Russell and Carnap as well as in philosophy of mathematics and philosophy of science.

ERICH H. RECK is Associate Professor of Philosophy, University of California at Riverside. He works in the areas of early analytic philosophy, philosophy of mathematics, and philosophy of logic and has edited or co-edited three books, one on early analytic philosophy, another (with S. Awodey) *Frege's Lectures on Logic*, and most recently (with M. Beaney) *Gottlob: Critical Assessments of Leading Philosophers*, 4 vols.

ALAN W. RICHARDSON is Asssociate Professor in Department of Philosophy at the University of British Columbia. He is the author of *Carnap's Construction of the World* and the co-editor of three volumes on logical empiricism, most recently (with T. Uebel) *The Cambridge Companion to Logical Empiricism*.

THOMAS RICKETTS is Professor of Philosophy at the University of Pittsburgh. He is the author of numerous articles on the development of analytic philosophy, especially Frege, Russell, Wittgenstein, Carnap, and Quine.

THOMAS RYCKMAN is Lecturer in the Philosophy Department, Stanford University. He is the author of many works in philosophy of science and most recently of *The Reign of Relativity: Philosophy in Physics, 1915–1925*.

THOMAS UEBEL is Professor and Head of Philosophy, University of Manchester. His research interests include general epistemology, philosophy of science, and the history of analytic philosophy. Besides many publications in these areas he is the author of *Overcoming*

Logical Positivism from Within and (with N. Cartwright *et al.*) *Otto Neurath: Philosophy Between Science and Politics.*

SANDY ZABELL is Professor of Statistics and Mathematics, Northwestern University. His research interests revolve around mathematical probability and Bayesian statistics and their history, philosophical foundations, and legal applications. His publications include *Symmetry and its Discontents.*

EDITORS' NOTE

ACKNOWLEDGMENTS

We would like to thank our editor at Cambridge University Press, Hilary Gaskin, whose encouragement and patience made this book possible. Thanks also to Mia McNulty, who helped us with the technical aspects of editing and who put in hundreds of hours on the combined bibliography. And as always our thanks in more ways than we can adequately express to Graciela De Pierris and Jane Maienschein.

NOTE ON REFERENCES

In the text we have given citations by author, date, and page (and/or section) numbers. Sometimes two dates are given, separated by slashes. The first date, including a letter if any, identifies a unique entry in the combined bibliography. The second date would then refer to a later edition given within that same bibliographic entry. Where one set of page numbers is given but two dates, the page numbers refer to the later edition in the citation. In a few cases page numbers for both editions are given, and those are also separated by slashes and refer to the corresponding editions. Section numbers, of course, are assumed not to change among editions. Thus, for example, "(Carnap, 1934c/1937, 245–246/317–319)" refers both to pages 245–246 of Carnap's (1934c) *LogischeSyntax der Sprache* and pages 317–319 of its 1937 English translation, *The Logical Syntax of Language*.

PREFACE: CARNAP'S POSTHUMOUS CAREER

RICHARD CREATH

When Carnap died in 1970 he was widely honored both as a philosopher of historic importance and as a human being. But even those who so honored him thought that his most characteristic ideas and the major works in which he had expressed them were either seriously flawed or just plain wrong. Worse, his work no longer led the ongoing development of the field. Philosophy had moved on.

As you will see in the following chapters the current picture of Carnap is very different. His views now seem subtler and more defensible. And even if contemporary philosophers still find much to disagree with, they also find that he has much to say that is relevant and useful in their ongoing struggle with philosophic issues. Here I consider the question of how we got from there to here, that is, from the picture of Carnap that was widespread in 1970 to the image that emerges in this volume.

The central answer, of course, is that the change resulted from the work of a great many philosophers and historians on both sides of the Atlantic. Much of this has been done by the authors of the chapters in this volume, and the extensive bibliography is a useful guide to even more. In a brief preface such as this, though, it is not really possible to summarize such a substantial body of work. Besides, you have before you splendid examples of that research, and it would be better to go directly to that. So here I concentrate on developments that have facilitated that research rather than the research itself. And the only persons I will mention by name are no longer living. We have come a long way since 1970, and to see how far we need to see more clearly how things looked then.

The rejection of Carnap's ideas in the period immediately after his death ran across the full gamut of his work. Due to the influential

xiii

work of W. V. Quine and Nelson Goodman, the *Aufbau* was viewed as primarily aiming ontologically to reduce all scientific objects to sense data, a reduction that was even in principle doomed to fail. The idea of trying to distinguish claims that have genuine empirical content by means of a verificationist or empiricist criterion of significance was thought to be a complete dead end. In this Popper's misrepresentations of Carnap played a significant role. *The Logical Syntax of Language* was thought mainly to argue that semantics (and pragmatics) were neither necessary nor philosophically useful. Its central "Principle of Tolerance" had been forgotten. Carnap's analytic/synthetic distinction was recognized as one of the main pillars of his philosophy, but it was thought that Quine had shown the distinction to be wholly untenable. In probability theory Carnap had convinced many that an epistemic notion was needed in addition to a notion of chance. But even those who sided with Carnap on that issue viewed his idea that there could be objective, though language relative, prior probabilities as misguided. So his views on probability were largely superceded by what is variously called subjectivism or personal probability theories. Finally, in the aftermath of Thomas Kuhn's enormously successful *The Structure of Scientific Revolutions* Carnap was thought to have believed erroneously that our judgments at the observational level are certain and theory independent, that the conception of scientific rationality we use is eternal and unchanging, and that theoretical objects such as atoms and electrons are to be rejected in favor of observable entities, whether those are the sturdy objects of common sense or some sort of phenomenal entities.

Philosophy, of course, is a heterogeneous enterprise. If the preceding describes the prevailing opinion, there were holdouts against it. Of course, many of these holdouts encouraged the systematic reconsideration that has ensued. In any case, the portrait that would be drawn of Carnap now, as one can see from the following pages, is very different and much more nuanced. On some issues we now believe that Carnap's opinions were not what we had earlier thought that they were. On others our evaluation of them or of the arguments against them has changed. And on these and other issues we now see that various aspects of Carnap's work provide useful suggestions for how to approach contemporary issues. That there should be changes in our understanding and evaluation of Carnap is not surprising; after all, philosophy moves on. But the depth and breadth of the transformation here could scarcely have been anticipated in 1970.

In the 1970s two developments were well under way that would encourage researchers to look at Carnap again from a new perspective. One of these was the slow emergence of a sub-field of philosophy devoted to the historical study of twentieth-century analytic philosophy. This arose independently in a number of centers, but one of the most important formed around Burton Dreben at Harvard. As a teacher and colleague he wielded an influence far beyond his written publications. He convinced many younger scholars to take the history of such areas as logic, philosophy of mathematics, and philosophy of language over the last hundred years as philosophically important and fruitful areas for research. Before Dreben many philosophers sharply distinguished between doing philosophy and doing the history of philosophy, so a genuinely philosophic interest in historical study was rare. And a community of scholars amounting to a sub-discipline interested in the history of analytic philosophy was non-existent. Again, Harvard was not the only place that such historical interests were stirring, but it was perhaps the one most directly focused on twentieth-century analytic philosophy.

The second development was the creation of important archives on both sides of the Atlantic. Wittgenstein's papers had long been widely available even in microfilm form. In 1968 The Bertrand Russell Archive was started at McMaster University in Canada. Russell was still alive and sold to McMaster the vast bulk of his manuscripts and other memorabilia. The collection was significantly added to thereafter. In 1978 another archival collection, The Vienna Circle Foundation, was established to house the papers of Moritz Schlick and Otto Neurath. Now housed at the Rijksarchief in Noord-Holland (Haarlem), the archive was created by Henk L. Mulder, who had earlier acquired and conserved these papers.

From the point of view of reexamining Carnap, the most important archive is the Rudolf Carnap Collection, founded in 1974 at the University of Pittsburgh. It includes Carnap's personal library, much of it heavily annotated, some 10,000 letters, and masses of notes, manuscripts, and other materials. A large body of photographs and other personal material has since been added to the collection. Moreover, the Carnap Collection formed the nucleus of a larger archive, the Archives of Scientific Philosophy, that now holds the papers of

Bruno de Finetti, Carl Hempel, Richard Jeffrey, Frank Ramsay, Hans Reichenbach, Wilfrid Sellars, and others. This magnificent collection and others like it around the world (including a smaller body of Carnap material at UCLA), together with the published record, have made real historical scholarship possible.

By the late 1980s the rise in historical interest and the staggering body of new archival material was producing a steady stream of new research results appearing in mainstream journals, for example, in a special issue of *Nous* (1987) edited by Alberto Coffa. 1991, however, was a landmark year. It was the centennial of the birth of both Rudolf Carnap and Hans Reichenbach. There was a special issue of *Erkenntnis* for the two men and two special issues of *Synthese*, one for each. There were major international conferences in Los Angeles, Boston, and Konstanz, Germany, as well as many special sessions at philosophical meetings around the world.

1991 also saw the founding of the Institute Vienna Circle. The Institute has been extremely active in hosting conferences, running seminars, classes, and a summer school, and vigorously supporting research and publication. It has been and remains one of the primary European venues to have both crystallized and encouraged the revival of interest in the Circle, including of course Carnap.

Finally, in this banner year, Cambridge University Press brought out Alberto Coffa's long-awaited *The Semantic Tradition from Kant to Carnap: To the Vienna Station*. Coffa had died at the end of 1984 just after completing a penultimate draft. One reviewer called the book ". . . the first comprehensive treatment of the development of logical positivism that is rigorous and sophisticated from both a historical and technical point of view." The book has provoked much vigorous discussion in a fruitful way, and it has enabled many of its readers to see that serious philosophy and careful history can not only coexist in the same work, but reinforce one another.

The stream of papers, books, conferences, and seminars has only grown since 1991. A new sub-field of philosophy, twentieth-century analytic history, has now been recognized. The study of Carnap is a significant part of that sub-field and is strengthened by an increasingly sophisticated understanding of Carnap's contemporaries. Indeed, as of this writing, *The Cambridge Companion to Logical Empiricism* is about to appear.

Among the most important developments currently under way is the republication by Open Court Publishing Company of all the work that Carnap published in his lifetime into a *Collected Works of Rudolf Carnap*. All of the work will appear in English and also in the original language if that is different. This is a massive undertaking, comprising some thirteen volumes, and it will take well over a decade to complete. The first volumes of the *Collected Works* should appear in 2007 or 2008. On its completion the set will provide ready access to all of Carnap's published writings, and the introductory essays will make his ideas accessible to a contemporary audience.

The book you now hold, *The Cambridge Companion to Carnap*, is itself a major step in the continuing reappraisal of Carnap's legacy. As Michael Friedman's introduction shows, Carnap's philosophic interests were broad, deep, and even revolutionary. As the chapters that follow demonstrate, Carnap's ideas continue to guide illuminating research. Philosophy still moves on – now enriched and inspired by a fuller appreciation of Carnap's legacy.

Introduction: Carnap's revolution in philosophy

Rudolf Carnap (1891–1970) was a giant of twentieth-century philosophy. He was one of the leading figures of the logical empiricist movement associated with the Vienna Circle and one of the leaders of the analytic tradition more generally. In particular, the defining debates of this tradition involved, at its inception, Gottlob Frege, Bertrand Russell, Carnap, and Ludwig Wittgenstein, and, in a later phase, Carnap and Willard Van Orman Quine. Moreover, Carnap was engaged in significant philosophical interaction with some of the leaders of the continental tradition, including Edmund Husserl and Martin Heidegger. Finally, Carnap was a central participant in key episodes in the development of modern logic associated with Kurt Gödel and Alfred Tarski; and, after emigrating to the United States, he also interacted with important American pragmatist philosophers such as Charles Morris and John Dewey. He made major contributions to philosophy of science and philosophy of logic, and, perhaps most importantly, to our understanding of the nature of philosophy as a discipline. It is impossible adequately to understand twentieth-century philosophy without appreciating Carnap's central position within it.

Yet the general understanding of Carnap's place within twentieth-century philosophy among philosophers on both sides of the Atlantic is at present severely limited, and for two interrelated reasons. On the one hand, Carnap tends to be exclusively identified with logical empiricism, and this movement, in turn, tends to be exclusively identified with a rather naïve version of empiricist foundationalism or phenomenalistic reductionism, according to which all (synthetic) knowledge of the world is to rest on a certain basis of immediately given sensory experience. Logical empiricism, understood in this way, is then widely viewed as a failed philosophical project – whose failure, moreover, is conclusively documented in Carnap's own failure to execute it in precise logical terms in *Der logische Aufbau der Welt* (the logical structure of the world) (1928). On the other hand, Quine's celebrated paper "Two Dogmas of Empiricism" (1951) is widely thought to have definitively demolished the "first dogma" of logical empiricism – that there is a clear and sharp distinction between formal or analytic truth (in logic and mathematics), on the one side, and factual or synthetic truth (in empirical natural science), on the other. (The "second dogma" is phenomenalistic reductionism, and Quine famously claims that it and the first dogma are "at root identical.") Since the analytic/synthetic distinction becomes absolutely central to Carnap's philosophy from the period of *Logical Syntax of Language* (1934c/1937) onwards, there is a widespread tendency to conclude that there is now nothing left in Carnap's philosophy worth considering.

Beginning in the 1970s and early 1980s, as Richard Creath explains in his Preface, increasing numbers of scholars on both sides of the Atlantic have made groundbreaking contributions towards reevaluating Carnap's central philosophical significance. It has emerged that the widespread conception of Carnap's philosophy just presented involves very serious misunderstandings and, in the end, amounts to little more than a caricature. Indeed, this is not especially surprising when we appreciate that the (mis-)conception in question derives from polemical discussions of logical empiricism – both for and against – rather than serious scholarly investigations of Carnap's own work in its historical and philosophical context. In particular, the standard picture of the logical empiricist movement and Carnap's place within it derives, in large part, from A. J. Ayer's militantly pro-logical-empiricist polemic in *Language, Truth and Logic* (1936), written after visiting the leading members of the Circle in Vienna; and the standard picture of the significance and fate of Carnap's analytic/synthetic distinction derives, as just noted, from Quine's polemical attack in 1951 – where Quine, after having studied with Carnap in Europe in the 1930s, now stakes out a new philosophical direction for himself. Of course it does not follow that there is no truth at all in either polemically motivated picture, nor that we have nothing important to learn from Ayer's militant advocacy or Quine's critical attack. But it now appears, in light of the new research in question, that we have ample reason to pursue a more balanced and dispassionate understanding of Carnap's place within twentieth-century philosophy and its history.

The present volume aims to make the fruits of the recent renaissance in Carnap scholarship as widely available as possible. Some of the contributors discuss previously unknown or under-appreciated aspects of Carnap's work, such as his connections with the phenomenological tradition originating with Husserl (Thomas Ryckman), his interactions with Gödel and Tarski during the late 1920s and early 1930s, when our modern understanding of mathematical logic first crystallized (Erich Reck), or his relationship with the American pragmatist tradition of Morris and Dewey (Alan Richardson). But we are primarily concerned, in general, to expose the originality and depth of Carnap's overall position, which amounts to an entirely novel philosophical perspective on empiricism and the critique of metaphysics, on logicism and the analytic/synthetic distinction, on the role of logic within philosophy as a discipline, and on the relationship between philosophy and the empirical sciences. The revolutionary character of Carnap's reconfiguration of these themes is completely obscured in the picture promulgated by Ayer, Quine, and many others, where Carnap, and the Vienna Circle more generally, are characteristically assimilated to well-worn versions of epistemological foundationalism associated with British empiricism. Carnap's position, it turns out, has virtually nothing to do with such views, and everything to do, instead, with a radically voluntaristic philosophy of what we might call logical pragmatism (see A. W. Carus's and Alan Richardson's contributions). Hence, even when more familiar topics are discussed here, such as Carnap's relationships with Frege (Gottfried Gabriel) and Russell (Christopher Pincock), his work in semantics and intensional logic (Steve Awodey), his contributions to philosophy of science (William Demopoulos) and probability and induction (S. L. Zabell), or his place within the Vienna Circle (Thomas Uebel), it is always with an eye to the deeply revolutionary character of his overall philosophical position.

CARNAP AND MODERN LOGIC

The leading theme of Carnap's philosophy, throughout his career, is the overriding philosophical importance of the modern mathematical logic created by Frege, with whom Carnap had studied at the University of Jena, and by Russell, from whom he had learned both the theory of logical types developed in *Principia Mathematica* and the great value to be gained by the application of modern logic to the problems of philosophy. Moreover, Carnap imbibed from them a logicist philosophy of mathematics – the view that, as Carnap (1963a, 12) puts it, "knowledge in mathematics is analytic in the general sense that it has essentially the same nature as knowledge in logic." For Carnap, however, the significance of this view is not that we can thereby justify or explain mathematical knowledge on the basis of another type of knowledge – logical knowledge – presumed to be antecedently (or better) understood, but rather that logic and mathematics together play a distinctively formal or inferential role in framing our empirical knowledge:

It is the task of logic and mathematics within the total system of knowledge to supply the forms of concepts, statements, and inferences, forms which are then applicable everywhere, hence also to non-logical knowledge. It follows from these considerations that the nature of logic and mathematics can be clearly understood only if close attention is given to their applications in non-logical fields, especially in empirical science . . . This point of view is an important factor in the motivation for some of my philosophical positions, for example, for the choice of forms of languages, for my emphasis on the fundamental distinction between logical and non-logical knowledge. (1963a, 12–13)

In particular, Carnap's emphasis on the importance of the analytic/synthetic distinction is in no way derived from a foundationalist epistemological program for pure logic and mathematics aiming to explain how logical and mathematical certainty is possible by appealing to truth-by-convention or truth-in-virtue-of-meaning. The point is rather that logic and mathematics, in their extraordinarily fruitful and indeed indispensable applications to empirical science, are thereby seen as purely formal, empty, and devoid of factual content.

Carnap's first book-length discussion of the application of mathematical logic to the problems of philosophy, explicitly following Russell's example in *Our Knowledge of the External World* (1914a), was, of course, *Der logische Aufbau der Welt* (1928). Carnap here develops a "constitutional system" in which all concepts of empirical science are defined or "constituted" in a step-wise progression of logical constructions extending up through the hierarchy of logical types, whose basis (individuals or objects of lowest type) is given by the subjective "elementary experiences" of a single cognitive subject. This project, however, is no more of a contribution to traditional foundationalist epistemology (here an empiricist foundationalism directed at our empirical knowledge) than is Carnap's logicist philosophy of logic and mathematics. The point is rather to depict, in the most general possible terms, the way in which the "forms of concepts" supplied by modern mathematical logic can in fact succeed in structuring our empirical knowledge. Carnap, in his student days at Jena, had also imbibed a healthy dose of Kantian and neo-Kantian philosophy, according to which empirical knowledge is itself only possible in virtue of a priori forms and principles antecedently supplied by thought. Here, in the *Aufbau*, Carnap defends an empiricist version of this conception, in so far as such (still indispensable) formal structuring is now seen – in virtue of modern mathematical logic (understood in a logicist context) – as *analytic* rather than *synthetic* a priori.

Carnap takes the subjective basis in "elementary experiences" he starts with to be entirely uncontroversial, in the sense that all current "epistemological tendencies" will agree with the order of "epistemic primacy" he depicts. In particular, Carnap does not assume that our knowledge of "elementary experiences" is any more certain than anything else, but merely that our actual empirical knowledge is in fact based, in the end, on precisely such subjective experiences. The point of depicting this order of logical construction rather than some other, therefore, is not so much to give a traditional empiricist justification for our knowledge of the external world as to exhibit what Carnap calls the "neutral basis" common to *all* epistemological views – whether empiricist, transcendental idealist, realist, or subjective idealist. Modern logic, now applied to the form of our empirical knowledge in general, allows us precisely and rigorously to dissolve the idle metaphysical disputes between such views (especially the dispute between realism and idealism) and, therefore, to import "the rigorous and responsible basic attitude of scientific researchers" into philosophy (see my own contribution).

Although the *Aufbau* was written largely in the years 1922–25, before Carnap moved to Vienna, it appeared in 1928 during the heyday of the Vienna Circle. In the meantime, however, modern mathematical logic had become embroiled in considerable turmoil due to a "foundations crisis" precipitated by the failure to achieve general agreement on a solution to the serious logical contradictions or paradoxes afflicting both Frege's original system presented in his *Basic Laws of Arithmetic* (1893/1903) and Cantorian set theory. (Paradigmatic, of course, was Russell's famous paradox of the "class of all classes that are not members of themselves," which cannot, on pain of contradiction, be either a member or a non-member of itself.) The theory of types of *Principia Mathematica* (on which Carnap had depended in the *Aufbau*) was supposed to provide a solution, but this turned out to require controversial axioms (such the axioms of infinity, reducibility, and choice) in order to recapture the mathematical laws of arithmetic (and analysis) Frege had derived. As a result, three opposing schools in the foundations of mathematics were articulated in the 1920s: logicism attempted to preserve the original Frege–Russell view; intuitionism, represented especially by L. E. J. Brouwer, developed a radical challenge to classical mathematics and logic based on a denial of the law of excluded middle applied to elements of infinite collections (like the natural numbers); formalism, represented by David Hilbert, then attempted to save classical mathematics and logic from Brouwer's challenge by developing a formal proof-theoretic consistency proof (in which the terms and sentences of classical logic and mathematics are now viewed as purely formal sequences of uninterpreted symbols) using only the more limited ("finitist") logico-mathematical methods sanctioned by Brouwer.

In the late 1920s and early 1930s, immediately after the publication of the *Aufbau*, Carnap, the Vienna Circle, and the whole brave new world of "scientific philosophy" became embroiled in this controversy as well. From the point of view of modern mathematical logic itself, the upshot was our now dominant view of the subject, which is due, in large part, to the fundamental results attained by Gödel and Tarski in the 1930s: Gödel's completeness theorem for first-order logic in 1930, his famous incompleteness theorems for arithmetic (and thus for higher-order logical systems, like *Principia Mathematica*, which contain arithmetic) in 1931, and Tarski's celebrated work on the semantical conception of truth in 1931–36 (which, in turn, led to the later development of contemporary model theory). It follows from Gödel's results, in particular, that Hilbert's proof-theoretic program for defending the consistency of classical logic and mathematics (sufficient to include arithmetic) cannot in fact be achieved (at least in Hilbert's original form), and, more generally, that no axiomatic (deductive) system for logic and mathematics (again sufficient to include arithmetic) can contain all the logico-mathematical truths – a result which severely challenges classical logicism as well, in so far as it had envisioned a single logical (deductive) system containing *all* of mathematics.

It has long been clear that Carnap was one of the very first philosophers to understand and appreciate these groundbreaking results. In particular, he interacted extensively with both Gödel and Tarski during the period in question, and he immediately put their results to use in the further development of his own philosophical position. It is well known, for example, that Gödel's results figure centrally in *Logical Syntax of Language* (1934c/1937), and that Tarski's work on the concept of truth provides the basis for Carnap's succeeding semantical period, beginning in the mid to late 1930s and extending throughout the 1940s and beyond. One of the most striking discoveries of recent scholarship, however, is that Carnap was not only a competent (and very early) apologist for and expositor of these results, but his own logical research in the late 1920s provided an important part of their background and immediate motivation (see Erich Reck's contribution). Carnap was then engaged in a systematic "investigation into general axiomatics," whose aim was to disentangle various concepts of consistency, completeness, and what we now call categoricity for axiomatic systems in general – and, on this basis, to prove general theorems about the relationships among these concepts. Although this work was never published (since it contained technical flaws and inadequacies which were later clarified in the work of Gödel and Tarski), it was then at the cutting edge of research into what we now call metamathematics, and it provided a crucial part of the background, in particular, for Gödel's own work in the early 1930s.

Logical Syntax was Carnap's philosophical response to this very complex situation in the evolving foundations of logic and mathematics, and, at the same time, the very first formulation of his mature philosophical position. The key innovation is a radically new approach to the philosophy of logic and mathematics based on what

Carnap calls the Principle of Tolerance (see Thomas Ricketts's contribution). There is no such thing as the unique, "correct" formulation of logic and mathematics, and there is no uniquely correct answer, in particular, to the dispute among the three foundational schools. Intuitionism is right to claim that we can coherently develop a formal system or calculus for logic and mathematics in which the law of excluded middle is no longer universally valid, and such a system, moreover, is less likely to be inconsistent (paradoxical) than the (logically stronger) classical system. Formalism is right to claim that we can fruitfully view logic and mathematics as purely syntactic formal systems and, more generally, that the metamathematical method, in which we sharply distinguish between the object-language or system under investigation and the meta-language in which our investigation is carried out, is indispensable for a rigorous formulation of logic. And logicism is right to claim, finally, that the best way to appreciate the distinctive character of logic and mathematics is within a formal system or calculus for the total language of empirical science which makes it clear, in particular, that, as Carnap (1963a, 12) puts it (see above), "knowledge in mathematics is analytic in the general sense that it has essentially the same nature as knowledge in logic." Now, in *Logical Syntax*, Carnap articulates this idea in terms of a clear and sharp distinction, within any such formal language, between the contentful terms of the empirical sciences ("descriptive terms") and the contentless terms of logic and mathematics ("logical terms").

The Principle of Tolerance, formulated against the background of the recent metamathematical results of Gödel and Tarski (which, as we now know, were themselves inspired, in part, by Carnap's own earlier proto-metamathematical research), thus gives new meaning and significance to Carnap's non-traditional understanding of logicism. For the point of viewing the terms of logic and mathematics as factually empty – and the propositions of logic and mathematics as therefore analytic – is now seen to lie precisely in our *freedom to choose* which system of logic and mathematics among the infinite number of possible such systems best serves the formal deductive needs of empirical science. The choice between classical logic and mathematics and intuitionism, for example, turns on the circumstance that classical mathematics is much easier to apply (in developing derivations) than intuitionist or constructive mathematics, while the latter, being logically weaker, is much less likely to result in contradiction. The choice between the two systems, from Carnap's new point of view, is therefore purely practical or pragmatic, and it should thus be sharply separated, in particular, from traditional metaphysical disputes about what mathematical entities "really are" (independent "Platonic" objects or mental constructions, for example) or which such entities "really exist" (for example, only natural numbers or also real numbers, that is, arbitrary sets of natural numbers). Carnap's aim, once again, is to use the new tools of modern mathematical logic (here the new tools of metamathematics) definitively to dissolve all such metaphysical disputes and to replace them, instead, with the much more rigorous, fruitful, and constructive project of language planning, language engineering. In this project, which Carnap now calls *Wissenschaftslogik* (the logic of science), our task is to develop and investigate a variety of formal deductive structures for application in the empirical sciences, where the only criteria for choosing one such structure over another are then purely practical or pragmatic; and it is *Wissenschaftslogik*, Carnap (1934c/1937, §72) explains, which now "takes the place of the inextricable tangle of problems known as philosophy."

CARNAP AND QUINE

The final paragraph of the last section of Quine's "Two Dogmas of Empiricism" (1951, §6, "Empiricism without the Dogmas") explicitly acknowledges that Carnap views the choice between different "language forms" or "scientific frameworks" as entirely pragmatic. The problem, in Quine's words, is that such "pragmatism leaves off at the imagined boundary between the analytic and the synthetic," so that, Quine continues, "[i]n repudiating such a boundary I espouse a more thorough pragmatism." In particular, according to the holistic empiricist epistemology Quine has just presented, all statements of science – statements of logic, mathematics, physics, or biology – equally face the "tribunal of experience" together. When faced with a "recalcitrant experience" in conflict with our total system, we then have a choice of where to make revisions: we normally try to make them as close as possible to the periphery of our overall "web of belief," but, when the conflict is particularly acute and persistent, for example, we can also revise the most abstract and general parts of science, including even the statements of logic and mathematics, lying at the center of this web. In all such cases our criteria of choice are, in the end, purely pragmatic, a matter of continually adjusting our overall web of belief to the flux of sensory experience so as to achieve the simplest total system best adapted to that experience. Therefore, Quine concludes, "[e]ach man is given a scientific heritage plus a continuing barrage of sensory stimulation; and the considerations which guide him in warping his scientific heritage to fit his continuing sensory promptings are, where rational, pragmatic."

The difference between Carnap's position and Quine's at this point is rather subtle. For, in a crucial section of *Logical Syntax* (1934c/1937, §82, "The Language of Physics"), Carnap makes two claims which sound rather similar to Quine's. First, Carnap adopts an holistic view of theory testing he associates with the names of Duhem and Poincaré: "*the test applies at bottom not to a single hypothesis but to the whole system of physics as a system of hypotheses.*" Second, Carnap also claims that, although when faced with an unsuccessful prediction of an observation sentence or "protocol sentence" (what Quine would call a "recalcitrant experience"), "some change must be made in the system," we always have, nonetheless, a choice of precisely where to make the needed revisions. In particular, both the fundamental principles of physics (which Carnap calls "P-rules") and the fundamental principles of logic and mathematics (which Carnap calls "L-rules") are subject to revision: "For instance, the P-rules can be altered in such a way that those particular primitive sentences are no longer valid; or the protocol-sentence can be taken as being non-valid; or again the L-rules which have been used in the deduction can also be changed." And, Carnap adds, "[t]here are no established rules for the kind of change which must be made." Indeed, in this regard there is only a difference of degree between the logico-mathematical sentences and the sentences of empirical physics:

No rule of the language of physics is definitive; all rules are laid down with the reservation that they may be altered as soon as it seems expedient to do so. This applies not only to the P-rules but also to the L-rules, including those of mathematics. In this respect, there are only differences in degree; certain rules are more difficult to renounce than others.

(This was written, I emphasize, some fifteen years before the publication of Quine's "Two Dogmas.") Where, then, does Carnap's pragmatism, in Quine's words, "leave off"?

Immediately following the last quoted passage, Carnap draws the line this way:

If, however, we assume that every new protocol-sentence which appears within a language is synthetic, there is this difference between an L-valid, and therefore analytic, sentence S_1 and a P-valid sentence S_2, namely, that such a new protocol-sentence – independently of whether it is acknowledged as valid or not – can be, at most, L-incompatible with S_2 but never with S_1. In spite of this, it may come about that, under the inducement of new protocol-sentences, we alter the language to such an extent that S_1 is no longer analytic. (1934c/1937, §82)

In other words, although both types of change in our total system induced by what Quine would call a "recalcitrant experience" are possible, and both involve broadly pragmatic considerations about the optimal overall arrangement of this total system, there is, for Carnap, a fundamental difference between the two: one involves changing the analytic sentences of the language, and thus the rules of logic and mathematics, whereas the other involves merely the synthetic sentences of empirical physics. Only the latter, on Carnap's view, have genuine factual content, and only the latter, accordingly, are the exclusive concern of the empirical scientist (here the physicist).

But now Carnap's position may easily begin to look arbitrary. If we admit that our ultimate epistemological arbiter amounts to broadly pragmatic considerations involving the optimal overall arrangement of our scientific system for both analytic and synthetic sentences, why in the world should we persist in maintaining a fundamental distinction between them? Are we not simply attaching arbitrary labels to different sentences, with no remaining epistemological significance? Are we not then ineluctably driven to the "more thorough," and apparently more radical, pragmatic empiricism defended by Quine?

THE LOGIC OF SCIENCE REPLACES EPISTEMOLOGY

It is just here, however, that the true philosophical radicalism of *Carnap's* position emerges. In 1936, at the very beginning of his semantical period, he published a paper (unfortunately never translated) entitled "Von der Erkenntnistheorie zur Wissenschaftslogik" (from epistemology to the logic of science). Here Carnap argues that all traditional epistemological projects, including his own earlier epistemological project in the *Aufbau*, must now be renounced as "unclear mixtures[s] of psychological and logical components." Whereas the broadly pragmatic and holistic epistemology Quine develops under the rubric of "empiricism without the dogmas" is intended as a replacement for, or reinterpretation of, what Quine takes to be the epistemology of logical empiricism (i.e., the *Aufbau*), Carnap (despite Quine's persistent attempts to associate him with varieties of epistemological foundationalism) is breaking decisively with the entire epistemological tradition. The logic of science, in Carnap's sense, is in no way concerned with either explaining or justifying scientific knowledge by exhibiting its ultimate basis (whatever this basis might be). It is concerned, instead, with developing a new role for philosophy vis-à-vis the empirical sciences that will maximally contribute to scientific progress while, at the same time, avoiding all the traditional metaphysical disputes and obscurities which have constituted (and, according to Carnap, continue to constitute) serious obstacles to progress in both philosophy and the sciences.

The first major publication of Carnap's semantical period was *Foundations of Logic and Mathematics* (1939), appearing in English in the first volume of the *International Encyclopedia of Unified Science* (the official monograph series of the Vienna Circle in exile). Here Carnap presents an especially clear and detailed account of the application of logic and mathematics in empirical science and, in particular, the central importance of the analytic/synthetic distinction therein. The application of logico-mathematical calculi in empirical science principally involves experimental procedures of counting and measurement (§§19, 23), whereby quantitatively formulated empirical laws yield testable statements about particular numerically specified outcomes via intervening logico-mathematical theorems. The scientific theory in question (in physics, for example) can thus be represented as an axiomatic system containing both logical and descriptive terms, where the logico-mathematical part of the system (containing only logical terms essentially) is, in its standard interpretation, analytic or L-true (in the semantical sense); and, because of the key role of numerical terms (including terms for real numbers) in the experimental procedure of measurement, this logico-mathematical part is most appropriately formulated as a higher-order system (§14, 18) (as opposed to an elementary or first-order logical system, §13) containing a sufficient amount of arithmetic and analysis.

Since Carnap is well aware, of course, that such higher-order logico-mathematical systems can and do lead to controversy, he immediately inserts a section on "The Controversies over 'Foundations' of Mathematics" (§20, compare §15). Carnap's response to these controversies, not surprisingly, is the Principle of Tolerance, now formulated in a clearly semantical way:

> Concerning mathematics as a pure calculus there are no sharp controversies. These arise as soon as mathematics is dealt with as a system of "knowledge"; in our terminology, as an interpreted system. Now, if we regard interpreted mathematics as an instrument of deduction within the field of empirical knowledge rather than as a system of information, then many of the controversial problems are recognized as being questions not of truth but of technical expedience. The question is: Which form of the mathematical system is technically most suitable for the purpose mentioned? Which one provides the greatest safety? If we compare, e.g., the systems of classical mathematics and of intuitionistic mathematics, we find that the first is much simpler and technically more efficient, while the second is more safe from surprising occurrences, e.g., contradictions. (1939, §20)

As we have already seen, therefore, Carnap's main reason for regarding interpreted mathematics – arithmetic and analysis in their customary interpretation – as analytic or devoid of factual content is that doing so shifts our attention away from "correctness" or truth and towards the purely pragmatic or technical problem of language planning.

The case of geometry, however, is essentially different (§21). Here, although it is perfectly possible to give a logical or analytic interpretation of a geometrical calculus (within analysis, for example, in terms of real number coordinates), the standard or customary intepretation is descriptive or synthetic – as a theory of actual space. But the great lesson of Albert Einstein's general theory of relativity (§22) is that the geometry of actual (physical) space is an empirical question and, in particular, that it is therefore necessary sharply to distinguish between mathematical geometry (given some logical interpretation) and physical geometry (under the customary descriptive interpretation). The latter, as Einstein clearly shows, is a posteriori and synthetic, whereas the former is a priori but purely analytic. Moreover, since physical geometry is a quantitative empirical theory like any other, the appropriate logico-mathematical framework within which it is to be axiomatized must also contain sufficient arithmetic and analysis. For Carnap, therefore, it follows from Einstein's work that the key difference between geometry, on the one side, and arithmetic and analysis, on the other, is that the former is synthetic (a posteriori) in its standard or customary interpretation while the latter are analytic. And it is this key difference Carnap has foremost in mind in his repeatedly expressed conviction, characteristic of his semantical period, that the distinction between analytic and synthetic truth "is indispensable for the logical analysis of science," so that "without [it] a satisfactory methodological analysis of science is not possible" (see 1942, xi; 1963d, 932; 1966/1974, 257).

The critical question, however, concerns what exactly Carnap means by a "satisfactory methodological analysis of science." And the point I most want to emphasize, once again, is that what Carnap has in mind is what he calls "the logic of science" (or "the logical analysis of science"), not any *epistemological* project. In particular, Carnap is not concerned, as is Quine, with developing a very general empiricist conception of justification or evidence simultaneously embracing scientific knowledge, common-sense knowledge, and logico-mathematical knowledge. Carnap is specifically concerned with the modern mathematical physical sciences, which are themselves only possible in the first place if we presuppose a certain amount of sophisticated modern mathematics (arithmetic and analysis) for their precise articulation and empirical testing. And the point of the logic of science, moreover, is not so much to describe the nature of science or scientific method as it has been practiced so far as to open up the possibility for a new kind of ongoing philosophical interaction with the sciences, which, in Carnap's eyes, promises to be particularly fruitful for both. Armed with the new logico-mathematical tools of modern logic (especially the new tools of metamathematics), the philosopher – that is, the logician of science – can participate, together with the scientists themselves, in the articulation, clarification, and development of formal inferential frameworks for articulating empirical theories and testing them by experimental methods. Unlike the empirical scientist, however, the logician of science, as such, is not concerned with then actually testing empirical theories within such inferential frameworks. Moreover, unlike the applied mathematician (who also develops formal methods for use in the empirical sciences), the logician of science has a characteristically philosophical interest in developing a systematic method for defusing unresolvable metaphysical controversies which, in Carnap's view, constitute an ever-present obstacle to progress in both the sciences and philosophy.

APPLICATIONS OF THE LOGIC OF SCIENCE: FOUNDATIONS OF MATHEMATICS, PHILOSOPHY OF SCIENCE, PROBABILITY AND INDUCTION

A particularly important fruitless controversy Carnap's new conception was originally intended to resolve, of course, was the "crisis" in mathematical logic and the foundations of mathematics of the 1920s. Mathematical logic itself successfully weathered this crisis, as we have seen, through the groundbreaking results of Gödel and Tarski in the early 1930s – results with which Carnap himself was very centrally involved. But Carnap, as we have also seen, aimed to develop a systematic diagnosis and remedy for all such metaphysical disputes using the Principle of Tolerance, according to which, in particular, we are to "regard interpreted mathematics as an instrument of deduction within the field of empirical knowledge rather than as a system of information." This proposal, which implements the analytic/synthetic distinction as Carnap has come to understand it, now belongs distinctively to the logic of science, for it is in precisely this way that we are now freed from unresolvable disputes in the foundations of mathematics so as to engage in language engineering for *empirical* science with only practical consequences in mind.

In further developing the logic of science in his semantical period, Carnap took inspiration from Einstein's general relativity. Einstein's new conception of physical geometry as fundamentally an empirical science was, as Einstein himself suggests, deeply indebted to the modern axiomatic conception of mathematical geometry associated with Hilbert. Indeed, Carnap (1966/1974, 257) is simply paraphrasing Einstein when he says that "the theory of relativity . . . could not have been developed if Einstein had not realized that the structure of physical space and time cannot be determined without physical tests," and claims that this illustrates the importance of "the sharp dividing line that must always be kept in mind between pure mathematics, with its many types of logically consistent geometries, and physics, in which only experiment and observation can determine which geometries can be applied most usefully to the physical world." From Carnap's point of view, therefore, Einstein's distinction between mathematical and physical geometry was an early anticipation of the fruitfulness of Carnapian logic of science – where, on the one hand, Einstein opened up the possibility of a radically new use of mathematics in empirical physics (general relativity) and, on the other, definitively cleared up the traditional dispute about Kantian synthetic a priori judgments. Indeed, an analogous logical clarification of geometry, aiming to dissolve persistent metaphysical disputes about the "true nature" of space in the light of modern mathematics, modern logic, and relativity theory, had already been the subject of Carnap's 1921–22 doctoral dissertation, although here a lingering attachment to the synthetic a priori still remained (see Thomas Mormann's contribution).

Carnap also clearly thought (although he never provided a detailed development of this idea) that the logic of science could be fruitfully applied to the problems of quantum theory as well. In particular, the final sections of *Foundations of Logic and Mathematics* (1939, §§24, 25) suggest that the vexed question of the "interpretation" of the wave-function can be resolved by appreciating that theories of modern mathematical physics operate with "abstract" terms which are implicitly defined, in the manner of Hilbert, in an axiomatic system (and thus require no "intuitive" or "visualizable" meaning) but which still relate to empirical phenomena (experimental measurements) indirectly. This appears, in fact, to be the origin of Carnap's later conception of the "partial interpretation" of theoretical terms, which eventually resulted in the Ramsey-sentence reconstruction of scientific theories – and theoretical analyticity – developed in Carnap (1966) (see William Demopoulos's contribution). Indeed, immediately following the passage quoted above about Einstein and general relativity, Carnap (1966/1974, 257–8) continues: "This distinction between analytic truth (which includes logical and mathematical truth) and factual truth is equally important today in quantum theory, as physicists explore the nature of elementary particles and search for a field theory that will bind quantum mechanics to relativity."

From the mid-1940s on, during the last twenty-five years of his long and fruitful career, Carnap worked principally on a new project in the logico-mathematical analysis of empirical science which he called the logical foundations of probability. He here turned his attention away from the more traditional deductive inferential frameworks on which he had so far primarily focused and towards the newer probabilistic and statistical frameworks now being constructed and applied with ever-increasing frequency in the physical, biological, and social sciences. Here, once again, Carnap, as logician of science par excellence, aimed fruitfully to engage with the scientists in question in clarifying existing statistical methods and developing new ones while, at the same time, dissolving residual metaphysical controversies (about the "true nature" of probability, objective or subjective, for example) which still threaten scientific progress. This project, from Carnap's own point of view, appears to have been quite successful. For, on the more philosophical side, Carnap's sharp distinction between two different concepts of probability – logical or epistemic (degree of confirmation) and empirical or physical (long-run relative frequency) – appears to have the same potential for defusing needless metaphysical disputes as the earlier distinction between mathematical and physical geometry. And, on the more technical side, Carnap's own positive contributions to the theory of statistical inference, although somewhat outside of the mainstream, did in fact interact fruitfully with other scientific work in the ongoing development of our formal inductive methods (see S. L. Zabell's contribution). Nothing more, from the point of view of Carnapian logic of science, could either be hoped for or achieved.

My extended discussion of the logic of science and the place of the analytic/synthetic distinction within it has been intended to illustrate what the point of the distinction is from Carnap's own point of view. This, as suggested at the beginning, has been largely obscured by the influence of Quine's sharp and striking criticisms, and, as I hope we are now in a position better to appreciate, they proceed from a philosophical perspective entirely foreign to Carnap himself. It does not follow, however, that there are no serious technical difficulties afflicting Carnap's project (see Steve Awodey's contribution for the problems involved in explicating L-truth within Carnap's semantical framework), nor that there is nothing in Quine's criticisms to challenge Carnap's overall philosophical perspective (see

Richard Creath's contribution). But perhaps the not inconsiderable pragmatic successes of Carnapian logic of science, on its own terms, do explain why Carnap (during the very period in which his work in inductive logic, in particular, was resulting in more and more genuine advances) never viewed either the difficulties in question or Quine's criticisms as fundamental obstacles to his philosophical program.

1 Carnap's intellectual development*

I. ORIGINS

The young Carnap is not easy to classify. He was neither really a scientist nor a proper philosopher. Among scientists he felt temperamentally at home, but he regretted the slovenliness of the enterprise. The officers at headquarters, he thought, needed to bring some order to operations on the front. Unfortunately these "officers" – the neo-Kantian philosophers whose lectures he attended in Jena and Freiburg before the First World War – seemed too unsure of the terrain to guide the scientific sappers in their spadework of intellectual trench warfare.

But Carnap did not reject the neo-Kantian tradition he grew up in. He assimilated a good deal of it. The impulse for the revival of Kant in mid-nineteenth-century Germany had originally come from the natural sciences rather than philosophy, particularly from the great physicist and physiologist Hermann von Helmholtz. He and the philosophers who followed his lead had wanted to complete the job of eliminating metaphysics that Kant, in their view, had left unfinished. Helmholtz's physiology of perception, they thought, could render the transcendental aesthetic metaphysically harmless. Though they held that the subjective *feelings* of spatiality and temporality are built into our perceptual system, just as Kant had argued, this did not mean that the *geometry* governing the perceived world was put there by human perception. We have no idea, Helmholtz said, whether physical space is Euclidean or non-Euclidean; this is an empirical question like any other, to be settled by going out and looking. So

* I am grateful to Steve Awodey, Richard Creath, Michael Friedman, and Erich Reck for extremely helpful comments on this chapter.

much, Helmholtz had thought, for Kant's best example of supposedly synthetic a priori knowledge.

The scientific neo-Kantians, then, had been Kantians without much of a synthetic a priori. In the first issue of their new *Quarterly for Scientific Philosophy*, the editor, Richard Avenarius, had argued for a thorough reform of philosophy, and the elimination of all the traditional metaphysical pseudo-problems. Though this school of neo-Kantianism established itself in Germany during the 1870s and 1880s, by the end of the century it had been displaced by a new generation of neo-Kantians who, without losing their interest in natural science, were more concerned to resurrect Kant's emphasis on the metaphysical *presuppositions* of science. And where Helmholtz had seen his sensory physiology as a *bridge* between the natural and human sciences, the new generation wanted to *limit* the claims of natural science and to explore the *different* procedures and standards of the human sciences.

Carnap's philosophy teachers were of this later school. He listened. But he also read the earlier neo-Kantians, as well as Mach and, more enthusiastically, Poincaré. Physics remained a priority; the structural approach of Kirchhoff and Hertz, which sought to reduce assumptions to a minimum, appealed to Carnap greatly. And he attended the lectures of an eccentric and reclusive mathematics professor, Gottlob Frege, who had invented a symbolic language in which, he claimed, he could lay bare the underlying structure of mathematical reasoning – which traditional Aristotelian logic could not.

Of at least equal importance to these more obviously "intellectual" influences, for Carnap's future development, was his intense participation in a student group around the Jena publisher Eugen Diederichs. This "Sera group" was affiliated with the larger German Youth Movement, a phenomenonon little studied by historians.[1] It seems to have been specifically Central European. It began, around the turn of the century, as a back-to-nature movement by German bourgeois schoolboys and students who rejected their parents'

---

[1] The workmanlike but narrowly focused book by Laqueur (1962) has little competition; Werner (2003) sheds significant light on the specifically Jena background of the Sera group. An impression of the atmosphere and rhetoric of the German Youth Movement can be gained from Chapter XIV of Thomas Mann's *Doctor Faustus*.

new-found material prosperity and their narrow conformism. It had no explicitly political agenda, more a cultural-political one; bands of students headed off into the countryside to experience nature and "authentic" peasant culture. They sang traditional German wandering songs. Youth Movement songbooks proliferated, as did "natural" diets and physical regimens. The "bourgeois" drugs – coffee, tobacco, alcohol – were proscribed. (Carnap never touched them for the rest of his life.) The Sera group organized excursions and processions to the hills around Jena in which improvised rituals, often drawing on archaic elements as well as traditional dances and costumes, played a central role. At Midsummer, for instance, a huge bonfire was built on a lonely hilltop after sunset. After the carefully orchestrated and ritualized feasting, dancing, and singing, couples jumped over the flames together holding hands, until the fire died down amidst the murmur of quiet conversation. As the sun appeared on the horizon, over the hills, the antiphonal hymn to the sun by St. Francis of Assisi was intoned, with Diederichs himself in the lead. Carnap much admired his creativity in making such events memorable (Carnap, UCLA RC1029/Box 2, CM3).

For Carnap, the lasting effect of these experiences was to give him the sense that the basic forms of human life are within human control; they do not have to be accepted from tradition or from existing conventions. This "voluntarism," as it has been called (Jeffrey, 1994), would prove to be of fundamental importance to Carnap's philosophy through all its phases. And though the Youth Movement "did not leave any externally visible achievements," Carnap later wrote, "the spirit that lived in this movement, which was like a religion without dogmas, remained a precious inheritance for everyone who had the good luck to take an active part in it. What remained was more than a mere reminiscence of an enjoyable time; it was rather an indestructible living strength which forever would influence one's reactions to all practical problems of life" (Carnap, UCLA RC1029/Box 2, CM3). Moreover, it was something he missed throughout his subsequent life:

After the war . . . the same spirit was still alive in the life of my newly founded family and in the relationships with friends. When I went to Vienna, however, the situation was different. I still preserved the same spirit in my personal attitude, but I missed it painfully in the social life with others. None of the members of the Vienna Circle had taken part in the Youth Movement, and I did not feel myself strong and productive enough to transform single-handedly the group of friends into a living community, sharing the style of life which I wanted. Although I was able to play a leading role in the philosophical work of the group, I was unable to fulfil the task of a missionary or a prophet. Thus I often felt as perhaps a man might feel who has lived in a strongly religious [and] inspired community and then sudddenly finds himself isolated in the Diaspora and feels himself not strong enough to convert the heathen. The same feeling I had in a still greater measure later in America, where the power of traditional social conventions is much stronger than it was in Vienna and where also the number of those who have at least sensed some dissatisfaction with the traditional forms of life is smaller than anywhere on the European continent. (Carnap, UCLA RC1029/Box 2, CM3)

Into this idyllic dawn of a new world erupted the unheralded disaster of August 1914 and the Great War. Carnap and his Sera friends dutifully enlisted and were not even unwilling combatants, at first. Only when they witnessed the scale of the slaughter did doubts arise. Like Wittgenstein on the eastern front, Carnap participated in many of the bloodiest engagements on the western front. Both young philosophers were profoundly alienated by the loathsomeness of the officer corps. Both were wounded, and decorated for bravery. But their reactions to this common experience could not have been more different. Wittgenstein read Tolstoy in the trenches, and discovered the merits of a mystical religious inwardness, which convinced him to withdraw from worldly involvement. Carnap read Einstein in the trenches, and discovered the general theory of relativity, whose merits he explained to his non-scientific friends. He also realized that it was precisely the German intelligentsia's traditional withdrawal from public life that had made it complicit in the bloodshed, standing idly by while the political classes had started a world war. The only answer, he realized, was active involvement – not just in politics as usually defined, but in politics at all levels, including the highest-level conceptual planning and organization of knowledge. For all the other social functions to work together, it was essential to arrive at a "structure of community" (*Gemeinschaftsgestalt*) that could serve to coordinate them so as "to remove [these tasks] from the realm of chaotic whim and subordinate them to goal-oriented reason" (Carnap, ASP RC 089-72-04 [1918], 18). (It is perhaps no accident that Carnap later used the same phrase to describe the goal of an envisaged comprehensive "system of knowledge.") This new resolve, growing directly out of the disaster of German defeat and guilt, merged with the voluntarism inspired by the Youth Movement to produce in Carnap a remarkably original species of utopianism. His earlier desire to bring some order into the chaotic slovenliness of science was transferred to the larger theatre of bringing order into the world as a whole – not just into knowledge but into practical life as well.

The more narrowly political component of this new resolve ("political" in the conventional sense) was easily implemented: Carnap joined the USPD, the far-left party of Rosa Luxemburg and Karl Liebknecht. He sent clandestine circular letters to friends at the front with excerpts from the foreign press. He wrote well-informed articles about such subjects as world government for underground leaflets such as the *Politische Rundbriefe*, which attempted to translate the values of the pre-war Youth Movement into political action.

But it was less obvious how to prosecute the "conceptual politics" on a higher plane, the planning and design of the "structure of community." His aspiration was clear: what was needed was a grand synoptic system of the sciences (a *System der Wissenschaftslehre*), an *overall* conceptual system that afforded a vantage point from which the whole of knowledge could be surveyed and organized, and from which individual claims or theories could be rationally judged. This was a self-consciously Leibnizian ideal of a *calculus philosophicus* or a universal characteristic. Frege (who had presented his *Begriffsschrift* as a first step toward realizing the Leibnizian dream) had given Carnap a concrete sense of how such a universal characteristic might look.

Carnap was unsure how to go about this project, though, within the "idealistic conception" he was attracted to at this time, derived from the "positivist idealism" of Hans Vaihinger, a neo-Kantian philosopher whose book *The Philosophy of As If* had generated a great deal of discussion after its publication in 1911. Vaihinger took an extreme positivist view of what we actually know: it is only the "chaos" of our immediately present sensations that we have direct access to. The "reality" we construct on this basis, whether in science or in everyday life, is not genuine knowledge but a tissue of useful *fictions* that we purposefully invent to get things done in the world and to serve our mental and social needs. He included in this category not just Kant's synthetic a priori propositions – the axioms of arithmetic, geometry, and mechanics, as well as the principles of causality and of the uniformity of nature. He also included much else, for example the fictions of religion, of natural justice and equal citizenship, of free will and moral reasons. It was essentially a pragmatist position, as Vaihinger himself recognized, though he thought James wrong to make utility a *standard* of true knowledge.[2] There is genuinely true knowledge, he maintained, however limited in scope, while the fictions, though useful, are *not* true. They are to be judged by practical results, not by cognitive standards.

Carnap's own "idealistic conception" took Vaihinger as a starting point, but extended the criterion of practical results to the cognitive realm itself. If I am to take some knowledge claim seriously, Carnap wrote to a friend, it has to reveal something about my own subjective world that I couldn't have discerned without it, and that I can put to the test within *my* world. The seeing person among the blind, for instance, can predict things about *their* world that they can put to the test; they find that he is generally right, so his knowledge claim is trustworthy. The same can't be said for the claims of the religious mystic you suggested I read, Carnap told his (religious) friend. The mystic can't tell me anything about *my world* that I don't already know without his supposed vision, and what he does claim I can't bear out (Carnap, ASP RC 081-48-04 [1921]).

But it proved difficult for Carnap to pursue his Leibnizian dream of a system of knowledge within this "idealistic" framework. He tried various ways of deducing a physical "reality" by *analysis* from the "chaos" of experience, even using a makeshift fuzzy logic at one point, but these efforts led nowhere. It seemed impossible to break out of the phenomenal "chaos" convincingly. But amidst all his other projects, the preoccupation with such an overall system did not let him go. "I worked on many special problems, always looking for new approaches and improved solutions," Carnap wrote of this period. "But in the background there was always the ultimate aim of the total system of all concepts. I believed that it should be possible, in principle, to give a logical reconstruction of the total system of the world as we know it" (Carnap, UCLA RC1029/Box 2, CM3, E4).

---

[2] Vaihinger appears to have been strongly influenced, at one remove, by the psychological theories of Alexander Bain, which were also an important influence on William James and C. S. Peirce. These connections are established by Ceynowa (1993).

II. THE *AUFBAU* PROJECT

In the winter of 1921–22 Carnap read a book that not only suggested how to overcome this basic obstacle to his project of a "total system of all concepts," but showed him how to describe at least one aspect of his new utopian mission in compelling terms. This book was Russell's *Our Knowledge of the External World as a Field for Scientific Method in Philosophy*. It ends with a ringing call to arms that stirred Carnap to resolve that this would henceforth be his task:

> The study of logic becomes the central study in philosophy: it gives the method of research just as mathematics give the method in physics . . . All this supposed knowledge in the traditional systems must be swept away, and a new beginning must be made . . . To the large and still growing body of men engaged in the pursuit of science . . . the new method, successful already in such time-honored problems as number, infinity, continuity, space, and time, should make an appeal which the older methods have wholly failed to make . . . The one and only condition, I believe, which is necessary to secure for philosophy in the near future an achievement surpassing all that has hitherto been accomplished by philosophers, is the creation of a school of men with scientific training and philosophical interests, unhampered by the traditions of the past, and not misled by the literary methods of those who copy the ancients in all except their merits. (Russell, 1914a, 242)

Regarding the "total system of all concepts," Russell gave him the crucial hint that the way to get from the chaos of experience to a "reality" was not by *analysis* of experience, but by *construction*, using a "principle of abstraction."[3] Experiences could be gathered into equivalence classes, e.g. a series of experiences of "red," at a certain position in the visual field, could be defined as equivalent. For the purposes of constructing a "real" world, this class can be regarded as an object; we can use the class itself in place of the quality. No actual quality, transcending momentary experience, need figure in subsequent steps to a "reality." The evanescence of "chaotic" experience is no longer a constraint. The problem of forcing the fluid

---

[3] "When a group of objects have that kind of similarity which we are inclined to attribute to possession of a common quality, the principle [of abstraction] shows that membership of the group will serve all the purposes of the supposed common quality, and that therefore, unless some common quality is actually known, the group or class of similar objects may be used to replace the common quality, which need not be assumed to exist" (Russell, 1914a, 44–45).

character of lived experience into the straitjacket of deductive relations disappears.

This also solved another problem. According to Vaihinger, the
"chaos" of subjective experience has no structure; nothing is "given"
but the undifferentiated chaos itself. No distinguishable "elements"
present themselves as naturally isolable from it or as available unambiguously in themselves, without calling on externally imposed fictions. (A somewhat less extreme version of this holistic starting point
had just been articulated by a new school of "Gestalt" psychologists (Ash, 1998).) Russell's principle of abstraction – his method
of substituting "logical constructions for inferred entities" (such as
qualities) – solved this problem. Instead of trying to isolate specific
elements within the undifferentiated "chaos," Carnap could obtain
the elements he sought by partitioning the entire "chaos" into just
two sectors, which he called the "living" and "dead" parts of experience. This one distinction allowed Carnap to arrange experiences
into a temporal sequence ("dead" experience belongs to the past;
"living" experience is present), and thus made it possible to identify
holistic "temporal cross-sections" of experience, in which the total
experience of a given specious present remains intact as a momentary whole. This chronological sequence of experiential time-slices
now gave Carnap the basic framework he needed for identifying
qualities as cross-temporal equivalence classes of particular aspects
within certain time-slices. The holistic time-slices of experience did
not need to be *analyzed*. Qualities and qualitative relations could,
rather, be *constructed* by defining equivalence classes of sufficiently
"similar" experience-aspects (e.g. approximations to "red" at certain
coordinates of the visual field) across a series of time-slices. ("Similarity" could be defined as precisely as needed.) The result of this
procedure – with "quality classes" standing in for qualities, and so on
– was therefore essentially what empiricists (like Hume or Mach) had
always hoped to achieve by analysis, but it was accomplished *without* analysis. Carnap called it "quasi-analysis." Once qualities had
been constructed, physical objects could be constructed as classes of
qualities, and the path to a "reality" was clear.

Carnap still followed Vaihinger in distinguishing sharply between
the direct, genuine, first-hand knowledge of the "chaos" and the
fictive, constructed nature of "reality." But he put the boundary
between them in a different place. This was because Carnap had

recently come across Edmund Husserl's group at the University of Freiburg, and thought their new "phenomenology" offered an escape route from Vaihinger's completely undifferentiated chaos. It gave certain basic distinctions *within* the chaos (such as that between "living" and "dead" experience) a degree of objectivity. These distinctions, then, were not "fictional" but actually extended the range of what could be genuinely *known*, even *without* fictions, just from the "chaos" itself. So Carnap's boundary between the immediately known "chaos" and the realm of fictitious construction was further out than Vaihinger's. But fictions were still needed to get from this immediately known *primary world* (of "chaos" supplied with a minimal, phenomenologically extrapolated structure) to a fictive *secondary world* of "reality" – such as the everyday world of physical objects and forces, or the abstract scientific world of fields and space-time coincidences, or some other construction. Carnap thought at this point that he could show on phenomenological grounds that the primary world was two-dimensional in all sense modalities (Carnap, 1924). So the stepping-off point from the fixed primary world to a freely choosable secondary world was located at the ascent from two to three dimensions. Within the primary world, the construction proceeded entirely by explicit definition, beginning from the qualities obtained by quasi-analysis. Secondary worlds, by contrast, are not uniquely determined. The construction of a secondary world proceeds, rather, by optimizing its "fit" to whichever fictions are chosen to guide the construction, subject to the *constraint* of the (fixed) primary world.

Regarding the choice among fictions to guide this ascent, Carnap remained as radically pragmatist as Vaihinger; the choice of fictions was entirely a matter of what was practically useful for some purpose. And if our purposes are served by the *scientific* secondary world, Carnap maintained, we need adopt only two fictions, corresponding roughly to Kant's categories of cause and substance: a principle of induction or uniformity of nature and a principle of "continuity," as Mach had called it – a principle that a certain cluster of perceptions grouped, for example, into a "physical object" remains constant while we are not perceiving it if it is still "the same" cluster (by defined standards) before and after the interruption.

It seemed, therefore, that the problems facing Carnap's dream of a "total system of all concepts" had been overcome. He could now go public with his grand plan to revolutionize the conceptual framework of knowledge. He immediately wrote up a sketch of the new "total system of all concepts" in a typescript which he gave the Vaihinger-inspired title *From the Chaos to Reality*. This was the germ of the constructive project he would later put forward in *The Logical Construction of the World* (usually called the *Aufbau* after its German title). He circulated the *Chaos to Reality* typescript to people who seemed interested in similar problems and organized a conference in Erlangen to discuss it – the first conference of "scientific philosophy." The participants, who previously had each been working alone, became a like-minded community. Carnap also talked to Hans Reichenbach and others about starting a new journal to propagate the new ethos. The program of "conceptual politics" was well under way.

III. THE VIENNA CIRCLE

The *Aufbau*, published in 1928, became the programmatic bible of the Vienna Circle, which Carnap joined in 1926 when Schlick recruited him to the University of Vienna. The *Aufbau* exemplified the Vienna Circle's goal of "rational reconstruction," the replacement of vague, informal concepts by precise ones defined in terms of a standard logical language in which all of knowledge could be expressed. The concept rationally reconstructed in the *Aufbau* was that of "empirical content" (or "empirical meaning"), which had long been of central importance for empiricists, from Locke to Mach, but had never been made logically precise.

Though the continuity of Carnap's constructional system between the *Chaos to Reality* typescript in 1922 and the *Aufbau* is undeniable, there were also some important changes. In the 1922 system, three components had worked somewhat uneasily together: (1) the *basis* of momentary time-slices of total experience, distilled from a chaotic primary world by phenomenological reflection; (2) the *fictions* that guided the construction of a secondary world from the primary world; and (3) the *logic* that connected the constructional steps. As Carnap continued to work on the system after 1922, these three parts came to seem less compatible with each other. Though he had greatly reduced the number of fictions from Vaihinger's heterogeneous jumble, the two he had chosen still seemed somewhat ad hoc.

And phenomenological reflection, though also a kind of "thought," did not operate mechanically, without mental assistance, as Frege's logical system was intended to. Logic and phenomenology seemed to be fundamentally different kinds of constructional procedure that could not be reduced to each other. If Carnap was to take seriously Russell's dictum that "logic gives the method of research," then everything that *could* be done by logic alone *had* to be done by logic alone. Accordingly, by 1925 Carnap gave up the distinction between "primary" and "secondary" worlds – i.e., between a single determinate "given" and optional "realities." Instead, he extended the logical construction *downwards* as far as possible to perform the tasks that had previously been left to phenomenology.

This displacement of phenomenology by logic led Carnap to minimize the number of relations required for the construction. By 1925 the number of basic relations had been reduced to five, and in the published *Aufbau* there is only a *single* basic relation – that of "remembered similarity" of quality-aspects across time-slices of experience. Indeed, the imperative to eliminate the subjective element altogether, and make the construction *entirely* logical, led Carnap to the extreme of suggesting that even this one remaining basic relation might be eliminated if we define it "implicitly," i.e., if we define it simply as "whatever basic relation leads to our existing body of scientific knowledge" (Carnap, 1928a/1967, §153).

For all these major changes Carnap did not, however, give up Vaihinger's pragmatist orientation. To make the fictions of cause and substance that guided the construction less ad hoc, Carnap suggested that they could be deduced from some "highest principle of constitution" which might, he thought, in turn be deducible from "whatever it is that knowledge contributes to the more comprehensive context of life purposes" (Carnap, 1928a/1967, §105). And he was careful to emphasize that the *Aufbau* construction was not the only possible one, but that other approaches might be appropriate to serve different purposes (Carnap, 1928a/1967, §59).[4]

The *Aufbau* construction gave the Vienna Circle a standard by which to judge any statement and determine whether it has meaning.

---

4 This aspect of the *Aufbau* is discussed in Michael Friedman's chapter in this volume, which shows that Carnap's early voluntarism was very much alive in this period, and also foreshadows the later, more systematic pluralism of the *Logical Syntax* (see below).

Carnap gave a popular lecture around this time in which he depicted the whole of human intellectual history, since the Greeks, as a struggle between the "critical intellect" and the "poetic imagination" over their respective claims to knowledge. In the ancient world, he said, the critical intellect had dealt poetic imagination a major blow with its concept of a single, all-encompassing physical space. In response to any mythical creature or entity the imagination might dream up, the critical intellect could now ask, "Where is it located in space?" – i.e., "Tell me exactly how I can get there from here." Imagination took to hiding its goblins and spirits in remote, inaccessible places, but this was only a stopgap. Eventually imagination struck back more forcefully by inventing *metaphysics*. It hit on the idea of a *non-material* God and other non-material entitities. This new kind of knowledge claim was quite plausible, Carnap said, because we often refer quite legitimately to non-material items like numbers, relations, and so on. Many thinking people were taken in. But now, Carnap triumphantly concluded, the critical intellect has found a tool to combat this ingenious maneuver. Just as the ancients had hit on the idea of an all-encompassing *physical* space, so now we, here in Vienna, have developed a single, all-encompassing *conceptual* space: the *Aufbau* system. This puts the burden on the poetic imagination to specify exactly how to get to any supposed non-material entity from "here" – from my own immediate experience (Carnap, 2005).[5] This was how the *Aufbau* system provided the basis for the Vienna Circle's campaign against metaphysics and traditional obscurantism.

IV. WITTGENSTEIN

When Carnap came to Vienna in 1926, the *Aufbau* was already substantially complete. In Carnap's mind, the *Aufbau* project had been only one aspect of the overarching task of rational reconstruction. The assumption had been that its construction of physical objects and theoretical entities would all be of a piece, so that these concrete and theoretical objects could also be cashed out again in terms of subjective experience. In 1926 Carnap had published a booklet

[5] As Michael Friedman's chapter in this volume makes clear, this was a retrospective simplification in the context of a popular lecture; the *Aufbau*'s actual approach to metaphysics is in fact considerably subtler.

on *Physical Concept Formation* that claimed a completely seamless intertranslatability between subjective experiences and the sets of 14-tuples in which, he said, the world could, against a set of background theories, be exhaustively described.

On arriving in Vienna, Carnap was confronted with a new influence that disrupted this harmony. The Circle was just in the process of reading Wittgenstein's *Tractatus Logico-Philosophicus* line by line, and Carnap came to share their appreciation of it. In their eyes, the *Tractatus* solved what historically had been the severest problem for empiricism – its inability to account for mathematics. Frege's critique of empiricist efforts (e.g. by John Stuart Mill) to found arithmetic on empirical generalizations had convinced them that a different approach was needed. But they also rejected Frege's and Russell's view that the laws of logic (and thus mathematics) governed the world, that they were laws of something – *everything* – out there. This seemed metaphysical to them, so they welcomed Wittgenstein's view that the laws of logic were, rather, about *nothing*; they were empty. These laws conveyed no information about the world, as they were "tautological" artifacts of the language itself and neither made nor excluded any assertions about anything that is or is not the case.

What gives a sentence meaning, Wittgenstein said, is that it is a logical "picture" of a fact. So all meaningful sentences had to be built up out of "atomic" sentences, picturing simplest facts, by truth-functional connectives. Since the number of observation sentences supporting a physical law could only ever be finite, this meant – to the Vienna Circle – that a *universal* law could not, strictly speaking, have meaning. So in Wittgenstein's framework, as they saw it, a law could be nothing more than the body of evidence for it. This made theoretical science as it had been done for the past few centuries impossible; it broke the seamless continuity Carnap had previously assumed between subjective experience and theoretical concepts.

But Wittgenstein's conception of meaning also raised a second problem for the Circle. Statements *about* language – like their own writings about the scientific language, including the *Aufbau* – could not be construed as truth-functional concatenations of atomic sentences, and were therefore also, strictly speaking, meaningless. Wittgenstein himself had arrived at this conclusion in the final sentences of the *Tractatus*, where he had declared his own book meaningless. What it had tried to say could not really be said, but could only "reveal itself." So although the Vienna Circle regarded the *Tractatus* as indispensable, they also realized that to do the job they required of it, its conception of language would have to be expanded to admit physical laws and metalinguistic "elucidations."

A central issue on this agenda was the status of *axiomatic* concepts. Hilbert had introduced the idea of a "metamathematics," in which statements *about* axiom systems (of set theory, of classical mathematics, of physics or other sciences) were formulated and proved. To fit these systems into Wittgenstein's conception, Carnap tried to show that such a meta-language was not ultimately essential, however useful it might be in mathematical practice, and that in principle only a single basic language would suffice. If he could succeed in this program, then the new work in meta-logic and meta-mathematics by Hilbert, Tarski, and Gödel would be consistent with Wittgenstein's theory of meaning. And both of the above two major problems would be solved: metalinguistic elucidations of Hilbert's kind would be shown to be legitimate (while ultimately dispensable), and the meaningfulness of the axiomatic concepts of classical mathematics and of physics would be guaranteed. Carnap devoted much of the years 1927–29 to this project, which resulted in a large manuscript called *Investigations in General Axiomatics*.

All this effort came to naught in early 1930 when Alfred Tarski visited the Vienna Circle, and in private conversations convinced Carnap that his single-language *Axiomatics* did not really capture the metamathematical concepts that Carnap had wanted to account for in a single language. Later that year, Gödel showed that arithmetic was incomplete – it contained sentences that, although true, could not be proved from its axioms. This contradicted one of the central theorems Carnap had arrived at in his *Axiomatics* manuscript.[6]

At the end of 1930, then, the Vienna program of rational reconstruction, with its crucial reliance on a single standard language, had run aground. The efforts to expand Wittgenstein's restrictive conception of language to allow universal laws and metalinguistic elucidations had come to nothing. And much of the damage had been done by mathematicians like Tarski and Gödel, who were using meta-languages in very precise and respectable ways, openly flouting Wittgenstein's claim that it was impossible to speak about language *in* language. Could the Vienna Circle's program somehow be rescued?

---

[6] See Awodey and Carus (2001) as well as Erich Reck's chapter in this volume.

V. SYNTAX

On 21 January 1931 Carnap had the flu. He hardly slept that night. As he lay awake an idea came to him, in a flash, that solved all his problems. The Wittgensteinian conception of meaning went overboard. We can forget about meaning, in fact, at least in our statements *about* the scientific language – our metalinguistic "elucidations." Though the scientific language itself had empirical meaning (in a way that remained to be clarified[7]), our elucidations of it do not refer to anything extra-linguistic. We are talking *always and only about language*. We should be careful not to talk about "facts" or about "things," but always confine ourselves to talking rather about "sentences" or "thing names." As Carnap would soon put it, we should restrict ourselves in principle to the "formal mode of speech" (sentences and names). The "material mode of speech" (facts and things) should be used only if we are sure we can translate what we are saying into the formal mode (Carnap, 1932a). From a technical, logical point of view, this was nothing new; Carnap was simply adopting the metalinguistic apparatus of Hilbert, Tarski, and Gödel. But he was applying this hitherto purely mathematical method to the whole of knowledge. Philosophy itself was to be rationally reconstructed in the formal mode of speech. What remained of philosophy was the metalinguistic "logic of science" (*Wissenschaftslogik*) that could be expressed in the formal mode.

Carnap immediately threw himself into creating the language for the formal mode of speech. Taking his cue from Hilbert's metamathematics, Carnap sought to strip this standard meta-language of all problematic assumptions. It would consist simply of strings of dots on a page, and the basic laws of arithmetic would arise unambiguously in the meta-language from the immediately evident patterns of dots (e.g. the commutative law from the perceptible equivalence of the number of dots counted from the left and from the right). A few months later, when he was presenting the new ideas to the Vienna Circle in June of 1931, Carnap found that he could not express certain essential concepts in this limited language, and turned instead to a more usual axiomatized arithmetic. This also had the advantage

---

[7] This question, to which Carnap (1932a) gave a preliminary, still rather *Aufbau*-oriented answer, aroused much controversy within the Circle – the celebrated "protocol sentence debate" (Uebel, 1992a).

that, by using Gödel's trick of arithmetizing syntax, Carnap could now express the syntax of the language (i.e., its logic) in the language itself, so the syntactic meta-language collapses into the object language, and there is only one language again after all.

Though some details still needed working out, Carnap was convinced he had what he needed – a canonical language for the formal mode of speech. This also gave him a new and different way of eliminating metaphysics, superceding the previous, Wittgensteinian way. The previous criterion had been a criterion for *meaning*. The new criterion was not. It required that any statement either be straightforwardly factual or be translatable into the formal mode of speech. An acceptable sentence had, in other words, to be statable in a "correct" language – the canonical language or an equivalent. Assuming that the kinks in his canonical language could be ironed out, Carnap thought it would be capable of expressing the entire language of physics, as well as containing its own meta-language. Since the Circle's "unity of science" program held that all knowledge was expressible in the language of physics, Carnap put his canonical language forward as a *universal language* (though not *the* universal language) for all of knowledge (Carnap, 1932a). Another way of expressing the new criterion, then, was that any acceptable statement must be phrased in the language of physics. The new ideas of January 1931 flowed into the stream of Carnap's discussions in the Circle, particularly with Neurath, to produce this new doctrine of *physicalism*.

But the demands on the "correct" language for the formal mode of speech were exorbitant. Though Carnap had wanted to keep it weak and uncontroversial, it also had to be capable of expressing all the mathematics needed for physics. On the other hand, its arithmetized syntax had to be capable of expressing the basic concept of "analytic truth," or there would be no way of saying whether a formal-mode statement "holds." Previously it had always been assumed that *provability* was the standard of mathematical truth, but now Gödel had shown that there are true sentences that are not provable. So a different criterion was needed, but one that would still – like provability – identify the logically true sentences solely by means of the formation and transformation rules of the language. Carnap did attempt such a criterion for "analyticity" in the first draft of his syntax book, written in late 1931 and the spring of 1932. He sent the typescript to Gödel, who pointed out that the new criterion was defective. In fact, Gödel added, it is *impossible* to give a correct definition of analyticity or logical truth in *any* meta-language that can be faithfully represented in the object language (e.g. by arithmetization). This is what we now know as Tarski's theorem on the indefinability of truth. So it turns out that Carnap's single-language approach will not work after all (Awodey and Carus, 2007).

Although Carnap, with Gödel's assistance, developed a new definition of analyticity, in a meta-language, this definition no longer had the privileged status that one in the *same language* (had it been possible) could have claimed. And indeed there is no basis for singling out any particular meta-language as more "suitable" or "natural" than any other. One option may turn out to be more *useful* than another, but there is no basis for privileging one of the many possible candidates as uniquely "correct." So the new definition of analyticity hardly seemed to matter anymore. Carnap was more impressed with the *language relativity* of any definition of truth or analyticity. The disputes about protocol sentences within the Circle merged in his mind with the disputes among intuitionists, logicists, and formalists in the philosophy of mathematics.

All these disputes, it suddenly seemed to him in the autumn of 1932, really just revolved around the question how to set up the *language*, and there was no right or wrong answer to such questions. He no longer saw any basis for choosing one solution as "correct." One could only try out different ways, and see which ones worked better. This new attitude, which first appeared in Carnap's reply to Neurath about protocol sentences in late 1932, received its definitive statement in the "Principle of Tolerance" enunciated in *The Logical Syntax of Language* in 1934. It was at this point in Carnap's development that the voluntarist and utopian convictions of his youth, partially submerged during the *Aufbau* period, finally found adequate *philosophical* expression. He spent the remainder of his career absorbing the consequences of this breakthrough, and cultivating a vast garden of language projects within the new freedom it afforded.

VI. SEMANTICS AND LATER PROJECTS

The syntax period was characterized by two major ideas. The first, from January 1931, had been the rejection of Wittgenstein's picture theory of meaning and its replacement by a sharp distinction between a language – a calculus, a purely formal symbol system – and its interpretation, as well as the requirement that a language be entirely specified by explicit rules. The second major idea, from October 1932, had been the Principle of Tolerance: no language is inherently definitive or "correct"; there is no logical "reality" for a language to "correspond to." In the published *Logical Syntax*, these two major ideas were enmeshed with the insistence on the "formal mode of speech" and the avoidance of meaning. As we saw, this had originally been *part* of the first idea (from January 1931). And it had remained high-profile in *Logical Syntax*. But within a year of the book's publication, it was dropped. Carnap accepted Tarski's new semantical accounts of designation and truth. The two major ideas, however, survived unscathed for the rest of Carnap's career. (So it is actually somewhat misleading to call them "syntactic.") What did not survive was the overreaction against "meaning" that accompanied the original insight – the exclusive emphasis on the "formal mode of speech." In distinguishing between a language and its interpretation, Carnap's first response had been to restrict extra-linguistic interpretation to the object language (and there to one particular – physicalistic – interpretation), and dispense with it entirely in the "elucidatory" meta-language. But this restriction was loosened when Tarski convinced him that interpretation could be completely specified by explicit rules (governing satisfaction, designation, and truth).

In a series of semantic works published in the late 1930s and the 1940s, Carnap tried to develop a *general* definition of "analyticity" that would distinguish analytic from synthetic sentences in a natural and obvious way. The shortcomings of these successive attempts were pointed out by Quine, and were often taken to undermine other parts of Carnap's view, e.g. the Principle of Tolerance itself. This was partly because Quine appears to have misunderstood Carnap's attempt at a general definition of analyticity as an attempt to give a language-*transcendent* definition. In fact, this was never at issue; Carnap was always clear that any definition had to be language-relative. But he hoped to find a simple definition that could hold over a large range of acceptable languages, and he did not succeed in this even to his own satisfaction.[8]

Carnap also tried unsuccessfully, over a number of years, to specify a strictly deductive logical relation between observation sentences

---

[8] See the chapter by Steve Awodey in this volume.

and theoretical sentences. After he abandoned the *Aufbau* effort to construct theories directly from subjective experience, a series of looser definitions of "empirical content" or "empirical reducibility" were given; the best-known of these were *Testability and Meaning* (Carnap, 1936–37) and "The Methodological Character of Theoretical Concepts" (Carnap, 1956). These attempts were also subjected to searching criticism, above all by Hempel. The lesson derived from this apparent failure has generally been to abandon the question altogether, unfortunately, instead of confining the pessimism to Carnap's particular approach, which sought to specify the semantics of theoretical sentences by their *deductive* relations to observation sentences.

Alongside this attempt to find deductive relations between observational and theoretical sentences, the later Carnap also explored the *inductive* relations between observation and empirical generalizations or hypotheses, as a distinct kind of purely logical relation. The last three decades of Carnap's life were largely devoted to the creation of an inductive logic, a language engineering project on a vast scale. He distinguished sharply between two informal uses of the word "probability": probability as relative frequency (of one kind of event or property relative to another) and probability as epistemic (applying to degrees of evidential support or of belief). His inductive logic was intended as an explication of the latter concept; it was to make precise the informal usage, in everyday *and* scientific life, by which the evidence is taken to "make" one empirical hypothesis "more likely" than another. This broad scope, Carnap hoped, would also make inductive logic usable by practicing scientists, to measure the probability of competing hypotheses with respect to the available evidence. Carnap's proposals attained some currency in the 1950s and 1960s and were considered by R. B. Braithwaite, for instance, to be the most promising route to a fundamental justification of J. M. Keynes's theory of probability (Braithwaite, 1973, xxi). While Carnap's own work on probability has not been in the mainstream of discussion for the past few decades, its spirit may be said to survive in the very active research community on Bayesian inference (Jeffrey, 1994).[9]

---

[9] This is also very much the tenor of S. L. Zabell's very informative contribution to this volume. Even some of Carnap's more particular proposals in support of his inductive logic have shown some life; a reformulated version of his "continuum of inductive methods," for instance, is given by Zabell (1997).

VII. THE IDEAL OF EXPLICATION

Even if all these major language projects are written off as failures, however, this would not discredit the larger vision or ideal of explication and language engineering that guided Carnap after 1935. He devoted little time to making this ideal explicit, so it must be gleaned indirectly from his approach to various language projects, and from occasional statements like the famous paper "Empiricism, Semantics, and Ontology" (Carnap, 1950a) or his replies to critics in the Schilpp volume (Carnap, 1963d), as well as from unpublished papers and notes.[10]

At the basis of this ideal is the utopian conception of highest-level "conceptual politics" that never left him after 1918. He believed that those who are fortunate enough to be able to devote their lives to thought and reflection have a responsibility to devise conceptual frameworks for the whole of knowledge that will maximize the usefulness of that knowledge for the human species – not for some particular use, but for all uses to which different humans put knowledge, especially the uses for the purpose of enlightenment, or liberation from unreflective tradition and conformity. In devising these frameworks we are constrained by certain obvious human limitations, but we should not allow ourselves to be constrained by the past – the languages handed down to us by our ancestors. Those give us a starting point, certainly, and we could get nowhere without that starting point, but we should not treat the puzzles and contradictions embedded in natural languages, or in historical languages of philosophy, with any undue reverence. In fact, we should liberate ourselves from them as far as possible when planning new and better frameworks of thought. Certainly our habitual ways of thinking and talking are deeply entrenched, and are hard for us to abandon, but in Carnap's view this is no reason to be constrained by them when we envision new ones.

There are three levels of language engineering or language study, in Carnap's mature conception: *syntax* considers languages in isolation from anything extra-linguistic they might be thought of as representing; *semantics* considers languages as representing

---

[10] This task is undertaken in Carus (2007), where detailed evidence for the brief exposition in this section will be found.

extra-linguistic things, but still in isolation from their actual uses by humans; and *pragmatics* considers languages in relation to their use contexts and their users. Each of these three (syntax, semantics, pragmatics) can be considered as *engineering* activities (the creation or discussion of new or improved languages) or as *empirical* studies (of existing languages). The engineering activity Carnap called "pure" syntax, semantics, or pragmatics, the empirical study he called "descriptive" syntax, semantics, or pragmatics. (Linguists generally engage in the *descriptive* syntax, semantics, and pragmatics of already existing natural languages, while logicians generally engage in the *pure* syntax and semantics of constructed languages.) Among the traditional sectors of philosophy, epistemology and methodology belong to pragmatics, while whatever remains of metaphysics and ontology belongs to semantics – though this now becomes a matter of *deciding* which entities to make fundamental to a language framework, given existing scientific knowledge, rather than *finding out* what those entities are or might be.

This voluntarist orientation remained fundamental. The notion that something beyond the scope of science might actually *be the case* seemed to Carnap a back door to the readmission of traditional prejudices and conformities of all kinds. Certainly we need to make assumptions, he acknowledged, but we can *decide* on these, and spell them out; they are not "out there" for us to *find*. On these grounds he deprecated Quine's preoccupation with ontology. It makes no sense to talk about "what there is," Carnap said, without specifying the language framework in which this is asserted; any such claim can only be understood or judged relative to a framework. It makes perfectly good sense to ask, *within* a framework that includes, say, the Zermelo-Frankel axioms for set theory, whether there are infinite numbers. Such "internal" questions have determinate answers. But it makes no sense, *outside* such a framework, to ask "just in general" whether "there are" infinite numbers. Not only is there no determinate answer, but there is no way to give such an "external" question itself any clear meaning. What we *can* ask instead is the *practical* question whether it is better (e.g. for use in science) to choose a linguistic framework that includes infinite numbers or one that does not. But this is not a question of ontology or semantics, this is a question of pragmatics, a question of *which language* we *want*.

The process by which the human species upgrades its messy and imprecise inherited languages to newly built and more precise ones Carnap called *explication*. He acknowledged that this is a piecemeal, not a revolutionary process. Humanity replaces its concepts a few at a time. An example Carnap often cited was the replacement of our vague, subjective, intuitive sense of "hot" and "cold" by the precise, quantitative concept of temperature, which we can define intersubjectively by reference to measurement devices. This concept not only takes the place of the former vague concepts for many purposes, but also gives us many capabilities the vague ones lacked. It can, for instance, provide an outside, objective framework or standard against which to judge subjective feelings; instead of just saying "I feel hot" or "I feel feverish," I can take my temperature and find out exactly how much higher it is than its ordinary level. So explication also provides a framework of objectivity that enables us to escape from a merely subjective view of the world. But the replacement of the vague, informal world-view by a framework of more objective concepts is piecemeal and iterative; temperature remains to be explicated within a more general framework of concepts.

Meanwhile, we live in a vaguely and fragmentarily understood world. Even the people working at the frontier of knowledge have to use a vernacular, a derivative of ordinary language, to discuss the application of the more precise calculi in which they frame their theories. Their vernacular will of course be cleaner and more precise than the vernacular of the society at large. In the scientific vernacular, all concepts used are intended in their scientifically rigorous meanings. (Behind a biologist's use of the word "light," for instance, lurks the entire current theory of quantum electrodynamics.) But many concepts even in this tidied-up vernacular have no such precise meanings. They may go on being used for generations before they are made precise. The concept of the derivative of a function, for instance, was put to good use for nearly two centuries before it was given a precise meaning by the work of Cauchy and Weierstrass.

Explication, which in Carnap's view is the main task of conceptual engineering, consists in the *replacement* of a vague concept – the *explicandum* – by a more precise one, the *explicatum*. The first step is the *clarification* of the explicandum, the establishment of some basic agreement, among those using the vague concept, what they mean by it. The next step is a proposal for its replacement, a proposed *explicatum*, which should have the most important uses that were agreed on in the clarification stage, but need not have all of them. It should also, if possible, be expressed in a language framework that makes precise and transparent its relation to other concepts. Many disciplines – especially those usually considered "scientific" – use provisionally canonical languages[11] in which they expect, or sometimes require, explications to be framed. Despite the continuing recourse to an ordinary language for practical everyday communication (as a sort of user interface), such a provisionally canonical language becomes the official first language, the gold standard for the genuine content of theoretical concepts in that discipline. For the purpose of determining just what knowledge the discipline actually possesses, the statement in that provisionally canonical language framework supercedes, for its users, all pedagogical or intuitive explanations in everyday language. There can be explicata in that language framework, then, that correspond to *no* explicanda in ordinary language. (And of course vice versa; there can be ordinary-language explicanda that correspond to no precise concepts.) Explications, then, do not just replace ordinary-language explicanda one by one; the entire system of interrelations holding them together is also replaced gradually by the provisionally canonical languages of science, giving rise to entirely new concepts (such as "cholesterol" or "tectonic plate") that have no obvious ordinary-language predecessors at all. From their acceptance within a discipline's canonical language, such concepts diffuse into that discipline's ordinary language and ultimately into wider use by the community of those who use the tidied-up scientific vernacular.

So far, explication sounds much like the previous Vienna Circle program of "rational reconstruction." There is certainly a continuity. But explication differs in one critical respect. Rational reconstruction was a one-way street; vernacular concepts were to be replaced, piece

---

[11] Such provisionally canonical languages have been called "paradigms" by Thomas Kuhn (1962). While Kuhn himself (along with much of the intellectual world) thought he was "refuting" logical empiricism, Carnap (editor of the series in which Kuhn's book appeared) thought Kuhn's book was fundamentally compatible with his own view (Reisch, 1991). As Michael Friedman remarks, "the accepted conventional wisdom concerning the relationship between Kuhn's theory of scientific revolutions and logical empiricist philosophy of science is seriously oversimplified and fundamentally misleading" (Friedman, 2003, 19).

by piece, with more precise ones. It was assumed that there was a single, definitive logical language in which this reconstruction could be achieved. But under the new regime of tolerance after 1932, there is no longer a single correct language. There is an infinity of possible languages, and the community must decide among them. Explication is therefore *dialectical*, as Howard Stein, a student of Carnap's, has pointed out (Stein, 1992), in a way that rational reconstruction was not. Knowledge has obvious and far-reaching effects on our practical life (more and more so, it seems, as history advances). It can, among other things, tell us about the likely consequences of various value systems and courses of action, far more than we could have known a few centuries ago. On the other hand, we use our *values* to decide on the language(s) in which we represent and understand our knowledge. This choice *among* languages is not one we can make *within* a given language framework. It is a practical choice, a choice involving values – whether it is a global adoption of one language system over another, or a local, piecemeal replacement of a single explicandum by an explicatum.

Not only do values and the realm of practice make a striking reappearance in Carnap's later thought, then,[12] but it is tightly *integrated* into his view of knowledge. Knowledge and values are implicitly portrayed in a continuous feedback relation to each other; knowledge shapes values and values shape knowledge. This dialectical conception would appear to make the late Carnap more radically "pragmatist" than, say, William James.[13] The voluntarist convictions of Carnap's youth, which found their adequate philosophical articulation in the Principle of Tolerance, were transformed and given their fullest expression in Carnap's mature ideal of explication, in which reason is not the slave of the passions, but an equal partner. Reason informs the passions (and the rest of life, the realm of practice), and the passions inform reason. Neither is subordinate.

---

[12] In the *Logical Syntax*, this new role for values and the practical realm was still largely implicit. It became more evident in the work on inductive logic, and was finally given a systematic exposition (Carnap, 1963f.).

[13] See Alan Richardson's contribution to this volume for a discussion of Carnap and American pragmatism.

2 Geometrical leitmotifs in Carnap's early philosophy

I. INTRODUCTION

Carnap was a leading figure of logical empiricism, but he did not begin as a logical empiricist. Hence, it is natural to ask how he became one. This question not only concerns the individual career of a distinguished philosopher, it is significant also for the wider question of how logical empiricism emerged in the general context of European philosophy in the early twentieth century.

Arguably, Carnap began his philosophical career as a neo-Kantian (cf. Coffa, 1991). But, as can be gleaned from his early writings, he was also influenced by scientists and philosophers such as Poincaré, Frege, Hilbert, Russell, Husserl, and Dingler, who did not belong to the Kantian tradition in the strict sense. Presently, the question of who influenced Carnap how is vigorously disputed among Carnap scholars (cf. Pincock, 2002). The aim of this chapter is not to take issue in this debate presenting a new candidate or offering new arguments in favor of one who is already in the race. Rather, I would like to concentrate on an influential factor of a different kind, namely, the influence philosophy of geometry had on Carnap's philosophy.

It is not difficult gathering evidence that philosophy of geometry was important for the early Carnap: his very first work, "Der Raum. Ein Beitrag zur Wissenschaftslehre" (1922), was a treatise on philosophy of geometry. As I want to show, "Raum" set the agenda for his philosophical work in the 1920s, and even the basic ideas of the constitution theory (Konstitutionstheorie) of Aufbau can be traced back to "Raum." More generally, Carnap's conventionalism, which marked his philosophical thought throughout his life, can be shown to have its roots in the geometrical conventionalism developed

43

in "Raum." Indeed, those scientists and philosophers who had an impact on his early thought did this mainly through the medium of (philosophy of) geometry. In sum, his philosophy of geometry may be interpreted as the overture in which many leitmotifs that pervaded his later philosophy appeared for the first time. One should note that these geometrical leitmotifs were operative before Carnap became a logical empiricist in the proper sense. Philosophy of geometry informed his philosophical thought in the logical empiricist as well as in the continental period. It belonged to the common ground of both currents. This makes philosophy of geometry a particularly interesting issue for the elucidation of the relation between logical empiricism and continental currents such as neo-Kantianism, phenomenology, and conventionalism.

The outline of this chapter is as follows: in section II we start with a brief discussion of "Raum," interpreting it as a typical piece of a Carnapian dissolution of philosophical disputes by a thoroughgoing logical analysis. Section III deals with the geometrical origins of Carnap's conventionalism that can be found in his thesis that the topological facts can be expressed by a conventionally chosen (geo)metrical structure in the same sense as one may choose German or English sentences to express the same propositions. The distinction between topological facts and their conventional metrical expressions is used by Carnap to put forward a partial rehabilitation of Kant's synthetic a priori. Section IV deals with Carnap's first attempt to generalize the results obtained in *Raum* to physics in general. Section V considers two examples of constitution systems dealing with the constitutional character of causality and the topological structure of space-time, respectively. Section VI treats the problem of "implicit definitions" that Carnap considered as paradigmatic for the formation of concepts (*Begriffsbildung*) of modern science in general. Section VII concludes with some general remarks on how the geometric leitmotifs left their mark on later stages of Carnap's philosophy.

II. CARNAP'S PHILOSOPHY OF GEOMETRY: SOME BASIC DISTINCTIONS

Carnap's first publication was his dissertation "Der Raum: Ein Beitrag zur Wissenschaftslehre" ("Space: A Contribution to the

Theory of Science") (1922) written in Jena under the supervision of the neo-Kantian Bruno Bauch.[1] In "Raum" Carnap intended to dissolve the conceptual muddle into which philosophy of geometry had been led by discoveries of non-Euclidean geometry and Einstein's relativistic theories.

Although space had been a problem for philosophy since its inception these events dramatically changed the agenda of philosophy of geometry and endowed this classical topic with new momentum. Mathematicians, physicists, and philosophers such as Poincaré, Hilbert, Helmholtz, Einstein, Schlick, Cassirer, and Husserl were engaged in the debate on space. "Raum" aimed to clarify this entangled discussion by pointing out that the protagonists had often talked about different things without realizing it. This led, Carnap argued, to unnecessary controversies that might be defused by carrying out a conceptual analysis that carefully distinguished between the different concepts of space that were used by the participants of the debate. For this purpose he distinguished between three notions of space that lead to three different epistemic enterprises:

(i)   formal space (formaler Raum)
(ii)   intuitive space (Anschauungsraum)
(iii)   physical space (physischer Raum)

Formal space is space in the sense of mathematics. It can be described as a relational structure defined by appropriate structural axioms, e.g. those Hilbert had proposed in his famous Grundlagen der Geometrie (Foundations of Geometry) (Hilbert, 1899). This structural conception of geometry implied, as Carnap repeatedly emphasized, that the objects the theory of formal space was speaking about were "meaningless relational terms for which one may substitute the most diverse kinds of things (numbers, colors,[2] degrees of kinship, circles, judgments, people, etc.) in so far as there are relations between them satisfying the particular formal conditions" (1922, 6).[3]

---

[1] There is an English translation of "Raum" by Michael Friedman and Peter Heath with the assistance of Alan Richardson. In the following this translation is used for the quotes of "Raum," the page references are to the German original.

[2] In "Der Raum" (1922, 10) Carnap discussed an example based on color strips that was to become of central importance for the constitutional method of "quasi-analysis" in Aufbau (1928/1967, §70; cf. also Mormann, 2003, 51f.).

[3] In Abriss (1929) he carried out this program for many other examples.

The concept of intuitive space in Carnap's sense combines elements of Kantian and Husserlian intuition in a peculiar blend. On the one hand, intuitive space is a structure whose particular nature we cannot fully specify. It can only be pointed at by certain contents of experience such as spatial forms and relations like points, linear segments, surface elements, etc. On the other hand, the basic properties and relations of intuitive space are independent of experience in the sense that their cognition is not, as with experiential propositions, made ever more secure by often repeated experience. Following Husserl, Carnap maintains that in intuitive space we are not dealing with facts in the sense of experiential reality, but rather with the essence (*eidos*) of certain data which can already be grasped in its particular nature by being given in a single instance (cf. 1922, 22). It is the task of philosophy (phenomenology) to show "which axioms about spatiality can be established by appeal to intuition" (1922, 23). Carnap's general answer is that intuition can only relate to the properties and relations of limited spatial regions. More specifically, he claimed that only the local[4] topological properties of space can be intuited, while "we have complete freedom with respect to the total structure we construct from these basic forms" (1922, 23).

Finally, physical space is constituted by actual spatial facts given in experience, for instance that a body touches another one, or that two bodies are separated from each other by a third one. In our contact with nature we experience, among other things, spatial relations such as "relations of before, within, between, near, far and so on. These relations will here be called physico-spatial. The theory of physical space . . . has the task of establishing which of these relations hold for the particular things that confront us in experience" (1922, 32).

The three kinds of space, and the three kinds of investigations that study them, should be strictly distinguished. Otherwise confusion and misunderstandings arise, as had been shown amply by the muddled debates on the nature of space. Certainly the most intriguing element of Carnap's account of geometry is the Husserlian component of intuitive space. In first approximation, intuitive space has the

---

[4] Actually Carnap did not distinguish between local and global topological properties, but from the context it is clear that he always meant "local topological properties" when he spoke of "topological properties."

role of mediating between formal space and physical space: "Cognition of physical space presupposes the cognition of intuitive space, and the latter . . . finds the pure form of its structure prefigured in formal space" (1922, 7). More precisely, he maintained that the three theories of space are related as follows: the theories of formal and intuitive space stand in the relation of specification, and the relation between the theories of intuitive and physical space is the relation of subordination. In Husserlian terminology, this hierarchy is said to correspond to the relations between formal ontology, regional ontology, and factual science (cf. Husserl, 1900–1901/1970, 303ff.).[5]

The subordination relation between intuitive and physical space implies that the cognition of physical space is based on a modified version of a Kantian synthetic a priori that determines its intuitive component. In contrast to Kant, however, this new a priori is no longer concerned with the full Euclidean structure of space, but only with the underlying topological structure. In other words, in "Raum" Carnap maintained the topological structure of Euclidean space to be a priori for cognition of physical space, since it captured the real "essence" of space. Based on these differentiations and modifications of Kant's original account, Carnap pleaded for a dissolution of the traditional dispute over the Kantian doctrine that cognition of space is based on the synthetic a priori of pure spatial intuition:

The old controversies between mathematicians, who disputed Kant's assertion, and philosophers, who defended it, were thus obviously unable to reach any result, because the two sides were not talking about the same object. The former had partly formal space in mind (e.g. Couturat) and partly physical space (Riemann, Helmholtz, Poincaré), the latter intuitive space. So both parties were correct and could have been easily reconciled if clarity had prevailed concerning the three different meanings of space. (Carnap, 1922, 47)

Whether this Kantian–Husserlian account of intuitive space is really feasible or not is hard to say, since Carnap is less than clear about it. One may well doubt if Kant's *reine Anschauung* can be equated with Husserl's *Wesenserschauung* as Carnap wants to make us believe. Fortunately, there is no need to dwell further on this problem here,

---

[5] Husserl's influence on Carnap's early philosophy has been recognized by various authors; for the *Aufbau* see Mayer (1992), and for "Raum" Sarkar (2003). See Thomas Ryckman's contribution to this volume for an extended discussion.

since already in the early 1920s Carnap abandoned the Husserlian positions of "Raum" and fell back on neo-Kantian or empiricist lines for which intuitions, be they Kantian or Husserlian ones, no longer played a role.

An early hint that intuition was to play a less important role in the future may be seen in the fact that already in "Raum" Carnap had to combine intuitive and conceptual moments in order to cope with the more general spatial structures needed in modern empirical science, in particular spaces of higher dimensions. Strictly speaking, Carnap claimed, intuition was restricted to limited areas of space, since we cannot intuit unlimited, infinite spaces of higher dimensions. Hence, axioms that intend to capture an intuition have to be axioms that refer to limited spatial regions only. Since intuition reigns only in finite regions, we are free to stipulate what are the global relations to hold in a space constructed from (possibly infinitely many) limited pieces in which intuition is assumed to hold.[6]

The distinction between formal, phenomenological, and physical space may be considered as the first example of a Carnapian conceptual analysis carried out in order to clarify the meaning of a problematic concept thereby avoiding unnecessary confusions. It would be a misunderstanding, however, to consider "Raum" simply as an exercise in classifying distinct notions of space and their relations. Under the classificatory surface are lurking substantial problems of philosophy that go well beyond the confines of philosophy of geometry proper, questions of epistemology and logic concerning the nature of theoretical concepts that left their mark on Carnap's thought throughout his life.

III. TOPOLOGICAL FACTS AND METRICAL CONVENTIONS

In this section we deal with the geometrical version of what was to become one of the most characteristic features of Carnap's thought throughout his entire philosophical career, to wit, his thoroughgoing conventionalism in matters of epistemology, philosophy of science,

---

[6] Carnap's account of this piecemeal construction of general spaces is rather sketchy and probably flawed mathematically. It is, however, well known in mathematics that the basic idea is feasible: the theory of manifolds deals with the problem of how general spaces (manifolds) can be built up in a piecemeal manner from limited regions of Euclidean spaces.

and even logic. All this began in "Raum" with the problem of conventionalism in the realm of geometry. More precisely, the problem of the relation between the metrical and the topological structure of space may be considered as the germ of Carnap's conventionalist attitude to be later generalized to cognition in general.

Arguably the most important source of inspiration for Carnap's geometric conventionalism was the French mathematician, physicist, and philosopher Henri Poincaré.[7] According to him, the axioms of geometry were neither synthetic judgments a priori nor experimental facts. Rather, they should be considered as stipulations based on agreement ("conventions") (cf. Poincare, 1902/1952, 51).

Poincaré's conventionalism with respect to the geometrical structure of space was based on his mathematical discovery that Euclidean space may be endowed with a Riemannian structure different from the standard one, namely a structure of constant negative curvature, nevertheless compatible with the standard topological structure of Euclidean space. This showed that one and the same topological space could be endowed with different geometrical structures, to wit, a Euclidean structure and a hyperbolic structure. The meaning of this mathematical fact may be explained in more vivid terms as follows:

Suppose . . . a world enclosed in a large sphere and subject to the following laws. The temperature is not uniform; it is greatest at the centre and gradually decreases as we move towards the circumference of the sphere, where it is absolute zero. The law of this temperature is as follows: if R be the radius of the sphere and r the distance of the point considered from the centre, the absolute temperature will be $R^2 - r^2$. Further, I will assume that in this world all bodies have the same coefficient of dilatation, so that the linear dilatation of any body transported from one point to another of different temperature is instantaneously in thermal equilibrium with its new environment. (Poincaré, 1902/1952, 65)

If Poincaré's world is visualized in Euclidean space E as the interior P of a large sphere S, to a spectator, who is not part of P, a rod transported toward the circumference of P will appear to shrink progressively. An inhabitant of P can therefore never reach its boundaries, all points on the circumference of P are at an infinite distance from any point within P, according to his experiences he is

<hr />

[7] On the influence of Dingler's "conventionalism" on Carnap's early philosophy see Wolters (1985).

living in an infinite world governed by the laws of hyperbolic (or Lobachevskian) geometry (cf. Zahar, 2001, 82f.).[8] Why does P matter for the problem of conventionalism? The striking answer is that the strange hyperbolic world P may be considered as simply a redescription of the Euclidean world we are all familiar with.[9] Carnap was very impressed by Poincaré's result; the bulk of the mathematical part of "Raum" is dedicated to the task of outdoing Poincaré by showing that Euclidean space E could not only be endowed with a Riemannian structure of constant *negative* curvature (as Poincaré had shown) but also with a structure of constant *positive* curvature.[10] This led him to conclude that only topological relations were matters of fact while metrical relations were mere conventions, resulting in the following extremely influential analogy (taken from Poincaré), which, in one form or other, was to appear again and again in the texts of the logical empiricists:

The transformation of a statement of matter of fact from one metrical space-form into another – e.g., from the Euclidean into one of the non-Euclidean – has been aptly compared to the translation of a proposition from one language into another. Now, just as the genuine sense of the proposition is not its presentation in one of these linguistic forms – for then its presentation in the other languages would have to appear as derivative and less original – but is merely that in the proposition which remains unaltered in translation; so too the sense of the statement of matter of fact is not one of its metrical presentations, but that which is common to all of them (the "invariants of topological transformations") – and that is precisely its presentation in merely topological form. (1922, 65)

In a slogan, then, Carnap's metrical conventionalism can be formulated as follows: the topological structure of space is to its metrical structure as the meaning of a proposition is to its specific expression

---

[8] This means mathematically that in Poincaré's world Euclid's 5th parallel axiom does not hold. It has to be replaced by the following one: Through a point P not on a line l pass two rays r_1 and r_2 which do not intersect l but such that every line between the two rays does intersect l (cf. Hilbert, 1899/1971).

[9] One may define continuous mappings P --- f --- >E and E --- g --- >P that preserve the underlying topological structure and are inverse to each other: f and g are 1-1 mappings such that inclusion and contact relations between regions of P and E are preserved, i.e., if two regions a and b of P are such that a is a part of b or a is in contact with b, then the same holds for their images f(a) and f(b) in E, and analogously for regions a' and b' of P mapped by g.

[10] This is impossible for mathematical reasons, at least if one assumes that the Riemannian metric is complete, as Carnap seemed to do.

in a given language (cf. Howard, 1996, 148). Or, with a slightly different emphasis: two metrical geometries are merely two descriptions of the same topological facts (cf. Carnap, 1966 150).

Specific arguments against Carnap's metrical conventionalism have been put forward by Ryckman (1996, 200) and Friedman (1999a, 71ff.), which argue, along different lines, that Carnap's account is not in line with the general theory of relativity. Moreover, one can argue that for purely mathematical reasons geometry fails to be a stronghold for conventionalism. One can show that Poincaré's result concerning the metrical structure of Euclidean spaces is not representative for manifolds in general: differential topology and related mathematical disciplines of twentieth-century mathematics have shown that the relation between the topological and geometrical structure of manifolds is extremely intricate (cf. Mormann 2006a). It is quite misleading to describe this relation in terms of a hierarchical conventionalism à la Carnap, according to which there is a bedrock of topological facts (*topologischer Tatbestand*) dealing with the topological structure of space-time, and then there are different "Euclidean" and "non-Euclidean languages" in which these facts are expressed.

Although these criticisms cast serious doubts on the feasibility of metrical conventionalism in geometry, they do not undermine the historico-philosophical fact that the geometrical motivation was of utmost importance for Carnap's more general conventionalist stance. For there is no doubt that Carnap took metrical conventionalism as the paradigm for conventionalism in general: the allegedly conventional character of the metrical with respect to the topological provided a central motivation for his attempts to generalize conventionalism beyond geometry that culminated in his "Principle of Tolerance," according to which even logic was considered to be conventional.

IV. THE PRINCIPLE OF MAXIMAL SIMPLICITY

Soon after *Raum* had appeared, in 1923, Carnap published the article "Über die Aufgabe der Physik"[11] ("Concerning the Task of Physics")

---

[11] There is a translation of "Über die Aufgabe der Physik" by the members of T. Ryckman's *Aufbau* Seminar at UC Berkeley, Spring 2000. In the following this translation is used for the quotes; the page references are to the German original.

in the renowned journal *Kant-Studien*. The intention of "Aufgabe" was to generalize the "critical conventionalism" of "Raum" from geometry to physics. This involved considering physics as an extension of physical geometry that not only dealt with laws of space and spatial measurement but also with that of time and action. Thereby the ken of conventionalism was extended so that it included not only spatial but also temporal and causal aspects of scientific knowledge. In line with "Raum," this amounted to partially saving a kind of Kantian a priori. In contrast to "Raum," however, Carnap did not ask Husserl for help in this venture. And this was for good reasons: although a modified synthetic a priori (that actually amounted to a topological one) might have had a certain appeal in geometry, the new developments in physics rendered it highly implausible that an analogous move could be successful there. In the 1920s no reasonable philosopher of science dared propose some substantial physical theory as a priori as Kant had claimed for Newtonian physics. If something like a physical synthetic a priori should survive in physics, it had to be of a radically different nature.

Carnap proposed an a priori that renounced all claims to necessity, but was to be interpreted as a purely hypothetical constitutional principle. This "movable" a priori was to become the primary source for introducing conventional components into the realm of physical knowledge. Thereby, a radical empiricist account of physics became untenable. Consequently, "Aufgabe" opened with the following explicitly anti-empiricist thesis:

> After the question concerning the sources of physical knowledge has been heatedly debated over a long time, perhaps today already it can be said that pure empiricism has lost its dominance. (Carnap, 1923, 90)

Radicalizing the approach of "Raum," conventions play a role not only for matters spatial but also for temporal and causal relations (1923, 98). Succinctly this is expressed by saying that conventions are important for the *Raumgesetz* (space postulate), *Zeitgesetz* (time postulate), and the *Wirkungsgesetz* (action postulate). Since the problem of the space postulate has already been dealt with extensively in "Raum," let us concentrate on some remarks concerning the time postulate and action postulate. The time postulate amounts to the stipulation of a *periodic* process, i.e., a clock. For such a stipulation conventional choices play a role analogous to those that govern the choice of a rigid body. The conventional character of the action postulate is more difficult to render plausible. Carnap argued that the action postulate exhibits a conventional character in so far as we have the choice either to prefer relatively simple action laws and are thereby committed to assume a relatively complicated distribution of acting substance, or to rely on complicated action laws that govern a relatively simple distribution of the acting substance.

The overarching rule governing the conventional formulations of the three postulates, is the *Einfachstheitsprinzip* (Principle of Maximal Simplicity) (PMS) (1923, 93). To put it bluntly, (PMS) required that the laws were to be chosen in such a way that the resulting theory was as simple as possible. This was, of course, not very exciting. The new twist that Carnap gave to this traditional account becomes visible only when one takes into account more precisely the structure of physical theory. For this purpose he proposed to consider a highly idealized "completed physics" as it would be available to a Laplacian demon who knows everything there is to know about a fully deterministic world. Such a *completed* physics, conceived as a "Great Book of Nature," consisted of three volumes:

The first volume . . . contains synthetic a priori propositions, although not exactly in the Kantian transcendental critical sense. For that would mean that they express the necessary conditions of the objects of experience, themselves conditioned through the forms of intuition and of thought. In that case, however, only one possible frame for the content of these volumes is given. In actuality its construction is left to our repeated choice.
. . .
The second volume establishes the mediation between the domain of perception and the domain that is the object of physical theories.
. . .
The third volume contains the description of the physical state of the world at any two points in time. (1923, 97)

After these elucidations concerning the structure of an ideal physics the problem of applying (PMS) can be described more precisely as the problem to which part of physics (PMS) should be applied. Hence, the problem of applying (PMS) may be formulated as follows:

"Does the requirement of maximal simplicity hold for the basic law or for the description of the state of the world made on the basis of this law?" (1923, 94)

An example from elementary geometry makes clear that the application of the Principle of Maximal Simplicity may yield different outcomes. Assume our task is to give an account of the spatial distribution of trees in a nursery. If we have no further information, we may be inclined to use the conceptually simplest coordinate system we have learned in high school, to wit, rectangular Cartesian coordinates, and describe the position of each tree by its coordinates in this system. It may be the case, however, that the trees are distributed in some oblique-angled system, in concentric circles or in some other way of this kind. In this case their positions could be expressed in Cartesian coordinates only in a rather complicated and roundabout way, and it might have been more economical to use a more complicated system of oblique or polar coordinates, although these systems are at first look more complicated than the Cartesian one.

As an example from physics Carnap mentioned the following case: if one takes into account only the axiomatic component of physical knowledge, the simplest system resulting from the application of (PMS) is traditional physics based on Euclidean geometry and Newtonian physics. Hence, if simplicity concerned only the basic axioms, Dingler would be justified in preferring the traditional theory to Einstein's new relativistic system (cf. 1923, 104). On the other hand, if (PMS) is applied to the second component of physical knowledge, things look different, since then the general theory of relativity scores best, while the traditional theories "become very complicated; e.g. to the electron there probably corresponds a spiral vortex ring of third order made up of ether particles" (1922, 105).[12]

Conventionality in the sense of Carnap has not much to do with arbitrariness and relativism. On the contrary, the conventional character of empirical knowledge helps enhance its rational character, since through this door philosophy of science enters the stage to play a role in the task of deciding which theory to take among several competing ones. If the basic principles of science – the space postulate, the time postulate, and the action postulate – are to be formulated according to the Principle of Maximal Simplicity, and if the application of this principle requires carefully reasoned methodological

---

[12] Carnap even proposed to replace the "untenable" distinction between "false" and "true" theories by a purely methodological one that distinguished between reasonably complex theories and "too complicated" ones (cf. 1923, 106).

choices, this calls for philosophy as methodology of science. In particular, Carnap considered the insight that philosophy of science could help explicate the various possibilities of building up the edifice of physics that result from the choices concerning the space postulate (*Raumgesetz*), time postulate (*Zeitgesetz*), and action postulates (*Wirkungsgesetz*) according to the overarching principle of (PMS):

Thus we have shown which decisions have to be made and which criteria have to be established in order to evaluate a physical theory and to decide between several competing theories, withdrawing the choice between competing theories from scientific instincts that have so far reigned supreme in this area, and put it under the reign of conscious principles of the theory of science [*Wissenschaftslehre*]. (1923, 107; translation altered)

Later, this thesis was reformulated and generalized in his theory of linguistic frameworks (cf. Carnap, 1950a), according to which the task of philosophy of science is to make proposals for the choice of convenient linguistic and ontological frameworks for doing science. Thereby the ideal philosopher of science could be characterized as an inventor of languages that could help formulate scientific knowledge in a perspicuous manner.

V. CONSTRUCTING WORLDS

Before Carnap built the world in 1928,[13] he had already been engaged in a variety of constitutional projects that did not concern the entire world, but whose scale had been a bit more modest. This plurality of "*Aufbau* projects"[14] shows that the task of constitution theory was a very general one dealing with many constitutional systems.

Indeed, the first *Aufbau* project can be found already in "Raum," which sketched the constitution of global space out of building blocks of small, intuitively graspable spatial regions. Here Carnap explicitly spoke of "the logical constitution of space from the elements

---

[13] This phrase is borrowed from the title of Wedberg (1973).
[14] The English translation "structure" for "Aufbau" in George's translation, *The Logical Structure of the World*, is positively misleading. "Aufbau" has a strong process component meaning "construction" in the active sense. For a thoroughgoing interpretation of the connotations of the emblematic notion of "Aufbau" in twentieth-century German culture see Galison (1996).

of sense perception" (1922, 82). In the mid-1920s other, more physics-oriented constitutional projects were under way: "Dreidimensionalität des Raumes und Kausalität" ("Three-dimensionality of Space and Causality") (1924) treated the constitution of several "secondary worlds" from the "primary world of sense impressions", and "Über die Abhängigkeit der Eigenschaften des Raumes von denen der Zeit" ("On the Dependency of the Properties of Space on those of Time") (1925) tackled the task of constructing the topological structure of space-time from the topological structure of time and the coincidence relation of world-lines. Although this work is certainly to be considered as an integral part of the *Aufbau* programme that characterized his philosophical agenda in 1920, world-lines and coincidences show up in the *Aufbau* only sporadically in examples and brief elucidating comments (cf.1928/1967, §15, §126, 133).

Let us first consider "Dreidimensionalität," where Carnap pursued a liberalized Machian approach that aimed to reconstruct from a "primary world of sense impressions the fictitious secondary worlds of things and of physics," in particular a three-dimensional structure (1924, 3). Compared with "Aufgabe" the conventionalist attitude in "Dreidimensionalität" is more radical and global: while in "Aufgabe" conventional choices were governed by the Principle of Maximal Simplicity, "Dreidimensionalität" stressed that convention-guided choices may occur at many junctures of the constitutional process. Thus, the results of these constitutional processes cannot be expected to yield unique results. For instance, starting with the constitutional base of "the primary world of sense impressions," two quite different constitutions can be carried out: the common-sense "world of things and causal relations" on the one hand, and the a-causal "physical world" on the other.

"Dreidimensionalität" is Carnap's only paper at this time where Humean ideas are clearly visible. Following Hume he claimed that causality was a fictitious moment not to be found among the basic experiences themselves (cf. Hume, 1748, II). Going further than Hume, Carnap contended that the fiction of causality and the fiction of the three-dimensionality of the experienced world are closely related: more precisely, the fiction of a three-dimensional world is said to be a logical consequence of the fiction of physical causality.

In "Dreidimensionalität" the base level from which all constitutions are carried out is the "primary world of sense impressions (*primäre Welt der Sinnesempfindungen*)." This domain exhibits a certain qualitative spatial and temporal order (some experiences are later than others, some may happen at the same place, others not, etc.) but still this experience is not articulated in terms of "things" and their "properties," and there do not exist causal relations between experiences that single out some as causes of others. Carnap insisted that this world of primary experiences is not a philosopher's abstraction, but really exists. He claimed that uninterpreted sensations without an objectual carrier, so to speak, really exist, for instance in very young children, or when we are not attentive, etc. From this weakly ordered primary world of sense impressions different "fictitious secondary worlds" may be constructed. Among them, the most important ones are the "world of things" and the "world of physics."[15] The world of things may be characterized as the world of common sense consisting of things and their properties, ordered in space and time in the familiar way, and moreover enjoying an articulated causal structure. This world is constructed from the world of primary experience by applying the categories of "substantiality" and "causality" in order to single out certain complexes of primary experiences as "causes" and others as "effects."

The world of things is, however, not the only secondary world that may be constructed from the primary world. There is also the world of physics lacking causal relations and, in its purest version, it becomes a purely relational structure whose terms have nothing to do with spatiality or temporality and lack any sensational character. Nor do the processes of the physical world involve any causal "activity"; rather, they exhibit dependencies expressed in certain mathematical-functional relations. For Carnap, both the scientific image (physics) *and* the manifest image (common-sense world) are fictions, in the sense that they are constituted from a basic primary level of primitive sense impressions. It would be a serious misunderstanding of Carnap's intentions to consider him as embracing a scientism according to which only the physical world is real. *Both* the "world of things" *and* the "world of physics" are constructs from the primary world. It would equally be a serious misunderstanding, however, to conceive these constructs as "*mere* fictions"

---

[15] The "world of things" and the "world of physics" may be considered as the structural precursors of the "thing language" and the "language of physics" that played an important role later (cf. for instance Carnap, 1950a).

in any metaphysically derogatory sense: Carnap (1924, 7) explicitly emphasizes that "the expression 'fiction' carries no metaphysically negative value character," and designates merely something that is constituted rather than primary.

In "Abhängigkeit" Carnap pursued a rather different constitutional project in the realm of physical geometry. This paper is an attempt to construct the topological properties of space from those of time and the incidence relation between world-lines. Carnap announced that even the metrical properties of space-time may be constructed from that base. At first sight, Carnap's proposal may look "bizarre" (Pincock, 2002, 8), but it is actually quite reasonable if we view it from the perspective of "Raum." There Carnap had pointed out that the essential structure of space was topological: metrical structure was conceived as only a conventional "form" of topological structure. The topological structure of space-time may be considered as similarly elusive, and it is natural to ask if it can be constructed from some underlying, more primitive structure. In "Abhängigkeit" Carnap intended to do just this, relying on the distinction between spatial and temporal dimensions in the theory of relativity. Although Carnap offered only a sketch, his approach seems feasible, at least if one works in the framework of the special theory of relativity, and it has some similarity with that of Robb (1914).

The constitutional system of "Abhängigkeit" is given by a class of basic elements and some relations defined for them: the class of base elements is defined as the set of world-lines of elementary particles, and the set of basic relations comprises the binary relations C (coincidence) and T (temporal precedence). The resulting system is called the C-T-system. More precisely, each world-line is to be conceptualized as a continuous series of states, to be interpreted as the temporally ordered states of an elementary particle. Note that this description implicitly relies on a topological structure of the world-lines due to the requirement of continuity. Each point of such a world-line may be called a world-point. We now need a relation between the world-lines of different particles by which possible interactions can be described, and this is provided by the coincidence relation C that determines which states of different world-lines are to be identified. In order that such an identification works, C has to be at least an equivalence relation. Moreover, in order that C and T smoothly collaborate, one has to assume that the intersection $C \cap T$ is empty, i.e., there do not exist two world states s *and* s* such that s temporally precedes s* and s and s* coincide (cf. Carnap, 1925). Given C and T, one can define a relation W such that a W b can be physically interpreted as "a physically influences b," i.e. causal connectibility (1925, 339), which can be used to define simultaneity and the differentiation between spacelike and timelike trajectories. Carnap's argumentation essentially amounts to the assertion that the light-cone structure of Minkowski space-time determines all of its geometrical properties, in particular the topology of its three-dimensional spatial slices.

The important point is that the C-T-system is a sketch of a constitutional system in its own right. It and the systems dealt with in "Dreidimensionalität" show evidence, once again, of the pluralism inherent in Carnap's constitutional approach. The "phenomenalist" system that eventually figured prominently in the *Aufbau* was one of many possible ones Carnap was investigating. Hence, it may be considered as an historical coincidence that for the *Aufbau* he chose such a phenomenalist system. Taking into account his early constitutional attempts reveals that the constitutional program had a much broader and more flexible scope than many critics of the *Aufbau* have realized. Success of this general program had relatively little to do with the phenomenalist example which got preferential treatment in the *Aufbau* (cf. Friedman, 1999a).

VI. CONCEPT CONSTITUTION AND FREE-FLOATING SYSTEMS

The problem of understanding geometrical concepts is naturally embedded in the more general task of providing a thoroughgoing philosophical understanding of scientific concept formation in general (cf. Carnap, 1926; Cassirer 1910/1953). Carnap had begun this endeavor in "Raum," and it continued to play a vital role in virtually every following work. In this section we will concentrate on the unduly neglected paper "Über eigentliche und uneigentliche Begriffe" ("On Proper and Improper Concepts," 1927).

As indicated already in its title, the main task of "Begriffe" was the distinction between two kinds of essentially different concepts, to wit, proper and improper ones. While proper concepts are a well-trodden topic of traditional logic and epistemology, improper concepts came into being only in the context of modern geometry and mathematics in the nineteenth and twentieth century. To set the stage, we begin with a brief discussion of Carnap's account of proper concepts, then the constitution of proper concept is dealt with, and finally the role of "free-floating" conceptual systems for constitutional theory is considered.

Taking Kant as his point of departure, Carnap proposed to conceive a (proper) concept as a predicate of possible judgments, or, in terms of modern logic, as a propositional function F. For him, the essential feature of a proper concept was that it is 2-valued. This means given an object *a*, either *a* is F or *a* is not F: *tertium non datur* (cf. Carnap, 1927, 1). Further, concepts appear as elements of conceptual systems, i.e., as belonging to an ensemble of concepts ordered "logically" in some way or other. Carnap assumed that concepts can be ordered in such a way that certain concepts are taken as basic in that all other concepts can be derived from them by explicit definitions: "In this way the concepts of any area of knowledge can be ordered in a "constitution system" ("Konstitutionssystem") (1927, 2).[16] For every defined concept C the explicit definitions by which it is tied to the basic concepts provide empirical clues that can be used to find out whether a given object is or is not C.

The relation between a conceptual system and its constitution system is elucidated by the following geometric metaphor:

By such a characterizing definition or "constitution" ("Konstitution") a concept is not treated exhaustively at all. Only its place in the system of concepts has been determined, just as metaphorically a place on the surface of the earth is determined by geographical longitude and latitude; its further properties have to be determined by empirical investigations, and represented in the theory of the domain in question. But in order that this representation refers to something determined, first the constitution (the geographical coordinates in the simile) have to be given. (1927, 4)

Such a "coordination" relies on a strict separation between the empirical and the analytical component of a concept. In §179 of the *Aufbau* this geographical simile appears again, and the separation in question is explicitly given as a distinction between analytic (conventional) aspects, on the one hand, and synthetic components of

---

[16] In "Begriffe" Carnap mentioned the forthcoming *Aufbau* as "the book in which the theory of constitution (*Konstitutionstheorie*)" will be presented.

empirical knowledge, on the other. Thus, the constitution of concepts in the sense of *Konstitutionstheorie* did not intend to reconstruct the entire concept, but only to give a set of characteristic features, its "coordinates," so to speak. This geometrical description of the function of a constitution system has been further elaborated by Nelson Goodman:

The function of a constructional system is not to recreate experience but rather to map it. The constructed concepts of a constructional system are not meant to replace the original concepts without rest. Rather, the constructional system is a map very much like the highly stylized railway maps or underground maps that give the user of such a map the necessary information to use such a railway system. (Goodman, 1963b, 552)

This conception of a constitution system makes clear that a rational reconstruction of a concept as a result of its logical analysis need not be similar to the un-analyzed concept, just as a sign on a map need not be similar to the place it denotes.

This becomes even more evident when we consider improper concepts and their role for the constitution of systems of (proper) concepts. In particular, for formal mathematical concepts such as "point," "line," or "number" the *tertium non datur* does not hold. For instance, to ask whether a given object is a natural number or not does not make sense on its own. Any countably infinite set **N** of entities may be rendered a set of "natural numbers" by stipulating a convenient "successor function" s: **N**→**N** satisfying Peano's axioms. In a similar vein, any set of entities may be rendered a set of geometrical points by appropriate stipulations. Hence, concepts such as "number" or "geometrical point" fail to be "proper concepts," they are only "improper concepts" or "variable concepts" (cf. 1927, 15).

The most important kind of concepts, for the sake of which all scientific research is carried out, are real concepts ("Realbegriffe") such as "vertebrate" or "Paris" (1927, 2). In this task formal concepts are used as tools to present knowledge of real concepts (1927, 24). Hence one may ask what improper concepts such as Peano numbers or Hilbertian lines and points are good for. Strictly speaking, they are not (proper) concepts at all, and so we need to explain why improper concepts are so important for empirical science. Real concepts (such as "vertebrate") have an empirical reference, since they are built up step by step and can be verified, at least in principle. By contrast the improper concepts are floating in the air,[17] so to speak, at least in the beginnings. They are introduced by an axiomatic system AS that does not immediately refer to reality. Strictly speaking, the axioms of this system do not form a theory (since they are not about anything), but only a theory-schema, an empty form for possible theories . . . But if in the system of knowledge a real concept appears that can empirically be shown to satisfy the formal requirements formulated by AS for the corresponding improper concept, then the AS has found a realization: in place of the improper concept that is a variable, one can insert the corresponding real concept . . . Through the contact of the real concept and the axioms . . . in one stroke the relation is established with the theory-scheme based on AS. The blood of empirical reality is streaming through this interface and flows to the most remote veins of this scheme, up to now empty, rendering it a full theory . . . Hence, the formulation of improper concepts and the derivation of the theorems valid for them means constructing empty theories in stock for later use. (1927, 23)

Hence, we may consider an axiom system of improper concepts as an uninterpreted calculus that becomes interpreted by appropriate coordination rules,[18] and the most important example of such a free-floating conceptual system for Carnap was Hilbert's relational system of Euclidean geometry (cf. Hilbert, 1899, and "Raum"). In general, relational mathematics with its improper concepts thus provided the formal tools of a general theory of constitution systems which could be used to rationally reconstruct the conceptual systems of our scientific knowledge.

VII. CONCLUSION

Carnap began his philosophical career in the context of scientifically minded German "Schulphilosophie." What distinguished him from other authors of this ilk were his sustained efforts to come to terms with the then contemporary technical situations in geometry,

---

[17] This phrase can already be found in Schlick's *General Theory of Knowledge* (Schlick, 1918).

[18] Carnap's talk about "realizations," "formal models," etc. may be taken as evidence that improper concepts had ushered him into the domain of semantics. He was to become fully aware of this fact only later. One should here take into account that his notions of syntax and semantics were different from the ones used today (cf. Coffa, 1991; Creath, 1991; Bonk and Mosterín, 2000; Awodey and Carus, 2004). See Erich Reck's and Steve Awodey's contributions to this volume for further discussion.

physics, and logic (cf. Richardson, 2003a, 174). This intimate relation with science may be considered as the characteristic feature of the emerging logical empiricism of which Carnap was to become a distinguished representative.

Overcoming philosophical problems by carefully distinguishing the meanings of concepts used by participants in philosophical disputes was a method Carnap would apply again and again in the future: for instance, the distinction between the material and the formal modes of speech (Carnap, 1934), and the distinction between different notions of confirmation or probability (cf. Carnap, 1936/1937 and 1950b). Of course, this attitude can be explained by Carnap's general predilection for logical analysis he clearly expressed on many occasions. As he says in his "Intellectual autobiography," after having read Russell he took "the application of the new logical instrument for the purposes of analyzing scientific concepts and of clarifying philosophical problems [as] the essential aim of [his] philosophical activity" (Carnap, 1963a, 13). What may be added is that this "new logical instrument" had not been forged in the void, as it were, but rather to cope with the very specific challenges that modern geometry and relational mathematics were posing for logic and philosophy.[19]

In the hands of Russell and Carnap, logical analysis always resulted in the construction of new conceptual systems. These constructions may be underdetermined by their base, i.e., usually it is possible to construct different systems from a given base as is shown by the various secondary worlds that can be constructed from the primary world of sense impressions (cf. "Dreidimensionalität," 1924). Carnap did not consider this plurality as a defect of his account, quite the contrary. Indeed, this essential plurality of constitutional systems may have led Carnap to the insight that the task of philosophy was not to argue for a single system as the only true one but to chart the "boundless ocean" of constitutional possibilities.

The plurality of possible systems naturally rendered conventions important. If several constitutions were possible, conventional choices had to be made. For Carnap, the first and most impressive example for such a choice was provided by Poincaré's

---

[19] Indeed, Russell had developed the theory of relations first to cope with problems of geometry; only later did he apply it to arithmetic and analysis.

distinct metrical structures for the underlying topological space of the Euclidean plane. The attempt to generalize the allegedly purely conventional relation between topological and geometrical structure to other fields may be considered as the driving force behind Carnap's conventionalism.

The geometrical origins of the characteristic lines of Carnap's thinking are more clearly visible in the early stages of his philosophical development;[20] later they are masked under a wealth of scholarly refinements and sophisticated transformations. Indeed, after the 1920s geometry virtually disappeared as an explicit theme from Carnap's philosophical work.[21] Nevertheless, the philosophical problems once put on his agenda by geometry remained central for his philosophy throughout. Philosophy of geometry thus provided the leitmotifs ("guiding principles") of his philosophy in a quite literal sense.[22]

[20] The emphasis in this chapter on the geometrical origins of Carnap's thought is not to be understood as denying the obvious importance of logic for him. On the contrary, there is a deep connection between logic and geometry. Hence, revealing the geometrical roots of his philosophy intends to contribute to a better understanding of the logical aspects as well.

[21] In Carnap's later work, philosophy of geometry surfaces explicitly only twice: in his "Reply" to Grünbaum's criticism of "Raum" (1963e) and in *Philosophical Foundations of Physics* (1966) where he discussed geometrical conventionalism in basically the same way as he had done in "Raum" more than forty years earlier.

[22] I would like to thank Michael Friedman for improving the English style and the clarity of the exposition of my contribution.

3   Carnap and Frege*

Rudolf Carnap is, along with Frege, Russell, and Wittgenstein, one of the outstanding representatives of analytic philosophy – indeed, its most radical, as shown by his attempt to reduce philosophy to the logic of science, thereby seeking to establish philosophy itself as a science. But if we want to understand Carnap, we have to examine the historical situation in which his thought developed. The founders of a new tradition often remain indebted to the tradition they seek to break with. Unlike those who come after them, they are conscious of their opposition to the older tradition, and even when it does not surface as a central theme, their ideas at least bear indirect witness to it. This is certainly true of Carnap, an analytic philosopher whose ideas are deeply rooted in continental European soil, drawing nourishment not only from the "dry" soil of science, but also from Carnap's "rich" experience as an active member of the German Youth Movement. After leaving Europe, Carnap more or less abandoned those roots for political reasons. But in his "Intellectual Autobiography," he does vouchsafe a few clues about early influences on his intellectual development during his student years and immediately thereafter (Carnap, 1963a, 3–13).

Carnap studied philosophy, physics, and mathematics at the Universities of Jena and Freiburg from the summer of 1910 to the summer of 1914, and again from the winter of 1918–19 to the summer of 1919. The lengthy interruption was due to his military service

* My thanks to Brady Bowman, André Carus, Michael Friedman, and Wolfgang Kienzler for helpful comments and suggestions for revisions to the original draft of this chapter, and particularly to André Carus for his stimulating criticisms and many suggestions for stylistic improvement. This chapter was translated from the German by Aaron Epstein and Christian Kästner.

between August 1914 and December 1918. In his "Autobiography," Carnap writes that his teachers in Jena were the philosopher Bruno Bauch, who was eventually to serve as an examiner for Carnap's dissertation "Der Raum," the educational thinker Herman Nohl, but above all the mathematician Gottlob Frege, to whom Carnap pays greatest tribute.

In what context did Carnap first become acquainted with Frege in Jena? He began by attending Frege's lectures on *Conceptual Notation* (*Begriffsschrift*), part I in the autumn and winter of 1910–11 and part II in the spring and summer of 1913. He also attended Frege's course on analytical mechanics, part I in the autumn and winter of 1912–13, and part II in the spring and summer of 1913. Finally, he attended Frege's course on *Logic in Mathematics* in the spring and summer of 1914. Carnap's notes on *Conceptual Notation* and *Logic in Mathematics* have survived and editions have been published in both German and English (Reck and Awodey, 2004). These lectures were Carnap's first contact with modern formal logic – a contact that came about, as Carnap himself admitted, out of pure curiosity, evoked by a friend's remark "that somebody had found it interesting" (1963a, 5).

I. LOGIC AND LOGICISM

Carnap's detailed notes on these lecture courses reveal both a sustained interest in modern logic, and an excellent understanding of it. In both lecture courses on *Conceptual Notation*, Carnap became particularly well acquainted with Frege's two-dimensional formalism of propositional logic as well as first-order and second-order predicate logic, together with its use in representing different mathematical concepts. For the most part, this formalism corresponds to what we find in Frege's *Grundgesetze der Arithmetik*. However, as a consequence of Russell's paradox, value ranges are now completely eliminated, and, along with them, extensions of concepts or classes – a change that Frege does not even mention. Carnap's lecture notes confirm his later recollection that Frege's lectures never discussed Russell's paradox or any "possible modifications of his system in order to eliminate it." This seems to have led Carnap to the optimistic view that Frege "was confident that a satisfactory way for overcoming the difficulty could be found" (Carnap, 1963a, 5).

He thus failed to perceive that Frege had already tacitly realized the negative implications of Russell's paradox. These were not relevant to logic in the narrow sense, but were very significant for logicism.

By eliminating the notion of extensions of concepts, Frege effectively abandoned the logicist program of providing a purely logical foundation for arithmetic, whereby numbers could be conceived as logical objects. In Part I of Frege's lecture course *Conceptual Notation*, statements involving number are analyzed as propositions not about objects, but about concepts. They have the form, "the number *n* belongs to the concept *F*." This implies that numbers themselves are to be construed as second-level concepts – ones expressing a property of first-level concepts. Thus the proposition that "the number o belongs to the concept *F*" means that the number of objects falling under the (first-level) concept *F* is o. Using the universal quantifier, Frege expresses this by negating for all objects whatsoever that they fall under the concept *F*: $\forall x \, \neg F(x)$. This formulation arises because Frege's symbolism does not introduce an existential quantifier, but rather expresses existence using the universal quantifier and the negation sign. This proposition is logically equivalent to the negative existential proposition: "It is not the case that there is an object falling under the concept *F*": $\neg \exists x \, F(x)$. The proposition that the number of objects falling under the concept *F* is 1 is represented in the following manner: "There is at least one object that falls under the concept *F*, and if two things fall under the concept *F*, then they are identical" (Reck and Awodey, 2004, 84). In other words: "There is one and only one object that falls under the concept *F*." Thus Frege returns to an interpretation which he had considered in his *Grundlagen der Arithmetik* but had then believed he had to reject because it was inconsistent with the view he then held that numbers are logical objects. In *Grundlagen*, Frege defines "the number 1 belongs to the concept *F*" as meaning "Whatever *a* may be, the proposition does not hold universally that *a* does not fall under *F*, and [. . .] from the propositions '*a* falls under *F*' and '*b* falls under *F*' it follows universally that *a* and *b* are the same" (Frege, 1884/1980, §55). Here Frege succeeds in avoiding the appearance of circularity in Carnap's notes, where the expression "two" occurs in the definiens. In today's logical formalism, the definition translates as $\neg \forall x \, \neg F(x) \, \& \, \forall x \forall y \, [(F(x) \, \& \, F(y)) \rightarrow x=y]$.

Carnap seems to have identified what Frege presented in the lecture course with Frege's original logicism. He himself appropriated this later presentation when he introduced numbers as second-level concepts. Even many years later, Carnap continued to regard it as essential to Fregean logicism that the logical analysis of number statements employ quantifiers (Carnap, 1993, 137f.) and he ignored the fact that Frege had given up the conception of statements of number as propositions about logical *objects* which had originally been of such importance to him. Frege had held this earlier view not just for logico-mathematical reasons, for example to ensure that numbers could serve as arguments of first-level functions; as we shall see later, Frege's early conception was also associated with a metaphysical program that was completely foreign to Carnap.

The early Carnap adopted the view about statements of number that he encountered in Frege's lectures, as we can easily gather from the fact that he defined "the number of the concept f is two," for example, as follows: "There is an x and there is a y such that x is not identical with y, x falls under f, y falls under f, and for every z it is the case that if z falls under f, z is identical with x or with y."[1] But in this connection he does not mention Frege's original objection, expressed in the *Grundlagen*, that, through definitions of this kind, the individual numbers o, 1, etc. are not defined, but only the phrases, "the number o belongs to [the concept F]," "the number 1 belongs to [the concept F]," etc. Such contextual definitions do not allow us "to distinguish o and 1 here as independent, reidentifiable objects" (Frege, 1884/1980, §56). It was not until later that Carnap recognized this point as differing from his own view (cf. Carnap, 1934c/1937, 138–140). In *Meaning and Necessity*, Carnap cites Frege's chief reason for not regarding numbers as second-level concepts or, as stated here, "as properties of properties": Frege thought "that cardinal numbers are independent entities, while properties are not," and Carnap explicitly adds that he finds this reasoning "far from convincing" (Carnap, 1947, 116). Thus he indirectly implies that he does not subscribe to Frege's categorial distinction between "complete (*abgeschlossenen*)" objects and "unsaturated (*ungesättigten*)" concepts.

---

[1] Carnap (1930a/1959, 21/141). Cf. Carnap (1947, 115). The formal presentation of 27–3 found here does not entirely correspond to the formulation in "The old and new logic," but the two are logically equivalent. Cf. also Carnap (1934c/1937, §38b); Carnap (1954/1968, 70).

It is of course possible that Carnap simply failed to grasp Frege's distinction correctly. The elucidations of the expression "unsaturated" that he offers in *Der logische Aufbau der Welt* would tend to support this view. There Carnap writes that Frege showed "that extension symbols, and thus class symbols, are *unsaturated* (*ungesättigte*) *symbols*." However, when Carnap refers to "incomplete symbols" here, he is using the term in Russell's sense, to refer to symbols that do not have independent meaning in themselves.[2] If we follow Russell, expressions for extensions of concepts are indeed *incomplete* symbols, but according to Frege they are not *unsaturated*, precisely because they designate complete objects.

This misunderstanding would still not explain, however, how Carnap could have thought that Frege treated the extensions of concepts as the reference or *Bedeutung* (Carnap translates this as "nominatum") of concept words or predicates (Carnap, 1947, 125). Since the publication of Frege's *Nachlass* we know that Frege felt constrained by his strict distinction between complete objects and unsaturated concepts to identify the *Bedeutungen* ("nominata") of concept words or predicates with the concepts themselves (cf. Frege, 1892a/1997). Carnap could have known this earlier, for his own notes on Frege's lecture course *Conceptual Notation* provide evidence for such a view (Reck and Awodey, 2004, 74). It is true that concept words which have different intensions (senses) but the same extension, such as "human" and "featherless biped," fulfill Frege's criterion for identity of *Bedeutung*: they can be substituted for one another in sentences without the *Bedeutung* of the sentence, its truth value, being altered. But Frege still would not have considered them as the *Bedeutungen* of predicative (unsaturated) concept words since extensions of concepts are objects and, as such, are complete and hence not unsaturated.

Although Carnap does not adopt Frege's distinction, he nonetheless tries to do justice to Frege's insistence that the use of numbers as arguments of first-level functions, especially the relation of equality, requires numbers to be considered as objects. Thus, within the framework of his "method of extension and intension," Carnap treats number expressions as second-level predicates, distinguishing between

---

[2] Carnap (1928a/1967, §33). In the English edition the idea is rendered by the expression "incomplete" instead of "unsaturated," which conceals Carnap's misunderstanding.

their intensions (as second-level properties) and their extensions (as second-level classes). In this way he ensures, in accordance with Frege's view, that "equality of numbers can be regarded as identity of certain entities, not of number intensions but of number extensions" (Carnap, 1947/1956, 117). Here, however, it must be pointed out that when Carnap speaks of entities, he is not to be understood metaphysically. The distinctions at issue are to be understood as holding only within a "linguistic framework," in this case, the framework of the method of extension and intension. Thus Carnap emphasizes that the acceptance of a linguistic framework, such as the framework of natural numbers, "must not be regarded as implying a metaphysical doctrine concerning the reality of the entities in question" (Carnap, 1950a/1956, 214).

II. METAPHYSICS

The greatest difference between Carnap and Frege lies in their assessment of metaphysics. Carnap deprecated metaphysics, even occasionally to the point of seeking its complete "elimination" by means of the logical analysis of language.[3] Frege, by contrast, uses logical analysis locally in order to criticize *particular* metaphysical statements and arguments, pointing out, for instance, that the ontological argument for the existence of God fails because it uses the concept of existence, a second-level concept, as a first-level concept. Carnap was already familiar with this analysis from Frege's lectures, and he emphasizes the fact in his memoirs (Carnap, 1963a, 1966; cf. Reck and Awodey, 2004, 80f.). In contrast to Carnap, however, Frege never makes any explicit reference to his position on metaphysics. Only when it comes to the relation between logic and metaphysics does he emphatically assert the independence of logic from metaphysical principles, insisting that, on the contrary, it is metaphysics that rests on the principles of logic (Frege, 1893, XIX).

To be sure, Frege was hardly an advocate of the speculative metaphysics that Carnap associated with the German Idealists Fichte, Schelling, and Hegel. Like his philosophy teacher Hermann Lotze, Frege belonged rather to a rationalist tradition going back to Leibniz, while his foundationalism regarding questions of validity bears

---

[3] Carnap (1932d/1959); further discussion in Gabriel (2003).

affinity to the neo-Kantians' interest in the theory of value (discussed below). Frege viewed himself as a logician first and foremost, and as such abstained from explicit metaphysical commitments; even so, his philosophical reflections on the theory of knowledge and ontology are shot through with assumptions and implications that are undoubtedly "metaphysical" in Carnap's sense. This is shown, for instance, by his defense of epistemological realism and his logical Platonism concerning the ontological status of numbers.

It is not quite clear whether Frege's metaphysical interests were the expression of a metaphysical need which his logicism was designed to satisfy, or whether they were themselves a consequence of his attempt to establish a logical foundation for arithmetic. In any case, these metaphysical interests are particularly apparent in *Grundlagen der Arithmetik*. With his introduction of numbers as logical objects, Frege contradicts the basic premise of Kant's critique of metaphysics, namely that we have no cognitive access to the realm of "intelligible objects." Kant considers objects to be intelligible "if they can be conceived of by reason alone and are not accessible to any of our sensible intuitions (*Anschauungen*)" (Kant, 1783/1950, §34, note). Frege holds numbers to be precisely such intelligible objects. Gaining knowledge of objects from formal logic is only possible if, in contrast to Kant's view, formal logic is granted content. Frege's logicism would be inconsistent with a merely formal view of logic.

The conditions of the possibility of knowledge of objects are formulated by Kant in his transcendental aesthetic and transcendental logic. In particular, Kant emphasizes the distinction between formal and transcendental logic, since, according to him, formal logic abstracts from all content and cannot provide the conditions for our thought relating to objects. Frege, by contrast, does not provide for a distinction between formal and transcendental logic; for him, the forms and categories of formal logic are the only categories of our thought. Carnap also broadly subscribes to this view, although he introduces some additional constraints. For Frege, only violations of logical syntax can be viewed as category mistakes. Thus a sentence such as "Julius Caesar exists" is senseless, since here an object appears as the argument of a second-level function, namely the concept of existence. In contrast, a sentence such as "Julius Caesar is a number" is not senseless (though false) since here the object forms the argument of a first-level function (first-level concept). Though Carnap excludes such cases as "confusions of spheres" (*Sphärenvermengungen*) (Carnap, 1928a/1967, §§29–31; cf. Klein, 2004), he follows Frege in treating formal logic as the basis for a system of categories, i.e., as a transcendental logic in Kant's sense. Again, however, Frege goes further than Kant would have allowed, since he believes that logic may serve not only as a "canon" of reason, but also as an "organon" of objective arithmetical truths. In this respect, Carnap remains closer to Kant. As Frege himself saw it, the philosophical result of his logicist foundations for arithmetic stand in sharp contrast to the Kantian view: "I must also contradict the generality of Kant's claim that without sensibility no object would be given to us. Zero and one are objects that cannot be given to us through the senses" (Frege, 1884/1997, §89, 123). For the later Carnap, such an ontological consequence cannot arise, since he only recognizes the existence of objects – indeed of entities in general – *internally*, that is, relative to a linguistic framework. Thus Carnap rejects Frege's most fundamental question, that of what numbers are. The only meaningful question for Carnap is: What linguistic rules apply to number expressions? (Carnap, 1934b, 22; cf. 1934c/1937, 310). In the context of his later semantic work, culminating in *Meaning and Necessity*, Carnap reaffirms the anti-metaphysical stance of *Scheinprobleme in der Philosophie* by discarding all *external* questions of existence, if they are taken as theoretical questions about the existence of entities *in themselves*, as pseudo-questions (Carnap, 1950a/1956, 219). He admits Platonic expressions, but only provided that no corresponding ontological commitments are recognized.

Meaning and Necessity contains Carnap's most detailed discussions of Frege's views. The distinction between sense (*Sinn*) and reference (*Bedeutung*) is taken up productively and reworked into Carnap's own distinction between "intension" and "extension." Here Frege's influence is most directly noticeable and is also explicitly acknowledged by Carnap (Carnap, 1963a, 63). In Carnap's *Nachlass*, there is a detailed handwritten excerpt from "Über Sinn und Bedeutung," replete with commentary, dating from the period during which *Meaning and Necessity* was written. With his focus on semantics from about 1935 on, Carnap abandons the earlier, purely syntactic method of *The Logical Syntax of Language*, or rather he supplements syntax with semantics. Carnap had already encountered an account of Frege's intensional semantics in part I of the lecture course *Conceptual Notation* (Reck and Awodey, 2004, 72–74). This had no effect, however, since Carnap, under the influence of Wittgenstein's *Tractatus*, initially subscribed to the thesis of extensionality, according to which all sentences can be turned into sentences about extensions (Carnap, 1928a/1967, §§43–45).

III. GEOMETRY

Carnap was influenced not only by Frege but also by his opposite number Hilbert, whose influence can already be discerned in Carnap's dissertation "Der Raum," which also briefly mentions Frege's criticism of Hilbert.[4] Here, Carnap distinguishes between three concepts of space: formal, intuitive, and physical. He thus departs from the Kantian position, according to which space is specifically a form of external intuition.[5]

Frege acknowledged the nature of Hilbert's conception of formal axiomatic systems very early on, although he did not approve of it. This was especially the case with respect to Hilbert's presentation of Euclidian geometry (Hilbert, 1899/1977), which Frege accurately characterized as completely dissolving any attachment to "spatial intuition," making geometry, like arithmetic, a "purely logical science" (Frege, 1900/1980, 43). Carnap, however, agreed with Hilbert in this respect, and he extended logicism to (mathematical) geometry also, here following Russell rather than Frege (Carnap, 1963a, 49–50; cf. Carnap, 1931; Russell, 1903, part VI). Frege himself had of course pursued a logicist program for arithmetic only, explicitly excluding geometry. In contrast to Hilbert, he subscribed to the Kantian view that geometry is the science of our (Euclidian) intuitive space and that as such it is based on synthetic a priori axioms. Carnap goes a certain distance, in his treatment of intuitive space, toward an attempt to do justice to this view. He also limits the scope of intuitive space, however, by distinguishing it from physical space. Later, Carnap would distinguish only between formal and physical geometry, the former being a logical (analytic a priori), the latter

---

[4] Carnap (1922, 78). A thorough familiarity with Frege's criticism is evidenced in handwritten excerpts (in the Carnap *Nachlass*) from Frege (1903).
[5] On Carnap's dissertation, see the discussion in Gabriel (2004), including the full text (in translation) of the assessment of the dissertation by Bruno Bauch, Carnap's doctoral supervisor. See also Mormann (this volume).

an empirical (synthetic a posteriori), discipline (Carnap, 1928a/1967, §107, 124–125).

Whatever view one ultimately takes of the Frege–Hilbert controversy, the fact remains that Frege astutely laid bare the limitations of Hilbert's original position. The particular target of Frege's criticism is the idea of definition by axioms – the assertion that formal axiomatic systems can *implicitly* define the basic concepts embedded in the axioms (such as "point," "straight," "plane," and "between"). Frege objects that it is misleading to speak of definitions here, since one has not yet determined the meaning of the corresponding expressions. Hilbert's axioms are not propositions, but merely propositional functions, and in propositional functions the basic expressions have no fixed meaning at all; they are merely variables. According to Frege, axiomatic systems in Hilbert's sense do not determine *first-level* basic concepts, as Hilbert believed, but rather (multi-place) *second-level* concepts. An axiom system with n first-level basic concepts determines a second-level n-*place* concept – a *structure*, as we would call it nowadays, which is only given contentual meaning by means of a semantic interpretation of the variables. Carnap would follow Frege in 1927 and relinquish the Hilbertian idea that axioms alone could indeed define the content of basic concepts; the so-called concepts of formal systems were not "proper" concepts but rather "improper" ones (Carnap, 1927; cf. Goldfarb, 1996, 216f.). As always with Carnap, however, this too remains largely a matter of linguistic convenience, and he views the contentual and formal views of the axioms as two equally valid alternatives (Carnap, 1929, 71), while stressing the practical advantages of Hilbert's view "of the axiomatic method" that guaranteed its "versatile use," which was responsible for its great "fruitfulness" in science (Carnap, 2000, 88).

But Carnap's view is not strictly formalist, either, in that he always has in mind possible *contentual* interpretations of formal systems. Carnap emphasizes that the *fruitfulness* of a formal system is shown only in its concrete use; he is thinking particularly of empirical applications in physics. In doing so, he echoes Frege's view "that the foundation problems of mathematics can be solved only if we look not just at pure mathematics but also at the use of mathematical concepts in factual sentences" (Carnap, 1963a, 48; cf. Awodey and Carus, 2001, 152). But their conceptions differ nonetheless. It is true that Frege, in his analysis of the number concept, takes as his starting point its "ordinary use" (*ursprüngliche Anwendungsweise*) in empirical statements of number such as "These are five trees" (Frege, 1884/1997, §46, 98). Here Frege has in mind the everyday use of the term, not its scientific use. As far as applicability is concerned, Frege emphasizes that arithmetic reigns over the entire "realm of the numerable," a realm encompassing not only "the actual (*Wirkliche*)," but "everything thinkable" (Frege, 1884/1997, §14, 95).

Throughout his life, Carnap repeatedly sought to reconcile Hilbert's formalism and Frege's logicism – or what he held to be Frege's logicism.[6] By accommodating Frege's critical reconstruction of Hilbert's position within his own project of making the axiomatic method precise, he became the first to do justice to Frege's objections to Hilbert. Particularly among mathematicians, there is a widely held but mistaken belief that Frege did not understand Hilbert's ideas.[7] In his desire to reconcile the differences between Hilbert's and Frege's views, Carnap later minimized them, sometimes almost to the point of glossing over them entirely. In 1943, for instance, he wrote, "The elaboration of the formal method [i.e. the syntactical method] in logic is chiefly due to the works of Frege, Hilbert and their followers" (Carnap, 1943, X). At the same time, however, in the period leading up to *Meaning and Necessity*, Carnap invokes Frege's authority to help justify his newly developed semantic method, which represented a significant departure from his earlier view in *The Logical Syntax of Language*. There he had stated that logic "can only be studied with any degree of accuracy when it is applied, not to judgments (thoughts, or the content of thoughts) but rather to linguistic expressions, of which sentences are the most important, because only for them is it possible to lay down sharply defined rules" (Carnap, 1934c/1937, 1). This statement from *Logical Syntax* directly contradicts the view of Frege, who had always emphasized that his "conceptual notation" (*Begriffsschrift*) aimed to be not merely a logical calculus, but rather a *characteristica universalis* in Leibniz's sense, or more precisely a "*judgment* notation" (*Urteilsschrift*). Now, however, we find Carnap declaring, "It was Frege (1893), above all, who recognized the importance of the formal method and carried it through in an exact way, while simultaneously insisting that a logical

---

[6] Thus already in Carnap (1930b, 309f.). Cf. Carnap (1963a, 48).
[7] Cf. Freudenthal (1962, 618). Cf., in contrast, Kambartel (1968).

system should not be regarded merely as a formal calculus but should, *in addition*, be understood as expressing thoughts" (Carnap, 1943, 6, added emphasis). But this description of Frege's position is not quite correct either. For Frege, there is no such thing as a semantic interpretation of a formal calculus, as it were after the fact and somehow "in addition" to it: in inference, one always proceeds from one set of contentual judgments to another set of contentual judgments.

In this connection, Carnap's modification of the Fregean distinction between a designator (*Zeichen*) and its designatum (*Bezeichnetes* or *Bedeutung*) is also noteworthy. Reinterpreting it in the framework of his own distinction between an object language and a syntax language or meta-language (Carnap, 1947/1956, 4), Carnap turns Frege's distinction into a difference "between an object symbol (*Objektzeichen*) and its designation (*Bezeichnung*)" (Carnap, 1934c/1937, 158). While it is true that Frege, too, carefully distinguished between these two, Carnap's interpretation stands Frege's distinction on its head; for Frege's distinction was directed against precisely the formalistic conception of mathematics, which he criticized for confusing designator and designatum (Frege, 1893, vol. I, 4).

Carnap regards the contradiction between logicism and formalism as an apparent one – a difference which is "not a question of philosophical significance, but only one of technical expedience" (Carnap, 1934c/1937, 327). Ultimately Carnap is interested in transforming the opposition between philosophical views into a difference between languages which do not exclude each other. This was a central preoccupation throughout Carnap's career, later finding its definitive formulation in the "Principle of Tolerance" and in his "semantic" phase taking the form of admitting ontological questions either as strictly *internal* questions or as purely practical questions of language choice.

To sum up what has been said so far, Carnap understands logic as a calculus, or rather (taking into account his Principle of Tolerance) as a plurality of calculi, in abstraction from all content. For Carnap, as for Wittgenstein, logic is tautological. Frege would necessarily have rejected such a view as incompatible with his goal of deriving arithmetical *content* from a logic which for him was the only available logic. Carnap's logicism is, for arithmetic, a logicism without logical objects and thus without logical content. Frege's logicism is a quite specific contentual program, while Carnap's logicism is part of a pluralistic and formalistic program, even if he does admit the need for an additional contentual interpretation. In a program such as Carnap's, the geometry of formal space can be as readily accommodated as arithmetic. The only requirement is that *formal* structures be logically representable.

IV. EMPIRICISM, *LEBENSPHILOSOPHIE*, AND THE NEO-KANTIAN PHILOSOPHY OF VALUE

When it came to the actual realization of Carnap's program (except for the case of *Meaning and Necessity*), authors such as Russell, Wittgenstein, and Hilbert were probably more influential on him than Frege. But this did not prevent Carnap from appropriating Frege for his own purposes. Throughout his life, Carnap repeatedly referred to Frege in his writings. But his reading of Frege was systematically guided by his own interests, and these often did not correspond to those of Frege himself. Despite these differences, however, Carnap almost always refers to Frege in an affirmative way. He does so even when he takes a view opposite to Frege's on fundamental questions and even when he adopts a quite different philosophical orientation. There were four very substantial differences between Carnap and Frege: Carnap's empiricism; Carnap's view that formal reasoning in logic (and thus arithmetic) can be detached from its content; Carnap's inclusion of geometry in logicism, following Russell; and Carnap's dismissal of ontological concerns as pseudo-questions.

His lasting respect for Frege, which he maintained despite their differences, is based on Frege's achievements in the foundation of modern logic and the use of this logic in philosophical analysis "to break the power of words over the human mind" (Frege, 1879/1997, VI/50). Carnap and Frege shared the project of a scientific philosophy and a philosophy of science grounded in logic. Thus in hindsight Carnap characterized Frege's influence as essentially methodological in nature: "From Frege I learned carefulness and clarity in the analysis of concepts and linguistic expressions" (Carnap, 1963a, 12). The employment of logic in a philosophical program that applied it to the empirical world (such as logical empiricism), on the other hand, was not on Frege's agenda. Of course, his original criticism was leveled against a latently or openly psychologistic, naturalistic variety of empiricism that had lost sight of the Kantian distinction between questions of validity and questions of genesis. Concretely, it was mainly directed against John Stuart Mill's mistaken view that the laws of arithmetic are inductive truths (cf. Frege, 1884, §§9–11). In this matter, Frege and Carnap were in complete agreement (Carnap, 1963a, 47, 64f.). Carnap's logical empiricism did not arise out of nineteenth-century empiricism, but out of turn-of-the-century neo-Kantianism. This is most clearly apparent in the constitution (or rational reconstruction) program in *Der logische Aufbau der Welt* and in the distinction between analytic a priori and synthetic a posteriori knowledge. Carnap's scientific philosophy may thus be seen as neo-Kantianism minus the synthetic a priori and the philosophy of value.

To complete our discussion, therefore, we must examine the role played by the philosophy of value in Carnap and Frege. Neither considers philosophical issues that go beyond logic and the philosophy of science, such as questions of ethics and aesthetics. Carnap refuses to consider them on principle, since he regards normative statements, in so far as they are valuations rather than merely conventional stipulations, as (cognitively) meaningless.[8] Carnap's rejection of the philosophy of value aligns him with a philosopher to whom he was otherwise deeply opposed, Martin Heidegger. Friedrich Nietzsche and the *Lebensphilosophie* of Wilhelm Dilthey exercised an influence on both men, although in Carnap's published works this early but significant influence is only discernible upon close reading. It is reflected in the personal gratitude expressed toward Herman Nohl in his autobiography (Carnap, 1963a, 4). The most significant traces of this influence, however, can be found in his remarks on metaphysics as expression of an attitude towards life (*Lebensgefühl*).[9] These remarks suggest that, in addition to his philosophical *reasons*, extra-philosophical *motives* played a decisive role in Carnap's strict rejection of all metaphysics, although such motives cannot be subjected to an argumentative examination of their validity, but rather require a psychological explanation of their origin.[10]

---

[8] Carnap (1932d/1959, 77). Carnap later modified this view; see e.g. Carnap (1963d, 1000f., 1009–1013).

[9] Carnap (1932d/1959), especially the concluding Section 7.

[10] Cf. detailed discussion in Gabriel (2004).

In contrast to Carnap, Frege did not reject normative ethical and aesthetic questions as meaningless; they simply lay outside his field of work. There is no indication that he believed such questions to be pseudo-problems. On the contrary, in the tradition of value-theoretical neo-Kantianism with which he was linked through his teacher Hermann Lotze, Frege subscribed to the standard division of the philosophical disciplines into logic, ethics, and aesthetics, with the corresponding value triad of Truth, Goodness, and Beauty: "Just as 'beautiful' points the way for aesthetics and 'good' for ethics, so does the word 'true' for logic" (Frege, 1918/1997, 325). And when Frege emphasizes logic's "affinity" with ethics (Frege, 1979, 4), he is investing it with a value-theoretical interpretation.

Frege's concept of truth values is usually seen as merely setting up an analogy to the mathematical concept of values of functions, and in Frege's writings on formal logic this view generally prevails. As is well known, the introduction of truth values enables us to extend the concept of function to logic in its entirety and hence completely to replace the traditional subject-predicate structure of judgments with the argument-function structure of propositions. Frege goes about this by initially defining concepts as functions whose value (for all acceptable arguments) is one of the two possible truth values (Frege, 1891/1997, 139). In a further step, Frege admits truth values as arguments also, thereby arriving at the analysis of propositional connectives (such as "not," "and," "or," "if, then," etc.) as truth functions, namely as those functions which not only have truth values as their values, but also take them as arguments.[11] Frege thus succeeds in defining the other connectives in terms of the conditional and negation. This is the conception that Frege imparted to Carnap in his lectures on *Conceptual Notation*.[12]

With all due recognition of the function-theoretical significance of the notion of truth value, I would suggest that the value-theoretical aspect not be entirely overlooked. I regard this aspect as especially evident in Frege's arguments for identifying the *Bedeutung* of a sentence with its truth value. Here Frege makes use of the secondary

---

[11] Frege (1891/1997, 143 and 147); for further details, Frege (1893/1903, Vol. I, 9f. and 20f.).

[12] Cf. Reck and Awodey (2004, 77). The peculiarity that Frege admits not only truth values, but any objects as arguments for truth functions (cf. p. 73), receives no consideration by Carnap (nor subsequently by others).

meaning of "to have meaning" (*Bedeutung haben*), namely, "to be important" (*wichtig sein*) or "to have value" (*Wert haben*), in order to establish a connection between meaning (*Bedeutung*) and value (*Wert*): "The thought loses value for us as soon as we recognize that the *Bedeutung* of one of its parts is missing."[13] Particularly in the Anglo-Saxon tradition, in which "Bedeutung" is translated as "reference," this important nuance is lost. This nuance – and thus the value-theoretical interpretation – provides, in Frege's argumentation, the actual justification for introducing truth *values*.

The introduction of the term "truth value," on the analogy to "value" in its aesthetic and ethical sense, can be traced to the neo-Kantian Wilhelm Windelband, who stated that the logical value of truth (*Wahrheitswert*) "is to be coordinated with the other values" (cf. Windelband, 1884, 174). Carnap was familiar with the value-theoretical tradition of neo-Kantianism through his philosophy teacher Bruno Bauch in Jena. Bauch had been a student of Heinrich Rickert, himself a student of Windelband. Although Bauch was able to reconcile the two main neo-Kantian traditions, the Marburg School (Paul Natorp and Hermann Cohen) and the Southwest School (Windelband and Rickert), in the end the value-theoretical orientation of his teacher Rickert was for him the one that prevailed.[14] During his studies in Freiburg (1911–12), Carnap attended Rickert's lectures with great enthusiasm. This influence is still visible in the *Aufbau*, where the "constitution of values" is specifically allowed for (Carnap, 1928a/1967, §152; cf. Mormann, 2006b, 182). Rickert had elaborated Windelband's value-theoretical approach to the logical theory of judgment, establishing, in addition to a moral conscience, an "intellectual conscience" which "directs our cognition, as the moral conscience directs our actions" (Rickert, 1892, 89). Carnap's later rejection of such a position in his formulation of the Principle of Tolerance may thus be seen as a response to the philosophy of the Southwest School: "In logic, there are no morals" (Carnap, 1934c/1937, 52).

---

[13] Frege (1892b/1997, 157). The first to note this aspect was probably Angelelli (1982).
[14] On Bauch, cf. Schlotter (2004, particularly 178–182) regarding the Carnap–Bauch relationship.

4 Carnap and Husserl

I. INTRODUCTION

From a contemporary vantage point, the conjunction may appear puzzling. What *could* Carnap – anti-metaphysical logician, student and "legitimate successor" of Frege[1] – possibly have in common with the founder of transcendental phenomenology? Yet, as Michael Dummett has observed, the German philosophy student of 1903 likely regarded Husserl and Frege as mathematician-philosophers remarkably similar in interests and outlook (Dummett, 1993, 26). To be sure, subsequent developments pushed apart the incipient programs of phenomenology and analytic philosophy. Husserl turned to "transcendental subjectivity" in 1905–1907, whereas analytic philosophy around 1930 took a "linguistic turn" precisely to distinguish its methods from those placing cognitive reliance upon intuition or individual subjectivity. Then again, the 1927 publication of Heidegger's *Being and Time* inexorably changed perceptions of phenomenology as having acquired an expressly "existential" and "ontological" orientation, preempting and obscuring its original Husserlian impulses towards logic and the foundations of mathematics. Epitomizing this history in a memorable metaphor, Dummett notes that the respective influences of Frege, the "grandfather of analytic philosophy," and Husserl, a patriarch of "continental philosophy," run through twentieth-century philosophy like the Rhine and Danube, mighty rivers rising close together, briefly running parallel but then diverging to widely separate seas. Extending the metaphor a bit further, Carnap is a central current flowing into

---

[1] The characterization as Frege's "legitimate successor" is found in Beth (1963).

one of these seas, while Heidegger is the torrent surging into the other.

However vivid the image of radical divergence, closer examination reveals notable analogies. Both Husserl and Carnap consistently eschew philosophical theses in favor of their "explication" (Beaney, 2004, 117–150). Both reject traditional philosophy by inverting its priorities, setting considerations of meaning over those of being, formulating questions not about what exists but about the meaning of existence claims. In this regard, both represent what Alberto Coffa terms a "semantic idealism," where the focus of criticism of realism shifts from traditional idealism to considerations of meaning, from questions about the nature of the real to how to make sense or speak with objective significance (Coffa, 1991, 232). For both Husserl and for Carnap, at least up until the mid-1930s when he renounced the very project of epistemology, the fundamental problem of the theory of knowledge concerns how the unquestioned objectivity of the physical sciences arises despite the origin of all cognition in private subjective experience. Both provide a kind of "Copernican turn," rejecting "externalist" accounts of knowledge as uncritical manifestations of realist metaphysics while giving "internalist" accounts of reference, meaning, and truth as conditions of possibility of any particular inquiry. To be sure, Husserl, like Kant, envisages the phenomenological critique of knowledge as making way for a clarified conception of metaphysics, whereas Carnap eventually pares philosophy down to the "logic of science" (*Wissenschaftslogik*). Nevertheless, there is tacit agreement that questions concerning "the riddles of life," whether considered part of philosophy or not, must be understood in terms "that can have a possible sense for us" (Husserl, 1929, §64; Carnap, 1928, §183).

Just as these metaphilosophical and methodological parallels between Carnap and Husserl have long been occluded, the fundamental divergence between them has also been correspondingly misjudged. It is certainly not to be found in the accusations of psychologism or sheer obscurantism levied by some of the logical empiricists and their descendants against phenomenology (though not by Carnap himself).[2] It is not to be found, as Dummett maintains, in Husserl's

---

[2] See Husserl (1921, vi/English translation 1970, 663); for discussion, see Ryckman (2005, 113–114). Despite the affiliation to phenomenology of eminent scientific

generalization of meaning to all intentional acts, nor in the oft-cited "linguistic turn" not taken by phenomenology – which is a symptom and not a cause. Rather, the fundamental divergence originates in Frege's and Husserl's distinct briefs against logical psychologism and, in particular, in Husserl's insistence that the concepts and modes of formal reasoning in logic and mathematics require epistemic supplementation or clarification beyond that contained in the principles and laws of formal logic (and mathematics) itself. For Husserl, a necessary *transcendental logical* justification is to be found through phenomenological analysis of "transcendental subjectivity," the primary locus of formation ("constitution") of all objective meaning and thus all objects *qua* objects of knowledge. Accordingly, exploration of the intricate relationship between Carnap and Husserl must first journey back to the 1890s, still in Carnap's infancy, to the ostensibly similar but in fact quite distinct criticisms of psychologism levied by Husserl and Frege. From these emerge radically different appraisals of the office and autonomy of formal logic in the "constitution" of meaning and objectivity.

II. AGAINST PSYCHOLOGISM

The rapid rise of scientific psychology in Germany in the second half of the nineteenth century prompted a renewed challenge to the sharp separation between logic and psychology ordained by Kant. With characteristic forthrightness, John Stuart Mill had already deemed logic to be a chapter of psychology:

(Logic) is not a science distinct from, and coordinate with, Psychology. So far as it is a science at all, it is a part, or branch, of Psychology ... Its theoretical grounds are wholly borrowed from Psychology, and include as much of that science as is required to justify the rules of the art. (Mill, 1865, 359)

A centerpiece of late nineteenth-century materialism and naturalism, the reduction of logic to psychology was the research program

figures (e.g. the mathematician Hermann Weyl), phenomenology was subject to caricature within logical empiricism; witness Zilsel's (1941, 31) claim that the phenomenological method of *Wesensschau* is "meant to supplant causal investigation" in a manner "familiar to prescientific civilizations." Beth's (1963, 471, note 10) passing reference to "the reactionary tendency inherent in phenomenology" is perhaps broadly indicative.

of numerous psychologists and psychologistic logicians, who sought to show that the principles and laws of logic are rooted in empirical psychological (and ultimately, biological and chemical) laws governing actual mental processes. Accordingly, even the basic principles of logic (including non-contradiction) were regarded as being about, and drawing their evidence from, a range of facts comprising the particular mental acts and processes of empirical cognizing subjects. The rejection of such views, first by Frege and then by Husserl, drew upon the anti-psychologism of Rudolph Hermann Lotze (1817–1881), and both Frege and Husserl accordingly attacked the psychological logicians' attempts to ground the objective and a priori validity of logical and mathematical principles or laws in the mental acts or psychic experiences (*Erlebnisse*) of the judging or reasoning subject. But here the similarities end.

II.1 Frege and Carnap

Frege's criticism will be familiar to analytic philosophers (Frege, 1893/1967, xv–xxvi/13–25). The laws of logic are not psychological laws, empirical generalizations describing how individuals actually reason, but are "laws prescribing the way one ought to think," universal laws of truth concerning what obtains with the utmost generality for all rational thinking. The domain of logic is neither more nor less than *objective thought*, considered solely with regard to truth and falsity. Descriptions of the mental are to be purged altogether from logic, where "psychological considerations have no more place . . . than they do in astronomy or geology." Indeed, logic is *sui generis*: a request for the justification of a law of logic is either answered by reduction to another law of logic or is not to be answered at all. Any attempted extra-logical justification of logic must either be based on intuition, following rationalism, or empirical psychology. But neither option is suitable since both are irreducibly private, subjective, and arbitrary. Moreover, Frege regarded such attempted justifications as inevitably circular, since logical laws and principles are presupposed by any rational inquiry.[3] This

---

[3] Frege (1893/1967, xv/12) termed the laws of logic "the most general laws, which prescribe universally the way in which one ought to think if one is to think at all." See Lotze (1874, §332).

logocentrism is coupled with an objectivist and realist epistemology: knowledge is "an activity that does not create what is known but grasps what is already there," and, accordingly, "what is true" is "objective and independent of the judging subject." As the terminology of "grasping" suggests, Frege thus purchases his characterization of knowledge of logical and mathematical objects at the cost of a Platonism about abstract objects, in particular, thoughts (*Gedanken*).[4] Thoughts (e.g. the Pythagorean theorem) are not constituents of the stream of consciousness, but propositional bearers of truth values, objects of belief existing independently of being "grasped" by any subject. For a belief to be true, it must stand in a certain relation to a proposition that is true or false, according to whether it accurately represents some aspect of a mind-independent reality.

Carnap inherited the broad contours, though by no means all, of Frege's logocentrism, drawing no distinction between psychological and transcendental subjectivity in rejecting both. In his "Intellectual Autobiography," Frege's influence is cited as decisive for Carnap's understanding of the thesis of logicism, that the concepts of mathematics can be defined from logical concepts and the truths of mathematics are in principle the same as logical truths (Carnap, 1963a, 46). However, Carnap initially took up Wittgenstein's view of logical and mathematical truths as tautologies, and later emphasized that they are analytic propositions, true in virtue of their form alone. Lacking all content, logic and mathematics are deemed "sciences having no proper subject matter analogous to the material of the empirical sciences." In *Logical Syntax of Language* (1937, hereafter *LSL*; original German edition 1934), Carnap criticized an ostensibly Fregean conception of mathematics and logic as comprised of "pseudo-object sentences" (see §3). Nonetheless, Carnap consistently contrasts an "objectivist conception" of deductive logic *à la* Frege with subjectivist conceptions that refer to the principles of logic as forms or laws of thinking. In this respect, logical concepts are placed on a par with

---

[4] Frege (1918/1984, 74/368): "We do not *have* a thought as we have, say, a sense-impression, but we also do not *see* a thought as we see, say, a star. So it is advisable to choose a special expression; the word 'grasp' (*fassen*) suggests itself for the purpose. To the grasping of thoughts there must then correspond a special mental capacity, the power of thinking. In thinking we do not produce thoughts, we grasp them." Sluga's (1980, 120) view that Frege, as Lotze, was an epistemological, not an ontological Platonist, is extensively disputed in Dummett (1981).

physical concepts in lacking all relation to mental processes: the meta-logical statement "*j* is a consequence of *i*," just as "this stone is heavier than that," is "complete without regard to the properties or the behavior of any person" (Carnap, 1950b, 38–40).

For Carnap, the most salient aspect of Frege's anti-psychologism involves the proscription of any extra-logical epistemic justification of logic. To be sure, Carnap's Principle of Tolerance (*LSL*, §17) marks a significant departure. Whereas, according to Frege's "logical monotheism" (Ricketts, 1994, 185), a unique set of logical principles and laws are constitutive of rational thought, Carnap advances logical pluralism: different logics are perfectly acceptable, and choice among them is to be made on pragmatic grounds relative to particular inquiries. Logical truths are analytic truths within a particular *linguistic framework*, and the sole significance of logic and mathematics for empirical science lies in their use in showing how statements of science with a particular empirical content can be transformed from one form into another. Epistemic justification of a linguistic framework can only be relative, for it must presuppose some relation of *logical consequence* explicated within one linguistic framework or another (see §4). Yet this relativization is coupled with a *nonpareil* attempt to implement Russell's thesis of modern logic "as the essence of philosophy" (Russell, 1914a, chapter 2). In the heyday of the Vienna Circle in the early 1930s, Carnap limited philosophy to purely syntactic descriptions of linguistic frameworks for the rational reconstruction of particular inquiries. Distinguishing between "pure" and "applied" logic – the construction of formal symbolic systems and the logical analysis, on this basis, of empirical scientific theories (*Wissenschaftslogik*) – Carnap considered these activities to exhaust the scientific content of philosophy. His well-known declaration that *"we pursue Logical Analysis but no Philosophy"* thus retains much of the Fregean conception of formal logic as the sole regulative resource for inquiry (Carnap, 1932a/1934, 32 and 29).

II.2 Husserl

While a young mathematics Ph.D. in Vienna, Husserl's interests turned to philosophy under the influence of Franz Brentano. Inspired by the latter's injunction that philosophy can and must become scientific, Husserl's philosophical career began in earnest pursuit of

Brentano's goal of showing that philosophy and logic are grounded in the laws of an empirical descriptive psychology (Rollinger, 2004). This is a principal thesis of his first book, *The Philosophy of Arithmetic* (1891), dedicated to Brentano. But Husserl's failure clearly to distinguish between numbers as *ideal* objects and as *ideas* or *representations* (*Vorstellungen*) in the cognitive acts of counting, collecting, and comparing was subjected to a withering review by Frege in 1894. It has been long and widely believed that Frege's caustic criticism converted Husserl from seeking a psychological foundation for logic and that subsequently Husserl joined Frege in a common critique of that program (Farber, 1943, 54–58; Føllesdal, 1958). Husserl indeed frankly criticized his earlier psychologism in the first volume (*Prolegomena to a Pure Logic*) of his *Logical Investigations* (1900–1901), but the alleged role of Frege in Husserl's conversion is puzzlingly not documented there, being limited to a footnote in which Husserl retracted his criticism of Frege's anti-psychologism while warmly commending the reader to the "Preface" of Frege's *Grundgesetze* (Husserl, 1900–1901, Bd. I, §46). Nevertheless, although this might be due to an understandable sensitivity on the issue, recent studies argue in favor of Husserl's own later claim that he came independently to the rejection of psychologism in logic for reasons immanent within his own agenda.[5] Like Frege, the *Prolegomena* argues that psychologism in logic inexorably leads to skepticism and relativism. Yet, in contrast to Frege, Husserl regards the distinction between the descriptive and the normative as having little to do with the critique of psychologism, as can be seen in the fact that the psychological logicians themselves supply various accounts of how normative principles of logic could arise from psychological descriptions of certain aspects of the process of thinking. Instead, Husserl maintains that all normative sciences depend on theoretical sciences and, in particular, that applied logic, the technique of reasoning for a practical purpose is itself grounded on a very general theoretical science termed, following Kant and Lotze, "Pure Logic." The basic error of psychologism is its conflation of these, resulting in a misinterpretation of the pure laws of logic as empirical

---

[5] Husserl (1929, §27). The case for Husserl's autonomous development is argued in Willard (1984, chapter III), and Mohanty (1982); see, however, the reply to Mohanty of Føllesdal (1982).

laws of psychology. Moreover, already in the early 1890s, and perhaps even by 1891, Husserl had acquired the un-Fregean view that the fundamental contrast between logic and psychology lies in the fact that logical and mathematical objects are presented to the mind in a quite specific fashion which lends them an identity distinct from the various individual psychic acts through which they are "given." But then it was incumbent upon Husserl to say something specific about this special mode of "givenness." Husserl's alternative to Frege's anti-psychologism took its inspiration from the property of the ideal objects of a pure logic Lotze had termed "validity."

Kant, as we said, recognized a subject matter called "pure logic": a system of completely formal propositions demonstrated a priori, independent of all intuitive or representational content. In his *Logik*, Lotze enormously broadened the Kantian conception to encompass all forms of concepts, judgments, laws, and inferences. The subject matter of pure logic is comprised by a "systematic series of forms of thought," ideals manifesting the mind's "inherent impulse" to show "the coherence of all that co-exists" (Lotze, 1880/1888, §§112, 151). Both Frege and Husserl drew upon Lotze's sharp distinction between (subjective and particular) representations of a given object and the logical idea (*Idee*) or thought (*Gedanke*) that is "constitutive" of the object (by giving "its law").[6] *Ideen* are objective in the sense that they are independent of particular thinking subjects, and Fregean senses (*Sinne*) and thoughts (*Gedanken*) are objective in just this sense – almost certainly revealing a Lotzean influence. However, swept under the carpet by Frege's term "grasping" but of fundamental significance for Husserl is Lotze's account of how such shared objective content is possible: the self-identical content of an idea (*Idee*), its independence from actual instances in speech or thinking, has no *real existence* (*Wirklichkeit*) but only an *ideal being* or *validity* (*Geltung*) (Lotze, 1880/1888, §316). Leaving the latter

---

[6] Lotze (1874/1884, §§20–32, 129, 125). See Husserl (1900–1901, Bd. II, §59) and, far more explicitly, Husserl (1939/1975, 128–129/36): "For the fully conscious and radical turn and for the accompanying 'Platonism,' I must credit the study of Lotze's logic." Earlier in this text (§4), Husserl noted: "My so-called 'Platonism' does not consist in some sort of metaphysical or epistemological substructures, hypostases, or theories but rather in the simple reference to a type of original 'givens' which usually, however, are falsely explained away." Frege was not so explicit, and the nature of Lotze's influence on Frege is disputed; see Sluga (1980) and Dummett (1981).

conception unexplained,[7] Lotze thus interpreted Plato's doctrine of Ideas in a de-ontologized fashion, linking it to the philosophy of Kant in a "transcendental Platonism" wherein the systematic forms of thought comprising "pure logic" are ideal and independent of particular thinkers but not of mind altogether.[8] In a sense to be further articulated by Husserl, "pure logic" is "formal" in that it is regarded as the science of these ideal *forms of thought*.

As programmatically outlined in Husserl's *Prolegomena* (Husserl, 1900–1901, Bd. I, §§40, 47–48, 50, 54, and 56–57), "pure logic" is the domain of concepts such as *truth, object, sense, proposition, syllogism, ground*, and *consequence*. Inspired by the Leibnizean idea of a *mathesis universalis*, it considers "pure logico-grammatical forms" without regard to the actual knowing, judging, inferring, representing, and proving of any individual cognizing subject. The laws of pure logic obtain whether or not anyone has insight into them. They possess "'eternal' validity" (*"ewige" Geltung*), a validity guaranteed a priori through knowledge of their conceptual essence; and this knowledge, in turn, is obtained from intuition of categorial forms to which nothing perceptual corresponds (see below). An initial task of pure logic is the determination and clarification of pure categories of meaning, grammatical constraints governing meaningful sentences (Bar-Hillel, 1956). But its highest (and still to be completed) task is the articulation of a theory of the possible forms of theories, a conceptual skeleton of the conditions of possibility of theory in general. Moreover, the idea of such a theory, a *"pure theory of manifolds,"* is explicitly modeled on developments in nineteenth-century mathematics, in particular on the notion of manifold (*Mannigfaltigkeit*) arising from generalized geometries: the n-dimensional manifolds of Riemann and Helmholtz, Grassmann's *Ausdehnungslehre*, Hamilton's quaternions, Lie's continuous transformation groups, and also Cantor's theory of sets. However, Husserl's term "manifold"

---

[7] Lotze (1880/1888, §316): "And finally we must not ask what in its turn is meant by validity (*Geltung*), as if the meaning which the word clearly conveys to us can be deduced from some different conception … As little as we can say how it happens that anything *is* or *occurs*, so little can we explain how it comes about that a truth has validity; the latter conception has to be regarded as much as the former as ultimate and underivable, a conception of which everyone may know what he means by it, but which cannot be constructed out of any constituent elements that do not already contain it."

[8] Lotze (1880, §317). On the term "transcendental Platonism," see Gabriel (2002, 41).

signifies more generally any possible domain of knowledge that can be brought into an axiomatic deductive formulation, whose objects are determined only by the *forms* of the laws (axioms and theorems) governing them – pure forms emancipated from any content. A particular scientific theory would then be a specialization of its corresponding ideal theory form, a species within a common genus wherein the essential types of possible theory are elaborated and their relations to one another made explicit. The highest genus of such theory forms is that of a *definite manifold*, akin to the Hilbertian notion (developed at roughly the same time, in Hilbert's *Foundations of Geometry*, 1899) of a (finitely axiomatizable) *consistent complete theory*.[9] Within Husserlian pure logic, however, the method of investigation is that of *Erkenntniskritik* (critique of knowledge), an inquiry into the essence of theory and what makes theory possible in the first place. Only by complementing the *ars inventiva* of the mathematician with investigations of a pure logic, in particular, can theoretical insight be gained into all relations of essence of theory in general. By attaining *insight* into these *essences*, through *intuitive representation* of essences in *adequate* or *categorial Ideation*, concepts are fixed or determined with ever-increasing precision and generality.

For Husserl the ideality and a priori truth characteristic of propositions about the abstract objects of logic and mathematics involve a type of evidence presented only in directed intentional acts of categorial or "essential" intuition, intuitions that "give" an "essence" (an abstract object) immediately and directly as an intentional unity, a unity of meaning. In this way, intricate patterns of "validity-foundings" (*Geltungsfundierungen*) can be described, showing how certain validities are founded upon or presuppose others (Husserl, 1954/1970, §55). By refashioning Lotze's inchoate doctrine of validity into the phenomenological method of "essential intuition" (*Wesensschau, Wesenserschauung*), Husserl's earlier analyses of the

---

[9] Husserl (1900, §§ 69–70). Majer (1997) argues that two distinct meta-logical notions are involved; Husserl's pertains to the *deductive completeness* of an axiomatized domain (every well-formed formula of the descriptive language is either a consequence of the axioms, or it contradicts them) while Hilbert's notion of completeness expresses, in modern terms, the *categoricity* of an axiom system, that any two models of the axioms are isomorphic. See also Hill (1995). Mahnke (1923) is an early text tracing parallels between Husserl and Hilbert.

psychological origin of the basic concepts of arithmetic (unity, aggregate, cardinal number, etc.) are transformed into descriptive phenomenological analyses of structures of intentionality underlying the ideal validity of the objects of logic and mathematics. Thus, whereas Frege (and, following him, Carnap) understood late nineteenth-century mathematical developments (primarily the "rigorization" and eventual "arithmetization" of analysis) as pointing in the direction of a logical foundation for mathematics (arithmetic and analysis) making no reference to intuition whatsoever, Husserl drew from a different, more geometrical strand in articulating a foundation in "essential intuition" for the basic laws of logic themselves.

III. CONSTITUTION

III.1 Parallels and analogies

For transcendental phenomenology, and for the Carnap of *Der logische Aufbau der Welt* (1928), objects of cognition are neither posited nor given, but "constituted" from the given. Considerable difficulties in understanding "that elusive notion" (Coffa, 1991, 231) have led to the widespread misunderstanding that each of these constitutive projects is foundationalist: phenomenalist reductionism in the case of *Aufbau*, a revival of Cartesian rationalism based on "a priori intuition of essence" in that of Husserl. Yet neither is foundationalist in the traditional sense, attempting to justify our knowledge on a basis of indubitable certainties. Rather, both begin with the assumption that objective cognition is, from the standpoint of "constitution," the product of conceptual determination. Constitution is then a reflective or reconstructive methodology describing how the meaning of objective scientific concepts can arise from the "given" subjective contents of first-person experience.[10] The parallels are not perhaps surprising: Carnap wrote the first draft of *Aufbau* between 1922 and 1925 while living in Buchenbach, near Freiburg, where Husserl taught, and he attended Husserl's seminars in the summer

---

[10] Carnap (1928/1967, §2); Cf. Husserl (1911/1965, 299/87): "How can experience as consciousness give or contact an object? . . . How is natural science to be comprehensible in absolutely every case, to the extent that it pretends at every step to posit and to know a nature that is in itself – in itself in opposition to the subjective flow of consciousness?"

semesters of 1924 and 1925.[11] In particular, Carnap regarded *Aufbau* as a contribution towards a *mathesis of lived experience* – which he (mistakenly) believed to be a goal of phenomenology – undertaken in non-phenomenological, formal-logical terms.

For Husserl, transcendental phenomenology is constitutional analysis; that is, the intentional analysis of how an object is continuously constituted, with respect to its sense and validity, in the interconnections of all acts of consciousness directed towards it. But this is not to say that the object, whose sense may be that of a (mind-) transcendent object, is *produced* by consciousness, as subjective idealism absurdly maintains.[12] Rather, constitution is a matter of "sense-bestowal through transcendental subjectivity," and the task of constitutive analysis is to investigate how objects, exclusively considered as accomplishments of intentional acts, are ongoing unities of "sense-formation" arising against the background of previous sense-formations. In this sense, transcendental constitution presupposes a purely methodological "phenomenological reduction," leaving the world of objects of science and everyday life "as is" but suspending or "putting out of action" the usual assumptions regarding the mind-independent existence of these objects. It is the attempt to understand the meaning of "mind-independent" being as arising within an object's "sedimented" sense-history, a history to be transcendentally reconstructed and clarified as an accumulating achievement within conscious experience in the broadest sense.

The *Aufbau*, by contrast, presupposes only the theory of logical types of Whitehead and Russell's *Principia Mathematica* as the objectifying framework of a theory of constitution, lending the term "constitution" a precise meaning within the language of logic. It articulates the goal of a "rational reconstruction" of the (simply assumed) system of scientific knowledge via an extensional "constitution system of concepts" (*Konstitutionssystem der Begriffe*) wherein each scientific concept is definable in constructive step-by-step fashion from concepts of lower levels, ultimately from primitive concepts pertaining to the subjective sensory data or "elementary experiences" of a single subject. On account of the transitivity

---

[11] See Spiegelberg (1981). Mormann (2000) speculates that Carnap moved to Buchenbach, near Freiburg, in 1922 to be in a position to interact and study with Husserl.

[12] For discussion, see Føllesdal (1974, 1998).

of reducibility, the principal thesis of Carnap's "constitution theory" (*Konstitutionstheorie*) states that any scientific concept can be reduced, via logical chains of definition, to the primitive ones, thus reconstructing each concept in the epistemically privileged terms of first-person experiential content while simultaneously avoiding all (purely subjective) ostensive definitions (§§1, 13–16). Logical construction thus provides "a rational justification of intuition," and "intuitive understanding" is everywhere replaced with "discursive reasoning" (§§54, 100, 143). This automatically excludes any extralogical justification of logical laws and principles.

Carnap's term *Konstitutionstheorie* requires comment. In the English translation (1967) by Rolf George, it is rendered as "construction theory," following the example of Nelson Goodman in his *The Structure of Appearance* (1951). Since Goodman's book remains the only detailed attempt to explicitly implement a phenomenalist reductionism using the tools of modern logic (as, it was wrongly assumed, Carnap had outlined in the *Aufbau*), "construction theory" had already acquired an established usage in the literature of analytic philosophy. Carnap's *Konstitutionstheorie*, however, does not connote a "logical construction of the world" from primitive phenomenal experience but rather that objects of cognition *are constituted* in explicit agreement with the fundamental thesis of transcendental idealism; it is an "analysis of reality" showing how the intersubjective, objective world of science arises despite the subjective origin of all cognition in the contents of first-person experience (§§2–3, 177). The term "construction theory" therefore gives a misleading impression of the philosophical context in which the book was written, and so of the book's intent. That context, as has been made abundantly clear, is, in the main, a neo-Kantian "scientific philosophy" in transition under the twin pressures of modern logic and the new physics of relativity theory (Coffa, 1991; Sauer, 1985; Friedman, 1987, 1992a; Richardson, 1998).

Despite the ineluctable divide between Carnap and Husserl over the methodological primacy of logic *vis-à-vis* intuition, both constitutive analyses profess metaphysical "neutrality" between realism and idealism, phenomenalism and materialism. Constitution is expressly understood as a meta-level, purely immanent methodological reworking of actual cognition: "rational reconstruction" for Carnap, transcendental reflection consequent on the phenomenological reduction for Husserl. At this level, *being an object* is identical with *being constituted*, and so only an internal constitution-theoretic concept of reality can be meaningful, whereas an external "metaphysical" one cannot. Carnap's extensional concepts and Husserl's abstract intensional entities (*noemata*) go proxy for objects in the ordinary sense, and the constitution of objectivity is a *semantic analysis* leaving entirely intact the practicing scientist's default realism towards the objects of science ("the natural attitude" for Husserl, the use of "realistic language" in *Aufbau*). Both Carnap and Husserl assume that the use of realistic language in science is practical and justifiable in its own terms but this usage is distinct from, and does not imply, the metaphysical thesis of realism.[13] Similarly, at the meta-level of constitutive analysis or constitution theory, the task of epistemology lies neither in the refutation of skepticism (as with foundationalism), nor in the justification of first-order scientific knowledge claims (as with empiricism or positivism), but in answering the question: *How is objectivity constituted?*

This common problematic occasions direct parallels between *Aufbau*, where works of Husserl are strategically cited, and the phenomenological method (Mayer, 1992; Roy, 2004). Most salient is Carnap's choice of an "autopsychological basis," an initially autonomous realm of experiences of a single subject taken simply as they are, bracketed from all assumptions of the reality or non-reality of the objects alleged to be their "causes" (Carnap, 1928/1967, §64). In addition, a postulate of "methodological solipsism" enjoins that this starting point is independent of any particular cognizing subject. While the level-by-level logical constructions of *Aufbau* must then take place in a corresponding sequence (e.g. "my body" is constructed before other physical objects or cognitive subjects – the realm of the "heteropsychological"), nothing about these constructions depends on the peculiar character of a given individual's experience. To be sure, in *Aufbau* "egocentricity is not an original property of the given" in so far as the self or ego is regarded extensionally as just the class of basic elementary experiences (Carnap, 1928/1967,

---

[13] Carnap (1928, §§52, 178); Husserl (1950/1983, §§27–30) famously locates everyday life, as well as the practice of natural science (and even mathematics), within "the natural attitude" (or "arithmetical attitude") which can, and does, remain undisturbed by phenomenological reflection.

§§65, 163), whereas, in Husserl, transcendental subjectivity pertains
to a "transcendental ego" revealed by phenomenological reduction.
However, in accounting for the ultimate origins of objective cognition in subjective experience, both adopt the anti-naturalistic position that consciousness, or first-person experience, is not itself expli-
cable in terms of empirically confirmed psycho-physical laws. For
Husserl, such a procedure would be clearly circular; for Carnap,
it would violate the order in which objects are to be successively
built up within a constitutional system based on the postulate of
"epistemic primacy." Nonetheless, there is still a vast abyss separating the constitutive approach of *Aufbau* from transcendental
phenomenology.

III.2 *Experience*

The heart of the difference lies in nearly incommensurable notions
of experience. According to phenomenology, consciousness is intentional, in that it is always *of an object*. Perceptual acts are but a
species of a wider genus of intentional acts with the descriptively
characteristic *noetic-noematic* structure of intentionality. In particular, perception of an object is always "adumbrational," i.e., it
involves a "halo" of anticipated further aspects and determinations,
a rich but not-yet-specified complex. In a somewhat paradoxical formulation, "perception essentially contains indeterminables, but it
contains them as determinables" (Husserl, 1952, 222). In the simplest case of a sensibly given object "in space," the perceptual constitution of the object does not involve bringing the raw material
of sense perception (*hyletic data*) under concepts; rather, this data,
setting boundary conditions for interpretation, is but an integrated
component of a more comprehensive intentional experience, an act
of consciousness directed in a particular manner by its temporal
meaning-giving aspect (*noesis*). With this perceptual act is correlated a meaning (*noema*), an abstract intensional entity (a generalization of the notion of linguistic meaning) structuring all experience
of this object. The object is constituted through various perceptual *noemata*, interconnected components of the *noema* configur-
ing the experience and thus uniquely determining the object of an
act (cf. Føllesdal, 1969, 1990). The unity and coherence of such an

intentional process is not absolute but can be "destroyed" through unfulfilled expectations or incongruous aspects (e.g. illusions, hallucinations), leading to new *noeses* and a (possibly radical) revision of the *noema*, constituting a new object. We become fully cognizant of *noema* and how they structure experience only when, following the phenomenological reduction, they themselves become the objects of acts of a special kind, of reflection at the transcendental level of phenomenological or constitutional analysis.

For empiricism, experience is conceived in terms of the sensory evidence of outer perception and pertains only to statements of alleged matters of fact – if such a statement is meaningful at all, its meaning will consist precisely in the possibility of sensory evidence that confirms or disconfirms it. Yet the atomistic character of the standard empiricist conception of experience is rejected in *Aufbau*, where, in addition to the formal logical apparatus of *Principia Mathematica*, Carnap posits only one undefined empirical concept, the dyadic basic relation Rs defined for the domain of "elementary experiences." With explicit reference to both Gestalt psychology and phenomenology, these are momentary holistic slices of the stream of "lived experience" *(Erlebnis)*. For Carnap, each instance of the relation Rs ("recollection of similarity") involves a current elementary experience e_i, the retention or reproduction of a past elementary experience e_j, a comparison of e_j and e_i, and the recognition that there is a *partial* similarity between e_j and e_i. Tacitly presupposed is the identity of consciousness linking these four moments into a single cognitively meaningful relation, and thus time order and similarity already appear primitively in the explication of Rs (Carnap, 1928/1967, §§89, 117; §§110, 120. Cf. Sauer, 1985, 29–30). For Carnap, elementary experiences in themselves are not *of objects* (for these are to be constituted) and do not have parts; a specific logical method of "quasi-analysis" is employed even to distinguish the five sensory modalities employed in subsequent constitutions. An elaborate analysis must be performed to single out sensory particulars within the total impression of an elementary experience (e.g. to distinguish the constituent notes within a given chord). In this sense, quasi-analysis is a logical and extensional surrogate for phenomenology's *noetic-noematic* interpretation of perception, and *Aufbau's* "rational justification of intuition" begins at the very first stage.

III.3 Structure

For Husserl, logical and mathematical concepts, no less than others, must be submitted to phenomenological analysis and clarification (see §4). But in *Aufbau* logic provides the objectifying framework for rational reconstruction of all statements of empirical science. The fundamental problem of constitutional analysis is to reconstruct a path from the "lived experience" of a cognizing subject to objective knowledge, i.e., intersubjective *purely structural* statements about the world. Carnap's guiding assumption is that the gap between the "primary" world of subjective experience and the "secondary" world of objective science can be bridged by a radical implementation of Russell's "supreme maxim of scientific philosophizing" – "Wherever possible, logical constructions are to be substituted for inferred entities" – which serves as the epigram to *Aufbau*. In particular, objectivity is explicated in terms of Russell's notion of structure (isomorphism of relations): scientific objectivity is achieved through logical structure since only such structure can have an intersubjectively communicable meaning. In place of the now officially proscribed synthetic a priori judgments of the Kantian tradition (§§106, 179), the notion of logical structure is both necessary and sufficient for *Aufbau*'s constitution of objectivity: "*Each scientific statement can in principle be so transformed so that it is nothing but a structure statement*" (§16). Statements about individual empirical objects at a given level are to be reconstructed as *Kennzeichnungen* ("indicator signs"), relational descriptions that, if true, are true of one and only one object. Such descriptions, constituted by different epistemic subjects, are nonetheless relationally isomorphic and so pick out the same objects.

Carnap maintains that it lies in the "essence of an experience to refer intentionally to something." Yet, according to *Aufbau*'s purely extensional method of constitution, there is no fundamental distinction between individual and general concepts; the former pertain to certain relation extensions called "temporal" and "spatial," the latter to all others. Consideration of the most general qualities belonging to an object (its "essence" in phenomenological terms) is reconstructed as the object's "constitutional essence," the explicit indication of the truth criteria for all sentences regarding the object. Ultimately such criteria are to be reductively rendered as originally given states of affairs (*Ur-Sachverhalte*), the pairs of elementary experiences under the relation *Rs* that are either true or false of the object (§161). In tacit agreement with Husserl, as against Brentano, that the existence or non-existence of the intentional object is of no concern for the immediate character of the experience, Carnap departs from both in maintaining that the intentional relation has no special or privileged status, deconstructing the relation of intentionality in particular (§164). From the standpoint of constitution theory, the intentional relation merely obtains between an experience and an order of experiences, i.e., it is a sub-class of the relation between an element and a relational structure of a certain sort.

We can now see why Carnap considered *Aufbau* in connection with Husserl's idea of a mathesis of lived experience (*mathesis der Erlebnisse*).[14] By effectively assuming logic as a priori (as analytic or stipulational), the method of rational reconstruction can reject all appeals to intuition (as evidence) while retaining an autopsychological subject as the *fons et origo* of all evidential meaning in science. Despite the often very striking similarities and analogies between *Aufbau* and phenomenology, this fundamental divergence should not be obscured: *Aufbau* is a de-transcendentalized surrogate, substituting chains of definitions within an extensional logical system for the progressive steps of intentional phenomenological constitution.

IV. MEANING AND REFERENCE

In the first of his *Logical Investigations*, Husserl introduces a tripartite distinction between "expression," "meaning," and "object" reminiscent of, though not identical to, Frege's (1892b) distinction between a "sign," its "sense," and its "reference."[15] Dummett has argued that Husserl's phenomenological generalization (in the *Ideen I*) of the Fregean notion of meaning (*Sinn*) to all intentional mental acts created an insurmountable barrier preventing Husserl from taking the "linguistic turn" so critical for analytic philosophy. However, Parsons has pointed out that the requisite generalization of

---

[14] Carnap (1928/1967, §3). In his (1950/1983, §75), Husserl entertains the idea of a *Mathesis der Erlebnisse*, not as a "goal," as Carnap states, but as a counterpart to descriptive phenomenology where "pure and strict ideals (mathematical objects) occur in place of immediately intuitive givens."

[15] Frege (1892b/1984). For discussion, see the papers in Dreyfus (1982).

the notion of meaning, though not yet the term *noema*, was already present in the pre-transcendental-phenomenological Fifth Logical Investigation (§20) of 1901. Accordingly, it is not the generalization of meaning *per se* that separates Husserl from analytic philosophy but rather his "Cartesianism" – the constitutive analyses of "pure consciousness" together with the assumption that it is possible to express the meaning of intentional acts without any presuppositions about reference.[16] Yet Husserl's method is not Cartesian in the sense of doubting whether there are non-immanent objects external to a cognizing consciousness to which reference can be made. Rather, an intentional analysis of the semantic relation of reference shows it to be thoroughly mediated by, and inseparable from, cognitive access to the object presented through particular modes of sense-bestowal, the object as necessarily presented in some context of cognitive experience. The "world" comprising the referents of linguistic expressions is never a world of bare objects, but of objects clothed in senses bestowed by the intentional acts of cognition, perception, belief, willing, and so on. Of course, this kind of analysis still violates what Dummett calls "the fundamental axiom of analytical philosophy," that "the only route to the analysis of thought goes through the analysis of language" (Dummett, 1993, 128).

While such an "internalist" conception of reference indeed separates Husserl from classical analytical philosophy of language (whose roots lie in Frege and Russell), this is also true of Carnap from the mid-1930s on. Initially carrying his anti-metaphysical campaign into the language of science by subjecting it to logical, more specifically, syntactical analysis, Carnap distinguishes between "pseudo-object" and "formal" statements. The former are misleading "*quasi syntactical sentences of the material mode of speech*" which are "formulated as though they refer (either partially or exclusively) to objects, while in reality they refer to syntactic forms and specifically to forms of objects with which they appear to deal" (*LSL*, 285). As an example of a "pseudo-object" sentence,

"Five is not a thing but a *number*,"

seems to tell us that the term "five" does not designate things but numbers, and hence presupposes a semantic relation of designation

---

[16] Parsons (2001, 129); Parsons regards this assumption as "highly contestable."

between words and an ontology of things and numbers. But when reformulated in the "formal mode," the legitimate (anti-metaphysical) sense of the sentence is conveyed by

"'Five' is not a thing-word, but a number-word,"

which no longer misleads us, in particular, into thinking that we are dealing with extra-linguistic objects such as things and numbers instead of numerical expressions and thing-designations. This explication of so-called "pseudo-object sentences" stands fully on a par with Husserl's distinction between the "natural attitude" and the critical or philosophical attitude. These are not "philosophical objections," but rather elucidations intended to bring out hidden metaphysical assumptions buried, for good reason, in ordinary practices. Neither proposes to extirpate such practices within science or inquiry but rather, "leaving them as they are," to adopt a reflective standpoint calling attention to their potentially misleading character. While in *LSL* Carnap views the method of anti-metaphysical philosophy as exclusively comprised of syntactical researches (§82), the end result is notably similar to the crucial methodological step of the phenomenological reduction, a "bracketing" of all existential presuppositions of ordinary and scientific assertions.

Coupled with Carnap's metaphysically deflationary account of reference are several attempts to explicate Fregean senses within scientific philosophy via various intersubjectivizing strategies. His formalist conception of meaning of the mid-1930s assumes that sense or meaning can be made fully objective by distinguishing the content expressed by a sentence (*logische Gehalt*) from the subjective images different language users associate with the sentence (*Vorstellungsgehalt*). A sentence's logical content (its propositional meaning, as it were) consists of the class of sentences that may be inferred from it, and "sameness of meaning" or "sameness of content" of two sentences is defined by the extensional equivalence of the classes of propositions derivable from each. While this inferentialist account intersubjectivizes meaning, setting it apart from the subjective images and conceptions that particular language users associate with a sentence, Carnap's later "method of intension and extension" takes an apparent stride towards Fregean and Husserlian abstract semantic objects. Here, as in Frege, the extension of a sentence is its truth value, while its meaning or intension is the proposition expressed by it. A proposition is neither a linguistic expression, nor a subjective mental occurrence; rather, it is meaning in the strict sense, an objective extra-linguistic entity viewed, *à la* Husserl, as akin to Bolzano's "proposition in itself," as that which is grasped when we understand a sentence (Carnap, 1942, 235; Husserl, 1903/1981, 154, English translation). But sameness of intension, for Carnap, is relative to a particular linguistic framework: two sentences have the same meaning if and only if they are *L-equivalent*. Just as the earlier formalist account of meaning rested on inferences licensed by a notion of logical consequence, so here Carnap's intensionalism relies on framework relative *L-equivalence* or *analyticity*. In light of the Principle of Tolerance, and in sharp contrast to Frege, intersubjectivity of meaning is explicated in terms of – and is always relative to – a shared linguistic framework.

V. LOGIC AND MATHEMATICS

According to Husserl, phenomenology was transformed from a "purely descriptive psychology" to transcendental phenomenology by pursuit of the main themes of the *Logical Investigations* (Husserl, 1961, 28). Whereas the logician is concerned with a priori truths of ideal objectivities (just as the number theorist is concerned with numbers and the truths of arithmetic), the thesis of intentionality led to the view that meaning-constituting experiences (if only of an idealized subject) are necessarily correlated with any object of knowledge. Thus, the phenomenological discovery of the meaning-constituting acts of consciousness in the context of mathematical and logical idealities was extended to all objects. Through a step-by-step progression of acts of reflection undertaken within inner intuition, each directed upon a normally unthematized particular conscious experience, the character and limitations of such exhibited are successively exhibited, together with their possible interconnections to strata more deeply embedded in pre-conscious experience. The goal is to uncover and bring to full consciousness the multiplicity and structure of the subjective acts through which the intended objects are invested with objective meaning.

Only in later works did Husserl consider extending the phenomenological reduction, the *epoché*, "to formal logic and *mathesis* in its entirety." By making these objects *"essentially evident by observing consciousness itself* in its pure immanence," transcendental phenomenology seeks to discover the "transcendental subjectivity" underlying the objects of logic and mathematics, "the *a priori* other side of genuine objectivity" (Husserl, 1950/1983, §59; 1929/1970, §100). As in Kant, it then becomes the task of a *transcendental* logic to seek "in subjectivity, or more precisely, the correlation between subjectivity and the objective, the ultimate determination of the sense of objectivity, as apprehended in cognition" (Husserl, 1956, 386). These correlations of the formal objects of logic and mathematics with subjective processes of experiencing are treated schematically in the *Logical Investigations* but elaborated far more extensively in *Formal and Transcendental Logic* (1929) as well as other writings that remained unpublished in Husserl's lifetime (Husserl, 1939/1973; 1966/2001). Transcendental logic is "foundational" only in a novel sense: its aim is the *clarification* of the fundamental concepts of logic and mathematics by showing how the *sense* of these ideal objectivities arises within "transcendental subjectivity," "originary" sense-bestowing acts of consciousness. Increasingly prominent in these last writings, the account of the constitution of logical and mathematical objects within transcendental subjectivity ultimately rests upon the phenomenological description of the "life-world" (*Lebenswelt*), the world of ordinary activities and beliefs whose pre-logical validities act as grounds for the logical ones (Husserl, 1954/1970, §34). Through the phenomenological reduction, these practices, as intentional acts, become the objects of phenomenological reflection disclosing how their *noema* arise, structuring the experience characteristic of the life-world. In particular, Husserl famously argues that geometry originates within meaning conferring acts, revealed through phenomenological investigation of the life-world (Husserl, 1954/1970, 365–386 (*Beilage III*)/ 353–378, Appendix VI).

Carnap, to the contrary, was the twentieth-century's foremost exponent of a "self-sufficient" formal-mathematical logic – without transcendental or any other foundation – as the core of scientific philosophy. And, almost certainly, Husserl's critical characterization of this viewpoint had Carnap foremost in mind:

The supposedly completely self-sufficient logic that modern mathematical logicians (*Logistiker*) think they are able to develop, even calling it a truly scientific philosophy, namely, as the universal *a priori* fundamental science for all objective sciences, is nothing but a naïveté. (Husserl, 1954/1970, §36)

Continuing Frege's brief against any extra-logical foundation for logic, Carnap departed not only from Husserl but also from Russell, for whom logical and mathematical objects, and universals generally, are known "by acquaintance," a quasi-intuitional mode of epistemic immediacy. To be sure, in "Der Raum" (1922), Carnap recognized a necessary cognitive role for intuition (which he even identified with Husserlian *Wesenserschauung*) in establishing certain topological "matters of fact" comprising the a priori order structure of *intuitive space* presupposed by the empirically determined metrical structure of *physical space* (where both are distinct from *abstract formal spaces* constructed within the logic of relations). But this was youthful exuberance, and Carnap soon put it behind him. Moreover, whereas Frege simply assumed a Kantian account of geometry in terms of pure spatial intuition but departed from Kant in placing the sciences of number (arithmetic, analysis) entirely within the province of formal logic, Carnap, beginning in the *Aufbau*, extended Frege's logicism, following *Principia Mathematica*, to all of mathematics: "Mathematics forms a branch of logistics (i.e., it does not require any new basic concepts)" (§107). However, whereas Whitehead and Russell, in order to carry out the reduction of mathematics to logic, had padded the latter with axioms not obviously logical (such as the axioms of choice and infinity), Carnap's logicism is rather an attempt to circumvent questions regarding the *nature of logic* in favor of a general consideration of how, from basic logical concepts, it may be possible to construct all logical and mathematical objects.

Carnap's mature views on logic and the foundations of mathematics center on the notion of *analyticity* that is not absolute but *relative to a language* or, as he preferred, *to a linguistic framework L*. Logical and mathematical truths are now *L-truths* based upon the *L-rules* "constitutive" of that framework. Such rules delimit the kind and range of meaningful expressions and are presupposed in determining relations of logical implication among empirical statements. Having no content, logical truths do not express "facts" at all. But the most striking aspect of the Principle of Tolerance is that there can no longer be a language-transcendent notion of "facts" in any sense. All linguistic description of "matters of fact" is relative to the analytic/synthetic distinction of a linguistic framework, according to which the logical and mathematical part of the language is analytic. Such a system of analytic entailments furnishes the a priori logical structure for the "synthetic" statements that can be formulated within the non-logical descriptive vocabulary of the framework. So it is that, on adopting this "Principle of Conventionality" (Carnap, 1942, 247), Carnap effectively abandons any commitment to a language-transcendent empiricism.

Yet adequate explication of the framework-constitutive concept of analyticity – of "analytic-in-L, for variable L," as Quine famously put it – became all the more pressing. And here Carnap faced a dilemma. He could restrict his linguistic analyses to *language systems* with precisely formulated semantical rules within the Fregean tradition of *Begriffsschrift* – a purely formal concept language entirely severed from intuition – forbidding any extra-logical supplementation or clarification. But then the program of constructing language systems for analysis of the language of science largely lacked a target, for he had to allow that in the empirical sciences the requisite degree of explicitness concerning linguistic rules did not really obtain, even in physics. As Carnap admitted, any explication of *analyticity* could only be as exact and explicit as these very rules.[17] Thus, while admitting that semantical concepts need not possess "a prior pragmatical counterpart," Carnap turned from the "pure semantics" of constructed language systems to "pragmatical investigation of natural languages." In effect, this was to accept Quine's challenge to provide scientific legitimation for semantic intensional notions like *analyticity* in "empirical, behavioristic criteria." Yet here Carnap found himself on a slippery slope, improvidently linking the meaningfulness of mathematics and the necessity of logico-mathematical truth with procedures for testing hypotheses "not . . . essentially different from those customarily given for procedures in psychology, linguistics and anthropology" (Carnap, 1963a, 67; 1955, esp. 234–235 and 240). This was all the opening Quine's insistence on the irremediable vagueness of the notion of analyticity and his skepticism

---

[17] See Carnap's letter to Quine of 23 January 1943, and his manuscript "Quine on Analyticity," dated 3 February 1952; both in Carnap and Quine (1990, 302–310 and 427–432).

about mentalistic semantics ever needed.[18] Quinean holism and the view of logic and mathematics as merely deeply entrenched regions within an ever-changing web of belief was the inevitable result. From the perspective of transcendental phenomenology, Quinean naturalism then appears as the necessary outcome of "a logic that does not understand itself" (Husserl, 1954/1970, §55).

[18] Quine (1951).

5 Carnap, Russell, and the external world*

I.

As he approached his 71st birthday Carnap wrote a warm letter to Bertrand Russell (1872–1970), who was about to turn 90. Dated 12 May 1962, it notes that Russell's "books had indeed a stronger influence on my philosophical thinking than those of any other philosopher" and mentions "the inspiring effect on me of your appeal for a new method in philosophy, on the last pages of your book *Our Knowledge of the External World*" (Russell, 1967–1969, 1998, 626). Russell responded a few weeks later in equally affectionate terms: "I believe that your efforts to bring clarity and precision to philosophy will have an everlasting effect on the thinking of men . . . Nothing would be more fitting than that you should successfully realise your theory of inductive probability" (Russell, 1967–1969, 1998, 627; cf. ASP RC 090-06-07).

Here we have the final exchange in a correspondence that stretched back to 1921, when Carnap sent Russell a copy of his doctoral dissertation on space (Carnap, 1922). To appreciate its significance, we need to first briefly review Russell's intellectual career. He is widely seen as the most important early figure of analytic philosophy, who, along with G. E. Moore in the late 1890s, broke with the Hegelian idealism of Bradley and McTaggart and fashioned a new pluralistic and realistic approach to traditional metaphysical and epistemological disputes. From 1900 until 1910 Russell sought to transform this realist philosophy into a philosophy of logic and

* Parts of this chapter were presented at Wayne State and I would like to thank the audience for their questions and suggestions. The chapter also benefited a great deal from William Demopoulos's and Michael Friedman's detailed comments.

mathematics adequate to justify logicism, the view that mathematical concepts are just logical concepts and that logical axioms and definitions are sufficient to derive all of mathematics. When the first volume of the three-volume collaborative work with A. N. Whitehead, *Principia Mathematica*, appeared in 1910, though, Russell set his sights on more traditional topics. We will focus on his discussions of experience, knowledge, and language, first, in such works as *Problems of Philosophy* (1912), *Our Knowledge of the External World as a Field for Scientific Method in Philosophy* (1914a) and then in *The Analysis of Mind* (1921) and *The Analysis of Matter* (1927). Later in life Russell returned to some of these issues in his *An Inquiry into Meaning and Truth* (1940) and *Human Knowledge: Its Scope and Limits* (1948) (see Griffin, 2003).

Russell's work defies concise summary and, given Carnap's productivity, it is not any easier to review the various twists and turns in the Russell–Carnap philosophical relationship. One feature of this relationship is clear, though. Despite the warm words exchanged above, Russell and Carnap were constantly at odds on a number of fundamental philosophical issues. What is striking about their relationship is that these deep divisions were apparently overlooked in their early exchanges in the 1920s. By the 1930s and 1940s it must have been clear to both that their views were incompatible. Still, there is little outward sign of these conflicts and, especially in their autobiographical writings, the tendency is towards flattery over philosophical engagement.

After summarizing and criticizing Quine's own somewhat self-serving reconstruction of the Russell–Carnap relationship, I turn to the more subtle proposal first offered by Demopoulos and Friedman in their paper "Bertrand Russell's *The Analysis of Matter*: Its Historical Context and Contemporary Interest" (1985). The link noted by Demopoulos and Friedman then frames my survey of the later developments of Carnap and Russell. Here we find Russell filling out his proposals from the 1920s in a fairly straightforward manner, while Carnap adopts a series of increasingly radical proposals to overcome the problems of traditional philosophy. From where Carnap ends up in the 1950 paper "Empiricism, Semantics, and Ontology," Russell's views on experience, language, and metaphysics look outdated and confused.

One central theme of my discussion is Russell's underlying realistic metaphysics and a distinct commitment to the truth of our scientific theories. These more traditional philosophical positions clashed with Carnap's attempts at metaphysical neutrality and an associated conventionalism, first about the laws of physics, and then, later, even about the logical rules of his linguistic frameworks. We will see that right around the time when Russell finally presented a fully articulated account of his new approach to scientific knowledge, in *Human Knowledge*, Carnap offered instead a dramatically altered picture of what the philosophy of science should be.

II.

Quine's interpretation of Carnap's 1928 *Aufbau* was formed at the latest by 1936, and remained constant throughout his later writings, including 1951's "Two Dogmas of Empiricism" and the 1968 essay "Epistemology Naturalized" (Carnap and Quine, 1990, 204). Most famously, in "Two Dogmas," Quine writes: "Radical reductionism, conceived now with statements as units, set itself the task of specifying a sense-datum language and showing how to translate the rest of significant discourse, statement by statement, into it. Carnap embarked on this project in the *Aufbau*" (Quine, 1951/1963/1980, 39). The explicit claim that this sort of project was also Russell's project is made later in "Epistemology Naturalized." There Quine presents empiricist reductionism as the last, best hope for traditional epistemology. Focusing on the "conceptual" side of epistemology, in which we attempt to clarify "concepts by defining them" (Quine, 1969, 69), Quine mentions Russell's *Our Knowledge* "and elsewhere" and boldly states, "To account for the external world as a logical construct of sense data – such, in Russell's terms, was the program. It was Carnap, in his *Der logische Aufbau der Welt* of 1928, who came nearest to executing it" (Quine, 1969, 74). Thus, according to Quine, both Russell and Carnap sought to explicitly define all concepts using only the resources of the new logic of *Principia Mathematica* and concepts that applied to sense data. This kind of reduction, had it succeeded, would have vindicated the empiricist over the rationalist and placed all scientific concepts on the surest foundation available, namely, immediate experience. Carnap is to be praised for his rigorous attempt at constructing such a chain of definitions, whereas Russell in *Our Knowledge* stopped at informal descriptions of how various concepts might be defined.

There is some *prima facie* evidence in favor of Quine's assimilation of Russell and Carnap to reductive empiricism. For, beginning in 1914 with the book *Our Knowledge* and papers such as "The Relation of Sense-Data to Physics," "On Scientific Method in Philosophy," and "The Ultimate Constituents of Matter," Russell defended what he called "[t]he supreme maxim in scientific philosophizing": "Wherever possible, logical constructions are to be substituted for inferred entities" (Russell, 1914b/1986, 11). The core example of such constructions that Russell invariably invokes is Frege's definition of the natural numbers in terms of classes. Instead of assuming that natural numbers exist, we should instead define entities with the requisite properties in terms of resources that are uncontroversially available (Russell, 1914a, 199–205). In epistemological matters, the supreme maxim marks a shift from 1912's *Problems of Philosophy*, in which we are asked to infer the existence of matter as the cause of our sensory experiences. In 1914 Russell attempts to define matter, the points of space and the instants of time in terms of those very sensory experiences. Carnap signals his agreement with Russell here, it seems, when he invokes Russell's supreme maxim as the epigraph to the *Aufbau*. His autobiographical remarks about learning "a new method in philosophy" from Russell also fit Quine's proposal.

However, recent work by Michael Friedman and Alan Richardson on Carnap's *Aufbau* has shown that Carnap was never a reductive empiricist (cf. Friedman, 1999a; Richardson, 1998). The appeal of the reductive empiricist project was its promise of defining all concepts in sensory terms, and thereby securing their validity. Friedman points out that Carnap never motivates his definitions in these terms:

Carnap nowhere employs the traditional epistemological vocabulary of "certainty," "justification," "doubt," and so on in the *Aufbau*. [footnote removed] He nowhere says that knowledge of autopsychological objects is more certain or more secure than knowledge of physical objects, and the distinction between "hard data" and "soft data" central to Russell's motivation for his construction of the external world is entirely foreign to the *Aufbau*.[1]

---

[1] M. Friedman (1999a, 119). In the footnote that I have suppressed Friedman notes Carnap's different attitude in *Pseudoproblems in Philosophy* (1928b/1967). For a contrasting view see Jonathan Y. Tsou (2003).

Friedman and Richardson have also drawn attention to Carnap's claim that immediate experience is subjective and unreliable and to Carnap's use of definitions that go beyond the explicit definitions that reductive empiricism would demand. Quine takes this last shortcoming, and the failure of Carnap's definitions to pass a translation test, as evidence that Carnap's project failed. Friedman and Richardson rightly urge us to drop the assumption that the *Aufbau* ever was part of a reductive empiricist project in the first place.

While there is a more venerable tradition of taking Russell as a reductive empiricist,[2] I want to argue now that this has little more textual support than the similar attitude towards Carnap's *Aufbau*. Such an interpretation of Russell ignores his decidedly anti-empiricist view that we can be acquainted with entities that traditional empiricism rejects, such as universals and relations. As these entities are allowed as constituents of propositions that we can understand, Russell has no qualms in believing certain empirically unverifiable statements. Russell never tired of opposing his various realist metaphysics, such as "logical atomism" or "neutral monism," to alternative metaphysical positions. Indeed, Russell presents *Our Knowledge* (1914a, 4) as part of a case for logical atomism and in lecture II, "Logic as the Essence of Philosophy," argues against traditional empiricism: "if there is any knowledge of general truths at all, there must be *some* knowledge of general truths which is independent of empirical evidence, i.e. does not depend on the data of sense" (1914a, 56).

This willingness to transcend the limits imposed by reductive empiricism is also shown by the specific logical constructions that Russell offers. As we saw Friedman note above, Russell begins his discussion of "the external world" with a distinction between hard and soft data. The data here are those beliefs that we find ourselves accepting at the beginning of our epistemological investigations, and include common sense as well as scientific beliefs. Data are ranked in terms of "hardness" based on how well they stand up to critical scrutiny. Such scrutiny leaves "The hardest of hard data[, which] are of two sorts: the particular facts of sense, and the general truths of

---

[2] See, for example, Russell (1986).

logic."[3] Less firm, but still statements that we wish to preserve in some form, are the belief in other minds and the laws of physics. Russell's goal is to give some interpretation to talk of these things that goes beyond the hard data, and this is where his logical constructions play a crucial role. In lecture III Russell limits himself to the construction of ordinary things like pennies and tables out of the series of their aspects, and to placing these things in a public "perspective space." These constructions invoke perspectives of a thing in addition to the perspectives occupied by actual observers. These "unperceived perspectives" have contents analogous to sense data, or what are elsewhere called "sensibilia" (Russell, 1914b/1986, 9). The character of sensibilia are fixed using the laws of perspective and the properties of the occupied perspectives. This procedure is fundamentally defective, though, for, as Russell seems to sometimes recognize, it is not possible to connect the perspective on a thing at different times without appealing to the laws of physics (Russell, 1914a, 109). The problem is that the laws of physics are stated in terms of matter, spatial points, and temporal instants that Russell has yet to construct.

Matter, points, and instants are constructed in lecture IV, where genuine material particles are now defined as "those series of aspects which obey the laws of physics" (1914a, 110). These laws are taken for granted on the basis of the empirical success of science: "the empirical successes of the conception of matter show that there must be some legitimate conception which fulfills roughly the same functions" (1914a, 105). Temporal instants offer the most straightforward construction here. Russell takes for granted that each person perceives events of finite duration as well as the temporal relations of simultaneity (which includes partial overlap), earlier and later. He then notes that if we make certain assumptions about these relations we can construct instants as sets of events such that "no event outside the group is simultaneous with all of them, but all the events inside the group are simultaneous with each other" (1914a, 118). These assumptions include "if, given any two events [a and b] of which one [a] wholly precedes the other [b], there are events wholly

---

[3] Russell (1914a, 70). It is important to note that this critical scrutiny does not satisfy the skeptic. Indeed, Russell insists that skepticism is "logically irrefutable." See Russell (1914a, 67).

after the one [a] and simultaneous with something wholly before the other [b]," which ensures that the series of instants is dense, or in Russell's terms, compact (1914a, 120). Clearly, Russell must posit events that go beyond what it appears one individual is experiencing, although all of the posited events remain of finite temporal duration. The construction of spatial points is more complicated due to the need to secure a three-dimensional space. There Russell invokes Whitehead's notion of enclosure series and more elaborate assumptions about sense data.[4]

Two points about these constructions are crucial in order to appreciate Russell's project in *Our Knowledge*. First, the constructed instants are only acceptable because they can be ordered by a temporal relation defined in terms of the temporal relations made available in experience: "one instant is before another if the group [set] which is the one instant contains an event which is earlier than, but not simultaneous with, some event in the group [set] which is the other instant" (1914a, 119). This is essential to Russell's use of these instants to date events in line with the laws of physics. Second, there is a gap between the instants that comprise what Russell calls "local time" and the "one all-embracing time" of physics. The special theory of relativity "does not destroy the possibility of correlating different local times" although Russell nowhere explains how his private instants are to be collected across subjects (1914a, 104; cf. Russell, 1927, 208). It seems clear, though, that the embedding could only succeed if additional unperceived perspectives were posited, each with their own "local times."

Here I think we see two senses in which we might call Russell a realist. First, and most obviously, he is a realist because he thinks that idealism of any kind is false and that the opposite metaphysical position is true. This metaphysical realism, as I will call it, is reflected in Russell's analysis of experience. Sensory experience involves a relation between a subject and sense data that are logically independent of this experience. Sense data may not exist for long, but they are not mental for Russell in the sense of being essentially tied to a subject. This conception of experience is what makes

---

[4] The counterintuitive consequences of these constructions are recognized only later in Russell (1914a, 149). A helpful paper on these and later constructions is Anderson (1989).

it an option for him to posit sense-data-like entities (sensibilia) that are never experienced (see Hylton, 1990, esp. chapter 4). A second, distinct, sense of realism, theoretical realism, concerns Russell's attitude towards our pre-philosophical commitments, what we are here terming the soft data. For Russell, both the soft and hard data have a default presumption in favor of their truth. Earlier, in *Problems of Philosophy*, Russell had said, using "instinctive beliefs" for what are later termed "data," "There can never be any reason for rejecting one instinctive belief except that it clashes with others; thus if they are found to harmonize, the whole system becomes worthy of acceptance" (Russell, 1912/1967, 12). Thus, epistemology should begin with these commitments and seek to preserve them, even at the cost of invoking an elaborately constructed "penny" to clarify my belief in pennies. When it comes to the laws of physics, sensibilia that go beyond the hard data are invoked to preserve these laws by piecemeal constructions of matter, points, and instants. Theoretical realism is independent of metaphysical realism as someone could deny that the objects of sensory experience are truly independent of the subject and yet accept that our scientific theories contain truths about these objects. One might think here of Kant's empirical realism about Newtonian physics that was combined with his transcendental idealism about the physical world.

We see, then, that when Russell is faced with the choice between providing adequate logical constructions and adhering to reductive empiricist restrictions, he opts for the former and universals, relations, and sensibilia. Just as in the case of Carnap's *Aufbau*, Quine would conclude that Russell's reductive empiricist project was a failure. With Friedman and Richardson on Carnap, though, I suggest that Russell was never trying to give constructions that would satisfy the reductive empiricist.

III.

Carnap's estimation of the connection between his *Aufbau* and Russell's own work is clearly set out in a letter from 11 August 1928 to Russell that accompanied a copy of the *Aufbau*.[5] It shows a somewhat distorted conception of Russell's goals:

---

[5] For Carnap's prior contacts with Russell, see Pincock (2002).

I believe [myself] to have made here a step towards the goal that you also bear in mind: clarification of epistemological problems (and the removal of metaphysical problems) with the aid that the new logic, particularly through your own works, provides. I would like already here to indicate two points on which I had to depart from your view. These points of difference do not rest on differences in basic attitude, which appears to me thoroughly in agreement. The differences arise rather just because I have attempted to carry out your basic view in a more consistent way than has happened before. I believe I am here "more Russellian than Russell." (ASP RC 102-68-24)

One of the differences mentioned in the letter is also noted in §3 of the *Aufbau*: Carnap's constructions appeal only to the experiences of one individual, whereas Russell draws on the sense data of all agents, and even sensibilia. The second difference concerns Russell's metaphysical realism. For Carnap, the concept of a thing existing independently of all minds cannot be constructed in a construction system and so it is "a nonrational, metaphysical concept" (Carnap, 1928/1967, §176). Carnap is confused about Russell's stand on this issue:

It seems that we agree with Russell [Scientif.] 120 ff. in the indicated conception that the concept of nonempirical reality cannot be constructed. However, this does not seem to be consistent with the fact that, in Russell, questions of the following kind are frequently posed, which (independently of how they are answered) imply a realistic persuasion: whether physical things exist when they are not observed; whether other persons exist; whether classes exist; etc. ([Scientif.] 123, [Mind] 308, [External W.] 126, [Sense-Data] 157 and elsewhere). Cf. also Weyl [Handb.][6]

On the anti-metaphysical side, Carnap seems to refer to Russell's point about the words "real" and "independent": "if either side in the controversy of realism is asked to define these two words, their answer is pretty sure to embody confusions such as logical analysis will reveal" (Russell, 1914c/1986, 71). Immediately after some clarification, though, Russell reaffirms his metaphysical realism via the commitment to sensibilia: "objects of perception do not persist unchanged at times when they are not perceived, although probably objects more or less resembling them do exist at such times . . .

---

[6] Carnap (1928/1967, §176). Carnap's references here are, respectively, to Russell (1914c, 1921, 1914a, 1914b) and Weyl (1927).

[and] in the establishment of such laws [governing the objects of perception] the propositions of physics do not presuppose any propositions of psychology or even the existence of mind" (Russell, 1914c/1986, 72).

To help unravel the mystery of exactly where Carnap and Russell diverge, we need to draw on a second, more nuanced, reconstruction of the Carnap–Russell relationship in the 1920s: Demopoulos and Friedman's "Bertrand Russell's *The Analysis of Matter*: Its Historical Context and Contemporary Interest."[7] They find a shared "theory of theoretical knowledge" in Russell's 1927 *Analysis of Matter* and Carnap's *Aufbau* linking scientific knowledge to knowledge of structure. On this theory, which I will call the structuralist theory, while there may be some things of which we can know the intrinsic, non-structural properties, when it comes to the theoretical entities of the sciences, we are restricted to a knowledge of the formal properties of their relations to other things. Russell and Carnap presented this theory in a particularly precise way, compared to their predecessors, because they used the new logic of *Principia Mathematica* to describe this structural knowledge. Thus, Russell writes "Wherever we can infer from perceptions, it is only structure that we can validly infer; and structure is what can be expressed by mathematical logic" (Russell, 1927, 254, quoted in Demopoulos and Friedman, 1985, 623). Focusing on the subjectivity of private experience, Carnap deploys this theory to explain how scientific knowledge can be objective:

The series of experiences is different for each subject. If we want to achieve, in spite of this, agreement in the names for the entities which are constructed on the basis of these experiences, then this cannot be done by reference to the completely divergent content, but only through the formal description of the structure of these entities. (Carnap, 1928a/1967, §16, quoted in Demopoulos and Friedman, 1985, 626)

So, for Carnap, each subject can employ the same constructional definitions and arrive at intersubjective agreement about all scientific matters only because scientific matters never turn on the intrinsic nature or feel of an individual's experiences.

Russell's evolution from the supreme maxim and *Our Knowledge* to the structuralist theory and *Analysis of Matter* is a complex affair.

---

[7] Demopoulos and Friedman (1985). I have also drawn on M. Friedman (1999a); Demopoulos (2003a, 2003b).

On the mental side Russell abandons the earlier account of sensation in terms of a relation between subject and sense datum in favor of a neutral monist metaphysics of events. Perceived events or "percepts" are now used to logically construct both the subject and the physical objects that science requires. In line with this change, Russell posits unperceived events in the *Analysis of Matter* that play the crucial role that sensibilia had played earlier. Now experiencing a percept is viewed as the final event in a causal chain radiating outwards from an unperceived event.

It is the changes in contemporary physics, though, that lead to the biggest shifts in the details of Russell's constructions, most notably Einstein's general theory of relativity. The piecemeal constructions of matter, points of space and instants of time of *Our Knowledge* are replaced by the construction of the "point-instants" (Russell, 1927, 294) of space-time and a much more geometrical conception of matter. Russell's structuralist theory is a natural consequence of this, although I will suggest briefly in the next section that it was something of an overreaction. To see how the general theory of relativity might suggest the structuralist theory for Russell we need to see how the construction of point-instants differs from the earlier construction of instants. The perceived temporal relation of simultaneity between two events is no longer sufficient so Russell employs instead as his "fundamental relation" a five-term relation of co-punctuality "which holds between five events when there is a region common to all of them" (Russell, 1927, 299). The point-instants are then defined as maximally large sets of events such that any five are co-punctual. This five-term relation of overlap is a natural generalization of the two-term relation used in *Our Knowledge*. The key difference is that only the five-term relation allows for the appropriate ordering of the constructed point-instants in the four-dimensional manifold of the space-time of general relativity. A key step here is Russell's proof, in chapter 29, that certain assumptions about co-punctuality ensure that the point-instants can be collected together into neighborhoods satisfying the axioms for a four-dimensional topological manifold. With this topological structure in place, the metric of space-time is fixed by the arrangement of matter in line with Einstein's field equations.

What results from all this is a much more abstract characterization of the space-time of physics than we had in *Our Knowledge*.

Percepts are presented as a sub-class of the posited events, but the constructions depend entirely on the otherwise unspecified topological relation of co-punctuality. This gap between our private experience and the physical world has clear implications for communication between individuals. Russell claims that I need not doubt that other minds have experiences, but to the extent that I can ascribe content to their utterances about the physical world, it must be in terms of the formal, structural features that I know about. This point is noted eight years earlier in *Introduction to Mathematical Philosophy*, where Russell states that even for those who oppose a phenomenal, private world of experience to an objective world that transcends these experiences "every proposition having a communicable significance must be true of both [phenomenal and objective] worlds or of neither: the only difference must lie in just that essence of individuality which always eludes words and baffles description, but which, for that very reason, is irrelevant to science" (Russell, 1919, 61).

While it is clear that Carnap accepts this structuralist theory in the *Aufbau*, his reasons for doing so were quite different than Russell's. Once we get clear on these differences, the gulf between Russell and Carnap will become manifest. Thus in §16, "All Scientific Statements are Structure Statements," Carnap first quotes Poincaré's remark in the *Value of Science* that "only the relations between sensations have an objective value," but complains that this still

does not go far enough. From the relations, we must go on to the structures of relations if we want to reach totally formalized entities. Relations themselves, in their qualitative peculiarity, are not intersubjectively communicable. It was not until Russell ([Math. Phil.] 62f.) that the importance of structure for the achievement of objectivity was pointed out.[8]

I take this reference to Poincaré to be a crucial clue. For, following Poincaré, Carnap defends a decidedly conventionalist attitude towards physics. Indeed, Russell complains both that "Poincaré is Kantian" and that for Poincaré "almost all the mathematical part of physics is merely conventional" (Russell, 1914a/1926, 123). Neither Carnap nor Poincaré was a realist in either of the two senses noted above. First, Carnap correctly sees that Russell's attitude towards

---

[8] Carnap (1928/1967, §16). Carnap here refers to the 1923 German translation of Russell's *Introduction to Mathematical Philosophy* (1919).

sense data is a sign of metaphysical realism, and so rejects as unclear Russell's view that sense data are logically independent of the subject. If taken as a statement rejecting both realism and idealism, Carnap would have accepted the remark that Poincaré makes in the *Value of Science*, shortly after articulating his structuralism, that "a reality completely independent of the mind which conceives it, sees or feels it, is an impossibility" (Poincaré, 1913, 209). As Russell's remarks about Poincaré make clear, though, Russell can only interpret a rejection of realism as an adoption of idealism of some kind.

Second, and directly related to the differences between Carnap's and Russell's constructions, Carnap does not take Russell's hard and soft data for granted as genuine, factual claims. Throughout the 1920s, in the *Aufbau* and in papers before, Carnap adopted a conventionalist attitude towards the laws and the space-time manifold of physics. In the *Aufbau*, for example, the physical world is a wholly mathematical entity made up of quadruples of real numbers with additional numerical state magnitudes attached. The state magnitudes are assigned using the qualities assigned to the points in the associated perceptual world, which are themselves quadruples of real numbers. Carnap insists that this perceptual–physical correlation is not unique, but is on the contrary conventionally chosen to allow a fully law-governed, deterministic domain.[9] So, for Carnap, our scientific theories are not accorded the status of truths to be interpreted by positing genuine entities like space-time points or matter. Instead, any construction, including a wholly mathematical construction, can be used to interpret these conventionally adopted theories. Russell could not countenance such a rejection of theoretical realism, and he somewhat unfairly assimilates conventionalism about scientific theories to metaphysical idealism.

Carnap's rejection of Russell's theoretical realism allows him to construct his physical world without Russell's sensibilia. Russell struggles over how to relate experiences to the points of space and the instants of time, or the point-instants of the *Analysis of Matter*, so that the laws of physics can be given an empirical interpretation, i.e., an interpretation involving non-mathematical entities. Carnap will adopt the same laws and view them as conventions applying to the

---

[9] For further discussion see Richardson (1998, esp. 70–75 & 159–172).

wholly mathematical physical domain as long as they help make the physical world deterministic. Russell begins with the assumption that accepted laws, as part of the soft data, should be preserved. In place of Russell's soft data, Carnap offers stipulations.

We can better understand Carnap's and Russell's respective development in the thirties and forties by drawing on another aspect of Demopoulos and Friedman's paper: their argument that an objection originally raised by the mathematician Newman to Russell's structuralism in 1928 decisively sinks both Russell's and Carnap's projects. Newman argued that the claim that a physical domain satisfies a wholly structural description is trivially satisfied when certain cardinality assumptions are met. As our theoretical knowledge about the physical world is not supposed to be trivial, the structuralist theory is untenable. To see the problem recall the collection of events that Russell posited in his construction of the point-instants of space-time. If we can know from our percepts only that the events E that give rise to our percepts have some particular structure, then our knowledge can be captured in a sentence of the form: "There is some relation R and formal properties $S_1, \ldots, S_n$ such that $S_1(R)$ & $\ldots$ & $S_n(R)$ & $R(E)$." Newman showed, however, that this claim is nearly trivially satisfied no matter which formal properties we ascribe to R. In contemporary set-theoretic terms, the full structure of E is guaranteed to have a set corresponding to a relation with the required formal properties. The only restriction is that E have an appropriate cardinality.[10]

Initially, it might not be clear how this is an objection to Carnap's structuralism, for, as we have seen, his physical world *is* just a mathematical entity. Carnap must grant that it is trivial that there is such a mathematical entity, although this does not imply that it is trivial that this entity is correlated in a certain definite way with a perceptual world of qualities. Demopoulos and Friedman do not focus on this issue, but rather on what implications Carnap's structuralism has for the basic relation of his construction system. Unlike Russell, who allows knowledge of the intrinsic properties and relations between percepts, Carnap offers constructions even within the

---

[10] Ketland (2004). Compare also William Demopoulos's contribution to this volume, concerning Carnap's later use of Ramsey sentences in the reconstruction of scientific theories.

realm of one individual's experiences. All that Carnap assumes is a single relation of recollected similarity Rs, defined on the domain of an individual's total momentary experiences. This allows him to define many sensory properties and relations that Russell takes as basic, e.g. colors. Still, Carnap's primitive relation Rs sits poorly with the structuralist theory as it looks like this relation remains wholly private and subjective. This leads Carnap to try to eliminate Rs by a definite description given in wholly logical terms: Rs is defined as the relation on experiences that gives rise to a particular definition with special structural properties.[11] The Newman problem is that such a description will be trivially satisfied and so will not be unique. Carnap shows some awareness of this in the sections where he tries to eliminate Rs, but in the end he adopts the unacceptable proposal that a basic property of foundedness will, when included in the definition of Rs, ensure uniqueness and thus avoid triviality.[12]

It should now be clear, then, how far apart Carnap and Russell really were at this point, and yet how similar they might have appeared to each other. From the beginning, Russell posited entities and adopted a realistic attitude towards them in order to fill out his logical constructions to preserve the soft data, including the laws of physics. The details are quite different in 1927's *Analysis of Matter*, but the project remains the same. By 1927, though, physics itself has pushed Russell into a structuralist theory of scientific knowledge and a new metaphysics of events. Carnap, meanwhile, is reluctant to simply take for granted the objective status of the experiences of individuals, and so carries out his constructions even in the realm of one individual's experiences. In the construction of the physical world, Carnap's structuralism fits in well with a conventionalism that views space-time as a wholly mathematical entity. Only with something like the structuralist theory in place, with its agnosticism about the intrinsic features of space-time, is it reasonable to maintain that we are free to construct space-time out of mathematical materials. Thus in a way Carnap is more Russellian than Russell in that he is able to construct more by positing less. This may account for Russell's remark in a letter to Carnap from 1929 that the *Aufbau's*

---

[11] More specifically, as the relation on the elementary experiences that endows the color solid, defined in §118, with three dimensions. See §155.

[12] I pursue the response that Carnap does not need to define Rs, and so avoids the Newman problem, in Pincock (2005).

"views are those which I ought to hold, in the sense that they are the logical working out of premises which I accept" (ASP RC 102-68-18). At the same time, Russell's metaphysical and theoretical realism is inconsistent with the anti-metaphysical program of the *Aufbau*. The different roots of Carnap's and Russell's structuralism precluded agreement on the appropriate constraints for the construction of the external world. Russell's philosophical commitments forced him to view any qualms about metaphysical or theoretical realism as signs of latent idealism. Conventionalism about the laws of physics or the structure of space-time is a prime example of this.[13] For Carnap, conventionalism offered a nuanced way to both purge science of metaphysical debates altogether and find a special place for scientific laws in our scientific theories. These differences between Russell and Carnap, restricted at this stage of their respective developments to the arcane realm of the laws of physics, were to expand rapidly to include the nature of language and knowledge generally.

IV.

Russell responded to Newman's objections in a letter from 1928, which reads in part:

I had assumed that there might be co-punctuality between percepts and non-percepts, and even that one could pass by a finite number of steps from one event to another comprescent with it, from one end of the universe to the other. And co-punctuality I regarded as a relation which might exist among percepts and is itself perceptible.[14]

Russell never says this in *Analysis of Matter*, although he often invokes this two-term relation of comprescence or partial overlap between events and explicitly states that he is assuming that unperceived events can also be comprescent (Russell, 1927, 306; see also 384–385). The view described in the letter would adequately respond to Newman's objections as long as Russell could either explain how co-punctuality was perceptible or define his key relation of co-punctuality in terms of the clearly perceptible relation of

---

[13] Another is pragmatism. Compare Alan Richardson's contribution to this volume on the relationship between Carnap and American pragmatism.

[14] The entire letter is reprinted in Russell (1967–1969/1998, 413–414) and partially quoted in Demopoulos and Friedman (1985, 631–632).

compresence. For, on this amended view, scientific knowledge is not merely "There is some relation R and formal properties $S_1, \ldots, S_n$ such that $S_1(R) \& \ldots \& S_n(R) \& R(E)$," but rather "$S_1(C) \& \ldots \& S_n(C) \& C(E)$," where C is a definite relation whose intrinsic properties we are aware of in experience. This non-structural claim is no longer trivial. It remains to a certain extent structural, as it is consistent with our ignorance of some of the intrinsic properties of E, but the fixed relation C blocks Newman's set-theoretic construction.

In general, Russell seems content to offer only an indirect justification for these assumptions that go beyond our immediate experience. He tries to isolate a minimal set of entities and assumptions about these entities that are sufficient to interpret our scientific beliefs, what in *Our Knowledge* were called the soft data. By *Human Knowledge* in 1948, Russell has come up with a list of five such postulates. These are not justified independently, but only in terms of the reorganization of our knowledge that they allow. Among these postulates we find a "postulate of quasi-permanence" which posits qualitatively similar events in the neighborhood of a given event A (Russell, 1948, 488). Russell may have this postulate in mind when he gives "an ostensive definition from experience" of compresence and then notes his assumption "that this relation, which I know in my own experience, can also hold between events that are not experienced, and can be the relation by which space-time order is constructed" (Russell, 1948, 329–330). Thus, as in *Our Knowledge*, Russell assumes what is needed to preserve the laws of physics. While by *Human Knowledge* he has abandoned the wholly structuralist view of *Analysis of Matter*, he retains the basic motivations of that view. This is that experience is the basis for our knowledge of the external world, but that it must be supplemented by non-experiential assumptions.[15]

Shortly after the *Aufbau* and for the rest of his life, Carnap decisively and explicitly separated empirical issues about knowledge from logical questions about scientific confirmation. Russell's conception of scientific knowledge thus appears as an intolerable mixture of empirical and logical questions. While I will use these changes as points of comparison with Russell's views, I certainly do not think

---

[15] Thus I am forced to disagree with Demopoulos and Friedman when they complain that "all the [relevant] elements of the earlier and later theories are the same" (1985, 632). My proposed interpretation of Russell is essentially option (ii) from Demopoulos (2003a, 398).

that Russell was a motivating factor for Carnap's later views. Indeed, it is very hard to determine what combination of factors internal to Carnap's own thinking and stemming from interactions with other philosophers were responsible for these changes. In relation to Russell, the most significant change was the rejection of confirmation as a relation between experiences and sentences in favor of the view that confirmation is properly seen as a logical relation between sentences. This more syntactic approach to confirmation was tied to Carnap's Principle of Tolerance that extended a kind of conventionalism even to the basic logical rules for a language. Later, after semantic concepts were reintroduced, these innovations led to Carnap's distinction between internal, theoretical questions and external, pragmatic questions. While Russell complained loudly about these changes, from Carnap's perspective Russell's objections failed to engage with the truly radical turn that Carnap was trying to take.

Apparently responding to the criticisms of Neurath, Carnap first adopted a physicalist language in order to escape the dangers of subjectivity associated with the psychological language of private experiences. But by the 1932 paper "On Protocol Sentences" even physicalism was viewed as too restrictive. There Carnap criticized Neurath for insisting that all protocol sentences, that is, sentences representing basic elements of our scientific knowledge, must take a definite form. Instead, "their exact characterization are, it seems to me, not answered by assertions but rather by postulations" (Carnap, 1932c/1987, 458). These postulations of different languages are not restricted by some domain of pre-established facts about how experience really relates to language. Carnap eventually came to believe that that sort of question was too psychological to be of any relevance to resolving the logical question of scientific confirmation. Thus, most stridently in the 1935 paper "From the Theory of Knowledge to the Logic of Science," Carnap claims:

It seems to me that *theory of knowledge* is in its previous form *an unclear mixture of psychological and logical elements*. That holds as well for the work of our circle, not excluding my own earlier work. There thus arises much unclarity and misunderstanding. From these we see how important it is in so-called epistemological discussions to be explicit as to whether logical or psychological questions are meant.[16]

---

[16] Carnap, "Von Erkenntnistheorie zur Wissenschaftslogik," quoted and partially translated by T. Ricketts (2003, 259).

Genuine questions about confirmation need to be pursued in isolation from psychological distractions that appeals to experience invariably involve. The Principle of Tolerance of *Logical Syntax of Language* that "It is not our business to set up prohibitions, but to arrive at conventions" (Carnap, 1934c/1937, §17) eventually comes into play here. Different languages are studied to see how the sentences that are designated as the protocol sentences of the language logically relate to the other sentences. It is only by restricting our attention to these sorts of questions that a non-psychological epistemology can be preserved.

Russell attended the 1935 Paris conference at which Carnap presented this paper,[17] and responded most fully to Carnap's program for the logic of science in his 1940 William James lectures, *Inquiry into Meaning and Truth*. These lectures were delivered at Harvard in the fall of 1940, after a series of seminars at Chicago and Los Angeles in 1938–39 and 1939–40 respectively. In the preface Russell offers this summary of his views: "I am, as regards method, more in sympathy with the logical positivists than with any other existing school. I differ from them, however, in attaching more importance than they do to the work of Berkeley and Hume" (Russell, 1940, Preface). Two main points of disagreement with Carnap, on the relation between language and experience, on the one hand, and language and metaphysics, on the other, run throughout the book. In the last chapter Russell offers what is "in some sense, the goal of all our discussions":

that complete metaphysical agnosticism is not compatible with the maintenance of linguistic propositions. Some modern philosophers hold that we know much about language, but nothing about anything else. This view forgets that language is an empirical phenomena like another [sic], and that a man who is metaphysically agnostic must deny that he knows when he uses a word. For my part, I believe that, partly by means of the study of syntax, we can arrive at considerable knowledge concerning the structure of the world. (Russell, 1940, 347)

Russell reasons as follows: on the assumption that "language is an empirical phenomenon like another," philosophers should approach the study of language just as they approach physics. We must look at the empirical results discovered by scientists and try to provide a

---

[17] For a picture of Russell and Carnap in Paris, see Stadler (2001, 368).

clearer and more unified account of how these results are possible. What is a word, for example, and how can we use words to communicate or to express truths? Russell charges that "some modern philosophers" are unable to answer these questions because they try to stop with the sentences themselves and remain "metaphysically agnostic."

That Russell has Carnap in mind here is made clearer earlier in the book. In chapter 22, "Significance and Verification," Russell discusses Carnap's long 1936 paper "Testability and Meaning." After reviewing Carnap's proposal there for moving from the strict criteria of meaning as verification to the looser conception of testability, Russell notes that

I have not been contending that what Carnap says is mistaken, but only that there are certain prior questions to be considered, and that, while they are ignored, the relation of empirical knowledge to non-linguistic occurrences cannot be properly understood. It is chiefly in attaching importance to these prior questions that I differ from the logical positivists. (Russell, 1940, 314)

These non-linguistic occurrences are experiences that cause me to assent to things like "this is red" or "that is bright" and, for Russell, unless Carnap and others can explain what is going on in such cases, they are unable to get beyond language to the real world.

This passage makes clear exactly what aspect of Berkeley and Hume might have appealed to Russell. It was certainly not their anti-metaphysical tendencies, but rather their focus on experience and its role in our knowledge. Russell believes that if Carnap paid attention to how we use language, and what experiences prompt us to assent to what sentences, then his account of confirmation would be much improved. It is also here, and in the account of words themselves, that Russell sees hidden metaphysical commitments in Carnap's writings. For Carnap, Russell is just talking about the wrong thing. Experience–language relations surely exist, but they are psychological relations to be studied empirically and a distraction from the primary tasks of the logic of science and confirmation, e.g. formulating languages with precisely defined confirmation relations. We cannot treat language use as an "empirical phenomenon like another" and hope to get to the bottom of what sentences give a reason to believe other sentences, i.e., the logical question of confirmation. More generally, in his syntax period, Carnap completely rejects any non-syntactic investigation of language as irrelevant to his log-ical investigations. Tolerance implies that it is wrong to think that the facts in a pre-linguistic world constrain the forms that our lan-guage could take. Empirical questions, like which formal language approximates to the language behavior of scientists, can only be pro-ductively posed after the formal languages have been defined and investigated.

Right around the time *Inquiry into Meaning and Truth* was being written, though, Carnap was entering a final, more liberal, phase of his thinking during which semantics was allowed into the field of philosophical investigation. It is tempting to think that these changes would bring Carnap and Russell closer together philosoph-ically. In fact, in the most concise and mature presentation of this later approach, the 1950 paper "Empiricism, Semantics, and Ontol-ogy," we find Carnap offering a rare criticism of Russell. Recall that now semantic claims are allowed, for example, about what a linguis-tic item means, but that these semantic claims must be relativized to a linguistic framework. Once a linguistic framework is accepted, we can ask questions using it, including, if the framework has the appropriate resources, what its terms refer to. This does not settle the question of whether or not the terms *really* refer to my experiences or whether there are experiences, independently of any linguistic framework, and Carnap continues to insist that this sort of external question is a pseudo-question. Instead, the only external questions about linguistic frameworks that are allowed are about their practi-cal suitability in a world like ours: "To decree dogmatic prohibitions of certain linguistic forms instead of testing them by their success or failure in practical use, is worse than futile; it is positively harmful because it may obstruct scientific progress" (Carnap, 1950a, 40).

Carnap here criticizes Russell's theory of propositions from *Inquiry*, according to which every significant sentence expresses a proposition and propositions are mental events. Russell bases this theory of propositions on the need to find entities of the same general category for both true and false sentences (Russell, 1940, 170–189; cf. Carnap, 1947/1956, §6). Carnap's objections are based not on a conflicting theory of propositions, but rather draw on some rules that he thinks are sufficient to introduce propositional variables into a linguistic framework. These rules fix a proposition for every sen-tence, regardless of its truth value. They imply that propositions are not mental events because otherwise existential statements would be of the form: "If the mental state of the person in question fulfills such and such conditions, then there is a p such that . . ." The fact that no references to mental conditions occur in existential statements [involving propositions] (. . .) shows that propositions are not mental entities. (Carnap, 1950a, 26–27)

Additional claims about propositions that go beyond the rules of the linguistic framework can only be ordinary internal claims about propositions. Russell's proposed discovery of the essence of propositions is thus based on confusion (cf. Carnap, 1950a, 36).

V.

We see, then, that Carnap and Russell always disagreed on a number of fundamental philosophical issues, and that though these disagreements were somewhat obscured in the 1920s, by the 1940s the gap between Russell and Carnap had grown so large that both men must have clearly recognized it. Oversimplifying somewhat, it was Russell's metaphysical and theoretical realism, born in his struggle against idealism, that set his views in opposition to Carnap. Russell continued to think of philosophical problems as genuine questions with determinate answers. Carnap clearly rejected this by insisting on the need to specify a linguistic framework prior to any scientific or "metaphysical" investigations.

There is one final element of Carnap's later philosophy that might provide a kind of accommodation for Russell's insistence on experience, namely Carnap's views on pragmatics. Drawing on Charles Morris's three-fold division of investigations of language into syntax, semantics, and pragmatics, Carnap presents semantics as an abstraction away from the actual use of language by speakers studied by pragmatics. Thus, pragmatical investigations include "a physiological analysis of the processes in the speaking organs and in the nervous system connected with speaking activities; a psychological analysis of the relations between speaking behavior and other behavior" (Carnap, 1942, 10). These are of course the sorts of things that Russell saw as crucial to understanding the importance of language for philosophy. When at his most tolerant, Carnap would have to accept these investigations as a necessary part of the study of language. His semantic investigations, carried out in abstraction from pragmatics, presuppose that in the end, the connections between some of Carnap's languages and the actual use of English, say, can be made.

This recognition of pragmatics should not blind us to the fact that for Carnap all scientific investigation, and so all pragmatics, can take place only from within a linguistic framework. This means that even if Russell's views on language and experience could find a place in Carnap's philosophy, they would not have the same import for Carnap as they had for Russell. Russell thought he was discovering the truth about how experience relates to language, the world, and our knowledge, and that these truths were not in any way tied to the choice of a particular linguistic framework. Russell's attitude mirrors the qualms that many feel about Carnap's "Empiricism, Semantics, and Ontology." It is not surprising to find philosophers today siding with Russell's more traditional attitude towards philosophical problems, as it allows the philosopher to claim that she is discovering genuine facts about the world. While Carnap's semantic investigations remain influential, one cannot help feeling that Russell's prediction that Carnap would have "an everlasting effect on the thinking of men" has been borne out in a way that Carnap himself would have regretted.

MICHAEL FRIEDMAN

6 The *Aufbau* and the rejection of metaphysics

Der logische Aufbau der Welt (The logical construction of the world),
first published in 1928, is a founding document of the analytic tradition in philosophy. During the heyday of the Vienna Circle, in the late
1920s and early 1930s, it served, along with Wittgenstein's *Tractatus
Logico-Philosophicus* (1921), as one of the twin testaments of logical
empiricism. In the immediately following period, however, marked
by the rise of Nazism and the Second World War, many of the leading
representatives of logical empiricism, including Carnap, emigrated
to the English-speaking world, and the *Aufbau* went largely unread.
Indeed, the second German edition appeared only in 1961, and it was
not translated into English until 1967 – four years after the appearance of the Carnap volume in the *Library of Living Philosophers*.[1]
Meanwhile, a small number of prominent English-speaking philosophers did learn about Carnap and the Vienna Circle, and they articulated an initial understanding of Carnap's *Aufbau* against which they
then reacted both constructively and critically. A. J. Ayer's *Language,
Truth and Logic* (1936) appealed centrally to the *Aufbau* in enunciat-
ing a notorious attack on all traditional metaphysics as meaningless,
based on the principle of verifiability. W. V. Quine studied with Carnap in the early 1930s, and he later made the *Aufbau* a central object
of criticism – rejecting the "dogma" of phenomenalistic reductionism – in his celebrated paper "Two Dogmas of Empiricism" (1951).

[1] Carnap explains in the Preface to the second edition that not only the printed copies
but also the printer's plates of the first edition were destroyed during the war. The
English version is *The Logical Structure of the World*, trans. R. George (1967). I
have deviated from this translation at a number of points: most notably, I use "constitution" in place of George's "construction." My "construction" is typically the
translation of *Aufbau* or, when indicated, of *Konstruktion*.

129

Quine's colleague Nelson Goodman, by contrast, strongly approved of phenomenalistic reductionism, and he attempted both to expound and to improve on the *Aufbau* in *The Structure of Appearance* (1951).

A central theme running through this English-language reception is that the *Aufbau* belongs squarely within the tradition of modern philosophical empiricism, extending back to the British empiricists and epitomized more recently in Bertrand Russell's *Our Knowledge of the External World* (1914a).[2] Whereas the British empiricists had insisted that the meaning of all our ideas is derived from preceding sensory impressions, Russell had given a precise logical twist to this conviction in his program for "logically constructing" all scientific concepts on the basis of sense data. The main achievement of the *Aufbau*, accordingly, is to have attempted actually to carry out Russell's program in logical detail.[3] The twin testaments of logical empiricism are then seen as related thus: whereas Wittgenstein's *Tractatus* had shown that all meaningful propositions are logical truth-functions of "elementary propositions," Carnap had shown how all scientific concepts are logically reducible to "elementary experiences" – thereby instituting, for the first time, a precise empiricist criterion of cognitive meaning or significance.[4]

It is no wonder, then, that Ayer begins his attack on traditional metaphysics, in the Preface to the first edition of *Language, Truth and Logic*, by explaining (1936, 31) that "[t]he views which are put forward in this treatise derive from the doctrines of Bertrand Russell and Wittgenstein, which are themselves the logical outcome of the empiricism of Berkeley and David Hume." He then states the principle of verifiability and sketches the basic idea of the resulting critique of metaphysics:

---

[2] According to Quine (1951/1963, 39): "[Carnap] was the first empiricist who, not content with asserting the reducibility of science to terms of immediate experience, took serious steps toward carrying out the reduction." According to Goodman (1963b, 558): "[The *Aufbau*] belongs very much in the main tradition of modern philosophy, and carries forward a little the efforts of the British Empiricists of the 18th Century."

[3] According to Quine (1969, 74): "To account for the external world as a logical construct of sense data – such, in Russell's terms, was the program. It was Carnap, in his *Der logische Aufbau der Welt* of 1928, who came nearest to executing it."

[4] This conception of how Carnap and Wittgenstein were combined within the Circle is prominent in Kraft (1950).

If a putative proposition fails to satisfy this [verifiability] principle, and is not a tautology, then I hold that it is metaphysical, and that, being metaphysical, it is neither true nor false but literally senseless. It will be found that much of what ordinarily passes for philosophy is metaphysical according to this criterion, and, in particular, that it can not be significantly asserted that there is a non-empirical world of values, or that men have immortal souls, or that there is a transcendent God. (Ayer, 1936, 31)

Ayer concludes by recording his main intellectual debts (1936, 32): "The philosophers with whom I am in the closest agreement are those who compose the 'Viennese Circle,' under the leadership of Moritz Schlick, and are commonly known as the logical positivists [; a]nd of these I owe most to Rudolf Carnap."

Recent scholarship, not surprisingly, has gone far beyond this initial reception of the *Aufbau*, and has posed, in particular, serious problems for a straightforwardly phenomenalistic reading. Nevertheless, it must still be admitted that the more traditional picture contains at least an important kernel of truth. Indeed, Carnap later describes his original work on the *Aufbau* (in the years 1922–25) quite similarly:

Inspired by Russell's description of the aim and the method of future philosophy [in *Our Knowledge of the External World*], I made numerous attempts at analyzing the concepts of ordinary language relating to things in our environment and their observable properties and relations, and at constructing definitions of these concepts with the help of symbolic logic . . . My use of this method was probably influenced by Mach and phenomenalist philosophers. But it seemed to me that I was the first who took the doctrine of these philosophers seriously. I was not content with their customary general statements like "A material body is a complex of visual, tactile, and other sensations," but tried actually to construct these complexes in order to show their structure. For the description of the structure of any complex, the new logic of relations as in *Principia Mathematica* seemed to me just the required tool. (1963a, 16)

Thus, Carnap himself describes his project as a more logically rigorous and detailed implementation of the doctrines of phenomenalistic reductionism, just as the traditional picture holds.

Moreover, Carnap then touches on the resulting critique of metaphysics:

[R]egarding the criticism of traditional metaphysics, in the *Aufbau* I merely refrained from taking sides; I added that, if one proceeds from the discussion of language forms to that of the corresponding metaphysical theses about the reality or unreality of some kind of entities, he steps beyond the bounds of science. I shall later speak of the development towards a more radical anti-metaphysical position. (1963a, 18–19)

And this "more radical" position is later described as follows:

The most decisive development in my view of metaphysics occurred later, in the Vienna period, chiefly under the influence of Wittgenstein. I came to hold the view that many theses of traditional metaphysics are not only useless, but even devoid of cognitive content . . . Even the apparent questions to which these sentences allegedly give either an affirmative or a negative answer, e.g., the question "is the external world real?" are not genuine questions but pseudo-questions. The view that these sentences and questions are non-cognitive was based on Wittgenstein's principle of verifiability. (1963a, 45)

Thus, whereas Carnap's main work on the *Aufbau* was completed, as noted, in the years 1922–25, the assimilation of the *Aufbau* within the Vienna Circle, and its integration, in particular, with the views of Wittgenstein's *Tractatus*, occurred after Carnap moved to Vienna in 1926. So far, therefore, the traditional picture of how the *Aufbau* was combined with the *Tractatus* to yield a critique of metaphysics based on phenomenalistic reductionism and the principle of verifiability appears to be perfectly correct.

It is striking, however, that Carnap does not ascribe such a critique of metaphysics to the *Aufbau* itself: on the contrary, he explicitly says that this kind of "more radical" critique was formulated only after the *Aufbau* was assimilated within the Circle. But the *Aufbau* is by no means silent on the vices of traditional metaphysical philosophy, and it formulates its own characteristic version of a critical rejection of metaphysics. In particular, whereas the main body of the *Aufbau* is devoted to an explanation of the new discipline of "constitutional theory [*Konstitutionstheorie*]" and the outline of a particular "constitutional system [*Konstitutionssystem*]," the concluding part V engages in a "clarification of some philosophical problems on the basis of constitutional theory." Chapter V. A considers "some problems of essence," chapter V. B considers the "psycho-physical problem," and chapters V. C, D consider the "problem of reality."

In each case Carnap distinguishes "constitutional" and "metaphysical" versions of the problem in question, argues that the first finds a place within the constitutional system he outlines while the latter does not, and concludes that the first can be treated with the methods of "rational science" while the latter cannot. The clear implication is that metaphysics can in no way be conceived as "rational," "conceptual," or "theoretical" knowledge – as opposed, say, to mere "intuitive faith" (§181).

I will here examine the *Aufbau*'s critical rejection of metaphysics on its own terms. I will focus, in particular, on Carnap's treatment of the problem of reality: the dispute between philosophical realism and idealism about which entities and processes – physical or psychological, objective or subjective – are ultimately real. That this particular metaphysical problem was especially important to him is indicated by the circumstance that Carnap devotes two full chapters to it, and it is precisely this problem which is emphasized in the two passages from Carnap (1963a) cited above. Moreover, in tracing Carnap's discussion of this problem throughout the text of the *Aufbau* (in both part V and the preceding parts), we will end up confronting most of the important issues discussed by both Carnap himself and later interpreters. After a brief outline of the *Aufbau*'s constitutional system, therefore, I will turn to a more detailed examination of the text through the lens of the problem of reality.

I. THE CONSTITUTIONAL SYSTEM

The *Aufbau*, as noted, explains a new philosophical discipline Carnap calls constitutional theory and presents a particular constitutional system against the background of this general theory. The system Carnap chooses to investigate in detail is one in which "[all] scientific concepts are reduced to the 'given'" (§3): it proceeds from an "autopsychological basis" wherein "the choice of basic elements is limited to such psychological objects that belong to only one subject" (§63). More precisely, the basic elements consist of the conscious psychological states or "experiences" of a single subject (§64) – which Carnap, more technically, refers to as the "elementary experiences" (§67). Constitutional theory also envisions other possible constitutional systems, however: notably, a system with "general-psychological basis," in which scientific concepts are reduced to the experiences of all subjects (§63), and a system with "physical basis," in which scientific concepts are reduced to the fundamental concepts of physics (§62). What is common to every such system is the idea that all scientific concepts are to be defined or "constituted" from a small number of basic or fundamental concepts:

A constitutional system does not only have the task, like other conceptual systems, of classifying concepts in various types and investigating the differences and mutual relations of these types. Rather, concepts are to be step-wise derived or "constituted" from certain basic concepts, so that a *genealogical tree of concepts* results in which every concept finds its determinate place. That such a derivation of all concepts from a few basic concepts is possible is the main thesis of constitutional theory, through which it is distinguished from most other theories of objects. (§1)[5]

The general discipline of constitutional theory therefore has the task of investigating all possible forms of step-wise definitional systems of concepts: all possible "reductionistic" "system forms" (§46, compare §§59, 60).

Whereas the particular system Carnap presents certainly corresponds to the traditional demands of phenomenalistic reductionism, other systems are equally important for constitutional theory. Among the alternatives to the system with autopsychological basis, Carnap takes the system with physical basis to be most important. This is because such a system "has that domain (namely the physical) as basic domain which is the only one endowed with a univocal law-governedness of its processes" and therefore "presents the most appropriate order of concepts from the point of view of factual science [*Realwissenschaft*]" (§59). Indeed, Carnap was dissatisfied with the title of the *Aufbau* for this reason, and he at one time envisioned a second work that was to supplement what we now know as the *Aufbau* by presenting the same kind of detailed development of a physicalistic system. This work was to be entitled *Wirklichkeitslogik* or *Der logische Aufbau der Welt*, whereas what we now know as the

---

[5] The notion of a "theory of objects [*Gegenstandstheorie*]" refers to Meinong's *Gegenstandstheorie* (Carnap, 1928a/1967, §§3, 93, 172), which investigates all objects of thought as such. As Carnap explains (§1): "The expression '*object*' is here used always in the widest possible sense, namely, for anything about which a statement can be made. Therefore, we count among the objects not only things, but also properties and relationships, classes and relations, states and processes – moreover, the real and the unreal."

Aufbau was to be entitled *Erkenntnislogik* or *Der logische Aufbau der Erkenntnis.*[6]

The general framework for articulating any and all constitutional systems is the logic of Whitehead and Russell's *Principia Mathematica* (1910–13), which Carnap takes (at the time of the *Aufbau*) to be the definitive formulation of the modern symbolic or mathematical logic first invented by his teacher Gottlob Frege. The most distinctive feature of this logical framework, as Carnap understands it, is its use of what we now call the simple theory of types: the basic or fundamental objects considered (whatever they may be) are *individuals* belonging to the first level of an ordered hierarchy of logical types, properties of or relations between these objects are considered as *classes* of individuals (or, in the case of relations, classes of ordered pairs, etc. of individuals) belonging to the second level of our hierarchy, the third level then consists of *classes of classes* of individuals (and similarly in the case of relations), and so on. The entire universe of objects is thereby stratified into what Carnap calls "object spheres" (§29) associated with different "constitutional levels" (§41), where objects of a given level (logical type) are classes of objects (or relations between objects) of the next lower level. In the particular case of the autopsychological system, therefore, the basic objects or individuals are the elementary experiences, and all other objects of the system – first the other autopsychological objects, and then the physical and what Carnap calls "heteropsychological" objects (involving experiences of persons different from the initial subject) – appear at successively higher constitutional levels in the hierarchy of logical types.

We begin with the elementary experiences (holistic momentary cross-sections of the total stream of experience) ordered by a (holistically conceived) "basic relation" of remembrance-of-part-similarity-in-some-arbitrary-respect (§§67, 75–78).[7] The main formal problem within the autopsychological realm is then to differentiate, on this initially holistic basis, the particular sense qualities and sense modalities from one another. In grouping elementary experiences into

---

[6] Carnap expresses these qualms about the title of the *Aufbau* in correspondence with Reichenbach and Schlick in 1925–27. See Coffa (1991, 231, n. 11).

[7] Carnap explains in §67 that this choice of a *holistic* experiential basis – "in opposition to an 'atomizing' tendency of psychology and an epistemology which takes such psychic 'atoms' as simple sensations as elements" (as, for example, in Mach) – is influenced by contemporary Gestalt psychology.

classes (and classes of classes, and so on) via the one given relation of similarity and a complicated procedure of "quasi-analysis" (§68–74),[8] Carnap defines first the "quality classes" ("points" in a sensory field or modality such as the visual, auditory, or tactual fields) and then the "sense classes" (the sensory modalities themselves) (§§81, 85). The sense classes are not yet distinguished from one another, however, and Carnap then defines the *visual field* as the unique sense class possessing exactly five dimensions (two of spatial location and three of color quality) (§§86, 88–90). This definition, which concludes the constitution of the autopsychological realm, is paradigmatic of what Carnap calls a "purely structural definite description [*rein struk-turelle Kennzeichnung*]" – which, in particular, makes no reference to the subjective felt qualities of the visual as opposed to other sensory fields (§91). Carnap holds, more generally, that the possibility of all truly objective science (here, the sciences of "psychology" and "phenomenology," §§93, 106) depends on the possibility of defining all objects of study in this way (§§13–16).

Carnap next explains (much more briefly and sketchily) how to step beyond the domain of the autopsychological into the physical and heteropsychological realms. We begin by defining the "visual things" as the result of an embedding of the visual fields of our initial subject into a four-dimensional, so far purely mathematical continuous number-manifold ($\mathbf{R}^4$),[9] whereby colored points of these visual fields are projected along "lines of sight" onto colored surfaces in such a way that principles of constancy and continuity are maximally satisfied (§§125–128). And, in an analogous fashion, we define the "physical things" or objects of mathematical physics as the result of a "physico-qualitative coordination": we coordinate purely numerical "physical state magnitudes" (representing, for example,

---

[8] Carnap explains in §73 that the procedure of quasi-analysis is a generalization of the "principle of abstraction" employed by Frege and Russell in the definition of cardinal number. Thus, the Frege–Russell definition of cardinal number (which is the paradigm, for both Russell and Carnap, of the program of "logical construction" in general) uses the equivalence relation of equinumerosity between classes (whose members thereby stand in a relation of one-to-one correspondence) in defining a cardinal number as a class of equinumerous classes. Carnap's procedure of quasi-analysis attempts to do something analogous for *non-transitive* relations of similarity.

[9] The real numbers ($\mathbf{R}$) are constructed from the natural numbers (the finite Frege–Russell cardinal numbers) in the standard way, thereby implementing Frege–Russell logicism for all the objects of pure mathematics (§107).

the electro-magnetic field) with sensible qualities in such a way that the laws and methodological principles of the relevant sciences (here, the electro-magnetic theory of light and color) are maximally satisfied (§136).[10] Finally, we constitute the heteropsychological realm by constructing other subjects of experience analogous to the initial subject (i.e., systems of elementary experiences coordinated to "other" human bodies), and by then constructing an "intersubjective world" common to all such subjects obtained by an abstraction (via an equivalence relation) from the resulting diversity in points of view (§§140–150).[11]

We have now obtained all the objects of science by a step-wise constructive procedure extending successively up through the hierarchy of logical types. This means, in particular, that we can, according to Carnap, do equal justice to both "reductionist" and "anti-reductionist" philosophical attitudes. For example, we define the psychological states of other subjects in terms of their bodily (and linguistic) behavior, and the heteropsychological objects in question are thereby defined in terms of physical objects (§§57, 58). However, since the heteropsychological objects still constitute a distinct object sphere (a distinct series of constitutional levels) in comparison with the physical objects, it is by no means true that heteropsychological objects are "nothing but" physical objects. As Carnap himself puts it, the hierarchy of constitutional levels thereby allows us to do justice to both "the unity of the object domain" and "the multiplicity of independent object types" (§41). Similarly, we can maintain that "cultural objects [*geistige Gegenstände*]" (such as institutions) are constituted from heteropsychological objects (in terms of groups of people and their psychological states) while still preserving the autonomy of the "cultural sciences [*Geisteswissenschaften*]" (§56); and so on.

II. REALISM, IDEALISM, AND "PHENOMENALISM"

Carnap begins his discussion of "the metaphysical problem of reality" (part V. D) with a description of the three metaphysical positions

---

[10] Carnap explains that this constitution of the world of physics is based on his earlier methodological studies Carnap (1923 and 1924).

[11] According to Carnap, *only* the purely abstract world of physics (and not the qualitative world of common-sense perceptual experience) "provides the possibility of a univocal, consistent intersubjectivization" (§136, compare §133).

from which he wants to distance himself: "realism, idealism, and phenomenalism" (§175). He then argues that these positions, in so far as they take themselves to be disagreeing with one another, are employing a "metaphysical concept of reality" which cannot be defined or constituted within rational science (§176). He concludes by arguing that "constitutional theory contradicts neither realism, idealism, nor phenomenalism" (§177), so that "the three tendencies diverge only in the metaphysical [domain]" (§178). In other words, since *"the so-called epistemological tendencies of realism, idealism, and phenomenalism agree within the domain of epistemology [Erkenntnistheorie]," "[t]hey first diverge in the domain of metaphysics and thus (if they are supposed to be epistemological tendencies) only as the result of a transgression of their boundaries"* (§178). In this way, as Carnap also puts it, *"[c]onstitutional theory presents the neutral foundation [neutrale Fundament] common to all"* (§178).

Carnap is not using the term "phenomenalism" here as we employ it today. Realism, as Carnap understands it, ascribes the metaphysical concept of (ultimate) reality – viz., "independence of the cognizing consciousness" (§176) – to physical and heteropsychological objects. "Subjective idealism" ascribes it to the heteropsychological but not the physical objects, whereas "solipsism" denies it to the heteropsychological objects as well. "Phenomenalism," however, agrees with realism about "the existence of realities outside of the autopsychological" but "denies such reality, like idealism, to the physical [objects]" – it rather pertains "to uncognizable 'things in themselves', of which the physical objects are appearances" (§175). Thus "phenomenalism" refers to a standard reading of Kantian transcendental idealism in terms of a dualism between phenomena (appearances) and noumena (things in themselves). What we call "phenomenalism" – the doctrine that physical objects can be constructed out of sense data – is therefore closer to what Carnap here calls "subjective idealism."[12]

That what we call "phenomenalism" corresponds to what Carnap calls "subjective idealism" is confirmed by the way Carnap

---

[12] To make matters even more confusing, Carnap (1963a, 16), as we have seen, uses "phenomenalism" in precisely our contemporary sense when retrospectively describing the *Aufbau*.

characterizes the agreement between constitutional theory and the latter doctrine (§177): "Constitutional theory and *subjective idealism* agree that all assertions about the objects of cognition can be transformed in principle into assertions about structural-complexes [*Strukturzusammenhänge*] of the given" (where Carnap also adds that "with *solipsism* constitutional theory shares the conception that this given [consists of] my experiences"). More interestingly, Carnap then explains (and in considerably more detail) the central points of agreement between constitutional theory and what he calls "transcendental idealism" (§177): "Constitutional theory and *transcendental idealism* agree in representing the following position: all objects of cognition are constituted (in idealistic language, are 'generated in thought [*im Denken erzeugt*]'); and, moreover, the constituted objects are only objects of cognition *qua* logical forms constructed in a determinate way." Although Carnap does not make this explicit here, the kind of "transcendental idealism" he has in mind would presumably go beyond the proper boundaries of constitutional theory either by affirming (with "phenomenalism") the reality of uncognizable things in themselves, or by denying (again with "phenomenalism") the (ultimate) reality of the *physical* objects thereby "generated in thought."

In fact, Carnap's use of the expression "generated in thought" allows us to pinpoint the variety of transcendental idealism in question as the "logical idealism" represented by the contemporary Marburg School of neo-Kantianism. Characteristic of this school is a "genetic [*erzeugende*]" conception of cognition, according to which the proper object of scientific knowledge is never actually "given [*gegeben*]," but is rather "set as a task [*aufgegeben*]" for science in an indefinitely extended process of logical construction and refinement. The proper object of science is a never-to-be-completed ideal X towards which this process is converging, and there is no sense, for the Marburg School, in which the objects of scientific knowledge are already there waiting to be recognized. That Carnap has this variety of transcendental idealism primarily in mind is further confirmed by his first mention of the opposition between realism and idealism in the *Aufbau*:

Are the constituted structures "generated in thought [*im Denken erzeugt*]," as the Marburg School teaches, or "only recognized [*nur erkannt*]" by thought, as realism asserts? Constitutional theory employs a neutral language; according to it the structures are neither "generated" nor "recognized," but rather "constituted"; and even at this early stage it cannot be too strongly emphasized that this word "constitution" is always meant completely *neutrally*. From the point of view of constitutional theory the dispute involving "generation" versus "recognition" is therefore an idle linguistic dispute. (§5)

Carnap diverges from the Marburg School, therefore, in so far as it *opposes* realism by asserting that it is incorrect to say that the objects of scientific knowledge are "recognized" by thought. This whole issue, for Carnap, represents no genuine substantive disagreement at all, but merely "an idle linguistic dispute."[13]

Nevertheless, if constitutional theory, as Carnap suggests, agrees with realism that there is a clear sense in which the objects of scientific knowledge are "recognized" by thought, it also agrees with the transcendental idealism of the Marburg School that there is an equally clear sense in which these very same objects are "generated in thought." Carnap further clarifies this sense when he first introduces the basic elements and relation of his constitutional system:

The merit of having discovered the necessary basis of the constitutional system thereby belongs to two entirely different, and often mutually hostile, philosophical tendencies. *Positivism* has stressed that the sole *material* for cognition lies in the undigested [*unverarbeitet*] experiential *given*; here is to be sought the *basic elements* of the constitutional system. *Transcendental idealism*, however, especially the neo-Kantian tendency (Rickert, Cassirer, Bauch), has rightly emphasized that these elements do not suffice; *order-posits* [*Ordnungssetzungen*] must be added, our "basic relations." (§75)

---

[13] Carnap's divergence from the Marburg School is even more specific, for he explicitly rejects the "genetic" conception of the object of scientific knowledge (§179): "According to the conception of the *Marburg School* . . . the object is the eternal X, its determination is an incompletable task. In opposition to this it is to be noted that finitely many determinations suffice for the constitution of the object – and thus for its univocal definite description [*eindeutigen Kennzeichnung*] among the objects in general. Once such a definite description is set up the object is no longer an X, but something univocally determined – whose complete description [*Beschreibung*] then certainly still remains an incompleteable task." Carnap's view that every object of cognition is defined or constituted in a *finite* number of logical steps (and thus at a specific finite rank in the hierarchy of logical types) decisively separates him from the Marburg School, and allows him, in particular, to say that there is nothing incorrect in asserting that such objects of cognition are also "recognized" by thought.

Whereas "positivism" (as represented especially by §§3, 176) is correct that the so far unstructured "experiential given" comprises the basic objects of the system, "transcendental idealism" is equally correct that cognition necessarily requires that the given in question then be logically structured.[14] Such logical structuring, for Carnap, proceeds by means of the basic relation, whereby we successively ascend through the hierarchy of logical types in defining classes (and classes of classes, and so on) of the basic elements.

As noted above, the definitions employed in the *Aufbau* are what Carnap calls purely structural definite descriptions (such as the definition of the visual field, for example), which characterize the object in question as the unique object thereby arising in the hierarchy of logical types possessing certain purely formal structural properties (here, the property of having five dimensions). Only this type of definition, for Carnap, secures the *objectivity* of scientific knowledge (§§13–16), and it is precisely here, as Carnap stresses in §177, that constitutional theory comes closest to the "logical idealism" of the Marburg School – according to which "the constituted objects are only objects of cognition *qua* logical forms constructed in a determinate way." Indeed, Carnap even goes so far as to extend this requirement to the basic elements as well (§177): "They are, to be sure, taken as basis as unanalyzed unities, but they are then furnished with various properties and analyzed into (quasi-)constituents (§116); first hereby, and thus also first as constituted objects, do they become objects of cognition properly speaking – and, indeed, objects of psychology." Section 116 presents the formal constitution of "sensations" as concrete instantiations of the already defined abstract sensory qualities ("quality classes"): a sensation is an ordered pair consisting of an elementary experience plus a quality class to which it belongs. Moreover, as Carnap explains in the informal exposition of §93: "In contrast to sensations, which belong to the object-domain of psychology, qualities belong to the domain of phenomenology or the *theory of objects* [*Gegenstandstheorie*]." Thus, all objects of

---

[14] Ernst Cassirer was the leading contemporary representative of the Marburg School of neo-Kantianism. Bruno Bauch (with whom Carnap himself had studied at Jena) was a student of Heinrich Rickert, the leading contemporary representative of the Southwest School of neo-Kantianism. Carnap is here not distinguishing between these schools. For further discussion see Friedman (1999a, chapter 6, including the Postscript) and Friedman (2000, chapters 3 and 5).

scientific cognition (whether of psychology, phenomenology, or any other scientific discipline) must be constituted as "logical forms." There is no room within rational science for any "undigested" or logically unstructured entities at all, and this is in fact a central and very important point of agreement between Carnapian constitutional theory and contemporary transcendental idealism – which point, in particular, decisively separates Carnap's project from the "positivist" phenomenalist program represented by Mach (compare note 7 above).[15]

III. THE LANGUAGES OF REALISM AND IDEALISM

In §5, which first introduces – and dismisses – the traditional philosophical opposition between realism and idealism, Carnap begins by arguing that "[s]ince we always employ the expression 'object' here in the widest sense (§1) [see note 5 above], then to every concept there belongs one and only one object, 'its object' (not to be confused with the objects that fall *under* the concept)." In particular, a concept defined within the theory of types results in a corresponding *class*, where the objects falling under the concept then appear as *elements* of this class. And, since all objects in the domain of a constitutional system (aside from the basic elements themselves) are in fact constructed as classes, "it signifies no logical difference whether a certain object-sign means the concept or the object, or whether a sentence holds for concepts or for objects." Thus, when Carnap then introduces the opposition between realism and idealism in §5, he first explains that "[t]hese two parallel languages, which speak of objects and of concepts and still say the same thing, are fundamentally the *languages of realism and idealism*." The opposition between "generation" and "recognition" is "an idle linguistic dispute," therefore, precisely because constitutional theory itself

---

[15] This point of agreement is the basis for the recent flowering of Kantian and neo-Kantian readings of the *Aufbau*. For further discussion and references, see the works cited in note 14 above, and also Richardson (1998). Not surprisingly, this literature has also stimulated a return to more standard empiricist readings – for example, Hudson (1994). What we are now seeing is that Carnap is in fact completely neutral between Kantianism and empiricism (in so far as they remain within "the domain of epistemology" and do not transgress their proper boundaries) – a point already strongly emphasized in Friedman (1992a).

"employs a *neutral* language" (emphasis added) – in which the structures in question (conceived either as concepts or as objects) are simply "constituted."

In order adequately to understand (and ultimately dissolve) the dispute between realism and idealism, we must thus distinguish between three different languages: the languages of realism and idealism themselves, and the completely neutral language of constitutional theory. It is striking, then, that §95 introduces an analogous distinction. To begin with, "[t]*he fundamental language of the constitutional system is the symbolic language of logistic*" (that is, the language of *Principia Mathematica*, §107), whereas "[t]he remaining . . . languages only provide translations of the logical fundamental language." And, among the latter, we have both "the *realistic language [realistische Sprache]*, as is usual in the factual sciences [*Realwissenschaften*]," and "the *language of a fictional construction [Sprache einer fiktiven Konstruktion]*."[16] In the latter, in particular, we view the strictly logical constitutional definitions (first language) "*as operational rules for a constructive procedure*," whereby "we have the task of prescribing for a given subject, designated as A, step-by-step operations through which A can arrive at certain schemata (the 'inventory lists') corresponding to the individual objects to be constituted (§102)" (§99).

Although "[t]*he proper language of the constitutional system is the symbolic language of logistic*" (§96), the other two languages still have their legitimate uses. In particular, the realistic language "serves primarily for the easier recognition of the *contentual* correctness of the constitution, whether the intended, known object is in fact encountered through the constitutional definition (§98)" (§95). Since the whole point of the constitutional system is to order and systematize the already existing concepts of the factual sciences, "the constituted structure is supposed to be erected as a rational reconstruction of a structure that is already constituted, in daily life or science, in a partly intuitive and partly rational manner" (§98). A translation of the strict constitutional definition into the realistic language allows us to verify that this desideratum has in fact

---

[16] Carnap actually describes *four* languages, but his second language is just a simple translation into words of the "logistic language" – thus, instead of formally displaying in symbols the transitivity of a given relation R, for example, we simply say "R is transitive." So this language is of no particular interest here.

been fulfilled, in so far as *an already known object* is thereby recognized as corresponding to it. By contrast, the language of a fictional construction "serves especially for the easier, intuitive recognition of the *formal* correctness of the constitution, for verifying whether every constitutional definition is constructive (i.e., not ambiguous, not empty, and purely extensional) (§§99, 101, 102)" (§95). The point, briefly, is that every such definition, from a purely formal point of view, "must not designate more than one object, but also at least one" (§96), and the "inventory list" (purely extensional description of a class) created in the language of a fictional construction corresponds to a *"definite description of an object"* (§102). This language thereby facilitates the intuitive recognition that a purely structural definite description is formally correct – by representing the subject A as faced, for example, with the totality of sense-classes resulting from quasi-analysis at a given stage, on the basis of which one and only one such class (the visual field) can then be picked out as five-dimensional (§115).[17]

Carnap does not explicitly identify the language of a fictional construction as *idealistic*. However, in view of the importance of purely structural definite descriptions in Carnap's conception of the central points of agreement between constitutional theory and transcendental idealism ("the constituted objects are only objects of cognition *qua* logical forms constructed in a determinate way"), such an identification appears to be by no means inappropriate. Carnap's

---

[17] Carnap reemphasizes the fundamental importance of purely structural definite descriptions in this connection in §159: "As was explained earlier (§13), a definite description [*Kennzeichnung*] involves designation of an object by means of overlapping classes to which it belongs, or by relations to other objects, or even by pure structural description [*Beschreibung*] of its place in a relational system, in such a way that the description pertains only to it and to no other object. We have seen what fundamental significance belongs to definite descriptions in precisely constitutional theory; indeed, the constitutional system consists of nothing else but such definite descriptions in the form of constitutional definitions." The requirement of *extensionality* mentioned in §95 really adds nothing to the requirements of existence and uniqueness; for, as Carnap explains in §96, the methods of extensional definition by class and relation abstraction (which are fundamental to the formalism of the logistic language) are designed precisely to fulfill these (prior) two requirements: "[The] requirement of 'constructivity' [is] easily and so to speak automatically [fulfilled] by the application of the logical forms for introducing classes or relations and for univocal definite description of individuals. That by these forms univocality and logical existence are guaranteed is known from logistic; for the forms are fashioned in view of these required properties."

further discussion makes it all but irresistible. For, in the language of a fictional construction, we represent our subject A as undertaking a "synthesis of cognition [*Erkenntnissynthese*]" starting from the "given" (§100), on the basis of "synthetic components, and thus the constitutional forms" (§101). Moreover, since "[b]y *categories* are understood the forms of synthesis of the manifold of intuition to unity of the object," and since "[t]he manifold of intuition is called in constitutional theory 'the given,' 'the basic elements'" while "[t]he synthesis of this manifold to unity of an object is here designated as constitution of the object from the given" (§83), it follows that we can, if we like, view our subject A as undertaking a "synthesis of cognition" by means of "categories." There can be very little doubt, then, that the language of a fictional construction is precisely the language of (transcendental) idealism. Whereas in the realistic language we view our constitutional definitions as capturing or representing independently given objects (the already familiar objects of the factual sciences), in the idealistic language we view our constitutional definitions as synthesizing or generating objects via the operations or constructions of a cognitive subject.

The central point, however, is that the language of a fictional construction is indeed purely "auxiliary" or "fictional." The cognitive subject A, the step-by-step construction from the given, and the operations or acts of synthesis are all strictly speaking fictions, by which the underlying constitutional definitions are heuristically expressed "as palpable processes" (§99): "It is to be emphasized that *the constitutional system itself has nothing to do with these fictions;* they are referred only to the [third] language, and this serves only the didactic purpose of illustration." Similarly, although Carnap intends to give a rational reconstruction of the actual (empirical) process of cognition, he is careful to point out that the constitutional system itself involves no psychological processes whatsoever:

Since the constitution indicates this function [a particular psycho-physical correlation], the course of the process of cognition is not somehow falsely presented through the constitution (namely, as a rational-discursive [process] instead of an intuitive one). (The latter occurs only in the language of a fictional construction, which can be given alongside as an intuitive aid.) The constitution itself indicates no process at all, but only the logical function in question. (§143)

For Carnap, the fundamental language is always the purely formal logical language of *Principia Mathematica* – wherein no cognitive subjects, no synthetic processes, and no acts or operations of construction are in fact to be found. On the contrary, in the strict "constitutional language" we have only a purely logical sequence of definitions formulated in a type-theoretic language containing a single non-logical primitive.[18]

The sense in which the notion of "constitution" is completely neutral between "generation" and "recognition," therefore, is that "to constitute," for Carnap, simply means *to define* in the type-theoretic language of *Principia Mathematica*. Although the particular form these definitions take (as purely structural definite descriptions) implies that we can describe the objects of cognition "*in idealistic language*" (my emphasis) as "generated in thought," we transgress our proper boundaries and fall into metaphysics if we go on to conclude that the objects of cognition are "really" generated by our cognitive processes and thus have no "reality" outside these processes. Similarly, since the constitutional system is not, as it were, free floating, but is rather intended to capture the objects (and concepts) already recognized in the existing factual sciences, the naturally realistic language of these sciences plays an important role as a necessary check on the contentual correctness of the strict constitutional definitions. Once again, however, we transgress our proper boundaries and fall into metaphysics if we go on to conclude that the objects of scientific cognition are "real" in some ultimate sense of "independence of the cognizing consciousness" (§§52, 178). They are of course "real" in the "constitutional" or "empirical" sense, as determined by the methods of the factual sciences themselves, but

---

[18] Since "the given has no subject" (§65), nothing corresponding to the cognitive subject A actually occurs in the constitutional system. Indeed, "my experiences" become attached to a subject only when "the domain of the autopsychological" is formally constituted (§132) *after* the constitution of "my body" as a physical thing (§129). The only subjects in Carnap's world are thus ordinary empirical subjects, and this may be part of the reason he refrains from explicitly associating the language of a fictional construction with transcendental idealism (which he does associate with a "transcendental subject" in §66). Compare the retrospective discussion in Carnap (1963a, 18) which describes the procedure of this language as "a reformulation of the [constitutional] definition as a rule of operation for a constructive procedure, applicable by anybody, be it Kant's transcendental subject or a computing machine."

this is something no self-respecting idealist (and certainly no transcendental idealist) wishes to deny (§§170, 176). It is in precisely this way, for Carnap, that the language of constitutional theory provides the "neutral foundation" which both realism and idealism share.

IV. THE REJECTION OF METAPHYSICS

What, then, is the basis for Carnap's anti-metaphysical attitude? We know that, in the *Aufbau*, it is not the principle of verifiability, because this principle, as Carnap himself says, was not actually formulated until after he moved to Vienna. Somewhat more surprisingly, however, although it is certainly true that the constitutional system of the *Aufbau* fulfills the demands, as Carnap understands them, of traditional empiricist reductionism, this also has very little to do with his rejection of metaphysics; in particular, it has very little to do with his decisive rejection of "the metaphysical concept of reality" in §176. For the (very brief) argument Carnap presents is simply that the notion of "independence of the cognizing consciousness" cannot be represented in constitutional theory in a way that is adequate to the dispute between realism and idealism. For example, if I try to cash this out in terms of independence from my will, it turns out that a physical body I hold in my hand is not "real," contrary to the position of realism; similarly, a physical object outside the reach of current technology (Carnap gives the example of a crater on the moon) turns out automatically to be "real," contrary to the position of idealism. Moreover, this result, as Carnap points out, does not depend on the specific form of constitutional system he has chosen develop:

This [result] does not only hold when a constitutional system of precisely the system form of our outline is taken as basis, rather, [it holds] with respect to any epistemic [*erkenntnismäßige*] constitutional system, and, in fact, with respect to a system that would not proceed from an autopsychological basis but from the experiences of all subjects or even from the physical [basis]. *The (second* [metaphysical]*) concept of reality cannot be constituted in an epistemic constitutional system; it is thereby characterized as a nonrational, metaphysical concept.* (§176)

The point, in particular, is that all the constitutional systems Carnap envisions are concerned, from the beginning, with the logical reconstruction and ordering of what Carnap calls "conceptual," "theoretical," or "rational" knowledge – that is, the knowledge already gathered by the empirical factual sciences.[19] The autopsychological system is one in which "[all] scientific concepts are reduced to the 'given'" (§3), while in the other two systems these same "scientific concepts" are reduced to the experiences of all subjects and the physical, respectively. Within the existing factual sciences we find an "empirical concept of reality" in accordance with which real and unreal objects of various types (physical, psychological, and cultural) can be distinguished from one another by established scientific procedures (§§170, 171), but the "metaphysical concept of reality," by the argument of §176, does not occur within these sciences.

To be sure, the autopsychological system is distinguished by representing the order of "epistemic primacy [erkenntnismäßige Primarität]" (§54), and that is why this system, unlike the others, counts as an "epistemic" system.[20] Moreover, Carnap explicitly says, in the above quotation from §176, that what characterizes a concept as "non-rational" and "metaphysical" is the failure to constitute it in an epistemic system. But this does not mean that a commitment to traditional empiricist reductionism forms the basis for Carnap's anti-metaphysical attitude after all. For, in the first place, Carnap takes the order of epistemic primacy to be entirely uncontroversial – entirely unaffected, in particular, by the traditional disputes between different epistemological tendencies.[21] And, in the second place, Carnap's epistemic system, as we have seen, does not exclusively

---

[19] See especially Carnap's discussion of "faith and knowledge [Glauben und Wissen]" in §181: "We hereby pronounce no value judgement about faith and intuition (in the irrational sense), neither negatively nor positively. They are areas of life, just like lyric and erotic, for example. Like these and all others, they can certainly become an object of science (for there is nothing that cannot become an object of science), but contentually they are completely different from science. These irrational areas on the one hand and science on the other can neither confirm nor contradict one another."

[20] I am indebted to Christopher Pincock for emphasizing this point to me – a point which I missed, for example, in Friedman (1987, note 32).

[21] Section 178 explains that the different epistemological tendencies agree that "all cognition traces back finally to my experiences, which are set into relation, connected, and worked up; thus cognition can attain in a logical progress to the various structures of my consciousness, then to the physical objects, further with their help to the structures of consciousness of the heteropsychological and thus to the cultural objects."

represent the particular standpoint of phenomenalistic empiricism, but rather the "neutral foundation" common to *all* epistemological tendencies. The privileged role of epistemic constitutional systems in Carnap's characterization of "metaphysical" simply reflects his commitment to a very general form of empiricism which holds – uncontroversially – that all knowledge in the empirical factual sciences indeed begins with subjective experience.

Does Carnap's argument in §176 therefore beg the question against metaphysics on behalf of the factual sciences? There is an important sense in which this is true. But let us look at how Carnap describes his anti-metaphysical attitude at the time of writing the *Aufbau*:

Even in the pre-Vienna period, most of the controversies in traditional metaphysics appeared to me sterile and useless. When I compared this kind of argumentation with investigations and discussions in empirical science or in the logical analysis of language, I was often struck by the vagueness of the concepts used and by the inconclusive nature of the arguments. I was depressed by disputations in which the opponents talked at cross purposes; there seemed hardly any chance of mutual understanding, let alone of agreement, because there was not even a common criterion for deciding the controversy. (1963a, 44–45)

From the very beginning, then, Carnap was forcibly struck by the obvious *de facto* differences between the scientific and (traditional) philosophical enterprises, especially by the obvious lack of "mutual understanding" – the tendency to talk "at cross purposes" – endemic to the latter.

This emphatically does not mean, however, that Carnap simply lost all interest in philosophical discussion. On the contrary, as he makes very clear in the same context, he rather developed his own characteristic philosophical perspective:

Since my student years, I have liked to talk with friends about general problems in science and practical life, and these discussions often led to philosophical questions. My friends were philosophically interested, yet most of them were not professional philosophers, but worked either in the natural sciences or in the humanities. Only much later, when I was working on the *Logischer Aufbau*, did I become aware that in talks with my various friends I had used different philosophical languages, adapting myself to their ways of thinking and speaking. With one friend I might talk in a language that could be characterized as realistic or even materialistic; here we looked at the world as consisting of bodies, bodies as consisting of atoms . . . In a talk with another friend, I might adapt myself to his idealistic kind of language. We would consider the question of how things are to be constituted on the basis of the given . . .

I was surprised to find that this variety in my ways of speaking appeared to some to be objectionable and even inconsistent. I had acquired insights valuable for my own thinking from philosophers and scientists of a great variety of philosophical creeds. When asked which philosophical position I myself held, I was unable to answer. I could only say that my general way of thinking was closer to that of physicists and of those philosophers who are in contact with scientific work. Only gradually, in the course of the years, did I recognize clearly that my way of thinking was neutral with respect to the traditional controversies, e.g., realism vs. idealism, nominalism vs. Platonism (realism of universals), materialism vs. spiritualism, and so on. When I developed the system of the *Aufbau*, it actually did not matter to me which of the various forms of philosophical language I used, because to me they were merely modes of speech, and not formulations of positions. Indeed, in the book itself, in the description of the system of construction or constitution, I used in addition to the neutral language of symbolic logic three other languages, in order to facilitate the understanding for the reader; namely, first, a simple translation of the symbolic formula of definition into the word language; second, a corresponding formulation in the realistic language as it is customary in natural science; and third, a reformulation of the definition as a rule of operation for a constructive procedure[.] (1963a, 17–18)[22]

As we have seen, Carnap, in the *Aufbau*, is by no means uninterested in the traditional metaphysical dispute between realism and idealism. On the contrary, he devotes considerable ingenuity and philosophical imagination to crafting logical reconstructions of these positions which capture what he takes to be correct and uncontroversial in them – so long, that is, as they do not transgress their proper boundaries. And, in particular, by thereby capturing the "neutral foundation" common to both, the constitutional system dissolves any possibility of fruitless metaphysical controversy while simultaneously explaining their undoubted significance and utility as "modes of speech."

---

[22] On the number of alternative languages (three or four), see note 16 above; for the continuation of the last sentence, see note 18.

Moreover, and at the same time, Carnap thereby turns philosophy into a scientific discipline – a subject with its own technical instrument (the mathematical logic of *Principia Mathematica*) and its own technical problems to solve (the formal problems of constitutional theory). As Carnap explains in the Preface to the first edition (1928, ix–x [xvi–xvii]): "The new type of philosophy has arisen in close contact with work in the special sciences, especially mathematics and physics[; and t]his has the consequence that we strive to make the rigorous and responsible basic attitude of scientific researchers also the basic attitude of workers in philosophy, whereas the attitude of the old type of philosophers is more similar to a poetic [attitude]." The new mathematical logic of Frege and Russell can thus finally bring peace and progress to the discipline of philosophy, analogous to the peace and progress that already reigns, in Carnap's view, within the existing scientific disciplines. Indeed, although Carnap was certainly very interested in Russell's construction of physical objects from sense data in *Our Knowledge of the External World*, what impressed him most was Russell's overarching conception of "logic as the essence of philosophy" – as the basis, in particular, for a radically new type of "scientific philosophy."[23]

Carnap explains in the continuation of the passage quoted above that this fundamental anti-metaphysical orientation remained constant throughout his career:

This neutral attitude toward the various philosophical forms of language, based on the principle that everyone is free to use the language most suited to his purpose, has remained the same throughout my life. It was formulated as "principle of tolerance" in *Logical Syntax* and I still hold it today, e.g., with respect to the contemporary controversy about a nominalist or Platonic language. (1963a, 18)

In *Logical Syntax of Language* (1934c) Carnap reconceives disputes between different "philosophical languages" (in particular, the dispute between different positions or "schools" in the foundations of

---

[23] The full title of Russell's book is *Our Knowledge of the External World as a Field for Scientific Method in Philosophy*. Compare Carnap (1963a, 13), which applauds Russell's call for a new "logical-analytic method of philosophy" and concludes, after quoting from Russell's stirring methodological call to arms in the final pages: "I felt as if this appeal had been directed to me personally. To work in this spirit would be my task from now on!"

mathematics) as *proposals* for formulating the total language of science on the basis of one or another logical calculus (intuitionistic or classical, for example). In "Empiricism, Semantics, and Ontology" (1950a) Carnap attempts to dissolve the then contemporary dispute between himself and Quine about the use of "abstract objects" in semantics by suggesting that all such philosophical controversies about "existence" (of abstract objects in general, physical objects in general, and so on) really concern the practical or "external" question of which "linguistic framework" to adopt, not any genuinely "theoretical" question of what entities actually exist. Quine, the convinced philosophical empiricist and ontological minimalist, would have none of this – a fact which left Carnap, the rigorously antimetaphysical advocate of philosophical tolerance, both pained and puzzled. But what is most striking, from our present point of view, are the deep continuities between Carnap's position here and his much earlier attempt definitively to dissolve the philosophical problem of "realism" in the *Aufbau*.

7 Carnap and the Vienna Circle: rational reconstructionism refined

I. INTRODUCTION

Rudolf Carnap is today the best known representative of the Vienna Circle, even though he was neither its nominal leader (Moritz Schlick), nor its effective founder (Hans Hahn), nor its most prolific writer and propagandist (Otto Neurath). The reason for Carnap's prominence lies in two books – *The Logical Construction of the World* (1928, better known as the *Aufbau*) and *The Logical Syntax of Language* (1934c, translated in 1937) – and a series of papers – including "The Elimination of Metaphysics Through Logical Analysis of Language" (1932d/1959) and "The Physical Language as the Universal Language of Science" (1932a, translated as *The Unity of Science*, 1934) – published between 1928 and 1936. In these works Carnap managed to articulate with until then unsurpassed clarity certain theses of extreme boldness and daring complexity that were closely associated with the Circle as a whole. Yet while he provided exemplary articulations of its members' characteristic convictions and also set themes for the Circle's continuing discussions, it must be stressed that the development of these theses was very much Carnap's own and that many of his positions encountered opposition even within the Circle itself. If one is then moved to add that there is more to the Vienna Circle's philosophy than Carnap's, one must also add that there is more to Rudolf Carnap than the Vienna Circle's influence.

That said, it is very hard indeed to imagine the mature Carnap without the background of the Vienna Circle. Carnap's philosophically deflationary attitude was largely of a piece with the Circle's anti-metaphysics. In turn, the Circle's modernist late Enlightenment

agenda provided him with the kind of intellectual companion-
ship that he valued most highly, and, in the Circle's scientifically
informed and lively discussion culture, his developing philosophy
found the critical support he needed to bring his projects to fruition.
That many of these specific projects were but temporary stopping
points and provisional articulations of his vision, which were soon
to be refashioned anew, was itself in the spirit of the collective
endeavor to which the Circle subscribed. Most significantly, however, it was Carnap's own attitude of philosophical tolerance – held,
as his autobiography tells us, since the days of his youth – that was
developed further in this period and gained its canonical formulation,
steeled in the furnace of the Circle's discussions. In the Vienna Circle
then, the philosopher Carnap came of age as he hardly would have
elsewhere.

In this chapter I shall consider Carnap's interaction with two other
leading members of the Circle, Moritz Schlick and Otto Neurath.
These two do not, of course, constitute Carnap's only interlocutors
within the Circle. Early on, Carnap discussed philosophical issues
frequently with Herbert Feigl and Friedrich Waismann, and the all-
important development of his *Logical Syntax* project profited from
discussions with Kurt Gödel, Karl Menger, and their former teacher
Hans Hahn. As the development of Carnap's philosophy of logic and
mathematics is analyzed in other chapters, I shall here concentrate
on the development of his general philosophy of science and conception of epistemology. It is particularly this aspect of Carnap's work
that is illuminated by considering his interaction with Schlick and
Neurath.

A central place in the development of Carnap's general epistemology is of course occupied by the *Aufbau*. Here again I must defer
to another chapter for a detailed discussion. What concerns me here
is how his general strategy of rational reconstruction fared in the
course of the Circle's discussions about the empirical base of science
which the *Aufbau* set off. Conditioned by different presuppositions,
Schlick and Neurath challenged different aspects of Carnap's rational reconstructionism. In his interaction with them we shall also see
Carnap's irenic tendencies fully displayed, even though he did not
remain wholly neutral. We shall also see him wavering before set-
tling on his own position. Caught between the demands of atomism
and holism, in the end Carnap characteristically disowned either's

pretense to "get to the bottom" of things and held that they were but different ways of conceptualizing or speaking.

II. CARNAP'S RELATIONS WITH SCHLICK AND NEURATH

The discussions in question constituted the so-called protocol sentence debate concerning which much has been written encouraging the false but still current caricature of logical empiricism as traditional foundationalism.[1] Looked at more carefully, however, the debate evidences a fundamental disagreement between leading protagonists that concerned the very core of "the" Circle's philosophy of science. Considering Carnap in this context helps to highlight how his distinctive form of doing scientific philosophy evolved and how it related to its apparent competitors in the Circle. His mature conception of philosophy as "logic of science" (early on even "syntax of science") differed from Schlick's project of clarifying meanings and Neurath's naturalistic approach to scientific theorizing. What is of particular interest is whether Carnap's conception is nevertheless compatible with one of them (and, if so, which one).

Considering Carnap in the protocol sentence debate also throws into relief his stance towards Wittgenstein. Whereas the development of his philosophy of formal science sees him reacting directly to the *Tractatus*, the development of his general conception of epistemology sees him dealing with Wittgenstein's shadow, as it were, the reactions to Wittgenstein's philosophy by Schlick and Neurath. Although he was neither a follower like Schlick nor an outright opponent like Neurath, but instead critically appreciative of the achievements of the *Tractatus* as well as its limits, Carnap nevertheless ended up in the anti-Wittgensteinian camp. Its members included also Hahn and Philipp Frank, who together with Neurath had formed the so-called first Vienna Circle before the First World War.[2] They rejected the doctrines of the *Tractatus* culminating in its paradoxical conclusion and they also broke with the Wittgensteinian orthodoxy

---

[1] To pick but one prominent example, see R. Rorty dismissing the "foundationalist motives of the logical empiricists" in his "Introduction" to Sellars (1956/1997, 5). Two recent accounts of the debate in its entirety, albeit from different vantage points, are Uebel (1992a) and Oberdan (1993).

[2] On the so-called first Vienna Circle, see Haller (1985/1991) and Uebel (2003).

of requiring conclusive verifiability as a criterion of cognitive significance.[3] (It may be noted that since Carnap, like Neurath and Hahn, placed no premium on faithfulness to Wittgenstein, charges that they misunderstood him are often besides the point: their intentions were far from exegetical.) Carnap (1963a, 47) designated this anti-Wittgensteinian camp in his autobiography as the "left wing" of the Vienna Circle. Other, less immediately philosophical aspects of Carnap's interactions with Schlick and Neurath become relevant here. For Carnap, each of them provided an entrance to different Viennese worlds: Schlick to the artistic-intellectual soirées of the liberal bourgeoisie, Neurath to the meetings and pedagogical fervor of the Socialist Workers' movement. Himself belonging to neither, Carnap was fascinated to witness both "Viennese Modernity" and "Red Vienna" in their final days. In the end, however, he appears to have been too "scientistic" in temperament for the salon culture and too "philosophical" in attitude for political activism.

In particular, Carnap's contribution to the struggle for what the Circle's manifesto called the "shaping of economic and social life according to rational principles" (Neurath, 1973, 318) was rather indirect. It lay in extremely abstract explorations of the plasticity of our conceptual frameworks and the conditions of their reconstructibility. However abstract, results here were urgently needed actually to carry out the program to "fashion intellectual tools for everyday life, for the daily life of the scholar but also for the daily life of all those who in some way join in working at the conscious re-shaping of life" (Neurath, 1973, 305). Carnap's constructivism not only expressed his modernist aesthetic, but was also consonant with his ethical-political attitude. His task was precisely to establish the consistency and philosophical value of the very idea that our conceptual frameworks were reconstructible in different ways and under intentional direction from within.[4]

As these brief remarks suggest, considering Carnap's philosophy through the lens of his relations to Schlick and Neurath would mean attending to a complex set of issues both philosophical and moral-political. Here I shall stick to the philosophical issues and focus

---

[3] On the latter break, which Carnap dated to "about 1931," see Carnap's remarks in (1934c/1937, §82, 321; 1936–37, 422n. and 33n.; and 1963a, 57–58).

[4] For more on the political dimension of the left Circle, see Uebel (2005b).

on the remarkable fact that it was the anti-Wittgensteinian camp within the Vienna Circle that developed anti-foundationalist epistemology and pioneered a deflationist version of neo-positivist antimetaphysics. My point will be that the process of Carnap's radicalization of his early diffidence towards metaphysical philosophy – his becoming an anti-foundationalist conventionalist empiricist – can be traced through his relations with Schlick and Neurath.

III. CARNAP AND SCHLICK: FORMAL RATIONAL RECONSTRUCTION CHALLENGED

Let me begin with Schlick, who, around 1930, professed a logical atomism of a rather attenuated form. Having originally approved of Carnap's *Aufbau* project – a footnote in his "Experience, Cognition, Metaphysics" of 1926 lauded Carnap's "acute and irrefutable remarks" (Schlick, 1979, 111) in his then still forthcoming book – by 1930 Schlick came to endorse a philosophical program that was sharply at variance with the logical reconstructionism that constituted Carnap's methodology in the *Aufbau*.

Carnap pursued the aim of furnishing an account of the nature of scientific knowledge adequate to the then latest advances by developing constructed languages for scientific disciplines. Over the course of his long career, Carnap changed his mind about the nature of the languages appropriate to the representation of scientific theories, but not about the strategy of providing so-called rational reconstructions of their logico-linguistic frameworks. The point lay in the clear exhibition of the meaning and empirical basis of scientific propositions. The *Aufbau* provides one such reconstruction of the concepts with which we form knowledge claims about the world, their relation to each other, and to the experientially given. As Carnap (Preface to 1st edition) put it, laying a "rational foundation" for the exercise of scientific concepts must be distinguished from investigations of how these concepts have actually been arrived at. Carnap here drew the methodological distinction later codified by Reichenbach (1938) between "context of justification" and "context of discovery," with philosophy proper being attentive only to the former.

Schlick had agreed with Carnap's thesis in the *Aufbau* that "all scientific statements must confine themselves to purely structural assertions" (Schlick, 1979, 111). This thesis, as Carnap (1928, §15) points out, is a radicalization of Schlick's method of providing implicit definitions for the non-observational, theoretical concepts of science in his *General Theory of Knowledge*. Intuition, the apprehension of the fleeting phenomenal contents of consciousness, was thereby reduced in importance for epistemology: while intuition provided for contact with the world, it was not intuitive content but logical form that carried the import of propositions. The question arose, however, what remained of philosophy once this perspective on cognitive meaning had been adopted. Having taken the linguistic turn of focusing not on the world itself directly but on ways in which we talk about the world, could philosophy now focus on logical form, as Carnap tried to do in the *Aufbau*?

Schlick's "The Turning Point of Philosophy" makes it clear that he was persuaded by Wittgenstein's *Tractatus* that such a procedure is illegitimate. With the latter, Schlick (1979, 156) held that logical form "can not in turn be presented on its own account." The picture theory of meaning of the *Tractatus* held that logical form was what a proposition must have in common with what is pictured in order to be able to picture it, but it also held that this logical form in turn could not be represented by propositions. The reason for this lay in the prescription of the theory of types that no proposition can speak about itself on pain of paradox. In order to represent the logical form of another proposition p', however, a proposition p would have to share that proposition's logical form and so be talking about itself.[5] So how could philosophy now proceed if Carnap's formal approach thus fails?

Schlick's answer was Wittgenstein's: what cannot be "said" (expressed propositionally) must be "shown" (demonstrated ostensively). When Schlick denied that there exist specifically philosophical truths he did not deny that there exists a characteristic activity of philosophy, separate from science (Schlick, 1979, 157–159). "Philosophy . . . is that activity whereby the meaning of statements is established or discovered. Philosophy elucidates statements, science verifies them. In the latter we are concerned with the truth of statements, but in the former with what they actually mean." Moreover, even "the giving of meaning to statements cannot . . . be

---

[5] See Wittgenstein (1922, 4.12, 2.172, and 3.332). I here follow the interpretation in Hart (1971).

done in turn by statements . . . The final giving of meaning therefore always takes place by means of actions," namely, ostensions. For Schlick, therefore, "philosophy is not a system of statements and not a science" because it concerns itself only with the elucidation of statements, not their verification. "Philosophy consists" in "acts of giving meaning."

Schlick's elucidatory approach to philosophy was not without problems of its own, however. What did it mean for him to assert (Schlick, 1979, 159) that "philosophy is called upon to provide the ultimate foundation of knowledge"? This sounds like a version of foundationalism, but we must remember that it was the determination of meaning that stood at the center of Schlick's concerns. Around 1930, it was merely due to the fact that, under Wittgenstein's influence, he held to a strict verificationist conception of meaning that Schlick's meaning determination strayed into foundationalist territory. Philosophy was to exhibit the given as the terminus of reduction chains by which every statement exhibited the path to its verification (Schlick, 1979, 157): "The act of verification . . . is the occurrence of a particular state-of-affairs, ascertained by observation and immediate experience." Since, moreover, philosophy's concern lies "with assertions which give all statements their meaning in an absolutely final sense" (1979, 159), Schlick even sounded like a proponent of traditional, infallibilist foundationalism. But this again would be to overlook his primary concern with what empirical knowledge presupposed: knowledge of meaning.

By 1930, then, Schlick disagreed with the *Aufbau* in two decisive respects. For the reasons given by Wittgenstein, philosophy could not consist in the explicit delineation of logical form, using the latter as the key to unlock the meaning contained in these structures. For Schlick (1979, 142), it became instead experiential "acts of giving or finding meaning which lend significance to all the words occurring in our statements." Moreover, where the *Aufbau* provided merely possible reduction chains for in-principle justifications of applying the symbolic system of our scientific theories, Schlick demanded ultimate meaning determinations that conclusively establish the actual applicability of our scientific symbol system. Both Schlick's overall method and its results differed from that of the *Aufbau*.

What was Carnap's own view of the challenge that Wittgenstein's view of logical form presented him with? Carnap's infrequent and rather innocent use of the notion of logical form in the *Aufbau* suggests that he did not share Wittgenstein's conception at the time of its writing. Carnap's response to the Wittgensteinian criticism rather came after the fact of his initial transgression of Tractarian strictures. But did Carnap accept for the *Aufbau* what Wittgenstein accepted for the *Tractatus*, namely, that it was strictly speaking meaningless? As Carnap never addressed the matter explicitly in print, we can only employ circumstantial evidence. This suggests that he tended to recast what he had done in the *Aufbau* as "eluci-dations," statements that are strictly speaking meaningless but are needed to explain the workings of meaningful statements. Thus even when Carnap began to envisage the so-called meta-logical investi-gations that were to lead to *Logical Syntax*, in the Circle meeting of 26 February 1931 he characterized Wittgenstein's elucidations as "seek[ing] to clarify the relation between the statements and the given."[6] Just that, of course, was also what the rational reconstruc-tions of the *Aufbau* did. To be sure, Carnap's elucidations were not acts of meaning determination ending with ostensive definitions (as in Schlick), but the reduction chains of the *Aufbau* terminating with formulas containing "recollection of similarity" as the only descrip-tive term. While Carnap could not resign himself to the idea that rational reconstructions should be strictly speaking meaningless, he did not yet know how to avoid this conclusion. It was only his metalogical investigations starting in early 1931 that allowed him to do so, and it was the distinction between the material and the formal mode of speech that provided the required relief. In particular, formal mode metalinguistic talk about the syntax of sentences or about words employed in them thereby became a part of proper scientific discourse; logical syntax could be propositionally expressed after all.

In recognizing this transitory period in Carnap's development we must not, however, assimilate his thinking too closely with that of his interlocutors. Thus he did not believe with Schlick and Wittgen-stein that it was possible to ground the meaningfulness of scien-tific statements philosophically (from outside of science), namely, by exhibiting their verification conditions through elucidatory acts. Rather, Carnap believed – from his confrontation of the Tractar-ian critique of his *Aufbau* until his discovery of the material and

---

[6] ASP RC 089-07-11. As translated in Stadler (2001, 256).

formal mode distinction – that the explication of scientific knowledge claims by rational reconstruction cannot itself proceed in terms of proper statements. Carnap did not give up his formalist approach during this episode but merely put it under elucidatory wraps.

IV. CARNAP AND NEURATH: METHODOLOGICAL SOLIPSISM UNDERMINED

Neurath pictured the trajectory of Carnap's development basically correctly when in mid-1932 he wrote to Carnap: "I'd prefer it if you as a centrist tending towards the left wing would give up the 'protocol statements without confirmation' and the parallel of 'intersubjective' and 'monologising' languages, etc., and would represent the Vienna Circle alongside those who have no truck with Wittgensteinian metaphysics."[7]

What Neurath referred to here was his own campaign against the stance of methodological solipsism that Carnap had adopted in the *Aufbau*, the assumption of the epistemic priority of phenomenal over physical object statements (Carnap, 1928, §66). Against this assumption, which Carnap deemed central from the epistemological point of view, Neurath had fielded explicit arguments since at least the "Besprechung über Physikalismus" of 4 March 1931.[8] Neurath's argument against methodological solipsism and for physicalism was tied up closely with his argument against the need for Wittgensteinian elucidations. But where Schlick's opposition to Carnap questioned the applicability of the method of rational reconstruction as such, Neurath only challenged its scope and how it was applied. With Carnap he insisted that rational reconstructions do not have the job of making intelligible from the outside how our cognition and language hooks on to the world, as it were, but only of showing from the inside how, shorn of irrelevant detail, the languages of science do their work. As Neurath (1983, 61) puts it (with multiply ambiguous overtones): "The possibility of science must become apparent in science itself."

---

[7] See Neurath's letter to Carnap, 27 July 1932 (ASP RC 029-12-38). Translations from archive materials (as well as from papers where no translation is indicated) are by the present author.

[8] For a discussion of this document (ASP RC 029-17-03), see Uebel (1992b).

The dispute that had been brewing between Neurath and Carnap for some time came to a head over the question of the content, form, and status of protocol statements, statements recording observational evidence in science and serving as checkpoints for theory acceptance. According to methodological solipsism as developed in the *Aufbau*, these statements spoke only of relations of recollected similarity between one individual's experiences. Apparently in response to Neurath's criticisms, Carnap granted a certain kind of primacy to the physicalist language but retained a separate protocol language for epistemological purposes. Carnap published these ideas in (the original of) "The Unity of Science," only to encounter reaffirmation of the opposition from Neurath in "Protocol Statements" that protocol languages separate from the physicalist language are neither needed nor ready to hand.

The quotation at the beginning of this section stems from this stage of their discussions. As it happened, Carnap did move left very soon. At first, in a paper published simultaneously with Neurath's restatement of his position in "Protocol Statements," Carnap, in "On Protocol Statements," outflanked even Neurath on what appeared to the latter as the lunatic fringe: now any concrete statement, even one not reporting observed states of affairs, could be deemed basic and made the checkpoint for the rest, a position which Neurath thought endangered empiricism. Later, in "Testability and Meaning," Carnap settled on a more traditionally physicalist position: protocol statements employ predicates that specify observable properties in accord with the best physiological-psychological account we can find. This position was closer to Neurath's but by no means identical with it.[9] The best way to convey their differences is to review their arguments as they stood at the time of Neurath's letter quoted above.

Neurath characterized physicalism as the claim that all the statements of empirical science used only spatio-temporal terms concerning spatio-temporal matters.[10] That unified science thus expresses everything in the intersubjective (and intersensual) language means, of course, that also the protocol sentences are expressed in it. As

---

[9] Even though since 1932 they were lumped together as "physicalists" by opponents, certain differences, of which they themselves were not always fully aware, persisted throughout. A detailed account of their different physicalisms is given in Uebel (2007).

[10] See, for example, Neurath (1973, 325–326, 359–360; 1983, 54, 61).

he put the "Neurath Principle" in a lecture of 29 March 1931 (Neurath, 1931c/1932, 312): "Every new statement must be compared with the system of statements and laws up to now. Either it will be integrated or rejected as incorrect, if one does not change the whole system."[11] No ultimate epistemological privilege accrues to protocol statements. Moreover, no simpler or more immediate language is available. Neurath's argument to this effect was first recorded in his "Besprechung über Physikalismus," then repeated in more or less cryptic form in various essays and lectures of the years 1931/32 and appealed to in several defenses of his position in later years. For example:

> only one language comes into question from the start, and that is the physicalist. One can learn the physicalist language from earliest childhood. *If someone makes predictions and wants to check them himself, he must count on changes in the system of his senses, he must use clocks and rulers;* in short, the person supposedly in isolation already makes use of the "intersensual" and "intersubjective" language. The forecaster of yesterday and the controller of today are, so two speak, two persons. (Neurath, 1983, 54–55, emphasis added)

Thus Neurath held that even a solitary thinker requires a system of symbolic represention for the ordering of his experiences over time that is intersubjective (and intersensual). Against Carnap's methodologically solipsist protocol language, Neurath argued that a language must be usable by one individual over time. (Phenomenal languages do not "come into question from the start" for they do not allow for mechanisms whereby the constancy of an individual's language use can be guaranteed which, in turn, is required for "checking" to take place.)

Neurath's highly condensed reasoning may be explicated as follows. To begin with, his "physicalistic" language includes ordinary talk of physical objects and events and also, given his anti-dualistic understanding of psychology, of psychological episodes understood as spatio-temporal phenomena. Now, if physicalistic statements like instrument readings need themselves be translated, in order to be meaningful statements, into phenomenal terms directly related to a scientist's experience, then no touchstone at all is available by which the constancy of his language use over time could be established.

---

[11] For the Neurath Principle, a.k.a the Quine–Duhem thesis, see Haller (1982/1991).

Neurath suggested that once on a solipsistic base there is no preventing solipsism of the present moment. The incoherence that threatens experience conceived of in this solipsistic fashion shows that constancy in the use of an individual over time can be established only by reference to the spatio-temporal determinations of physical states of affairs that the language speaks about. Now, if language use is so controllable, then that language is already intersubjective (and intersensual). So, if the protocol language is to be a usable language, it cannot be a phenomenalist one. The tempting line of reasoning from the corrigibility of statements about what our common experience is to the conclusion that the evidential basis for science must be sought in language that speaks only of the experience of an individual speaker cannot be right.

Consider now Carnap's position in *Unity*. Here physicalism means that the physical language (the language of present and future systematic physics) is (Carnap, 1932a/1934, 55) "a universal language," i.e. that

| *[formal mode of speech:]* | *[material mode of speech:]* |
| every statement can be translated into it. | every state of affairs can be expressed in it. |

Concerning such physical system statements, Carnap (1932a/1934, 42–44) asserts that their "verification is based upon 'protocol statements'" which "include statements belonging to the basic protocol or direct record of the scientists' experience." In Carnap's "schema," such "basic" or "primitive" protocol statements belong to a "primary" protocol language and exclude "all statements obtained indirectly," thus postulating "a sharp (theoretical) distinction between the raw material of scientific investigation and its organization." Hence (1932a/1934, 45):

| *[formal mode of speech:]* | *[material mode of speech:]* |
| The simplest statements in the protocol-language are . . . statements needing no justification and serving as foundation for all the remaining statements of science. | The simplest statements in the protocol language refer to the given, and describe directly given experience or phenomena, i.e. the simplest states of which knowledge can be had. |

So Carnap retained the idea of protocol languages separate from the physical language and, in essence the approach of methodological solipsism, namely, the assumption of the epistemic priority of experience statements over physical statements generally. Here, however, this epistemic priority did not necessarily mean epistemological phenomenalism, for now Carnap left open just what form the protocols had to take.[12] Instead he stressed that the intersubjectivity of the physicalist (system) language thus depended on the possibility (1932a/1934, 51) that

[formal mode of speech:]	[material mode of speech:]
... an inferential relation of the kind described holds between a statement p and each of the protocol languages of several persons.	... the state of affairs expressed by a statement p is verifiable in the manner described by several persons.

The inferential relation invoked in the formal mode of speech statement here is that of the deducibility of statements in the protocol languages of different speakers from the statement p. Importantly, Carnap allowed that in science this deducibility be mediated by hypotheses, and so he not only discounted conclusive verifiability as a criterion of cognitive significance in favor of confirmability (readmitting universal statements as meaningful), but he also recognized the epistemological holism that governed the acceptance of statements of the physical system language.[13]

Carnap argued that, given even only a relatively liberal version of verificationism, statements about mental states are unintelligible unless they refer to a person's behavioral dispositions or bodily state. Carnap first established that phenomenalistic protocol statements are verifiable and meaningful on the assumption of the intertranslatability of the psychological and physical languages. Then he assumed the standpoint of the phenomenalist opponent (which

---

[12] Carnap (1934a, 45–48). Carnap had adopted such a neutral stance already in "The Elimination of Metaphysics" (1932d/1959, 63), in contradistinction to the *Aufbau*-style conception still adopted in his "The Old and the New Logic" (1930a/1959, 143–144).

[13] (1932a/1934, 49). Note that Carnap's recognition of the implications of his move away from conclusive verifiability anticipates his long-overlooked but recently celebrated recognition of epistemological holism in *Logical Syntax*, §82, by two full years.

denies such intertranslatability) and established that in this case statements about other minds would be unverifiable and meaningless.[14] Carnap added (1932b/1959, 191): "The situation is the same with sentences about one's own mind," and argued that once we are able to confirm such a statement we are also able to confirm a statement about one's bodily state. Therefore, if the demand for intersubjective intelligibility is taken as axiomatic, there cannot be an ineluctably private language. So far, no significant disgreement between Carnap and Neurath has shown up. What prompted Neurath's misgivings, however, was that separate protocol languages appeared to allow for exemptions from the fallibilism that governed the scientific system language and introduced a troubling asymmetry in justification.

Carnap (1932b/1959, 170) asserts that the distinction between sentences about other minds and one's own mind is "indispensable" for the "epistemological analysis of subjective singular sentences." Here Carnap's distinction between statements in the "system language" of physics and the protocol statements for that system comes to the fore. A statement about my own mental state can be taken as either, but there still is an epistemological difference: as a system sentence, it "may, under certain circumstances be disavowed, whereas a protocol sentence, being an epistemological point of departure, cannot be rejected" (1932b/1959, 191). This statement is ambiguous. One could read it as saying that an "original" protocol statement cannot be rejected, but only its translation into a physical system statement. Or one could read it as saying that such protocol statements cannot be rejected only in the very process of testing being described, for then there are no other protocol statements around by comparision with which it would make sense to reject it.[15] Neurath opted for the critical reading and was able to discount the exculpatory one for good reason. For him, the very idea of such more or less private protocol languages was objectionable, for it faced an unenviable and entirely avoidable dilemma.

According to Carnap, statements in the primary protocol languages require translation into the physical system language to figure

[14] For step one, see Carnap (1932a/1934, 60–66 (recapitulated on 87–88)) and "Psychology" (1932b/1959, 170–173); for step two, see (1932a/1934, 78–82) and (1932b/1959, 173–177).
[15] This reading was suggested to me by Michael Friedman.

in intersubjective scientific practice. And this translation allows for the corrigibility of the scientific evidence statements of scientific practice. Nevertheless, physicalistic discourse must be reduced to the primary language of primitive protocol statements for purposes of justification. This means that speakers apprehend the meaning of that protocol language not in terms of its physicalistic interpretation, but directly in the terms of its possibly phenomenalistic surface reading. That is why Carnap made these languages "primary" and why he held that a person could only take their own protocol statements as checking points.[16] Now if, on the one hand, these protocol languages are construed along phenomenalist lines, a speaker's grasp of their meaning would be incorrigible. This conception retains a sense of privacy vulnerable to the argument Neurath had been pressing all along. For Neurath, a speaker's sense of the meaning of the expressions of his language is shaped in and by the process of communication: the self-understanding of an individual language user is as problematical as the understanding of other minds.[17] If, on the other hand, these primary protocol languages are construed as already physicalist, it becomes difficult to see what distinguishes their statements from system statements, so as to enable primitive protocols to remain unrevisable. Once part of the system language, protocol statements can of course be rejected on account of any contradiction, not only with other protocol statements. Unable to tie into scientific practice as we know it, Carnap's protocols remain problematic elucidations after all. Neurath was correct in detecting in Carnap's conception of separate protocol languages vestiges of the atomistic conception of knowledge that the *Tractatus* supported.

As noted above, Carnap abandoned his insistence on methodological solipsism even in its weakened sense and, in practice, he dropped the idea of protocol statements outside of the scientific system language from his rational reconstructions of scientific theories, beginning with his reply to Neurath in "On Protocol Statements." Yet he added (1932c/1987, 457): "this is a question not of two mutually

---

[16] This is asserted in the original (Carnap, 1932a, 461); in the translation (Carnap, 1932a/1934) this passage is dropped.

[17] Neurath's use of the rhetorical figure of Robinson Crusoe sought to emphasize that already an isolated epistemic agent requires the intersubjective language for the coherence of his experience – or, as he put it in a reprise of his argument (1983, 110): "even before Friday arrived."

inconsistent views, but rather two different methods for structuring the language of science which are both possible and legitimate." Carnap here first makes use of the famous Principle of Tolerance of *Logical Syntax* (1934c/1937, §17): "Everyone is at liberty to build up his own logic, i.e. his own form of language, as he wishes. All that is required of him is that, if he wishes to discuss it, he must state his methods clearly, and give syntactical rules instead of philosophical arguments." Applied to the question of protocol statements, this means that (1934c/1937, §82): "Syntactical rules will have to be stated concerning the forms which the protocol-sentences . . . may take." The issue is a pragmatic one of convenience, not a factual one. Preconceptions of a supposed epistemic order no longer dictate the answer about the questions of the form, content, and status of protocol statements.

Clearly, then, while his position did change, Carnap did not fully accept Neurath's argument.[18] The ultimate reason, it turns out, derives from Carnap's just emerging mature conception of the nature of philosophy (1934c/1937, §72): "The logic of science takes the place of the inextricable tangle of problems which is known as philosophy." From about mid-1932 until the fall of 1935, Carnap conceived of philosophy as the study of the "syntax" of the language of science (later semantics was included in the "logic of science"). This logic of language was continuous with philosophy in its apriorist method. That human beings cannot employ phenomenalist protocol languages in justificatory capacities would, if true, only provide empirical considerations that bear on possible applications of such models in epistemological contexts, but not on their logical probity itself. The logician of science was not debarred from considering them.

V. CARNAP CUTS LOOSE: POST-EPISTEMOLOGICAL DEFLATIONISM

Note that with his considered physicalist position just reviewed, Carnap had taken sides in the struggle between the different wings

---

[18] Carnap also did not accept Neurath's specific proposal for the precise form that protocol statements should take, either here or in his later "Testability and Meaning" (1936-37, 12-13). For a discussion of their more substantive differences in terms of what we might view as private language arguments of different strengths, see Uebel (1995).

of the Vienna Circle. Schlick showed little interest in Neurath's program of unified science and even felt moved to defend traditional philosophy in one of his very last papers (Schlick, 1979, 491–498). Therefore, he could not but view Carnap's physicalism with suspicion. Yet Carnap, as we saw, did not identify wholly with Neurathian physicalism either. With his papers at the 1935 Paris Congress on Unified Science, he can be seen to announce his independence from both of the warring factions.

In particular, Carnap's "Truth and Confirmation" carved out a position simultaneously distinct from both Schlick and Neurath.[19] They had become embroiled in 1934–35 in a confusing and somewhat confused controversy concerning what Schlick called "the foundations of knowledge."[20] Important at present is only that Schlick complicated the already fraught issue of the content, form, and status of protocol statements by connecting it with the traditional problem of truth: adopting a correspondence theory of statement and fact, Schlick attacked Neurath's supposed coherence theory of truth. Carnap, freshly converted by Tarski's truth definition for formal languages to the belief that the concept of truth was after all scientifically legitimate, asserted both that truth as a semantic notion must be distinguished from confirmation as a pragmatic notion and that it remained a mistake to "search for an absolute reality whose nature is assumed fixed independently of the language chose for its description" (1936c/1949, 126–127): "In translating one language into another the factual content of an empirical statement cannot always be preserved unchanged."

Carnap managed to upset both Schlick and Neurath. Schlick did not appreciate the fact that Carnap forbade unqualified comparisons of statements with facts. Moreover, against Carnap's conventionalist turn and especially his affirmation of the incommensurability of linguistic frameworks, Schlick insisted on a sharp division between

---

[19] Translated in Feigl and Sellars (1949, 119–127). (This translation also incorporates material from a later essay; the passages cited below appeared in the original.)

[20] The primary exhibits here are M. Schlick, "The Foundation of Knowledge" (1979, 370–387), and O. Neurath, "Radical Physicalism and 'the Real World'" (1983, 100–114). The debate continued with a slightly different emphasis in C. G. Hempel, "On the Logical Positivists' Theory of Truth" (1935a/2000, 9–21); M. Schlick, "Facts and Propositions" (1979, 400–404); C. G. Hempel, "Some Remarks on 'Facts and Propositions'" (2000, 21–25); M. Schlick, "On 'Affirmations'" (1979, 407–413).

conventional linguistic stipulation and factual invariance.[21] Neurath, for his part, was unhappy that Carnap insisted on the probity of talking about truth in a sense different from confirmation and soon began to voice his suspicion that the semantic conception readmitted metaphysics into the theory of science. Neurath's opposition was unfortunate: that was the last thing Carnap intended. Instead, by adopting Tarski's semantic conception of truth, Carnap sought to give precision to the Circle's opposition to metaphysics and allow it to survive the failure of reductivist verificationism he had begun to discern in another of his papers at the Paris Congress.[22]

Here it is helpful to recall that Carnap did not understand Tarski's theory of truth as a traditional correspondence theory where truth consists in a metaphysically significant agreement between statements or judgments and facts or the world.[23] Unlike Neurath, Carnap was not misled by Tarski's remark that he wished to pursue the intentions of the "so-called classical conception of truth," in opposition to the "utilitarian conception" as denoting a usefulness "in a certain respect" (Tarski, 1956, 183). After all, Tarski, did not provide an explication of what the classical notion of "correspondence with reality" might amount to, but only gave a definition of the predicate "true" for conservative metalinguistic extensions of formal languages and axiomatic theories. In Carnap's unchanged opposition to traditional (metaphysical) correspondence theories we find not only a continuity between his syntactic and his later semantic phase, but also the key to his understanding of the left Vienna Circle's anti-metaphysical campaign.[24] The metaphysics they attacked (besides the supra-scientific essentialism of old) was precisely the traditional correspondence conception of truth and of knowledge as expressed in traditional philosophical realism. (They also opposed their opposites, of course: coherence theory and idealism.)

[21] See Schlick (1979, 437–445), Carnap, "Truth and Confirmation" (1936c/1949), and the correspondence between them at the time, reviewed in Oberdan (1993, 138–142).
[22] Carnap's then new method of non-eliminative reductions was first presented in English in 1936–37.
[23] Carnap's understanding of Tarski's theory thus differs sharply from Popper's construal; cf. Popper (1963).
[24] For more on the left Circle's anti-correspondence version of anti-metaphysics, see Uebel (2004).

To see this in the case of Carnap, note that in his first statement of support for Tarski's theory, at the 1935 Paris Congress, Carnap stated that previous misgivings about the notion of truth had been prompted by now-allayed suspicions about its metaphysical nature. But there he also rejected the tendency to label the semantic conception "absolute" and instead noted that what accounts for the truth of a statement is not only the way the world is but also the structure and concepts of the language used. Accordingly, he rejected "comparisons" of statements with facts (1936c/1949, 119, 125–126). And, in his own volume for the International Encyclopedia of Unified Science, Carnap states (1939, 10): "Since to know the truth conditions of a sentence is to know what is asserted by it, the given semantical rules determine for every sentence of [a constructed language] what it asserts – in usual terms its 'meaning' – or, in other words, how it is to be translated into English." Carnap (1942, 26) makes his disquotational understanding of truth fully explicit: "we use the term here in such a sense that to assert that a sentence is true means the same as to assert the sentence itself." Finally, Carnap declares the "rules of truth" to be rules of disquotation (1955, 6): "We presuppose that a statement in [the meta-language] M saying that a certain sentence S1 is true means the same as the translation of this sentence [into the meta-language]."

It must be noted here that the interpretation of Carnap's understanding of truth remains a contested matter. On one view, Carnap accepts Tarski's semantics as a disquotational theory only and rejects the traditional idea of correspondence; on another, Carnap accepts a correspondence theory sufficiently robust to sustain scientific realism.[25] Typically, however, defenders of the latter reading subsequently feel compelled to revise or reject Carnap's mature distinction between internal and external questions.[26] For Carnap, existential questions are divided into two kinds, internal and external. The former concern questions about the existence of certain kinds of entities, questions asked within a logico-linguistic framework; the latter concern questions about "the existence or reality of the system of entities as a whole," questions asked outside of any particular

[25] For an example of the former, see Carus (1999); for the latter, see Niiniluoto (2003). This interpretive difference tends to echo that concerning Tarski's theory itself: see, for example, Sluga (1999) and Niiniluoto (1999), respectively.
[26] See, for example, Niiniluoto (2003, 20).

framework ("Empiricism, Semantics, and Ontology," 206). Carnap accepts the internal questions as legitimate and truth-evaluatable, but not the external questions. External questions are rather best understood as concerning the utility or convenience of adopting a logico-linguistic framework for talking about certain phenomena. For present purposes this means that, if the correspondence theory of truth is to sustain philosophical realist claims, then it must seek to answer external questions. Since Carnap did not use the theory of truth to this end, this strongly suggests that he did not understand truth in traditional correspondence terms.

What is metaphysical, for Carnap, is thus a certain conception of truth and scientific knowledge as well as the idea of philosophy as the pursuit of unconditional truth. No matter how cleansed it may be of intuitive content, Schlick's adoption of the Tractarian correspondence theory was in conflict with this view of Carnap's. His later adoption of the Wittgensteinian notions of "grammar" and "use" in the mid-1930s brought little change in this correspondentism. Also, as noted, Schlick recognized no incommensurabilities between languages, a feature central to Carnap's account. At the same time, however, even though Carnap did keep faith with the anti-metaphysical animadversions of his colleagues on the left wing of the Circle with his deflationist reading of Tarski's theory, this was not apparent to all.[27]

In yet another paper given at the Paris Congress, Carnap clarified that after the constructivist turn which his philosophy took in *Logical Syntax*, it did not remain limited to the purely syntactic and deductive reasoning there extolled. Philosophy became the logic of science in full generality, covering semantics as well and inductive as well as deductive logics: "the logical analysis of knowledge" concerned the analysis of "the sentences, theories and methods of science."[28] Conjoining a radically anti-psychologistic approach to

---

[27] In his ongoing debate with Neurath about truth and semantics, Carnap stressed that the semantic conception did not commit him to Aristotelian metaphysics. Carnap's rejection of Neurath's criticism of truth terms as "absolutist" is documented in note 9 of "Truth and Confirmation" (not in the original). On this debate, see also Mormann (1999).

[28] Carnap (1936b). As in Carnap (1934b), Carnap still speaks of "logical syntax," but a footnote implies that he now views Tarskian semantics as compatible with its basic outlook, as does, most explicitly, his contemporaneous "Truth and Confirmation."

epistemology with his Principle of Tolerance meant that philosophy could only offer different ways of conceptualizing the findings of first-order sciences. Philosophy makes "proposals" and explores conceptual possibilities.[29] Again, this is a quite different office for philosophy from the experiential determination of meanings envisaged by Schlick, and, while Neurath need not be disqualified from partaking in this conception of philosophy in principle, their divergent interests in fact became increasingly decisive.

Already in 1932 Neurath had declared that (1983, 67) "within a consistent physicalism there can be no 'theory of knowledge,' at least not in the traditional form. It could only consist in defense actions against metaphysics, i.e. unmasking meaningless terms. Some problems of the theory of knowledge will perhaps be transformable into empirical questions so that they can find a place within unified science." Note the two tasks here assigned to what could be called philosophy's successor discipline in unified science: unmasking meaningless terms and asking empirical questions about knowledge production. Both represent different aspects of what unified science contains alongside all the first-order disciplines: scientific metatheory. This higher-order theory of science comprises logical enquires as well as empirical ones.

Once Carnap had jettisoned in practice the epistemological-elucidatory ambitions that prompted his methodological solipsism, he affirmed, in *Logical Syntax*, a position that is partly consonant with Neurath's. Carnap saw the logic of science as replacing traditional philosophy because its methods of inquiry remained a priori: empirical concerns were not directly involved in the metalinguistic exploration of the multiplicity of logico-linguistic frameworks. What Carnap was able to add to Neurath's "defensive" task for the logic of science was his conventionalist constructivism concerning such alternative frameworks. This was a widening of the scope of scientific metatheory that Neurath happily accepted. Yet Carnap did not rule out all empirical concerns, as is clear from his remark that the logic of science is itself but part of a still more comprehensive enquiry, the "theory of science," which comprises also "empirical investigation of scientific activity," namely, "historical, sociological

[29] Borrowing from Robert Musil, Mormann (2000) calls Carnap's conception of philosophy a "science of possibilities" (*Möglichkeitswissenschaft*).

and, above all, psychological inquiries" (1934c/1937, §72). It is precisely this field that Neurath (1983, 169) differentiated from the logic of science as "the behaviouristics of scholars" and in which he located his own concerns with protocol statements. So both Carnap and Neurath recognized the need for logical *and* empirical branches of scientific metatheory, but they pursued their own detailed work in different branches.³⁰

Getting to this position of conceiving the differences in their philosophical conceptions as reflecting merely a division of labor was not easy. Nor was it, historically speaking, a stable position beyond the 1930s. Given their different orientations, disputes over what type of logical investigations should have priority – those that supported pragmatic investigations or those that remained free-standing, as it were – could and did occur. By the 1940s, Neurath's impatience with Carnap's semantics and Carnap's impatience with Neurath's anti-formalist orientation (which were invariably read as instances of intolerance on the part of the other) rendered further cooperation difficult. Their respective self-conceptions as primarily a mathematical logician of science and an empiricist pragmatist of science increasingly pulled them apart.

To conclude: in his Vienna Circle period, Carnap moved from a position of relative neutrality between Schlick and Neurath to one closer to Neurath amongst the anti-Wittgensteinians – before moving on beyond both of them. Carnap's characteristic move from epistemology to the logic of science represents a refinement of the rational reconstructionism that already characterized the *Aufbau*. (There it meant that epistemology abstracted from how subjects in practice justify their knowledge claims and considered only the logical requirements for the justification of their beliefs.) When Carnap abandoned epistemology for the logic of science, he did so under the banner of rejecting previously held "psychologistic" assumptions (e.g. the assumption of the epistemic priority of the phenomenal language or personal protocol languages). In so far as his work continued to concern justification, Carnap now abstracted altogether from justifications of their beliefs by individual subjects. Instead, Carnap concerned himself with propositional justification, the justification

---

³⁰ For an initial exploration of the compatibility between their mature conceptions, see Uebel (2001).

of potential knowledge claims by their evidence independently of their availability to actual epistemic subjects. From subject-centered rational reconstructions, Carnap moved to logical explications of knowledge claims independent of all epistemic subjects.[31]

[31] I wish to thank Michael Friedman for helpful comments and suggestions.

ERICH H. RECK[1]

8   Carnap and modern logic

A distinguishing feature of analytic philosophy, or at least of one central strand in it, is the use of modern logic for the purpose of clarifying and solving philosophical problems. The most prominent figure in this tradition was Bertrand Russell; and second only to Russell was Rudolf Carnap. Directly and strongly influenced by Russell, Carnap passed on this influence to legions of later philosophers, including such widely influential figures as W. V. O. Quine. It is well known that Carnap was a main expositor and promoter of modern logic, as illustrated by his textbooks on the subject, from *Abriss der Logistik* (1929) to *Einführung in die symbolische Logik* (1954). It is also well known that Carnap applied logic substantively, both in his own constructive endeavors in philosophy and in his criticism of metaphysics, as in *Der logische Aufbau der Welt* (1928a), "Überwindung der Metaphysik durch logische Analyse der Sprache" (1932d), and *Logische Syntax der Sprache* (1934c).

Less well known is the fact that, in addition, Carnap was actively engaged in research on pure logic and related questions in early metamathematics. In particular, during large parts of the 1920s – parallel and subsequent to his work on the *Aufbau* – Carnap was pursuing a major research project in this area. A main goal of this project was to

---

[1] In the present chapter I draw on a series of recent writings on Carnap (Bonk and Mosterin, 2000; Awodey and Carus, 2001; Awodey and Reck, 2002a; Awodey and Reck, 2002b; Goldfarb, 2003; Reck, 2004; Reck and Awodey, 2004; and Goldfarb, 2005). There are three ways in which I will try to advance the discussion: first, by emphasizing the uniqueness of the position Carnap occupied in the history of logic (sections I and II); second, by sharpening the focus on the notion of logical consequence (sections II and III); and third, by making explicit connections to Carnap's interests in the notion of mathematical truth (sections III and IV).

combine, and to reconcile, the approaches to logic and the foundations of mathematics he had encountered in interactions with Gottlob Frege and Bertrand Russell, on the one hand, and in the works of
David Hilbert and his followers, on the other. Carnap's project also
had direct connections to contemporary work by Abraham Fraenkel
on axiomatics, Kurt Gödel on incompleteness, and Alfred Tarski on
the foundations of meta-logical notions. Carnap was at the cutting
edge of research in modern logic during this period, both in terms of
his personal contacts and his own endeavors. While these endeavors
did not bear the systematic fruits he initially envisioned, they did
lead to some partial results; they also had a significant influence at
the time. It is this contribution by Carnap – a long-neglected side of
his career – to which I want to introduce the reader in the present
chapter.

In the first section of the chapter, Carnap will be introduced as
a student of modern logic. This will include a brief account of the
influence Frege and Russell had on him; but I will also describe his
early interest in the axiomatic method, especially in Hilbert's work.
In the second section, we will see how Carnap, attempting to synthesize these two major influences, was led to a project in "general
axiomatics." He was not the only person to be led in that direction,
as a look at related work by Fraenkel will illustrate. In the third
section, Carnap's project will be discussed in more detail, focusing
on a book manuscript, *Untersuchungen zur Allgemeinen Axiomatik*
(ASP RC 080-various), left unpublished by him, but recently edited
and made available in print (2000). This discussion will make explicit
some inherent limitations of, or problems with, Carnap's approach.
Recognition of these problems caused him to abandon the project
around 1930 – but not without first having influenced Gödel and
formed the basis for some interactions with Tarski. While it may
appear, at that point, that Carnap's 1920s project was mostly a failure, in the final section I will point out its interesting aftermath and
continuing significance.

I. CARNAP AS A STUDENT OF MODERN LOGIC

In his "Intellectual Autobiography" (1963a, 3ff.) Carnap tells us that
upon entering the University of Jena in 1910 his main interests were
first in philosophy and mathematics, then in philosophy and physics.

For a brief period he tried his hand at experimental work in physics, but he quickly turned towards more theoretical issues, including Kant's views about space and time and their relation to recent developments in physics. Early on, Carnap also attended three classes by Frege on logic and the foundations of mathematics: "Begriffsschrift I" (1910–11), "Begriffsschrift II" (1913), and "Logik in der Mathematik" (1913–14).[2] In these classes Carnap was introduced to modern logic, as originating in Frege's and Russell's works. This was quite unusual – not only were very few classes on modern logic taught anywhere at the time, Frege's particular classes, while offered regularly, were also attended by very few students.

While Carnap found Frege's classes fascinating, he didn't recognize the full significance of the logic he encountered in them right away, especially not its potential fruitfulness in addressing philosophical problems. As he explained later:

Although Frege gave quite a number of examples of interesting applications of his symbolism in mathematics, he usually did not discuss general philosophical problems. It is evident from his works that he saw the great philosophical importance of the new instrument which he had created, but he did not convey a clear impression of this to his students. Thus, although I was intensely interested in his system of logic, I was not aware at that time of its great philosophical significance. Only much later, after the first world war, when I read Frege's and Russell's books with greater attention, did I recognize the value of Frege's work not only for the foundations of mathematics, but for philosophy in general. (1963a, 6)

In addition, Carnap's attention was soon diverted by the outbreak of the First World War, which he experienced as an "incomprehensible catastrophe" (1963a, 9) and which took him away from the University of Jena as a soldier in the German army.

It was only after coming back from the war that Carnap could take up his academic interests again. In 1919, he started to study Whitehead and Russell's *Principia Mathematica* (1910–13). Frege had mentioned this work in his classes and, on the basis of what he had already learned, Carnap was able to assimilate its content by himself. Through Frege's influence, he was thus part of the first generation of thinkers on which *Principia* had an impact. From 1920 on, he also

---

[2] For Carnap's own notes from these classes, see Reck and Awodey (2004). For further discussion, see Reck (2004); but note that there are some inaccuracies in the corresponding dates given in that article.

returned to Frege's own writings and studied them carefully, especially *Die Grundgesetze der Arithmetik* (1893/1903), Frege's *magnum opus*. Later Carnap described the effect of these studies as follows:

> I began to apply symbolic notation, now more frequently in the *Principia* form than in Frege's, in my own thinking about philosophical problems or in the formulation of axiom systems. When I considered a concept or a proposition occurring in a scientific or philosophical discussion, I thought that I understood it clearly only if I felt that I could express it, if I wanted to, in symbolic language. I performed the actual symbolization, of course, only in special cases where it seemed necessary or useful. (1963a, 11)

Notice that, in direct connection with assimilating Frege's and Russell's works, Carnap mentions the goal of applying their logic "in the formulation of axiom systems." Carnap's first project for a dissertation, entitled "Axiomatic Foundations of Kinematics," stems from the same period. However, the two people at the University of Jena to whom he showed his proposal – the physicist Max Wien and the philosopher Bruno Bauch – both rejected it. Instead, Carnap chose another topic at the boundary between physics and philosophy for his dissertation. A revised version of it was published, soon thereafter, as "Der Raum" (1922).

Axiomatics was still involved in Carnap's new dissertation, although now in a different way. Geometry had long been presented axiomatically; but during the late nineteenth century, it had been recast in a more "formal" axiomatic way, culminating in Hilbert's well-known *Grundlagen der Geometrie* (1899). Similar approaches to other branches of mathematics, including arithmetic and analysis, had also gained prominence during this period, through works by Dedekind, Peano, Hilbert, and others.[3] Carnap's interest in axiomatics stemmed, directly or indirectly, from these mathematical sources. Indeed, later he often referred to Hilbert's *Grundlagen* in this connection, as well as to "Axiomatisches Denken" (1918), an article in which Hilbert reflects programmatically on the development of the axiomatic method in mathematics, mentioning physics along the way. An axiomatic approach to both mathematics and physics, as championed by Hilbert, was thus a central goal for Carnap from

---

[3] See Awodey and Reck (2002a) for an overview of these developments, with the focus on ensuing meta-logical and metamathematical questions that will become central below.

early on – in spite of the fact that both Frege and Russell had been critical of such an approach.[4]

After having finished "Der Raum," Carnap went on, in the early 1920s, to pursue two other research projects. The first was influenced by Russell's book *Our Knowledge of the External World* (1914a), which Carnap read with enthusiasm in 1921, and by his earlier studies of Kant and neo-Kantian views at the University of Jena. This project resulted in *Der logische Aufbau der Welt* (1928a). Carnap's second, but much less well-known project concerned pure logic and its applications to mathematics – my main topic. A tangible result of that second project was the publication of a small book, *Abriss der Logistik* (1929), one of the very first textbooks in modern logic. While published a year after Hilbert and Ackermann's more prominent *Grundzüge der theoretischen Logik* (1928), Carnap's *Abriss* – essentially finished in 1927, largely independent of *Grundzüge*, and circulated widely – also had significant influence, especially in Vienna, where Carnap taught at the time.

However, Carnap never presented *Abriss der Logistik* as a major intellectual achievement. It was not intended to be a substantive contribution to logic, but simply to make the tools of logic more widely accessible and to argue for their general usefulness. Moreover, *Abriss* was obviously quite derivative from *Principia Mathematica*, as Carnap himself was the first to emphasize. It had grown directly out of the notes he took when studying Whitehead and Russell's book in 1919–20, and Russell influenced it further through a correspondence Carnap initiated with him in 1921.[5] It thus appeared, at the time and later, that Carnap was merely popularizing (in *Abriss*) and applying (in *Aufbau*) Russell's new logic. Seen in this light, he was just one of a number of logicians who assimilated *Principia* in the late 1910s and early 1920s, a group that also included Hilbert and members of his school.[6]

However, this appearance is misleading in at least two respects. First, unlike almost all the other logicians in question, Carnap was

---

[4] For Frege's corresponding criticisms, see Reck and Awodey (2004, 135–166).
[5] In particular, Russell sent Carnap a hand-written 35-page summary of *Principia Mathematica*, in 1922, after Carnap had informed him of having trouble obtaining a copy of the book. For more on that summary, against the background of Carnap's general correspondence with Russell in the 1920s, see Reck (2004).
[6] For the assimilation of *Principia* in the Hilbert school, see Sieg (1999).

not only influenced by *Principia Mathematica* but also by Frege's earlier work. As we saw, he was influenced by the latter very directly – by attending Frege's classes, in 1910–14, and by studying his writings carefully, from 1920 on. Moreover, the particular way in which Frege had presented his logic in "Begriffsschrift I" and "Begriffsschrift II" made it natural for Carnap to adopt two stances that were unusual at the time: (i) from very early on, he worked with a higher-order logic based on simple types, as opposed to the ramified types of *Principia*; (ii) also from early on, Carnap used higher-order logic as an inferential framework, as opposed to a system for reconstructing all of mathematics within a corresponding theory of classes.[7] Influenced by Frege's critical discussion of Hilbert in "Logik in der Mathematik," there was also another difference: (iii) Carnap was more motivated than most to find a way of combining, and reconciling, the use of logic as a general inferential framework with a Hilbertian axiomatic approach.

This brings us to the second respect in which the appearance of Carnap as a mere popularizer and user of Russellian logic is misleading. He actually set out to provide, generally and systematically, a synthesis of Frege's and Russell's approach to logic, on the one hand, and Hilbert's approach to axiomatics, on the other.[8] This is what Carnap's second main research project from the 1920s was supposed to accomplish (thus aiming far beyond the more incidental, merely pedagogical role of *Abriss*). More concretely, this project was intended to result in a second research monograph (besides *Aufbau*), with the working title *Untersuchungen zur allgemeinen Axiomatik* (ASP RC 080-various). Carnap finished large parts of this monograph in manuscript form, which he then circulated among a group of logicians between 1928 and 1930. Many of Carnap's corresponding goals and themes were also mentioned in two little-known articles: "Eigentliche und uneigentliche Begriffe" (1927) and "Bericht über Untersuchungen zur allgemeinen Axiomatik" (1930c).

---

[7] Concerning the second point, Frege's presentation of logic in his lectures differs significantly from the presentations in his publications. In the latter, his logical system includes prominently a theory of classes, while in the former that theory is simply omitted; see Reck (2004) and Reck and Awodey (2004) for more.

[8] As he progressed, Carnap also tried to synthesize these two approaches with a third: constructivism, as championed by Kronecker, Brouwer, etc. I put this aspect aside in the present chapter since I take it to be less central for Carnap's work in the 1920s. See Bonk and Mosterin (2000) on this topic.

II. TOWARDS GENERAL AXIOMATICS

From Euclid's geometry on, the axiomatic method has been used for a number of different purposes. Traditionally, axiomatics was seen as a method for organizing the concepts and propositions of a science, such as geometry, in order to increase their clarity and certainty. While such goals are sometimes still appealed to in modern applications, they have become less central in the transformed axiomatics promoted by Hilbert and others. What has become crucial instead is the systematic investigation, by increasingly abstract and formal means, of three logical properties of an axiomatic system: (a) the independence of its axioms; (b) their consistency; and (c) their completeness.

In Hilbert's *Grundlagen*, the first of these properties is made especially prominent, largely as a response to nineteenth-century insights into the independence of Euclid's famous Parallel Postulate. Hilbert also spends considerable time establishing consistency results for his geometric axioms, more precisely relative consistency theorems (obtained by semantic means), as they are closely related to independence results in their method of proof. The issue of completeness comes up as well, but it is left unclear and unexplored in Hilbert's early writings – in spite of the fact that in Dedekind's earlier work on the natural numbers relevant results concerning what has come to be called "categoricity" had already been established. Indeed, the precise relation between "completeness" and "categoricity," or even the fact that they can be distinguished conceptually, was one of the issues left in need of clarification. Further progress in this connection was made in the early 1900s, in publications by E. V. Huntington, O. Veblen, and other "Postulate Theorists."[9] After that, it took until the 1920s for more systematic investigations to be attempted.

Research done by Hilbert and his school during the 1920s is known primarily for its sharp focus on consistency questions, now with the goal of obtaining absolute consistency proofs (by syntactic means), especially for arithmetic and analysis. While the issue of the completeness of axiomatic systems was not entirely ignored in the Hilbert school, it was another mathematician and logician who addressed it more fully and explicitly at the time: Abraham Fraenkel.

---

[9] See Scanlan (1991) and Awodey and Reck (2002a) for further discussion.

In the first edition of Fraenkel's *Einleitung in die Mengenlehre*, published in 1919, completeness does not yet play a prominent role; but in the second and revised edition (Fraenkel, 1923), there is a long section on "The Axiomatic Method" containing a detailed discussion. This discussion made an immediate and strong impression on Carnap, and he was soon exchanging ideas with Fraenkel about the topic, both in correspondence and in person.

What gradually became clear during this period, through Fraenkel's and subsequent work, was that several related notions of completeness should be clearly distinguished and their relationships then further investigated. A first important distinction is between the completeness of deductive systems, on the one hand, and the completeness of axiom systems for particular parts of mathematics, on the other. An example of the former is the completeness of (various deductive systems for) sentential and first-order logic, as established by Post (1921) and Gödel (1929), respectively, which was brought into sharper focus by Hilbert and his school during the 1920s in connection with the issue of "decidability."[10] The latter notion of completeness, concerning axiom systems for geometry, for the natural numbers, the real numbers, and so on turns out to be in need of additional distinctions and sub-division. And the core question in Carnap's exchanges with Fraenkel was precisely what exact form such sub-division should take.

Carnap first published ideas related to these exchanges in his article "Eigentliche und uneigentliche Begriffe" (1927); Fraenkel did so in the third, again revised, and significantly expanded edition of his *Einleitung* (1928). The two authors agreed on the need to distinguish between three notions of completeness for systems of axioms. Fraenkel now formulates these three notions as follows:

[T]he completeness of a system of axioms demands that the axioms encompass and govern the entire theory based on them in such a way that every question that belongs to and can be formulated in terms of the basic notions of the theory can be answered, one way or the other, in terms of deductive inferences from the axioms. Having this property would mean that one couldn't add any new axioms to the given system (without adding to the basic notions) so that the system was "complete" in that sense; since every relevant proposition that was not in contradiction with the system of

[10] See Zach (1999) for a discussion of early work in the Hilbert School on this topic.

axioms would already be a consequence and, thus, not independent, i.e., not an "axiom" . . .

Closely related to this first sense of completeness, but by far not as far reaching and easier to assess, is the following idea: . . . In general, a number of propositions that are inconsistent with each other and that can, thus, not be provable consequences of the same system of axioms can nevertheless be compatible with that system individually. Such a system of axioms leaves open whether certain relevant questions are to be answered positively or negatively; and it does so not just in the sense of deducibility by current or future mathematical means, but in an absolute sense (representable by independence proofs). A system of axioms of that kind is, then, with good reason, to be called incomplete . . .

Quite different, finally, is another sense of completeness, probably characterized explicitly for the first time by Veblen . . . According to it a system of axioms is to be called complete – also "categorical" (Veblen) or "monomorphic" (Feigl–Carnap) – if it determines the mathematical objects falling under it uniquely in the formal sense, i.e., such that between any two realizations one can always effect a transition by means of a 1–1 and isomorphic correlation. (Fraenkel, 1928, 347–349; my translation)

As the reference at the end of this passage indicates, Fraenkel saw himself as having benefited from his exchanges with Carnap. Other references make clear that with respect to Fraenkel's first notion of completeness, which both he and Carnap saw as closely connected with the notion of "decidability [*Entscheidungsdefinitheit*]," they felt indebted to Hilbert and his students, especially Heinrich Behmann and Hermann Weyl.[11]

From our present point of view, Fraenkel's three notions of completeness can be characterized, more briefly and in updated terminology, as follows:[12]

(1)   A system of axioms S is *deductively complete* if and only if for every proposition P in the relevant language either P or not-P is deducible from S.

(2)   A system of axioms S is *semantically complete* if and only if there is no proposition P in the relevant language such

---

[11] For Behmann's contributions to logic and metamathematics, see Mancosu (1999). For more on Carnap's and Fraenkel's indebtedness to both Behmann and Weyl, see Reck (2004).

[12] The terminology of "deductive completeness," "semantic completeness," and "categoricity" as used in the following definitions is not entirely standard. For further discussion, including some equivalent and historically significant variants, see Awodey and Reck (2002a).

that both S together with P and S together with not-P are satisfiable, i.e., have a model.

(3)   A system of axioms S is *categorical* (or *monomorphic*, as opposed to *polymorphic*) if and only if all models of S are isomorphic.

The main question then raised by Fraenkel, and seized upon by Carnap, is how these three notions are related. In the third edition of his book Fraenkel makes some general suggestions in this connection, but it is hard for him to be more conclusive. The reason, in hindsight, is that a precise answer requires the specification of a definite systematic background theory, and Fraenkel did not have such a theory at his disposal.

It is exactly at this point that Carnap, attempting to make further progress, is able to utilize what he learned earlier from Russell and, especially, from Frege. He proposes to reformulate Fraenkel's question within the framework of higher-order logic, specifically a system of higher-order logic with simple types understood purely inferentially – precisely as Carnap had encountered it in Frege's logic classes and as spelled out, subsequently, in *Abriss*. As noted above, neither Frege nor Russell had used their systems of higher-order logic for similar purposes, since both were fundamentally critical of the axiomatic method. Those interested in general axiomatics, like Hilbert, Behmann, Weyl, and Fraenkel, had also not yet made this synthesizing step, at least not systematically and in print.[13] Carnap, by contrast, was ideally situated to take this step, not only because of his close familiarity with Frege's and Russell's ideas and his interest in Hilbert's axiomatics, but also because of his active exchanges with Fraenkel.

Moreover, Carnap had further motivations for pursuing such a project stemming from his more general philosophical goals. First, some of the central ideas and methods of the *Allgemeine Axiomatik* project, such as the use of higher-order logic with simple types, are also present in the *Aufbau* project. Also, while the main focus in *Aufbau* is on empirical concepts, not on the concepts of logic and pure mathematics, axiomatically introduced concepts are not only important in pure mathematics, but have many fruitful applications in the empirical sciences as well, especially in the

---

[13] Alfred Tarski, who was doing independent work along related lines, is an exception; I will say more about him below.

axiomatic development of theories in physics. Second, from early on in his career Carnap was interested in explicating the notion of mathematical truth. Following Frege and Russell, he saw himself as a logicist, thus as defending the claim that mathematical truth and logical truth are fundamentally the same. The axiomatic method, as used by Dedekind, Peano, Hilbert, and others, seemed to provide another important approach to this issue; and in this respect as well Carnap's work on general axiomatics promised a way of combining the Fregean and the Hilbertian approaches. I will briefly return to these two additional topics later.

III. CARNAP'S APPROACH AND ITS LIMITATIONS

The part of Carnap's *Untersuchungen* that was worked out most fully by him, and then circulated among logicians between 1928 and 1930, is its part I. It begins with the following programmatic statement:

In the course of recent investigations into general properties of axiomatic systems such as: completeness, monomorphism (categoricity), decidability, consistency, etc., and into the problem of determining criteria for and the mutual relations between these properties, one thing has become increasingly clear: that the main difficulty with respect to these problems lies in the insufficient precision of the concepts used. The most important requirement for a fruitful treatment of them is: on the one hand, to establish explicitly the logical basis to be used in each case, as is usually not done with enough precision; and on the other hand, to give precise definitions for the concepts used on that basis. In what follows, my aim will be to satisfy those two requirements and, subsequently, to establish the fruitfulness of the established foundation by deriving a number of theorems of general axiomatics. (Carnap, 2000, 59: my translation)

Here we can already see how Carnap's project was meant to go beyond Fraenkel's: Fraenkel had not "established explicitly the logical basis to be used"; he had not given "precise definitions for the concepts used on that basis"; and he had not "derived a number of theorems of general axiomatics" (at least not the theorems Carnap had in mind). At the same time, Carnap's list of "completeness, monomorphism (categoricity), and decidability" conforms exactly to Fraenkel's threefold distinction (arranged in a different order). For the first notion, called "semantic completeness" above, Carnap also uses the term "non-forkability" (in the sense that a system S which is semantically complete is not "forkable" at any proposition P, i.e., does not "branch" in the sense specified in Definition (2)).

As already indicated, Carnap uses higher-order logic with simple types as the "logical basis" for his investigation. I will say more about the main "definitions of the concepts used on this basis" shortly. But to understand Carnap's goals, it is most helpful to go straight to the main "theorems of general axiomatics" he intended to establish. There are three core theorems which, from a contemporary point of view, would be formulated as follows:

THEOREM 1: An axiomatic system S is consistent (no contradiction is deducible from it) if and only if it is satisfiable, i.e., has a model.

THEOREM 2: An axiomatic system S is semantically complete (non-forkable) if and only if it is categorical (monomorphic).

THEOREM 3: An axiomatic system S is deductively complete if and only if it is semantically complete (non-forkable).[14]

Theorems 2 and 3 together would, if true, establish that all three notions of completeness distinguished by Fraenkel and Carnap are equivalent. Also, Theorem 1 (used by Carnap in his attempt to establish Theorem 3) may remind us of Gödel's later completeness theorem for first-order logic (Gödel 1929, 1930). It is important to keep in mind, however, that Carnap is working in higher-order logic, not in first-order logic. But then a red flag should go up immediately, since we now know that in that broader context Theorem 1 (understood in a contemporary sense) is not correct, since the "only if" part fails; likewise for Theorem 3.[15] (Theorem 2 is an interestingly different case, as we will see later.)

---

[14] Theorem 1 corresponds to Carnap's "Satz 2.4.9" (Carnap, 2000, 100), Theorem 2 to "Satz 3.4.10" (Carnap, 2000, 138), and Theorem 3 to "Satz 3.6.1" (Carnap, 2000, 144).

[15] Let PA be the higher-order Dedekind–Peano axioms (assumed to be consistent); let G be the sentence shown to be true but not provable from PA in Gödel's Incompleteness Theorem. Then PA together with $\sim G$ is consistent but not satisfiable. This shows that the "only if" part of Theorem 1 fails. As neither G nor $\sim G$ is provable, PA is not deductively complete; but it is semantically complete, because categorical. That shows that the "only if" part of Theorem 3 fails. For more background, see Awodey and Reck (2002a).

To assume, as Carnap obviously did, that all three "theorems" are capable of being established may look like an elementary blunder from our present point of view. But we need to keep in mind that we are looking at these issues with hindsight, from a perspective that has benefited from subsequent developments. Indeed, Gödel's famous Incompleteness Theorems, which show most directly that Theorems 1 and 3 are false (if understood in a contemporary sense), came as a big surprise to many when they were first announced, in 1930, and published, in 1931. In this sense, Carnap's misguided confidence in being able to establish his theorems may be compared to Hilbert's parallel confidence, repeatedly expressed by him in the 1920s, in being able to establish the consistency of arithmetic, analysis, and perhaps even set theory by "elementary means," a confidence also shattered by Gödel's results. Note also that, had Theorems 2 and 3 turned out to be true, this would have provided a clear and direct answer to Fraenkel's question about the relationship of his three notions of completeness. Yet something – indeed, several things – went wrong in Carnap's approach, and we now need to identify the main sources of the problems.

The most basic problem with Carnap's approach is that, despite his stated intention to give precise and workable definitions for his main concepts within an explicitly specified logical framework, the definitions he provides are not adequate for his own purposes. The core difficulty is that there is an ambiguity in his definition of the notion of deducibility, or of logical consequence more generally. Put briefly, Carnap works with the following notion (a descendant of Russell's notion of "formal implication"):

DEFINITION: The proposition $Q(t_1, \ldots, t_n)$ is a *logical consequence* of the proposition $P(t_1, \ldots, t_n)$ if and only if $\forall x_1 \ldots \forall x_n (P(x_1, \ldots, x_n) \supset Q(x_1, \ldots, x_n))$ holds.[16]

As an illustration, consider the case where $P(t_1, \ldots, t_n)$ is the conjunction of the Dedekind–Peano Axioms, $Q(t_1, \ldots, t_n)$ is some sentence of arithmetic, $t_1, \ldots, t_n$ are the basic constants used (here zero and successor), and everything else is defined in terms of them. The crucial question now is what "holding" is supposed to

---

[16] Quantifying out the constants $t_1, \ldots, t_n$ has an effect similar to the now standard idea of varying the interpretation for all the non-logical symbols in the language.

mean – a point left deliberately vague and indeterminate in our formulation of the definition. If we assume that it means "being deducible in the given formal system," then what we have, in effect, is the contemporary notion of syntactic consequence within higher-order logic. If we assume that "holding" means something like "being true" (in the "universal domain" assumed by Carnap, following Frege and Russell), then what we have is close to the contemporary notion of higher-order semantic consequence.

Let us call the two notions just distinguished "syntactic consequence" and "semantic consequence." In principle, it is possible to adopt either one. But which of them is Carnap working with, particularly when he talks about "deducibility"? From a contemporary point of view, one would expect him to work with syntactic consequence, especially since that seems to be the notion built into deductive completeness as used in Theorem 3. Recall also Fraenkel's informal characterization of deductive completeness in *Einleitung* (1928), as quoted above, which Carnap seems to want to explicate. Similarly, one would expect syntactic consequence to be built into Carnap's notion of consistency as occurring in Theorem 1. Overall, however, Carnap leans more towards semantic notions in *Allgemeine Axiomatik*, which points in the direction of semantic consequence; and in so far as this is the case, his explications of Fraenkel's distinctions are not adequate, especially that of deductive completeness. But most importantly, Carnap simply does not seem to be clear about the difference between syntactic and semantic consequence, both of which he can be read as invoking, at different points in his discussion, as if they were equivalent.[17] In other words, he is implicitly working with an inchoate amalgam of the two notions, and this is directly affecting his understanding of Theorems 1 and 3.

I have focused on Carnap's deficient understanding of the notion of deducibility, or of logical consequence more generally, which affects his treatment of deductive completeness, as well as his treatment of consistency. Beyond that, the notions of "model," "satisfiability," and "isomorphism," as built into his definitions of semantic completeness and categoricity, are also not treated in the now standard

---

17 See here, for example, Carnap (2000, 92–93), where he moves freely back and forth between the relation of logical consequence for P and Q as simply "holding [gelten]" and as "being provable."

way in *Allgemeine Axiomatik*. But this aspect is less consequential, and I will not go into the details here. Sufficient for present purposes is to note the following general point: because of the ambiguity in his core notions, Carnap's approach and his main theorems are problematic, especially Theorems 1 and 3. From a contemporary point of view they, too, turn out to be ambiguous (involving either syntactic or semantic consequence). Moreover, if one removes the ambiguity, then the two theorems either come out true but trivial, or false and refuted by Gödel's Incompleteness Theorems.[18]

Besides the specific problems pointed out so far, there is also a more general, though not unrelated, problem. Carnap tried to stay within a general Fregean and Russellian "universalist" approach to logic: he uses a single formal system, formulated in a fixed, all-encompassing background language, as the framework in which all logical reasoning is to take place. From within his framework he then tries to distinguish several notions of completeness, to define consistency, and so on.[19] But what these notions call for, from our point of view, is the distinction between object-language and meta-language – between statements within the object-language in which the axiom system is formulated and statements about this object-language from a metatheoretic standpoint. This distinction, as we now know, allows for clear definitions of both syntactic consequence and semantic consequence as precise metatheoretic notions; similarly for the other notions at issue. Carnap did not make such a distinction, and this may be seen as the deeper reason for the failure of his project.

This seems to be, in fact, exactly the conclusion to which Carnap himself would soon be led. But that happened only after showing his manuscript for part I to several logicians, including Fraenkel and

---

[18] If we work with semantic consequence throughout, then Theorems 1 and 3 are true but trivial. (This is the case not only if we use "universalist" semantic consequence along Carnap's lines, but also semantic consequence in the now standard "model-theoretic" sense.) If we work with syntactic consequence, then the "only if" parts of Theorems 1 and 3 are refuted by Gödel's Incompleteness Theorems; compare fn. 15.

[19] For instance, Carnap defines consistency for a (finite) system of axioms not metatheoretically, but as follows (notation updated): Suppose that $P(t_1, \ldots, t_n)$ is the conjunction of the given axioms. Then the axiom system is called *consistent* if and only if $\neg \exists Q \forall x_1 \ldots \forall x_n (P(x_1, \ldots, x_n) \supset (Q(x_1, \ldots, x_n) \wedge \neg Q(x_1, \ldots, x_n)))$

"holds" (same ambiguity as above); see Carnap (2000, 97).

Gödel, starting in 1928. He also presented the corresponding material publicly both in Vienna, in talks and in classes that same year, and at a conference in Prague, the "First Conference on Epistemology of the Exact Sciences," in 1929. The immediate responses to these presentations by Carnap were lively, especially at the Prague conference. As he wrote in a corresponding diary entry shortly thereafter:

My lecture: Investigations in General Axiomatics; just a brief summary. But the proof is requested, and acknowledged. Though it was late, a lively discussion on the basic issues afterwards; von Neumann, Zermelo, Hahn, Fraenkel said that a final judgment will only be possible when the complete proof [especially of Theorem 2 and 3 above] is available. Amazing interest in my Investigations. (Quoted in Awodey and Carus, 2001, 162)

The list of logicians mentioned here is impressive: von Neumann, Zermelo, Hahn, and Fraenkel. Apparently none of them saw right away what had gone wrong with Carnap's proof, or with his approach more generally. While this is probably due in part to the fact that Carnap only presented "a brief summary," the reaction also indicates that, at the time, the issues were not well understood more generally. In this sense, too, Carnap was presenting material at the cutting edge of research in logic and metamathematics.

The turning point for Carnap's project occurred in 1930. Two events were crucial. First, early in 1930 Alfred Tarski visited Vienna, and the two had several conversations, including on the topic at hand. After one of these conversations, Carnap wrote the following revealing remark in his diary:

Tarski visits me ... talked about my *Axiomatik*. It seems correct, but certain concepts don't capture what is intended; they must be defined metamathematically rather than mathematically. (Quoted in Awodey and Carus, 2001, 163)

Apparently Tarski – who already had made independent progress on how to frame, and then pursue, general questions in logic from a metatheoretic standpoint (although this work was only starting to become known outside Poland) – pointed out exactly the general problem with Carnap's approach as described above.

The second crucial event involved Kurt Gödel. During the second half of the 1920s Gödel was a research student at the University of Vienna, and Carnap had frequent conversations him, especially on logical matters. Gödel also attended Carnap's talks and classes in Vienna, in 1928, in which material from *Allgemeine Axiomatik* was presented, and he was one of the people who received a copy of Carnap's manuscript. Thus, the two had direct and prolonged contact in connection with exactly the issues under discussion in this chapter. At least partly influenced by that contact (partly also, as is well known, by work in the Hilbert school), Gödel then came up with his celebrated results: the Completeness Theorem for first-order logic and the Incompleteness Theorems for arithmetic and higher-order logic. The latter were first publicly announced at a conference in Königsberg, in the fall of 1930; but there is evidence that Gödel had told Carnap about them already earlier, during a conversation in August of that year. And while Carnap had problems following the details of the corresponding proofs initially, he recognized the importance of Gödel's results very quickly.[20]

When Gödel announced his Incompleteness Theorems for the first time publicly, at the Königsberg conference, it was in connection with his Completeness Theorem. After reporting on a proof of the latter in detail, he remarked:

I would furthermore like to call attention to an application that can be made of what has been proved [the Completeness Theorem] to the general theory of axiom systems. It concerns the concepts "decidable [*entscheidungsdefinit*]" and "monomorphic" . . . One would suspect that there is a close connection between these two concepts, yet up to now such a connection has eluded general formulation . . . In view of the developments presented here it can now be shown that, for a special class of axiom systems, namely those whose axioms can be expressed in the restricted functional calculus [i.e., first-order logic], decidability [*Entscheidungsdefinitheit*] always follows from monomorphism . . . If the completeness theorem could also be proved for the higher parts of logic (the extended functional calculus) [including the logic of *Principia Mathematica* and Carnap's simple type theory], then it would be shown in complete generality that decidability follows from monomorphism; and since we know, for example, that the Peano axiom system is monomorphic, from that the solvability of every problem of arithmetic and analysis in *Principia Mathematica* would follow.

---

[20] For more on the interactions between Carnap and Gödel in this connection, see Awodey and Carus (2001), Goldfarb (2003), and Goldfarb (2005).

Such an extension of the completeness theorem is, however, impossible, as I have recently proved; that is, there are mathematical problems which, though they can be expressed in *Principia Mathematica*, cannot be solved by the logical devices of *Principia Mathematica*. (Quoted in Goldfarb, 2005, 190–192; translation slightly amended)

Several details in this passage are significant in our context, since they show that Gödel's way of looking at the issue was very much influenced by Carnap's *Allgemeine Axiomatik* project. Note especially the terminology of "decidable" and "monomophic," as well as the question about the relation between these two notions. Note also Gödel's remark that "one would suspect that there is a close connection between these two notions." It seems that he thought his audience would agree that the latter was a natural suspicion – which, of course, made his "recent proof" that it is false more significant.

Thus, it was Tarski who first convinced Carnap, in early 1930, that his general framework was inadequate; but it was Gödel who directly showed him, later in 1930, that, even if the approach could be formulated adequately, several of Carnap's main theorems could not be salvaged. As a result of both of these blows, Carnap did not pursue part I of his project further after 1930 – the manuscript for it disappeared in a drawer, to be rediscovered and published only seven decades later. Indeed, Carnap became so convinced of the futility of this project that later, in his "Intellectual Autobiography" (1963a), he didn't even mention it. The only remaining traces were the corresponding remarks in "Eigentliche und uneigentliche Begriffe" (1927) and the summary in "Bericht über Untersuchungen zur allgemeinen Axiomatik" (1930c). It seems that the latter article had already gone into press when Carnap abandoned the project, so that its publication could no longer be prevented.

IV. AFTERMATH AND CONTINUING SIGNIFICANCE

At this point, the question arises why we should pay attention to *Allgemeine Axiomatik* today. Wasn't Carnap right to ignore it? It seems to me that, despite its general failure, the project is worthy of contemporary attention. Carnap was addressing important issues, issues that remain of interest for several reasons. Some of these involve technical, mathematical questions in general axiomatics; others have to do with Carnap himself, especially with a better understanding of the development of his views; yet others concern the history and philosophy of logic and metamathematics more generally.

A first observation to make in this connection is that from the perspective of a general investigation into the strengths and weaknesses of the axiomatic method the issues addressed by Carnap are undoubtedly central. More specifically, while in the work of Hilbert and his school the focus was on the notions of independence and consistency, the notion of completeness for systems of axioms is equally important – as acknowledged by everyone in the 1920s, including Hilbert himself. Moreover, this notion becomes particularly interesting within the higher-order logical framework adopted by Carnap. If we restrict ourselves to first-order logic, few mathematical theories are complete in any of the senses distinguished above. By contrast, in higher-order logic the axiomatic theories of the natural and real numbers, as well as of Euclidian geometry, are all semantically complete and categorical. For these reasons, higher-order logic seems to be the most natural framework for investigating notions of completeness.

As we have seen, Carnap thought that his three notions of completeness – "decidability" (deductive completeness), "nonforkability" (semantic completeness), and "monomorphism" (categoricity) – are all equivalent. This is wrong on several counts in the context of first-order logic. In the context of higher-order logic, the equivalence of deductive completeness and semantic completeness – asserted in Theorem 3 – is also false, as pointed out by Gödel at the Königsberg conference. To be more precise, while it is true that deductive completeness implies semantic completeness, Gödel's results refute the converse implication. However, what about the alleged equivalence of semantic completeness and categoricity in higher-order logic – Carnap's Theorem 2? This equivalence again involves two directions. One, from categoricity to semantic completeness, is correct and relatively easy to establish (not only for first-order logic, but also for higher-order logic). The other direction is much harder, and still not completely clarified. Here the question remains: Is it the case that an axiomatic system that is semantically complete is thereby also categorical? Carnap thought that the answer was positive, a claim we might therefore call "Carnap's Conjecture."[21]

Not only did Carnap think that this conjecture is true, he believed he had found a proof. Unfortunately, while neither the general inadequacy of his approach pointed out by Tarski nor the more specific results by Gödel immediately refute Carnap's work on this point, there is an additional weakness in his treatment not mentioned so far. Carnap made a subtle implicit assumption in his attempted proof that was later shown not to be true in general. With this assumption added the proof is correct, but it does not establish Carnap's Conjecture, only a partial, qualified result.[22] This leads to a new question: Might there not be some other proof of the conjecture, one not relying on any such additional assumption? As far as I am aware, this question is still unsettled, and so Carnap's Conjecture, in full generality, remains an open question.[23] What we have here is a natural and central question in general axiomatics still awaiting an answer, one to which a reconsideration of Carnap's 1920s project directly leads us and which may prove more tractable now.

I have concentrated so far on part I of *Allgemeine Axiomatik*, mostly because we only have this part available in print (as Carnap, 2000); but a few remarks about part II can illustrate further the remaining significance of Carnap's work. Here Carnap intended to address a number of further questions connected with his three notions of completeness, specifically questions involving "extremal axioms." An example of such an axiom is Hilbert's "Axiom of Completeness" in his axiomatization of Euclidian geometry, which can be considered a "maximality axiom"; another example is Dedekind's and Peano's induction axiom, forming part of their respective axiomatizations of arithmetic, which constitutes a "minimality axiom."

---

[21] It is implicitly assumed here, as it was during Carnap's time, that axiom systems have to be finite. Without that assumption the conjecture can be shown to be false; see Awodey and Reck (2002b, 83).

[22] Carnap assumed that every model of a higher-order theory is definable. This is made explicit in the correct, but restricted, version of the result published, a few years later, in Lindenbaum and Tarski (1935). For more on this issue, see Awodey and Reck (2002a) and, especially, Awodey and Reck (2002b).

[23] The conjecture is known to be true in some special cases, e.g., when working with simple type theory with no non-logical constants ("pure higher-order logic"); see Awodey and Carus (2001, 160–161).

As Carnap observed, both of these axioms lead to categorical theories. This suggests the question how and to what extent this phenomenon generalizes, i.e., whether other "extremal axioms" can be found that have the same effect and, if so, why they have that effect. Once again, this amounts to a natural and central question in general axiomatics, with many implications and subquestions.

While Carnap himself never reached a full answer to this question, he addressed parts of it successfully. He also rescued several of the results obtained here from the rubble of *Allgemeine Axiomatik* and published them a few years later in "Über Extremalaxiome" (1936), written in collaboration with Friedrich Bachmann. Like his other publications in logic from the period, this article did not draw a lot of attention, not least because the questions and results in it were now presented out of context; they thus lacked the support of the more general project within which Carnap studied them. Nevertheless, they led to a few subsequent investigations, e.g. in Fraenkel and Bar-Hillel's *Foundations of Set Theory* (1956). Also, given the recent broadening and branching out of logic, including a revival of higher-order logic (in computer science and category theory, among others), some of Carnap's results and conjectures in this connection too might prove fruitful for future research.[24]

As mentioned above, for Carnap the *Allgemeine Axiomatik* project also had broader philosophical significance, especially in two respects. First, he saw it as connected with general questions about the applicability of mathematical concepts to the empirical world, as investigated contemporaneously in *Der logische Aufbau der Welt*. This connection, in fact, was the main topic of the article "Eigentliche und uneigentliche Begriffe" (1927), in which Carnap argued that not only explicitly defined concepts, as treated in the *Aufbau*, but also concepts introduced by "complete" systems of axioms were of special importance for science, and thus in need of further clarification. Although this argument has not yet found much attention in the secondary literature, exploring it further might again prove fruitful in the future, now in connection with Carnap's views about empirical knowledge.[25]

---

[24] For more on this general issue, see Awodey and Reck (2002b).

[25] See Awodey and Carus (2001), in which this issue is emphasized. For a different perspective, and a rare earlier discussion of Carnap (1927), compare Goldfarb (1996).

Second and independently, Carnap also saw a direct connection between questions about completeness and the notion of mathematical truth, and thus the philosophy of mathematics. Here the basic idea – already implicit in earlier works on geometry by Hilbert and on the natural numbers by Dedekind and Peano – is this: If a mathematical theory can be based on a "complete" set of axioms, then the notion of truth in that area is captured fully in terms of the "logical consequences" of these axioms. After having learned, from Tarski and Gödel, about the problems with his treatment of completeness and logical consequence in *Allgemeine Axiomatik*, Carnap could, of course, no longer simply uphold this basic idea; at the very least, it needed to be modified and clarified. But that leads to the following question: Which modifications, if any, are possible? In other words, is there some less problematic variant of this approach that still provides us with an axiomatic, and broadly logicist, notion of mathematical truth?

The latter question remained very much a concern for Carnap after giving up his *Allgemeine Axiomatik* project in 1930. In response to Tarski's ideas, he now fully embraced the object- versus metalanguage distinction. Indeed, in his later reflections he characterized one of the main goals for his work in the early 1930s as follows:

One of my aims [at that point] was to make the metalanguage more precise, so that an exact conceptual system for metalogic could be constructed in it. Whereas Hilbert intended his metamathematics only for the specific purpose of proving the consistency of a mathematical system formulated in the object language, I aimed at the construction of a general theory of linguistic forms. (Carnap, 1963a, 53)

Carnap then attempted, on such a basis, to provide a post-Gödelian characterization of mathematical truth, one that takes full account of Gödel's Incompleteness Theorems. Indeed, the pursuit of this goal is a theme that connects many of Carnap's publications from the 1930s on: from *Die Logische Syntax der Sprache* (1934c) to "Die Antinomien und die Unvollständigkeit der Mathematik" (1934a) and "Ein Gültigkeitskriterium für die Sätze der klassischen Mathematik" (1935a), and even to later writings such as *Introduction to Semantics* (1942) and *Meaning and Necessity* (1947).[26] In these

---

[26] Both Carnap (1934a) and Carnap (1935a) were later worked into the augmented English edition of *Logische Syntax* (Carnap, 1934c/1937), as indicated on p. xi of its preface.

works, Carnap tried out a variety of ideas for how to capture the notion of mathematical truth along the general lines indicated above: broadly syntactic ideas, semantic ideas, infinitary logic, and even modal logic. Unfortunately, he never arrived at a satisfactory solution.

A full understanding of Carnap's views and their development will have to incorporate an account of his various attempts in this connection. This issue goes far beyond the bounds of the present chapter,[27] but let me make one further observation concerning it. While it is not inappropriate to think of these Carnapian investigations in the philosophy of mathematics as his response to Gödel's Incompleteness Theorems, a reconsideration of Carnap's earlier *Allgemeine Axiomatik* project reveals that their roots go back considerably further. They go deep into the 1920s, partly even the 1910s; and they consist of Carnap's early attempts at combining a Fregean and a Hilbertian point of view in logic and axiomatics. Thus, Gödel's results were not really the starting point in this connection. Rather, Gödel's results had special significance for Carnap precisely because of his own earlier work on logic and axiomatics. Moreover, that earlier work by Carnap provided a significant part of the framework within which Gödel himself proceeded.

This brings me to a final observation about the significance of the *Allgemeine Axiomatik* project, now for the history and philosophy of logic more generally. If, as I have argued, Carnap's project, despite its flaws, was at the cutting edge of research in logic and early metamathematics, then new light is shed on their development. It is often acknowledged that the 1920s was one of the most active and fertile decades in the rise of modern logic. But this is typically, and sometimes exclusively, acknowledged in connection with Hilbert's influential work (his quest for consistency proofs, his confrontation with Brouwer, and so on); and as a consequence, Gödel's theorems are interpreted as fitting into that development. While such an interpretation does shed significant light on the situation, paying attention to Carnap's *Allgemeine Axiomatik* project allows us to understand another, partly independent development also leading to Gödel. As a result, a fuller picture of the motivations for his celebrated results emerges. Gödel's work now appears as a node in a whole web of

---

[27] See Steve Awodey's contribution to this volume for a detailed discussion.

research during the 1920s and early 1930s, one that ties together not just Hilbert and Gödel, but also Frege, Russell, Fraenkel, and Tarski – with Carnap as a central mediating figure.[28]

[28] I am grateful to the editors, Michael Friedman and Richard Creath, for inviting me to contribute to this volume. Many thanks also to André Carus, William Demopoulos, Michael Friedman, and Paolo Mancosu for helpful comments on drafts of this chapter, as well as to Steve Awodey for collaborations that put me in a position to write it.

9 Tolerance and logicism: logical syntax and the philosophy of mathematics

The logical empiricism of the Vienna Circle presented itself as the reconciliation of a thoroughgoing empiricism as regards substantive knowledge with the certainty and necessity of mathematics. According to empiricism, sense experience is the only source of substantive knowledge of facts, but sense experience might always have been different from what it actually was. Moreover, anything we extrapolate from what we experience may be falsified by further experiences. Knowledge grounded in sense experience is thus knowledge of contingencies, and except perhaps for knowledge of what is immediately experienced ("Red here now"),[1] it is revisable on the basis of further experiences. In contrast, knowledge of mathematics appears to be unrevisably certain substantive knowledge of necessary truths. The contingencies of our sense experience thus seem to afford no basis for knowledge of mathematics. In a word, empiricism must be false, because mathematics is substantive a priori knowledge.

The logical empiricist approach to this dilemma is to deny that knowledge of mathematics is substantive knowledge. The apriority and necessity of mathematics is the apriority and necessity of logic. Logic is in its turn grounded in tacit conventions for the use of certain symbols, symbols that do not themselves stand for anything, like the signs for negation and conjunction. As Hans Hahn put it:

[Logic] *only deals with the way we talk about objects;* logic first comes into being through language. And the certainty and universal validity of a proposition of logic . . . flows precisely from this, that it says nothing about

---

[1] The existence of empirical certainties as a basis for factual knowledge is one of the central points of contention in the protocol sentence debate in the Vienna Circle. See Thomas Uebel's contribution to this volume for further discussion and references.

any objects . . . We learn – by training, as I should like to put it – to assign the designation "red" to some of these objects, and we make an agreement to assign the designation "not red" to any others. On the basis of this agreement we can now state the following proposition with absolute certainty: None of these objects is assigned both the designation "red" and the designation "not red," which is usually expressed briefly as follows: No object is both red and not red." (Hahn, 1933/1987, 29)

This reconciliation was to be achieved by a marriage of Russell's logic and Wittgenstein's *Tractatus*. Vienna took Whitehead and Russell's *Principia Mathematica* to make very plausible the reducibility of mathematics to logic, and Wittgenstein to have revealed that logical truths are empty tautologies that are true in virtue of language, not in virtue of representing facts. Their basic attitude is that Russell presents us with a new and powerful logic, while Wittgenstein decisively clarifies the essence of logic.

This marriage is troubled. The derivation of mathematics in *Principia* is achieved only by the use of three existence axioms whose lack of self-evidence arguably disqualifies them from the status of logical principles.[2] Nor do these axioms appear to be Tractarian tautologies. Indeed, in the *Tractatus* Wittgenstein rejects Frege's and Russell's logicist ambitions, and forwards an impenetrably terse, obscure account of the equations of arithmetic that distinguishes these equations from the tautologies of logic. Hahn realizes that logicism has not yet been fully validated, but is sanguine about its prospects:

Of course, the proof of the tautological character of mathematics is not yet complete on all points; . . . yet we have no doubt that the view that mathematics is tautological in character is essentially correct. (Hahn, 1933/1987, 35)[3]

After completing his dissertation, Carnap is concerned with the application of logic to the formalization of physical theory in order to address issues in the philosophy of science and theory of knowledge. *Der logische Aufbau der Welt* is the culmination of Carnap's efforts here. In *Aufbau*, Carnap accepts the simple theory of types as a formulation of logic, and casually assumes that all the mathematics

---

[2] These are the axioms of infinity, choice, and reducibility.
[3] Hahn appends a footnote to *Principia* to the second sentence. For a nuanced account of Hahn's philosophy of logic and mathematics and his contribution to the emergence of Carnap's Principle of Tolerance, see Uebel (2005a).

needed for natural science can be developed in this framework. He has no worked-out philosophy of logic. In the late 1920s, Carnap's attention turns to philosophy of mathematics and the difficulties with logicism. He hopes to combine basically Russell's logic with ideas inspired by Hilbert's metamathematics to develop an account of mathematics as a formal science rather than a factual science that will, nevertheless, do justice to its applications in the natural sciences. Carnap's efforts here were disrupted by Gödel's Incompleteness Theorem, which asserts that any consistent formalization of elementary arithmetic satisfying certain weak notational conditions is syntactically incomplete, and so fails to decide the truth or falsity of some arithmetical sentences.[4] The philosophy of logic and mathematics in *The Logical Syntax of Language* is Carnap's striking response to this complicated situation.

I.

In his Schilpp volume autobiography, Carnap confesses his aversion to the indecisive wrangling that, in his opinion, has traditionally pervaded philosophy:

> I was depressed by disputations in which opponents talked at cross purposes; there seemed hardly any chance of mutual understanding, let alone of agreement because there was not even a common criterion for deciding the controversy. (Carnap, 1963a, 45)

In the 1920s, in the wake of the logical paradoxes, the plethora of approaches to the foundations of mathematics threatened to turn logic and foundations of mathematics into another arena for fruitless contention. Russell's theory of types was not the only solution to the paradoxes. There were also various systems of axiomatic set theory. Within type-theoretic approaches to logic, advocates of impredicative higher-order quantification were opposed by those who permitted only predicative higher-order quantification, arguing that impredicative quantification was viciously circular.[5] Finally, there

---

[4] For a discussion of Carnap's evolving philosophy of logic leading up to *Logical Syntax*, see Goldfarb (1996), Awodey and Carus (forthcoming), and Erich Reck's contribution to this volume.

[5] Impredicative systems permit a predicate-variable to be instantiated by predicates that themselves contain predicate-variables with the same range as the original variable.

were the disputes over the legitimacy of non-constructive proofs in mathematics in which intuitionists went so far as to reject the unrestricted validity of the law of the excluded middle.

At the beginning of *Logical Syntax*, Carnap notes with satisfaction the progress logic had made in recent decades culminating in the work of Russell, but maintains that further progress has been limited by the view that any deviations from the Russellian standard "must be proved to be 'correct' and to constitute a faithful rendering of 'the true logic'" (Carnap, 1934c/1937, xiv). Carnap's proposes to surrender the ideal of single logic:

In [this book], the view will be maintained that we have in every respect complete freedom with regard to the forms of language; that both the forms of construction for sentences and the rules of transformation . . . may be chosen quite arbitrarily [*völlig frei*].

He contrasts his attitude with that of earlier thinkers:

Up to now, in constructing a language, the procedure has usually been, first to assign a meaning to the fundamental mathematico-logical symbols, and then to consider what sentences and inferences are seen to be logically correct in accordance with this meaning. (Carnap, 1934c/1937, xv)

It is easy to imagine Carnap here recollecting his logic classes with Frege. Frege devises a notation to give regular, unambiguous, perspicuous expression to logical notions, those notions that figure in thought and discourse on any topic whatsoever – so notation for the truth-functional connectives, the universal quantifier, and identity. He then sets forth the principles of demonstrative inference by selecting as axioms several self-evidently true formulas in his notation and by specifying several evidently truth-preserving notational manipulations of formulas as inference rules. These principles set the standards for logically valid reasoning. They are, Frege says, "boundary stones fixed in an eternal foundation that our thinking can overflow but never displace" (Frege, 1893, xvi). This logical project is framed by Frege's conception of thoughts as the objectively true or false, intersubjectively available contents grasped in thinking and put forward as true in assertions.

Carnap proposes to reverse Frege's procedure:

let any postulates [*Grundsätze*] and rules of inference be chosen at will; this choice gives the logical signs occurring in them the meaning they have. With this attitude, the conflict between different viewpoints on the problems of foundations of mathematics disappears. The mathematical part of the language can be set up as one or the other viewpoint prefers. There is here no question of "justification," but rather only the question of the syntactic consequences to which one or another choice leads, including the question of consistency. (Carnap, 1934c/1937, xv; my translation)

His idea is that the logician describes various possible languages. The logician is not to assume that the signs or characters of the language "possess a meaning" or "designate anything" (Carnap, 1934c/1937, §2, 5). Instead, possible languages are to be treated as calculi and described in notational terms, syntactic terms:

> The *syntax* of a language . . . is concerned, in general, with the *structures of possible serial orders* (of a definite kind) *of any elements whatsoever* . . . Pure syntax . . . is nothing more than combinatorial analysis, or, in other words, the geometry of finite, discrete, serial structures of a particular kind. (Carnap, 1934/1937, §2, 6–7)

First, the logician states formation rules that describe the series of signs that are well-formed formulas of the calculus. Second, she states transformation rules that define a logical consequence relation over these formulas. Notions of L-validity (analytic) and L-contravalid (contradictory) are defined in terms of the consequence relation. The L-determinate formulas of a calculus are those that are either L-valid or L-contravalid. The Carnapian logician aims to describe calculi that capture in syntactic terms the permissions and restrictions of various approaches in foundations of mathematics.

To illustrate the methods of logical syntax and their application to disputes in the philosophy of mathematics, Carnap devotes much of *Logical Syntax* to the description of two calculi. Language I is a version of primitive recursive arithmetic. Carnap takes it to represent the perspective of constructivists, including intuitionists.[6] Language II is the simple theory of types superimposed on elementary arithmetic (type ø arithmetic). This is the formal language that Gödel investigates in his incompleteness paper; it represents the perspective of classical mathematics with its non-constructive proofs. In

---

[6] Language I blocks non-constructive reasoning in that it expresses unbounded generalizations over positive integers only by use of free variables. Intuitionists would balk at accepting Language I as capturing their perspective; indeed, as Carnap recognizes, many would balk at identifying their perspective with any formalism. See Carnap (1934c/1937, §16).

contrast to Frege and Russell, Carnap does not separate out mathematical signs from logical signs, defining the former in terms of the latter. Both Languages I and II have primitive arithmetical signs.[7] Logicians may go on to investigate the consequences of these syntactic descriptions of various calculi, and so compare the calculi.

So far we just have pure syntax, a kind of abstract mathematical discipline. Carnap's correlative understanding of logicism and empiricism is bound up with his view of the potential use of a calculus as the language of science. Carnap describes the logical-mathematical core of his two formalisms. He introduces signs that are, extra-syntactically speaking, logical and mathematical signs. He sets up the consequence relation so that sentences constructed solely from these signs are L-determinate. Carnap envisions adding to his languages further predicates and functors, descriptive signs as opposed to logical signs. The consequence relation will link sentences containing these predicates to each other and to the logical core. We segregate a sub-class of descriptive predicates, the O-predicates. When we think of the calculus as a language in use, we imagine the O-predicates of the calculus to be observation predicates. In "Testability and Meaning," Carnap explains that an observation predicate of a used language is, as a first approximation, one that speakers of the language under suitable circumstances agree in applying or denying to demonstrated items on the basis of observation. The concept of an observation predicate thus belongs ". . . to a biological or psychological theory of language as a kind of human behavior, and especially as a kind of reaction to observation" (Carnap, 1936–1937, 454). We can now imagine investigators using the descriptive predicates to formulate theories. They then deduce from the theory consequences stated using the O-predicates. To evaluate the theory, they check whether the O-consequences of the theory agree with or contradict their observation reports made by use of the O-predicates. The theory is confirmed to the extent that its consequences for observation agree with the observation reports of investigators; it is falsified if the observation reports of investigators contradict some of its observational consequences.[8]

---

[7] See Carnap (1934c/1937, §84, especially 321). I return to this point below.
[8] Carnap allows that investigators may decide to give up the observation reports that contradict a theory. See Carnap (1934c/1937, §82, 318).

Beginning with "Testability and Meaning," Carnap attempts to demarcate in formal terms languages whose descriptive sentences are linked to observation predicates so as to render groups of descriptive sentences observationally testable in the way just sketched. These are Carnap's empiricist languages. We won't be concerned here with the details of Carnap's proposals, or the difficulties they face. Adoption of an empiricist language as the language of science gives clear-cut import to questions about the correctness of sentences in the calculus. A dispute concerning sentences constructed from logical-mathematical vocabulary should then be settled by reference just to the consequence relation of the language set forth in transformation rules. Debates about descriptive sentences should be settled by reference to the observational consequences of theories containing the sentences.

We can now appreciate better what Carnap's reversal of Frege's procedure comes to. In an empiricist language, the logical consequence relation of a calculus defines standards for the acceptance and rejection of sentences and theories formulated within the calculus and defines standards for a language-relative notion of cognitive correctness. Indeed, Carnap thinks that talk of truth or correctness becomes tolerably precise only in application to a formal language with its consequence relation. No such language-relative notion of correctness is applicable to the choice of a language with its constituting consequence relation. Here we have Carnap's leading idea: the Principle of Tolerance and an attendant sharp contrast between the adoption of a formal language as the language of science and the evaluation of sentences within that language as correct or incorrect. Carnap marks this contrast between the acceptance of a sentence within a language and the adoption of a language as the language for science by calling the latter a matter of convention. In *Logical Syntax*, he says:

The construction of the physical system is not effected in accordance with fixed rules, but by means of conventions [Festsetzungen]. These conventions . . . are, however, not arbitrary. The choice of them is influenced, in the first place, by certain practical methodological considerations (for instance, whether they make for simplicity, expedience, and fruitfulness in certain tasks). (Carnap, 1934/1937, §82, 320)

In later writings, Carnap drops talk of conventions, and contrasts instead the theoretical decision to accept a sentence within an adopted language with the practical decision to adopt a language:

To be sure, we have to face at this point an important question; but it is a practical, not a theoretical question; it is the question of whether or not to accept the new linguistic forms. The acceptance cannot be judged as being true or false because it is not an assertion. It can only be judged as being more or less expedient, fruitful, conducive to the aim for which the language is intended. (Carnap, 1950a/1956, 214)

The choice of a formal language as the language for science will be guided by the values and desiderata of the choosers. Carnap suggests that a choice between Languages I and II is a matter of weighing the greater security against inconsistency the weaker Language I provides against the convenience of the availability of the full resources of classical mathematics built into the stronger Language II (cf. Carnap, 1939, §20, 50f.; Carnap, 1963a, 49). Something similar holds for Carnap's empiricism. No fact makes the adoption of an empiricist language correct. The demarcation of empiricist languages clarifies the content of empiricism and thereby assists investigators who wish to evaluate descriptive theories and hypotheses on the basis of observation to avoid the distractions of irrelevant wrangling. Carnap accordingly advocates that candidate-languages for the language of science be restricted to empiricist languages, emphasizing the non-cognitive character of this empiricism (cf. Carnap, 1936–1937, 33).

The choice of a formal language as the language for science thus resembles the choice of rules for a game we intend to play. The rules define what is permitted in the course of the game. But no such question of legitimacy applies to the choice of these rules themselves. Rather, we construct the rules for the game by weighing various considerations in order to frame rules that define, say, an enjoyable, engaging, competitive activity whose course depends on a mixture of physical skill, quick wits, strategy, and luck. We may, in the light of our experience playing the game, decide to modify the rules, perhaps in far-reaching ways, and so to play a different game. Similarly, the option to change languages is always open as regards the choice of a language for science.

Carnap's conception of calculi and their use as possible languages of science offers a reconciliation of the apriority of mathematics with empiricism. The central aim in constructing a calculus to serve as the language of science is to make precise the standards for evaluating physical theories with their descriptive predicates by forging links between these theories and observation sentences constructed from the O-predicates. Carnap designs calculi whose L-consequence relation marks each logical-mathematical sentence either L-valid or L-contravalid. The predicates "L-valid" and "L-contravalid" thus play the role of a bivalent truth predicate over the logical-mathematical sentences of such a calculus. On the assumption that atomic sentences constructed from O-predicates are L-indeterminate, the logical-mathematical sentences of the calculus are not subject to empirical test. Rather, the L-validity (L-contravalidity) of these sentences is thus built into the calculus as an artifact of the consequence relation that secures the empirical testability of theories in the calculus. Carnap thus speaks of the logical-mathematical sentences of a calculus as notational auxiliaries to the L-indeterminate sentences, to the sentences used to formulate substantial, empirically testable theories:

> These auxiliary statements [*Hilfsätze*] have indeed no factual content or, to speak in the material idiom [*inhaltlich gesprochen*], they do not express any matter of fact, actual or non-actual. Rather they are, as it were, mere calculating devices [*bloße Rechenausdrücke*], but they are so constructed that they can be subjected to the same rules as the genuine (synthetic) statements. In this way, they are an easily applicable device [*handhabendes Hilfsmittel*] for operations with synthetic statements. (Carnap, 1935b/1953, 126)

The apriority and necessity of mathematics is then glossed by the status of L-valid mathematical sentences of a language as notational auxiliaries to the observationally testable sentences.[9]

What about the status of descriptions of calculi, of logical syntax itself? Carnap appreciates how formation rules, derivation rules, and indeed transformation rules generally are via Gödelization interpretable within a suitably strong arithmetic. So, logical syntax has the same status as arithmetic (Carnap, 1934c/1937, §19,

---

[9] In this paragraph, I am indebted to Michael Friedman, who has emphasized these points in his writings on Carnap. See especially Friedman (1999b, sec. iv, 215–220).

57). Carnap envisions that colloquial statements of arithmetic will be transformed into L-valid sentences on regimentation into a calculus.

II.

This view of mathematics as a notational auxiliary for empirical science faces a powerful objection due to Kurt Gödel.[10] Consideration of the objection will illuminate both the structure of Carnap's position and its deflationary character.

Gödel sees Carnap as offering a conventionalist account of mathematical truth and certainty. The correctness or truth of the observation reports by which descriptive theories are tested is a matter of their correspondence with empirical fact. In contrast, the correctness or truth of the valid sentences of a calculus is stipulated by the decision to adopt the calculus as the language for science. It is this truth by syntactic stipulation that makes these sentences notational auxiliaries to the sentences of empirical science. However, the truth of the valid sentences of a language can be stipulated by adoption of the calculus only if the atomic observation sentences are independent of the logic of the language. Only then will the valid sentences be notational auxiliaries for the descriptive sentences. So, as a prerequisite for stipulating the truth of the L-valid sentences of a calculus, we must show, as Gödel puts it, that the transformation rules are *admissible* in that they "do not imply the truth or falsity of any proposition expressing an empirical fact" (Gödel, 1995, 357). The transformation rules of a calculus are admissible only if the calculus is consistent, i.e., not every sentence is valid. Hence, a proof of the admissibility of transformation rules would be a proof of the consistency of the mathematics built into the calculus. However, on the basis of his Second Incompleteness Theorem, Gödel observes that a proof of the consistency of a calculus requires the use of mathematics in the meta-language stronger than the mathematics built into the calculus. So, in advance of the stipulation that confers truth on the valid sentences of a calculus, we must have available mathematics

---

[10] Gödel presents this objection in (1995). Although the essay was written for the Carnap–Schilpp volume, Gödel remained dissatisfied with the various versions of the essay and decided not to submit it.

at least comparable to that built into calculus. This mathematics must be non-conventional on pain of a vicious regress.

A number of passages in Carnap's writings suggest that in *Logical Syntax* he embraced a position subject to Gödel's criticism. For example, we find:

> In material interpretation, an analytic sentence is absolutely true whatever the empirical facts may be. Hence, it does not state anything about facts . . . A synthetic statement is sometimes true – namely, when certain facts exist – and sometimes false; hence it says something as to what facts exist. *Synthetic sentences* are the *genuine statements about reality*. (Carnap, 1934c/1937, §14, 41)

Nevertheless, I maintain that Carnap's position is not subject to Gödel's objection. Its avoidance of this pitfall exhibits its coherence and depth.

Gödel argues that a proof of admissibility is a prerequisite for adopting a calculus as the logic of science. This justificatory demand for a proof of admissibility in turn depends on the contrast between the factual truth and falsity of observation reports and the stipulated truth of the logic and mathematics built into the adopted calculus. For we cannot stipulate the truth of the logic and mathematics built into a calculus, if the stipulated truths would contradict the factual truth and falsity of observation reports. The requirement of an admissibility proof thus rests on a language-transcendent notion of empirical fact, of empirical truth and falsity, a notion that is not tied to a particular calculus. Such a language-transcendent notion of empirical fact imposes constraints on the choice of a calculus, making some choices incorrect because those choices stipulate sentences to be true which are in fact false.

I hold that Carnap, in advocating unconstrained tolerance in logic, rejects any language-transcendent notion of empirical fact or truth. We saw how Carnap, in "Testability and Meaning," characterizes observation predicates in behavioral terms, not semantic terms. Indeed, for Carnap talk of an observation report's being correct or true gets clear sense only in relation to a calculus with O-predicates that can be identified with the observation predicates that figure in the reports.[11] If a calculus is known to be inconsistent and so

---

[11] Carnap's attitude here is strikingly expressed in (1939, §4 , 6): "The facts [about linguistic behavior] do not determine whether the use of a certain expression is

inadmissible, then it would be self-defeating to adopt it as the language of science. We would then be committed to accepting all the sentences of the calculus irrespective of our observations, and the O-predicates of the calculus could not be identified with the predicates that figure in observation reports. Although it would be foolish to adopt such a calculus, we should not call the logic built into the calculus by the transformation rules "wrong" or "incorrect." To repeat: on Carnap's view, these terms of criticism become available only relative to a calculus and its envisioned use as the language of science.

Carnap is cognizant of the Second Incompleteness Theorem and its ramifications. He gives an informal consistency proof for Language II, but remarks:

> Even if [the proof] contains no formal errors, it gives us no absolute certainty that contradictions in the object-language II cannot arise. For, since the proof is carried out in a syntax-language which has richer resources than Language II, we are in no wise guaranteed against the appearance of contradictions in this syntax-language, and thus in our proof.[12]

Carnap himself places no justificatory weight on the proof. We can now appreciate the deflationary character of Carnap's philosophy of mathematics. Gödel's conventionalist target contrasts empirical truth with the truth conferred by conventional stipulation. Carnap rejects this contrast; he rejects any thick notion of truth-in-virtue-of. For him, what is clear in this contrast is captured in the distinction within an empiricist language between L-determinate and L-indeterminate sentences. Carnap thus does not present in *Logical Syntax* an account of the nature of mathematics, of our knowledge of mathematics, and of the applications of mathematics in empirical science comparable to the accounts developed by Kant, Mill, Frege, Wittgenstein, and Hilbert. Carnap rejects the questions these thinkers address. In a sense, he gives up philosophy of mathematics. He proposes the transformation of debates in the foundations

---

right or wrong but only how often it occurs and how often it leads to the effect intended, and the like. A question of right or wrong must always refer to a system of rules."

[12] Carnap (1934c/1937, §34i, 129). A couple of sentences earlier Carnap notes that his consistency proof with the resources it employs does not satisfy the constraints of Hilbert's program.

of mathematics into the elaboration and investigation of various calculi.[13]

A revealing illustration of Carnap's attitude comes at the end of *Logical Syntax* in a section entitled "The Foundational Problem of Mathematics," where Carnap responds to Frege's critique of formalism. The formalists treat arithmetic as a notational game in which the arithmetical signs have no meaning. Frege objects that the formalists can account neither for the use of these meaningless mathematical signs in meaningful empirical sentences reporting the results of counting and measurement, nor for logical links between sentences containing mathematical signs and those that do not.[14] In contrast, Frege's analysis of the meanings of mathematical signs applies to all their occurrences and forges the desired logical connections. Carnap reconciles logicism with formalism by observing that there are calculi in which the arithmetical signs are taken as primitive and treated as the formalist treats them, but in which the logical connections between pure arithmetic and counting – the ones which for Frege are consequences of his analysis of number – still hold. In such a calculus, the arithmetical signs are given "meaning" by the links forged by the consequence relation between sentences of pure arithmetic and empirical sentences reporting the results of counting and measurement. Carnap concludes:

> *The requirement of logicism* is then formulated in this way: *the task of the logical foundation for mathematics is not fulfilled by a metamathematics,* (*that is, a syntax for mathematics*) *alone, but only by a syntax for a total language which contains* [vereinigt] *both logico-mathematical sentences and synthetic sentences.* (Carnap, 1934c/1937, §84, 327)

Carnap's stance in *Logical Syntax* toward the disputes in the foundations of mathematics he encountered in the 1920s is then of a piece with his stance towards traditional philosophical debates. Cognitive enquiry should be viewed as either a matter of framing and observationally testing theories within an empiricist language or establishing the validity or contravalidity of logico-mathematical sentences within a calculus. Apart from this, there is only the

---

[13] For a striking example of Carnap's attitude, see his discussion of impredicative higher-order quantification in the final paragraph of Carnap (1934c/1937, §44).

[14] For example, the logical equivalence of "The number of F = 2" and "There are distinct x and y which are both F, and any F is identical with either x or y."

syntactic description and investigation of calculi, including those that are candidates for adoption as the language of science. Logical syntax itself can be interpreted in a suitably strong arithmetic, and so belongs to pure mathematics. Philosophical distinctions survive only to the extent that they are reconstructible in syntactic terms. The futile wrangling of philosophy is obviated by the collaborative scientific discipline of logical syntax applied to candidates for the language of science (Carnap, 1934c/1937, §§72, 73, and 86).

III.

The means Carnap uses to build logic-mathematics of varying strengths into calculi raise further questions about his project. I have repeatedly noted that the logical-mathematical sentences in any calculus that is a candidate language of science are to be either L-valid or L-contravalid. However, Carnap talks of specifying the logical consequence relation of a calculus by transformation rules, and he informally characterizes logical syntax as "*combinatorial analysis* . . . the *geometry* of finite, discrete, serial structures . . ." (Carnap, 1934c/1937, §2, 7). Carnap's rhetoric suggests that his transformation rules take the form of a standard formal system, with its effective specification of axioms and inference rules. Now according to Gödel's First Incompleteness Theorem, there is no consistent, complete formalization of elementary arithmetic. So, there are, with respect to any formalization of mathematics that incorporates arithmetic, arithmetical truths that are not derivable in the formalization. It then seems that in any suitably powerful consistent calculus, among the L-indeterminate sentences we will find some purely arithmetical sentences. Carnap would not want to take such formally undecidable sentences of pure arithmetic to be synthetic sentences that are empirically testable. But to pronounce them neither analytically true nor analytically false nor empirically testable would align them uncomfortably close to the pseudo-sentences of metaphysics.

Carnap was in close contact with Gödel in the late 1920s and early 1930s, and *Logical Syntax* exhibits a thorough appreciation of the Incompleteness Theorems.[15] Carnap observes that a formula

---

[15] For discussions of Gödel's and Carnap's interactions in this period, see Awodey and Carus (2001) and Goldfarb (2005).

is derivable if it is obtainable from given axioms by finitely many applications of effective inference rules. He then epitomizes Gödel's Theorem: "Only Gödel has shown that not all analytic sentences are derivable" (Carnap, 1934c/1937, §10, 28; my translation). If Carnap's transformation rules are to capture the mathematical truths express-ible in his sample calculi, they must then be something more than the effective specification of axioms and inference rules. For Lan-guage I, Carnap circumvents the limitations set forth in Gödel's The-orem by supplementing a standard characterization of derivability for primitive recursive arithmetic with a definition of consequence that incorporates an infinitary inference rule. For Language II, Car-nap gives a complicated definition of "analytic" which he subse-quently recognizes to be equivalent to a Tarskian truth-definition for the purely logico-mathematical sentences of Language II (Carnap, 1942, 247). Thanks then to the strength of the mathematics Carnap helps himself to in his syntax language, he is able to frame syntactic surrogates for "analytic" and "contradictory" that mimic bivalent truth- and falsity-predicates over the logico-mathematical sentences of Language II.

Carnap's rhetoric can then easily mislead contemporary readers. This rhetoric suggests to our ears that Carnapian calculi are for-mal systems whose logical syntax will be interpretable within a sub-system of elementary arithmetic. Carnap, however, accepts no limitations on the strength of the mathematical resources of syn-tax languages. In order to render the logico-mathematical sentences of a suitably powerful calculus determinate, and so to build some portion of mathematics into the calculus, the syntax language must exploit even stronger mathematics. Carnap is fully aware of the situa-tion (see 1934c/1937, §60c). When Carnap speaks generally of logical syntax as developed within arithmetic, he conceives of arithmetic as an open-ended mathematical discipline that includes, as we would put it, arbitrarily strong set theoretic principles. He recognizes that the informal syntax language used to describe a calculus can itself be formalized as a calculus in a still stronger syntax language, and he envisions a hierarchy of calculi, each incorporating a stronger arithmetic than its predecessor, commenting, "[E]verything mathe-matical can be formalized, but mathematics cannot be exhausted by one system; it requires an infinite series of ever richer languages" (Carnap, 1934c/1937, §60d, 222).

Carnap's clarity about the situation shows how far he is from embracing the conventionalist account of mathematical truth. It would be viciously circular to claim that mathematical truths are true in virtue of conventional stipulation, if the very framing of the stipulation requires the use of even stronger mathematics.[16] I have argued that in fact the specification of a calculus bears no justificatory or explanatory weight that engenders vicious circularity here. Carnap's aim is to come up with a syntactic surrogate for the distinction between analytically true-or-false sentences and synthetic sentences, one which will place what are, colloquially speaking, the purely mathematical sentences of a calculus in the first category. To this end, Carnap employs in his meta-language the necessary mathematical means. The question of the status of these means, of their analyticity, should it arise, may be addressed by identifying the syntax language with a further calculus, observing that the mathematics in the formalized syntax language is analytic. In doing this, we use a yet stronger syntax language to formalize the original syntax language. Thus, the mathematics used at each level can be retrospectively construed to be analytic. There is no *petitio* here. Rather, Carnap's position is self-supporting at each level.

Nevertheless, there is something disappointing about Carnap's procedure here. Carnap proclaims the Principle of Tolerance, but adds the requirement that investigators in discussing the language they have adopted should describe the construction of that language in syntactic terms. In this way, the consequence relation that is constitutive of the language is made explicit. We can then distinguish what adoption of the object language commits us to from what it leaves open. I have noted how Carnap's informal syntax language must implicitly employ even stronger mathematics than it explicitly builds into the object language in order to reproduce syntactically the true–false dichotomy over the logical-mathematical sentences. Our grasp of the logic-mathematics to which adoption of

---

[16] As Friedman has noted, this objection is distinct from Gödel's objection examined in the previous section. See Friedman (1999b, sec. i, 200–205). Gödel's criticism concerns, not the mathematics used to describe a calculus, but the mathematics required to prove the admissibility of the calculus. The objection under consideration here is close kin to Quine's point in part iii of Quine (1936/1976): any alleged conventional stipulation of quantificational logic must use quantificational logic to frame the stipulation.

the object language would commit us is only as good as our grasp on the logic-mathematics implicit in the informal syntax language. The clarification afforded by Carnapian descriptions of candidate languages for science in making implicit logical-mathematical commitments explicit thus appears slight (cf. Goldfarb and Ricketts, 1992, 72; Richardson, 1994, 94).

The strength of the syntax languages Carnap uses raises questions about the compatibility of his logicism with the Principle of Tolerance.[17] On the one hand, Carnap's logicism is a matter of the determinacy of logical-mathematical sentences within an empiricist language. The determinacy of these sentences explicates their status as notational auxiliaries to empirically testable theories in the language of science. On the other hand, adoption of the Principle of Tolerance is to give scientifically minded investigators a way to avoid fruitless, ill-defined wrangling over the foundations of mathematics. Proponents of different foundational approaches are to elaborate calculi that embody their outlook and restrictions. They then are to investigate the metamathematical properties of their calculi. These results will in turn figure in the advocacy of one or another calculus as the logical-mathematical core of the language of science. As adherents to Tolerance, the participants in this discussion will recognize that there is no right and wrong, no correct and incorrect in this choice. This vision of how adoption of Tolerance replaces sterile debates in foundations of mathematics with the construction and investigation of calculi appears to assume that proponents of different foundational approaches will share a common syntax language in which to present and discuss their proposed candidates for the language of science. We have seen, however, that Carnap's logicism requires the use of a very strong syntax language to describe a calculus that contains classical mathematics. Moreover, given the constraints of Carnap's logicism, even the syntax language for Language I, with its infinitary consequence rule, goes beyond anything most constructivists would accept. The price, then, of Carnap's logicism is the absence of a shared syntax language that affords proponents of different logics a common perspective from which to describe and acknowledge their differences. In this way, Carnap's logicism seems to block the conciliation that Tolerance offers.

---

[17] In (1999b, sec. vi, 226–231), Friedman argued that there is an incompatibility here.

Carnap himself shows no awareness of any difficulty here. Quite the contrary. In §45 of *Logical Syntax*, Carnap affirms that the Principle of Tolerance applies equally to the object language and the syntax language, while noting that adoption of a weak syntax language may bar the definition of various syntactic notions:

Our attitude towards the question of indefinite terms conforms to the principle of tolerance; in constructing a language we can either exclude such terms (as we have done in Language I) or admit them (as in Language II). It is a matter to be decided by convention . . . Now this holds equally for the terms of syntax. If we use a definite language in the formalization of a syntax (e.g., Language I in our formal construction), then only definite syntactical terms may be defined. Some important terms of the syntax of transformations are, however, indefinite (in general); as, for instance, "derivable," "demonstrable," and *a fortiori* "analytic," "contradictory," "synthetic," "consequence," "content," and so on. If we wish to introduce these terms also, we must employ an indefinite syntax-language (such as Language II).[18]

To understand Carnap's attitude here we need to consider both the status of Carnap's logism and the kind of conciliation the Principle of Tolerance offers proponents of different foundational approaches.

As already noted, Carnap is explicit that his empiricism is a proposal, not a thesis. It is the proposal that we restrict candidate languages of science to empiricist languages. I maintain that his logism also has the status of a proposal: it is the recommendation that candidate languages of science be restricted to those in which sentences constructed from just the logico-mathematical vocabulary are calculus-determinate. In Carnap's eyes, this explication of logism in the context of his explication of empiricist languages does not unduly constrain the choice of a language of science. After all, Carnap's Language I, with its very restricted mathematical resources, satisfies the requirements of logism. Indeed, it is an advantage of Carnap's proposal that it separates the explication of the special status of logic-mathematics from the question of the strength of logic-mathematics.

Of course, a proponent of a weak logic who is unwilling to use a stronger logic to set forth a proposed language of science that satisfies the requirements of Carnap's logism, let alone to contrast

18 Carnap (1934c/1937, §45, 165f.). An indefinite term in a syntax language is one for whose application there is no decision procedure.

her proposed logic with other stronger logics, will not be able to avail herself of Carnap's explication of the difference between mathematics and natural science. For the Carnapian, the attractions of this explication give such a constructively minded logician strong motivation to use stronger meta-languages to set forth and compare languages of science. Our tolerant, scientifically minded proponent of a weak logic may remain obdurate here. She then either owes her fellow logicians of science an alternative explication of the distinctive status of mathematics vis-à-vis natural science, or she must give up this explicatory task.[19] In any event, the reluctance of a proponent of a weak logic to accept Carnap's explication of logicism on account of the strong syntax language it requires does not give the Carnapian who has no such qualms a reason to reject Carnap's explication of logicism. Carnap first recommends the Principle of Tolerance to direct the energies of scientifically minded philosophers away from fruitless wrangling. To those who adopt it, Carnap recommends constraints on candidate languages of science. Of course, someone might reject these recommendations without giving up Tolerance. That's the point of calling them recommendations. Carnap's understanding of logicism and empiricism is framed by the Principle of Tolerance. There is no inconsistency or tension in Carnap's thought here.

Let us now turn to the conciliation of divergent foundational viewpoints that the Principle of Tolerance offers. Despite the name, the Principle of Tolerance is not itself a principle, a thesis that is correct or incorrect. It is rather an attitude that saps foundational debates. To take up the attitude of Tolerance is to accept that there is no correct or incorrect in the choice of a formalism as the language for science and so to give up any assumption of language-transcendent standards of truth and falsity. Hence, after adoption of Tolerance, there is no work of conciliation of divergent foundational positions that remains to be done. There is just the metamathematical investigation of various calculi and the advocacy on grounds of expediency of adoption of one or another calculus as the language of science.

Proponents of weaker logics who take up the attitude of Tolerance thus surrender the arguments they once advanced against the

---

[19] For a discussion of the drawbacks of explicating logicism in relatively weak logical terms, see Goldfarb and Ricketts (1992, pt. iii, 72–78).

use of stronger logics. There is nothing inconsistent or untoward in an advocate of weak logic for the language of science using a strong meta-language both to set forth her favored language and to compare it with other proposed languages for science. Nevertheless, a tolerant advocate of a weaker logic *may* balk at the use of a strong meta-language. Carnap always presents the biggest attraction of weaker logics to be the greater security they offer against inconsistency. This desire may operate, not only as regards the choice of a language for science, but also in meta-logical investigations. The refusal of our advocate of a weaker logic to use a strong meta-language does not, however, close off the prospect of metamathematical comparisons of calculi. In such circumstances, the discussants will have to restrict themselves to those descriptions of the languages under consideration that are available in a meta-language they all share. This may represent no serious loss, if, for example, their differences can be brought out by reference to the formal systems of derivation associated with each language under consideration. Of course, as Carnap notes, restriction to a weak syntax language may block some definitions and comparisons.[20]

There is one further point to be made on this topic. Carnap himself is not neutral as to the choice of the underlying logic for the language of science. He favors the adoption of a language that builds in classical mathematics. In advocating Tolerance, Carnap urges that the proponent of a strong logic for science need not answer the objections of constructively minded mathematicians. Carnap's philosophy of mathematics does not justify his own logical preference; it does, however, as Alan Richardson has noted, remove objections to it.[21] There is a parallel in Carnap's final attitude to the realism–idealism

[20] Carnap's only concrete treatment of this situation comes in (1963c, 872–873). There Carnap imagines a discussion between one logician who accepts only sets whose members are urelements and a second whose sets are themselves members of further sets. Carnap indicates that the first logician does not understand everything the second logician says, but notes that to some extent the two logicians can contrast their respective formalisms in terms that don't draw on the stronger set theory. Carnap's overarching point in the passage is to illustrate pseudo-statements (external statements) in ontology. In (1963d, 929f.), Carnap says that there is no common language for a classical mathematician to communicate her convictions to an intuitionistic mathematician.

[21] Richardson (1994) suggests that the hidden agenda of the Principle of Tolerance is to remove philosophical objections to the mathematics that the best contemporary natural science relies on.

debate.[22] Carnap thinks there is no well-defined question here; what is at issue is the choice of the form for an observation language in the language of science. In the protocol language debate, Carnap comes to favor use of a realistic observation language, one that speaks of observationally detectible qualities and relations of material bodies. His understanding of the realism–idealism debate removes idealist objections to this choice.

IV.

I have been describing Carnap's philosophy of mathematics in *Logical Syntax*. After 1936, under Tarski's influence, semantics comes to occupy the role previously played by syntax in Carnap's thought. From now on, Carnap will take the core of the description of a formal language to be a truth definition for the language. The calculi of *Logical Syntax* become the semantical systems of Carnap's later writings. I noted both the strength of Carnap's syntax, and how the logical syntax for strong calculi incorporates in effect a truth definition for their logical-mathematical portions. We should then be cautious in evaluating the significance of the shift to semantics, especially as regards Carnap's philosophy of mathematics. I shall argue that Carnap's view of mathematics as a notational auxiliary to empirical science remains basically unchanged.

To understand the significance of the switch to semantics for Carnap's philosophy of mathematics, we need first to consider a further aspect of Carnap's view of logic and mathematics in *Logical Syntax*. So far, I have presented Carnap as defining a consequence relation, a *logical* consequence relation, over the formulas of a calculus. This is more or less Carnap's procedure in describing Languages I and II.[23] However, in constructing a calculus as a candidate for the language of science, we may wish, in addition to logic-mathematics, to incorporate into the calculus a formalization of some body of empirical theory (cf. Carnap, 1934c/1937, §§40 and 57). This formalization can be described in syntactic terms – an important point to which we shall return. In the transformation rules of a calculus, we have then the L-rules, which mention primitive logical-mathematical

---

[22] I am indebted to Warren Goldfarb for this comparison.
[23] For Language II, Carnap defines "consequence in II" in terms of "analytic in II."

vocabulary, and P-rules, which mentions descriptive vocabulary. This division of primitive signs into logical and descriptive is given by a list supported only by some inchoate sense of the intended use of the signs, were the calculus to be adopted as the language of science.

Carnap wants to do better here. He supposes that we are given calculi by means of a specification of formation and transformation rules, but without any separation of the latter into L-rules and P-rules. The consequence relation over the formulas of the calculus cannot then be assumed to be restricted to logical consequence. Carnap offers a general syntactic criterion for the primitive logical signs of a calculus, and uses this definition to define L-consequence as a restriction of the consequence relation. Call a formula of a calculus *valid* (*not* L-valid), if it is a consequence of the null class of formulas; a formula is *contravalid*, if it has every formula as a consequence. Carnap's idea is that the transformation rules of a calculus fix the use of the logical-mathematical vocabulary in that every formula constructed solely from logical vocabulary is either valid or contravalid. In *Logical Syntax* (§50), Carnap accordingly defines the primitive logical vocabulary of the calculus along the following lines: the primitive logical vocabulary of the calculus is the largest vocabulary of uncompounded, undefined expressions such that there are sentences constructed solely from that vocabulary and any such sentence is valid or contravalid. The logical vocabulary of the calculus yields a notion of logical form that in turn can be used to characterize L-consequence in terms of consequence.[24]

Carnap's characterization leads to counterintuitive divisions of primitive signs into the logical and descriptive in many formalisms.[25] But let us put such objections to one side, and restrict attention to those calculi for which Carnap's characterization yields the desired distinction. The success of Carnap's explication of "logical sign" depends on the incompleteness of the classification of sentences as valid and contravalid, i.e., on their being sentences containing empirical vocabulary that are neither valid nor contravalid. Despite the mathematical strength Carnap permits in his syntax

---

[24] See Carnap (1934c/1937, §§51–52) for Carnap's general syntax definitions of L-consequence, analytic, and contradictory. Carnap characterizes both consequence and L-consequence as a relation between sets of formulas and individual formulas.

[25] For this sort of objection to Carnap, see Mac Lane (1938), Quine (1963/1976, §vii), and Creath (1996).

languages, he is confident that any syntactic definitions of "valid" and "contravalid" for a candidate language of science will be incomplete. Recall that the vocabulary of Carnap's syntax language is limited to arithmetic, including set theory. The syntax language thus lacks descriptive vocabulary. Carnap sees that with these resources we can reproduce the logical-mathematical distinctions of an object language in the syntax meta-language, and so in effect define "true" and "false" for the logical-mathematical part of the object language. But the only way Carnap sees to extend these definitions to descriptive sentences is simply to stipulate the validity of a syntactically specified class of sentences, thus incorporating some portion of currently accepted science into the valid object language formulas. Carnap reasonably thinks that this procedure is bound to leave some sentences containing descriptive predicates indeterminate, classifying them neither as valid nor as contravalid.[26] This is the point he makes in *Logical Syntax*, when he says:

> For truth and falsehood are not proper syntactical properties; whether a sentence is true or false cannot generally be seen by its design, that is to say, by the kinds and serial order of its symbols. [This fact has usually been overlooked by logicians, because, for the most part, they have been dealing not with descriptive but only with logical languages, and in relation to these, certainly "true" and "false" coincide with "analytic" and "contradictory," respectively, and are thus syntactical terms.][27]

Tarski shows how a bivalent truth predicate can be defined over both the logical-mathematical and the descriptive sentences in languages of interest to Carnap in a meta-language with the logical-mathematical resources of Carnap's syntax languages. Tarski's success comes at a price: a Tarskian truth definition must use descriptive predicates *in the meta-language* to specify satisfaction conditions for

---

[26] Suppose our language for science is a coordinate language in which fundamental physical magnitudes are functions that assign values to coordinates labeling space-time positions. There will then be an infinity of formulas, each of which assigns a value to a point. Carnap sees no way in a syntactic meta-language of reproducing the true–false dichotomy over these sentences.

[27] Carnap (1934c/1937, §60b, 216). This is the reason why Carnap in *Logical Syntax* maintains that the notion of truth, as opposed to logical truth (analyticity), is not a syntactic notion and so is irrelevant to logic and its application to the logic of science. For further discussion of this point and Carnap's reception of Tarski's technique for defining truth, see Ricketts (1996, especially §ii).

object language descriptive predicates. The truth predicate Tarski defines does not then count as syntactic by Carnap's standard. Still, the use of descriptive predicates to state satisfaction conditions for descriptive predicates is innocent enough, for Tarskian truth definitions build in no information about the extensions of descriptive predicates they use. From the perspective of Tarski's truth definitions, we see Carnap's general syntax definition of the logical/descriptive distinction in application to serious candidates for the language of science to depend on the wholesale exclusion of descriptive predicates from the meta-language, even in definitions and the extraction of logical consequences from definitions. Tarski's work renders this exclusion arbitrary. In order to avail himself of Tarskian truth definitions, Carnap permits the use of descriptive language in his meta-language. This use of descriptive predicates in the metalinguistic specification of a formal language constitutes in the first instance Carnap's shift from syntax to semantics.[28]

Carnap's leading idea after the adoption of semantics is that the truth of the L-valid sentences of an object language is logically implied *in the meta-language* by the truth definition for the object language.[29] Carnap's general post-syntax characterization of L-truth – the L-truths are the object language formulas whose truth is a logical consequence of the truth definition for the object language in the meta-language – cannot replace the old general syntax definition. For the new characterization is stated in a meta-meta-language and defines L-truth for the original object language in terms of logical consequence *for the meta-language*, a notion that itself stands in need of definition. What we have here is not a general definition of L-truth across languages but rather, Carnap tells us, an adequacy condition on definitions of L-truth.[30]

If we have isolated the logical vocabulary of a language, then we might adapt the definition of L-validity from *Logical Syntax* to define

---

[28] See Carnap (1939). In (1942), Carnap introduces an apparatus of intensional notions to describe semantical systems.

[29] The T-sentences for all object language sentences are deducible in the meta-language from the truth definition. In the case of logico-mathematical object language sentences, the right-hand side of the T-sentence is, for Carnap, a meta-language logical truth. Hence, the left-hand side of the T-sentence, the predication of truth to an object language formula, is a logical consequence of the truth definition.

[30] See Carnap (1942, 83–84).

L-truth for the language in terms of truth. The isolation of logical vocabulary gives us a notion of logical form for the sentences of the language. A sentence is L-true, if every sentence of the language that shares its logical form is true.[31] The problem, then, of a replacement for the general syntax characterization of L-notions reduces to the problem of replacing the general syntax definition of the logical-descriptive distinction. Carnap says of this problem:

> Here it is the question whether and how "logical" and "descriptive" can be defined on the basis of other semantical terms, e.g., "designation" and "true," so that the application of the general definition to any particular system will lead to a result which is in accordance with the intended distinction. A satisfactory solution is not yet known. (1942, 59)

Carnap never proposes a solution to this problem, and appears not to have pursued it further.[32] He never treats the absence of a general characterization of L-true and L-consequence as threatening his view of the logical-mathematical sentences of a candidate language of science as notational auxiliaries. Earlier in *Introduction to Semantics*, Carnap comments that in practice there is usually no dispute as to which primitive signs of a particular language are to be logical-mathematical and which are to be descriptive.[33] In any particular case, we can then make this distinction fully precise by lists. We can then go on to define L-truth for particular languages, at least extensional languages, along the lines just indicated, and so count all the purely mathematical sentences as L-true or L-false. This suffices, Carnap believes, to sustain his philosophy of mathematics.

At this point, we may, along with Quine, wonder whether there is anything of substance left in Carnap's position. In section vii of "Carnap and Logical Truth," Quine considers Carnap's general syntax definition of L-validity from *Logical Syntax*. Alluding to Tarskian truth definitions, Quine objects that if we add the descriptive vocabulary of our object language to the meta-language, we can broaden the compass of our demarcation of truth for the object language to embrace the sentences of "physics, economics, and anything else

---

[31] Carnap discusses a variant on this suggestion in (1942, §16, 86–87).
[32] For further discussion of the evolution of Carnap's views here after his adoption of semantical methods, see Ricketts (1996, §iii) and Steve Awodey's contribution to this volume.
[33] Carnap (1942, §13, 58; cf. 1942, §16, 84).

under the sun . . . No special trait of logic and mathematics has been singled out after all" (Quine, 1963/1976, 125). Moreover, Quine rejects Carnap's claim to have illuminated the status of logic and mathematics as notational auxiliaries on a language-by-language basis. Any list of vocabulary for a language can be used to introduce a notion of form. We can then use this notion of form and a truth predicate for the language to mark out the truths of the language that essentially contain the privileged vocabulary.[34] Suppose the vocabulary on our list excludes observation predicates. Then, if we wish, we can go on to hold observation to be irrelevant to the evaluation of the sentences in our favored class as true or false. But this is an attitude we take up towards the sentences of the favored class, not one revealed by its definition. No principled asymmetry between mathematics and non-observational sentences of empirical science has been established.

Quine is happy to deny that there is a sharp and principled epistemic difference between mathematics and natural science. In contrast, Carnap, like almost every mathematician, scientist, and philosopher in the modern era, recognizes a deep difference between mathematics and natural science: in a word, sense experience is relevant to science but irrelevant to mathematics. He aims to provide a way of understanding this difference that avoids the thickets of philosophical wrangling which have arisen from consideration of this difference. We have examined the explication of this difference Carnap provides via the description of various formal languages, possible languages for science, under the aegis of the attitude of Tolerance with the language-relativized understanding of truth that Tolerance enforces. However, given the resources Carnap deploys in order to build mathematics into his preferred formal languages, many will find Carnap's treatment of the difference between mathematics and natural science more a labeling than an explication, and so no more satisfying than Quine's denial of a sharp difference.[35]

---

[34] See Quine's characterization of logical truth in (1963/1976, §ii).
[35] I have benefited from comments from Michael Friedman and Warren Goldfarb on earlier versions of this chapter.

STEVE AWODEY*

10 Carnap's quest for analyticity: the *Studies in Semantics*[1]

I. FROM SYNTAX TO SEMANTICS

Carnap's project to construct a comprehensive language of science, which occupied his attention from about 1935 to 1945, was centered on his search for a satisfactory definition of logical truth, or *analyticity*. The need for such a definition grew out of the logical syntax program he had first conceived in early 1931, which dropped the conception of meaning of Wittgenstein's *Tractatus* (1922) and instead applied the metalinguistic methods of Hilbert, Tarski, and Gödel to the scientific language as a whole.[2]

Specifically, the need for a definition of analyticity had been precipitated by Gödel's Incompleteness Theorem, which had shown that there are apparently true sentences of arithmetic that are not logically provable, even given the axioms of arithmetic. Before this, the obvious criterion of logical and mathematical truth had always been provability, but Gödel had shown that this identification is unfounded and that logical and mathematical truth could not be understood as provability in a fixed axiom system. This not only threatened the logicist thesis of the logical character of all mathematical truth; it also called into question the fundamental tenet of logical empiricism that non-empirical (a priori) knowledge is analytic

---

* This chapter is closely related to a paper written in collaboration with André W. Carus, and still owes very much to him. I also thank Michael Friedman, Greg Frost-Arnold, and Leonard Linsky for helpful comments.
[1] Dedicated to Saunders Mac Lane.
[2] The story of this revolution in Carnap's thought, which came all at once on a sleepless night in January 1931, is told in full in the paper "Carnap's Dream: Wittgenstein, Gödel, and *Logical Syntax*" (Awodey and Carus, 2007), which is summarized in the first half of this section.

in the sense of being trivial and ultimately tautological. It was in this way, in fact, that the Vienna Circle developed a new "logical" brand of empiricism through a novel combination of two recent scientific advances: Wittgenstein's notion of tautology and Frege–Russell logicism. This new doctrine solved empiricism's traditional problem of the status of mathematics in a way that had not been conceivable before.

The Incompleteness Theorem, however, showed that mere logical provability would not suffice to characterize even the logical truths, if these were to include the truths of arithmetic. Carnap's logical syntax program needed to provide a criterion stronger than provability for logical and mathematical truth – which would determine the logical truth or falsity of every purely logical sentence. To this end, Carnap not only dropped Wittgenstein's conception of meaning, as given by the "picture theory" of the *Tractatus*, but went to the extreme of dropping *all* talk of "meaning" whatsoever. The philosophical meta-language, in this view, was restricted to statements about the formal, syntactic structure of the scientific language; it could say nothing about what linguistic signs "mean" or "refer to" outside of language. This restriction to the "formal mode of speech" was to be observed in formulating all concepts in the logic of science, including the concept of analyticity. In the "material mode of speech," by contrast, entities outside of language are also referred to, together with linguistic signs (e.g. "this paper is about Carnap"). Though perhaps unavoidable in everyday life, such talk was to be employed in the meta-language of science only when it was clear that it could be translated back into the formal mode ("this paper contains the word 'Carnap'").

This ensured that everything we could say in the philosophical meta-language would be strictly formal and devoid of all empirical content. Languages were constituted by rules – formation rules for well-formed formulas and transformation rules specifying how expressions of certain kinds could be transformed into other expressions. The purpose of a criterion of analyticity, then, was to specify the conditions under which an assertion in the scientific object language "holds" solely in virtue of these formal rules – in ordinary language, whether it is "logically true."

To see what Carnap was looking for, an analogy may help. The rules of a language have often been compared to the rules of a game, like chess. Think of the starting position of the pieces on the chess-board as the axioms, the permitted moves as the rules of inference, and a sequence of moves ending in checkmate as the proof of a theorem which is represented by the final position. But there are configurations of pieces on a chessboard constituting checkmate that can't be reached from the starting position by any sequence of permitted moves – such a position is the chess equivalent of an analytic sentence that can't be proved. In the same way, the desired definition of analyticity should be stated entirely in terms of purely formal properties, yet still be wider than the criteria for provability.

Carnap's first attempt to state such a formal criterion, in the first draft of *Logical Syntax of Language*, was intended to be definitive. He wanted to arrive at *the* correct definition of analyticity for the scientific language he was proposing. But this definition turned out to be defective, as Gödel pointed out to him in the autumn of 1932. The problem reduced to the fact that truth can only be defined in a meta-language having more expressive resources than the object language – which would become known to the world a few years later as Tarski's Theorem on the Indefinability of Truth.[3]

Carnap went back to work and came up with a new definition of analyticity, using a stronger meta-language. But he soon realized that this new definition was somewhat arbitrary, since it depended on the choice of a particular meta-language. No such definition, it seemed, was uniquely correct, canonical, or privileged. There might be a "natural" choice from some point of view (e.g. using third-order logic for the language of second-order logic) or one that was very useful for some particular purpose (e.g. using set theory for extensional languages), but this was far from being "correct" in the way he had originally sought. Having realized this, Carnap made his second big break with the Vienna Circle's past: now, in late 1932, he broke with the idea of "correctness" (and of a single, correct scientific language) altogether. The result was a thoroughgoing linguistic pluralism, together with the Principle of Tolerance, whereby the

---

[3] Carnap had attempted to give what we would now call a "substitutional" interpretation of higher-order quantification. Gödel pointed out that this cannot work for impredicative languages like the simple type theory that Carnap was using. See Gödel (2003, 346–356) for the exchange at issue, and Awodey and Carus (2007) for a fuller discussion.

language of science was freely choosable subject only to the condition of practical usefulness.

With this tectonic shift, the position of analyticity within the overall theory also changed fundamentally. Before this, the "correct" definition of analyticity had been something to be *discovered*, now it became something to be *specified*. Logical truth became a matter of convention, to be decided on grounds of utility and purpose. According to the Principle of Tolerance:

[We] *do not want to impose restrictions but to state conventions . . . In logic there are no morals.* Everyone can construct his logic, i.e. his language form, however he wants. If we wants to discuss it with us, though, he will have to make precise how we wants to set things up. He has to give syntactic rules rather than philosophical considerations. (Carnap, 1934c, 45)

But Carnap had barely published the final version of *Logical Syntax* (1934c), when he was already shocking his Vienna Circle friends by saying that the bad old word "meaning," which they had just agreed to proscribe, could now be used after all. After reading Tarski's famous paper on truth (Tarski, 1936a), he concluded that Tarski had offered a fitting replacement, defined by precise rules, of the common-sense concepts of "meaning" and "truth."[4] According to his own doctrine of Tolerance, these could therefore be readmitted, provided we agree to let our use of them be guided by Tarski's precise definitions. So we can now study not only the *syntax* of the scientific language, but also its *semantics*.

It may be that Carnap was led to accept Tarski's semantics, not only by adherence to the Principle of Tolerance, but also in the hope that he might use it to find a satisfactory general characterization of analyticity.[5] What is certain is that finding such a semantic characterization soon became the focus of his research. The definition of analyticity he had arrived at in *Logical Syntax* was, for the particular language Carnap was considering (arithmetic), essentially the same as Tarski's later definition of semantical truth. But Tarski's definition also encompassed languages of a more general kind, also containing non-logical (empirical) terms, and this well suited Carnap's purpose

---

4 Actually, Carnap was familiar with Tarski's work much earlier, from private conversations as well as the note Tarski (1932).

5 There is some evidence for this in the appendix to Carnap (1942), which indicates a number of difficulties with the syntax program that are solved by semantics.

of treating logic and mathematics as part of the larger language of total science. Thus, in accepting Tarski's semantics, Carnap had to directly face a problem he had already confronted (unsuccessfully, as we will see) in part IV of *Logical Syntax*: distinguishing *logical* truth in particular from general semantic truth in such more general languages.

In Tarski's theory of truth there was no inherent difference between mathematical and empirical truth.[6] The truth predicate applied equally to all sentences, without distinguishing a special class of "logical" sentences. What Carnap needed analyticity for in this new context was to distinguish the logical (and mathematical) from the empirical truths. This distinction, he thought, was not just an artifact of intuition, but had a fundamental practical importance for science. Einstein had said (in a passage often cited by Carnap): "Insofar as the sentences of mathematics refer to reality, they are not certain, and insofar as they are certain, they do not refer to reality . . . I place such a high value on this conception of geometry because without it, the discovery of the theory of relativity would have been impossible for me" (Einstein, 1921, 3–6).[7]

In his successive attempts to give a precise formulation of this distinction after 1935 Carnap seems to have been guided by two further pragmatic constraints, which together represent a sort of design preference for suitable languages of science. First, the analytic truths should capture at least customary logical reasoning. While it was certainly permissible to consider languages with wildly different logics, those Carnap actually considered were usually extensions of classical predicate logic, as is widely used in scientific and everyday reasoning. Second, Carnap required that the logical and mathematical sentences be *determinate*, in the sense that every sentence of logic

---

[6] One must distinguish between Tarski's definition of semantic truth and the later notion of "universal validity" in what is sometimes called "Tarskian semantics," i.e., model theory. I return to this point below.

[7] See, for example, Carnap (1966, 257): "In my opinion, a sharp analytic–synthetic distinction is of supreme importance for the philosophy of science. The theory of relativity could not have been developed if Einstein had not realized that the structure of physical space and time cannot be determined without physical tests. He saw clearly the sharp dividing line that must always be kept in mind between pure mathematics, with its many types of logically consistent geometries, and physics, in which only experiment and observation can determine which geometries can be applied most usefully to the physical world."

or mathematics should be either analytic or contradictory. This constraint of determinacy may originally have derived from Carnap's assumption of classical logic,[8] but was more likely due to his overarching intent to portray mathematics as *contentless* as required by logical empiricism's Wittgensteinian interpretation of Frege's logicism.[9] In the total language of science mathematics was to be a tool or instrument for reasoning about empirical data, the use of which should imply no new non-logical propositions. Requiring logical and mathematical sentences to be determinate was a way of ensuring that they had no empirical consequences or premises.

I shall return to these constraints in the concluding section. For now, I restrict attention to the quest for analyticity under these conditions. As we shall see, Carnap's successive attempts, using Tarskian semantics and modal logic, respectively, were hampered by an odd blindness to reapplying certain of his own ideas from earlier investigations. It remained for others to recognize how to put the pieces together in a way that would lead to important logical advances.

II. THE FIRST ATTEMPT: WHAT IS LOGIC?

In one of the very first reviews of *Logical Syntax*, the young Saunders Mac Lane pointed out that there is a fundamental flaw in the all-important, general definition of analyticity.[10] Carnap had, in

---

[8] See "Eigentliche und uneigentliche Begriffe" (Carnap, 1927) for a related discussion.

[9] Carnap's Wittgensteinian understanding of logicism survived his rejection of the *Tractatus* picture theory of meaning. See the well-known passage in Carnap (1963a, 25): "For me personally, Wittgenstein was perhaps the philosopher who, besides Russell and Frege, had the greatest influence on my thinking. The most important insight I gained from his work was the conception that the truth of logical statements is based only on their logical structure and on the meaning of the terms. Logical statements are true under all conceivable circumstances; thus their truth is independent of the contingent facts of the world. On the other hand, it follows that these statements do not say anything about the world and thus have no factual content."

[10] See Mac Lane (1938). The distinguished mathematician Saunders Mac Lane is known today as one of the co-inventors of category theory, an abstract approach to mathematical structures. When the English translation of *Logical Syntax* appeared in 1937, Mac Lane had just returned from David Hilbert's Göttingen – the world center of mathematics at the time – with a doctorate under Hermann Weyl and Paul Bernays, which he had earned with a thesis in logic.

effect, defined logical truth (L-truth) for the language of arithmetic recursively:

$a = b$ is *analytic*   iff $[a] = [b]$
$F(a)$ is *analytic*   iff $[a]$ is an element of $[F]$
$\neg P$ is *analytic*   iff P is not analytic
$P \,\&\, Q$ is *analytic*   iff P is analytic and Q is analytic
$(\forall x)F(x)$ is *analytic*   iff $F(a)$ is analytic for all numerical
                          constants a,

where $[a]$, $[b]$, and $[F]$ denote the interpretations of the symbols a, b, and F with respect to a given interpretation of the basic symbols (elements and sub-sets, respectively, of the given domain of quantification).[11] From a modern perspective, this is essentially the same procedure as Tarski's definition of truth *in a fixed interpretation* – but it is also suitable as a definition of *logical* truth because we are here dealing only with arithmetical terms, and the theory of arithmetic is categorical, so that *any* model of the axioms is isomorphic to the natural numbers. It therefore turns out that a sentence P of arithmetic is true in a given interpretation just if it is true in all interpretations, i.e., just if it is logically true. It then follows that any given sentence is either a logical truth or contradiction, i.e., all sentences are determinate, as a consequence of the law of excluded middle.

This special case was Carnap's starting point and paradigm in his later semantic investigations, but the special nature of arithmetic results in some features that are not typical of logical languages in general. In particular, this kind of recursive definition can be used to define semantic *truth in an interpretation* for more general languages but not *logical* truth. For instance, the sentence "Chicago is in Illinois" is not logically true, but neither is "Chicago is not in Illinois." Thus, for languages that may also include non-logical terms (like "Chicago"), it becomes essential for Carnap to be able to distinguish the logical from the non-logical or "descriptive" sentences. For then the "logical truths" will be simply those logical sentences that are true in virtue of the general recursive definition of truth. These

---

[11] The semantics for predicate quantification had originally caused the difficulty pointed out by Gödel, and is rather more complicated. Again, see Awodey and Carus (2007) for a fuller discussion.

sentences should still be determinate in general, independently of the interpretation of the non-logical terms.

In *Logical Syntax* Carnap had the ingenious idea of using determinacy to characterize the individual logical *symbols*, and then letting the logical sentences be those consisting entirely of such symbols:

> If a material interpretation is given for a language S, then the symbols, expressions, and sentences of S may be divided into logical and descriptive, i.e. those which have a purely logical, or mathematical, meaning and those which designate something extra-logical – such as empirical objects, properties, and so forth. This classification is not only inexact but also nonformal, and thus is not applicable in syntax. But if we reflect that all the connections between logico-mathematical terms are independent of extralinguistic factors, such as, for instance, empirical observations, and that they must be solely and completely determined by the transformation rules of the language, we find the formally expressible distinguishing peculiarity of logical symbols and expressions to consist in the fact that each sentence constructed solely from them is determinate. (Carnap, 1934c/1937, 177)

The idea is to define the logical symbols as the largest collection of symbols such that every sentence constructed only from them is determinate on the basis of the transformation rules.

Mac Lane showed that this definition is mathematically unworkable, at least along the lines laid out by Carnap.[12] Mac Lane also considered some possible modifications and demonstrated their defects as well. He concluded: "Such technical points might raise doubts as to the philosophical thesis Carnap wishes to establish here: that in any language whatsoever one can find a uniquely defined 'logical' part of the language, and that 'logic' and 'science' can be clearly distinguished."[13] As a result, Mac Lane proposed that the basic concepts of general syntax be treated "in a more postulational manner." Such an axiomatic approach to logical truth would indeed have been good Hilbertian practice (compare note 10 above), but it was incompatible

---

[12] The problem is that, in general, there is no *unique* such maximal set of symbols. While there are various different sets that are maximal, in the sense that they admit no further extension, the intersection of all such sets (as Carnap proposes) is itself no longer maximal. The situation is similar to one arising frequently in abstract algebra, as Mac Lane surely recognized.

[13] See Mac Lane (1938, 174; cf. 173–175). Of course, this would later be the nub of Quine's critique of Carnap's analytic synthetic–distinction (Quine, 1951), although Quine does not mention Mac Lane's prior work.

with the modified logicist program that Carnap had adopted after 1931 (see section IV below). In particular, Carnap's notion of logical truth had to be extensive enough to determine all propositions of logic and mathematics, but no conventional, deductive axiomatic system could do this in light of the incompleteness theorem. Moreover, the idea of axiomatizing logical truth directly seemed remote from Carnap's point of view and incompatible with the rest of his program.[14]

If he ignored Mac Lane's advice to take a more "postulational" approach, Carnap did grasp the problem of distinguishing the logical part of the language. Nevertheless, in his first semantical efforts he had little to offer by way of a solution. In *Foundations of Logic and Mathematics* (Carnap, 1939), where the new semantic point of view is first presented, a "logical" calculus is distinguished from other calculi simply in virtue of its "customary interpretation."[15] Soon thereafter Carnap embarked on the more ambitious *Studies in Semantics*. The first volume to be written, *Formalization of Logic* (Carnap, 1943), was devoted, among other things, to the problem of a semantic characterization of the formal logical operations.[16] The semantic notion of truth was investigated in *Introduction to Semantics* (Carnap, 1942), published before but written after *Formalization of Logic*. Finally, a different approach using modal logic was pursued in *Meaning and Necessity* (Carnap, 1947).

In the Appendix to *Introduction to Semantics*, where the modifications required to *Logical Syntax* are indicated, Carnap (1942, 247) writes: "The most important change concerns the distinction between logical and descriptive signs, and the related distinction between *logical and factual truth*. It seems to me at present that

---

[14] Quine (1951) disparages the arbitrariness of simply labeling certain sentences as "analytic." Mac Lane recognized the incompatibility of the proposed axiomatic approach with Carnap's modified logicism, and some 50 years later counted himself – along with Gödel, Quine, and Kuhn – as one of the "Four Assassins of Logical Empiricism" (in a conference talk at the University of Chicago in 1997 in honor of W. W. Tait).

[15] According to Carnap (1939, 29): "[t]his classification is rather rough and is only meant to serve as a temporary, practical purpose," but no improved or less "rough" criterion is to be found later in the book.

[16] The subject of this book, more generally, is the relation between the (syntactic) formalization of the logical operations and their semantics. See Belnap and Massey (1990) for one recent discussion.

these distinctions have to be made primarily in semantics, not in syntax" (Carnap, 1942, 47). Unfortunately, however, Carnap's treatment of this issue is one of the most unsatisfactory features of the book.

Following Tarski's early semantic theory, Carnap defines a "semantic system" as a formal language together with an interpretation in a meta-language determining which formal sentences are true and false. Thus, for example, suppose the formal language consists of:

Names: a, b, c
Predicates: $R(x,y), S(x)$
Logical symbols: $\neg$, &, v, $(\forall x)$,

and the interpretation in the meta-language English is:

a: Titisee
b: Chicago
c: Lake Michigan
$R(x,y)$: x is larger than y
$S(x)$: x is blue,

with the domain of quantification being taken as all physical objects. The logical symbols have the usual truth conditions:

$\neg A$ true   iff A false
A & B true   iff A true and B true
A v B true   iff A true or B true
$(\forall x)F(x)$ true   iff $[F](d)$ true for all objects d,

where $[F](d)$ means that the object d has the property $[F]$ interpreting the predicate F. The truth or falsity of atomic sentences is therefore determined by what is true in the meta-language (so that $S(a)$ is true, $S(b)$ is false, $S(c)$ is true, $R(a,b)$ is false, $R(c,a)$ is true, and so on), and the truth of logically complex sentences can then be worked out in the usual way. The meta-language itself could also be treated formally, but it is customarily treated informally (in English) by Carnap.

This method provides a characterization of the *true* sentences in a language, relative to the given semantic interpretation, but not of the logically true sentences. Carnap suggests that the latter are to be those that are true solely in virtue of the semantic rules for the logical constants, but he does not even try to develop this vague notion into a formal criterion. Strangely, the crucial problem of distinguishing the logically true sentences from those that are merely true is simply never satisfactorily resolved, as Carnap frequently admits:

The distinction between logical and descriptive signs and the distinction between logical and factual truth belong to the most important problems of logical analysis. Our previous discussion has shown the difficulties connected with the problem of a general formulation of these distinctions (§§13 and 16). This problem is very much in need of further investigation. (Carnap, 1942, 242–243)

Carnap's failure here is all the more disappointing in view of the fact that Tarski himself was quite skeptical about the possibility of distinguishing logical from factual truth in the context of his own semantic theory at the time.[17]

More generally, there are several serious problems afflicting Carnap's semantic program for defining analyticity. First, despite his efforts in *Formalization of Logic*, Mac Lane's problem of capturing the distinction between logical and descriptive symbols in a general way still remained:

So far we have discussed the distinction between logical and descriptive expressions only in the form in which it appears when we have to do with a particular semantical system, in other words, as a question of special semantics. The problem is more difficult in the form it takes in *general semantics*. Here it is the question whether and how "logical" and "descriptive" can be defined on the basis of other semantical terms, e.g. "designation" and "true," so that the application of the general definition to any particular system will lead to a result which is in accordance with the intended distinction. A satisfactory solution is not yet known. (Carnap, 1942, 59)

Second, how do we explain the all-important idea that the truth of a sentence "follows from the semantic rules alone"? Carnap's idea in *Logical Syntax* had been to identify the logical truths with the semantic truths consisting entirely of logical symbols. But, in the present context in which all terms are interpreted, this proves to be too narrow. Consider the difference between the sentences:

$$S(a) \qquad \text{true, because the Titisee is blue;}$$
$$\neg(S(a) \ \& \ \neg S(a)) \qquad \text{true, but not because of anything about the Titisee.}$$

---

[17] Carnap is clearly aware of his fundamental divergence from Tarski here in the Preface to *Introduction to Semantics* (Carnap, 1942, x–xi).

Carnap wants to say that the truth of the second sentence holds independently of the interpretation of the non-logical constants S and a occurring in it, and thus independently of the fact that the Titisee is blue: it will still hold if a is replaced by b, or $S(x)$ by $R(x, c)$, and so on. But it would of course fail to hold if the symbol & for conjunction were replaced by the symbol v for disjunction. Thus, the sentences "true in virtue of the semantic rules alone" *could* be described as those such that all substitutions for their *non-logical* symbols are true, but this again requires the distinction between logical and descriptive symbols.

Moreover, on the semantic approach it becomes necessary to *demonstrate* that logical truth does not depend on or imply factual truth, i.e., that it is truly *contentless*. This was to have been ensured in *Logical Syntax* by (1) the prohibition of extra-logical "meanings" combined with (2) the requirement of determinacy: analyticity is then empirically empty, since (by 1) no empirical facts are used in its specification, and (by 2) any consequence of an analytic proposition is analytic. Now, however, with the introduction of mixed logical and empirical concepts and propositions, together with the explicit use of extra-logical "meanings," there is a real danger that the two might become entangled. One solution would be to again require that every purely logical or mathematical sentence is "semantically determinate," i.e., either uniformly true or uniformly false under all *permissible* substitutions, for then its content (its consequence class) is trivial.

Even given the distinction between logical and descriptive symbols in order to identify the "permissible" substitutions, however, there is a still more fundamental problem with the general approach of Carnap's early semantical works. In order to determine logical truth (what we now call logical validity), it does not suffice, in general, simply to substitute different constant symbols and check the result in a *single* interpretation. Instead, the idea that the truth of a logically true sentence is independent of the interpretation of its non-logical symbols is captured, from a modern point of view, by considering the range of *all possible* interpretations of these symbols over *all possible* domains of quantification. It is only thus that we can show, for example, that every semantic consequence of a logical truth is itself a logical truth, thereby ensuring that logical truth is empirically empty. In the "model-theoretic" terms of modern logic, what is required is the difference between truth in a *particular* model and truth in *all* models.

But this idea of defining logical truth for a given language by considering the range of all possible semantic interpretations was simply absent from logic in the 1940s. Although this conception is now taken for granted, it was not present in Tarski's famous paper on truth (Tarski, 1936a), nor in his other works until around 1952.[18] Similarly, Carnap's semantic systems in the 1940s consist always of a language with a single fixed interpretation.[19] In Carnap's case, however, this omission is actually somewhat mysterious, since he himself had pioneered the notion of a "model" of a formal language in his failed work *Investigations in General Axiomatics* in 1927–30, before he had taken the post-1931 turn to syntax. In fact, he had even formulated the notion of logical entailment – "*A* implies *B*" – as, essentially, "every model of *A* is a model of *B*." Perhaps the difficulties in those early investigations made him overly cautious about later employing the notions developed there.[20] Yet, ironically, it was essentially Carnap's own earlier notion of logical entailment that others were eventually able to recognize as the key to the solution of Carnap's later problems, finally arriving at the modern notion of logical validity as "true in all models."[21]

Moreover, a fate quite similar to that of his near-definition of logical truth also befell his earlier *Logical Syntax* idea of characterizing the logical symbols as those occurring in the determinate sentences. For the intuition behind this property was later picked up and investigated by Tarski, and proposed as a characterization of the "logical" part of the language more generally. Specifically, the logical operations on any domain of variables have the special property that they are invariant under all permutations of that domain, regardless of

---

[18] See Hodges (1986). In fact, the idea seems first to have been suggested by Kemeny (1948), who was an associate of Carnap and was explicitly responding to Carnap's semantic work.

[19] On Carnap's failure to take the fully model-theoretic point of view compare Hintikka (1975a).

[20] The *Investigations in General Axiomatics* remained a fragment, and was left unpublished for good reasons, though a part of the manuscript was published long after Carnap's death (Carnap, 2000). See Erich Reck's contribution to this volume. See also Awodey and Carus (2001) for a general discussion of the *Axiomatics* project and its implications.

[21] See Kemeny (1948, 1956).

its size.[22] The analogy Tarski specifically had in mind was Klein's *Erlanger Program* of the late nineteenth century, in which geometries were to be characterized in terms of the features that remain invariant under different groups of linear transformations.[23] But it is clear that the idea fits very well with the work on characterizing logical symbols that Carnap had done a few years earlier, and once again represents a completion of that work by applying more sophisticated mathematical tools.

To judge by subsequent history, therefore, the definition of logical truth attempted in *Introduction to Semantics* was by no means a false start. In Carnap's own hands, however, it led nowhere. Moreover, even if understood in the present-day sense of logical validity ("true under all interpretations of the non-logical terms"), this characterization is still entirely dependent on the choice of methods used in the semantic meta-language. This is obvious at the level of higher-order languages (often used by Carnap), where the validity of the Axiom of Choice, for example, depends on whether that law is assumed in the meta-language. But even the notion of first-order logical validity depends, for example, on the law of excluded middle in the meta-language in order to "validate" that law in the object language.

Thus, the element of arbitrariness in the *Logical Syntax* definition of analyticity, which originally gave rise to the Principle of Tolerance, remains under the semantic approach. The logically true sentences of the object language are logically true only because they are *already* logically true in the meta-language. This "meta-linguistic relativity" is an inherent feature of the semantic approach, and it could not be remedied even by resolving all of the other problems we have described. Whether Carnap himself was satisfied with this

---

[22] To what extent invariance distinguishes *exactly* the logical operations remains an open question, subject to current investigation. See, for example, the discussion in Sher (1991).

[23] According to discussion notes in Carnap's *Nachlass* this idea appears to be due to the Polish mathematician Aleksander Wundheiler, rather than Tarski, who discussed it and related matters with Tarski, Carnap, and Quine at Harvard in 1940. ("Wundheiler: Can we perhaps characterize the difference between logic, mathematics, and physics through the transformation groups, just as we characterize projective, affine, and metrical geometry though transformation groups? Tarski: It is doubtful whether the concept of group helps much in this context." ASP RC 102-63-12.) Thanks to Greg Frost-Arnold for this point and citation.

outcome is not entirely clear, but it is a fact that he next pursued an entirely different approach involving intensional languages and modal logic.[24]

III. LATER ATTEMPTS: INTENSIONALITY AND NECESSITY

Although Frege's formal logic had been extensional, his investigation into the notions of *Sinn* and *Bedeutung* clearly indicated the possibility of a more rigorous treatment of intensions. Moreover, Russell's logic in *Principia Mathematica*, which Carnap had studied carefully, was of course explicitly intensional. Carnap himself had always been interested in intensional logics; there is a section on them in *Logical Syntax*, and the official position of *Introduction to Semantics* is that the meta-language is intensional. Although he had previously thought that intensional languages must be reducible to extensional languages (Carnap, 1934c/1937, §§68–69), in the 1940s Carnap considered the possibility that the distinction between analytic and synthetic might best be characterized in terms of a more precisely specified version of intensional identity and logical "necessity" (with empirical "contingency" corresponding to syntheticity). He developed a series of intensional and modal languages in which to frame this new proposal, whereby analyticity is to be defined in terms of intensional identity or logical necessity rather than truth.[25] The proposal was then explicitly put forward in his last major semantic work, *Meaning and Necessity: A Study in Semantics and Modal Logic* (Carnap, 1947).

According to the distinction between intension and extension, the predicate "*x* is blue" has the property of being blue as its intension and the class of all blue things as its extension; the sentence "Lake Michigan is blue" has that proposition as its intension and the truth value *True* as its extension; the name "Lake Michigan" has the meaning or sense of this name as its intension and a large body of water as its extension. Thus, for instance, the sentences "Lake Michigan is blue" and "Chicago is on Lake Michigan" have the same extension (*True*) but different intensions; while the sentences "Lake Michigan

---

[24] In his later "Empiricism, Semantics, and Ontology" (Carnap, 1950a), written squarely during his "intensional" phase, Carnap addresses this issue directly and explicitly embraces the relativity in question in the spirit of tolerance.

[25] The technical development of these systems was first presented in Carnap (1946).

is blue" and "Blue is the color of Lake Michigan" (presumably) agree in intension.

According to Carnap's new proposal, the notions of intension and logical truth (L-truth) can now be related as follows:

> Two expressions A and B *have the same extension* iff $A = B$ is true; they are then said to be *(extensionally) equivalent*.

> Two expressions A and B *have the same intension* iff $A = B$ is L-true; they are then said to be *(intensionally, or) L-equivalent*.

A context . . . X . . . is said to be *extensional* if its truth value is preserved by substitutions of equivalent expressions, *intensional* if its truth-value is preserved only by substitutions of L-equivalent expressions:

> *Extensional*:   . . . A . . . true and A is equivalent to B
> implies . . . B . . . true.
>
> *Intensional*:   . . . A . . . true and A is L-equivalent to B
> implies . . . B . . . true.

Thus, for instance, the context "X is blue" is extensional: e.g. "The second largest Great Lake is blue" follows from "Lake Michigan is blue." By contrast, "I believe X" is intensional, since "I believe Lake Michigan is blue" implies "I believe blue is the color of Lake Michigan" but not "I believe Chicago is on Lake Michigan."

One use of these distinctions is to solve apparent puzzles, such as that – sometimes known as the "antinomy of identity" – concerning the difference in meaning between the sentences "The morning star is the morning star" and "The morning star is the planet Venus." The first of these sentences is a matter of logic, while the second is an astronomical fact. A theory that distinguishes between intension and extension can account for this difference by positing that the expressions "morning star" and "Venus" have the same extension but different intensions.[26]

---

[26] A more subtle distinction – highlighted by what is sometimes called the "paradox of analysis" – concerns the difference in epistemological value of the sentences "The concept Brother is identical with the concept Brother" and "The concept Brother is identical with the concept Male Sibling." Each of these is (presumably) a matter of logic, but the second contains information not in the first. To address such cases Carnap develops a theory that distinguishes between intensional equivalence and the even stricter notion of intensional isomorphism (Carnap, 1956, §§14–15).

Carnap observes that modal terms like necessity and possibility also create intensional contexts. Consider for instance the following argument:

> 9 is necessarily less than 10.
> The number of planets is 9.
> Therefore, the number of planets is necessarily less than 10.

But how can the number of planets be a matter of necessity? The puzzle is resolved by recognizing that "necessarily X" is an intensional context, while "the number of planets" is only extensionally equivalent to 9 but not intensionally equivalent.

Not only are the notions of intension and extension definable from L-truth, but in fact they and the modal notions are all interdefinable. Thus, writing $N(A)$ for "A is necessary":

$N(A)$ is true   iff A is intensionally equivalent to *True* (which holds iff A is L-true),

so that one has:

$N(A = B)$ is true iff A is intensionally equivalent to B (i.e. $A = B$ is L-true).

In this way, the three distinctions intension vs. extension, analytic vs. synthetic, and necessity vs. possibility become just three sides of the same coin, as it were.[27]

Carnap was thus naturally led to propose using intensions rather than extensions in semantics. Predicates do not take sets of individuals but properties of individuals as semantic value, and the interpretations of sentences are propositions not truth values. Carnap again considers the possibility of reducing intensions to extensions but ultimately rejects it as unworkable.

Not until Kripke (1963) took up where Carnap left off was it known how to describe intensional and modal languages using extensional semantics.[28] Just as in the case of the characterization of logical truth

---

[27] Of course, this is only one of many different conceptions of necessity, corresponding to the idea that necessary truth is logical truth. It is distinguished from some other modal logics, e.g., by the law:

(S5) $P(A) \to NP(A)$

where $P(A)$ means "A is possible."

[28] In the Schilpp volume (Carnap, 1963d, 889–97) Carnap sketched another approach, which appears to suggest something more along the lines of Kripkean semantics.

as validity, the missing idea was again that of considering a range of different possible interpretations simultaneously. Indeed, given Carnap's treatment of the connection between L-truth and necessity, it was only a small step to the treatment of necessity as truth across a range of interpretations – truth "in all possible worlds" – once the notion of validity as truth in all models had been formulated. From this point of view, intensions occur as "varying extensions", i.e., as families of extensions, parameterized over some index set of "worlds." Pairs of expressions that always have the same semantic value (in all "possible worlds") are intensionally equivalent, then, and the sentences that are always true are just those that are L-true or analytic. This treatment not only provides semantics for intensional modal logic in an extensional meta-language, it does so in a way that is entirely in line with Carnap's approach to relating modality, intensionality, and logical truth.

But, once again, Carnap himself did not work out these consequences of his proposal, and this hampered his attempts to apply it to the case that was always at the forefront of his mind, the analysis of scientific theories. Here, as we have seen (compare note 7 above), he never gave up the hope that a useful and natural definition of analyticity would eventually be found. In his last years, Carnap seems to have moved towards the view that any definition of analyticity would at best be tentative or evolving. For any given language we can formulate a definition of analyticity that works pragmatically, in the sense that for its users the analytic sentences thus singled out depend on no facts in the extra-linguistic world. But we may eventually encounter borderline cases that result in confusions, and at this point we can revise our language or its definition of analyticity. We may never have a final or permanent explication, but we can go on using our makeshift explication for the time being while simultaneously improving it.[29]

IV. FROM LOGICAL TO STRUCTURAL EMPIRICISM

There is an almost tragic element in Carnap's forty-year quest for a definition of analyticity. His path is littered with inspired

---

[29] The most explicit statement of this view is not to be found in Carnap's own later writings, but in a conversation during the late 1960s reported by Bohnert (1975, 205–212).

suggestions which, had they been carried through, would have led to solutions later found by others, such as Tarski and Kripke. It remained then for others with a fresh perspective (and more sophisticated mathematical skills) to survey his successive attempts, to put them together in a new way, and to resolve the old problems. And it is worth emphasizing, finally, that the problems with which Carnap grappled in the 1940s have indeed been resolved – some in the immediate wake of his efforts and others only quite recently, using methods developed only in the last few years. The modern conception of logical validity as "truth in all models" is essentially the notion of analyticity later accepted by Carnap himself, and assumed in his discussions with Quine.[30] Moreover, as we saw in the foregoing section, the Kripkean semantics of modal logic, which takes necessity as truth in all possible worlds, essentially results from plugging the modern notion of logical validity into Carnap's own theory of necessity-as-analyticity (something Carnap himself seems eventually to have recognized: see note 28 above).

As good as they are as a starting point, however, these ideas do not address all the issues with which Carnap was struggling in the 1940s. As we have seen, the basic problem of distinguishing logical from descriptive truth and showing the former to be empirically empty, as well as what we have called "metalinguistic relativity," are not so much addressed in these schemes as they are simply ignored or taken as given. Both problems, however, are resolved by certain modern-day extensions of these ideas, as I will now briefly indicate.

The essential ingredient that was apparently missing from Carnap's early attempts, in both general semantics and modal logic, was the idea of allowing the interpretations of a given language to *vary* while the language itself is held fixed. The modern semantic notion of validity, as well as Kripkean semantics for modal logic, both employ this device in an essential way. Such a "variational" approach is taken even further in some quite recent logical research employing Mac Lane's theory of categories and functors. This approach not only subsumes the familiar characterizations of logical validity and modal necessity, but it also succeeds in distinguishing the logical constants

---

[30] This is clear from his remarks on the subject in the Schilpp volume (Carnap, 1963d, 900–905). The use of "meaning postulates" and other devices was intended to accommodate a more extensive notion of analyticity, partly in response to Quine's critique, including also synonymy in natural language.

from the descriptive vocabulary through invariance as proposed by Tarski. Moreover, this approach also provides an understanding of the incompleteness phenomenon in terms precisely of variation versus constancy: briefly, *provable* is equivalent to true in all "variable models," while *true but unprovable* is equivalent to true in the "constant models" only.[31] This addresses the problem of metalinguistic relativity as well, since the resulting notion of logical truth (in its most basic form) simply agrees with provability, and thus is essentially independent of the choice of meta-language. For more elaborate mathematics involving non-logical assumptions, an axiomatic (i.e., "postulational") approach very much in the spirit of Carnap's Principle of Tolerance then applies.[32]

This contemporary approach is incompatible, however, with one of Carnap's basic constraints: the determinateness of all logical and mathematical sentences. It turns out that also allowing some features of the mathematical universe (the cardinality of the continuum, for example) to vary – thus remaining logically indeterminate – can be a very useful and powerful device. Recall, however, that it was the contentlessness of logic and mathematics, derived from Carnap's Wittgensteinian understanding of Frege's logicism, which motivated the constraint of determinateness; for, using the classical law of excluded middle, determinateness follows from the independence of logic and mathematics from all empirical facts. Thus, in Carnap's own search for an explication of analyticity, the logicist tradition always remained his starting point. This was natural enough for a student of Frege, who, in Carnap's own words, had

strongly emphasized that the foundational problems of mathematics can only be solved if we look not solely at pure mathematics but also at the use of mathematical concepts in factual sentences. He had found his explication of cardinal numbers by asking himself the question: What does "five" mean in contexts like "I have five fingers on my right hand"? Since Schlick and I came to philosophy from physics, we looked at mathematics always from the point of view of its application in empirical science. (Carnap, 1963a, 48)

---

[31] See Awodey and Reck (2002a, 2002b) for a survey of the further development of some of Carnap's contributions to logic: Part II (2002b), in particular, outlines resolutions to some of Carnap's problems from a modern point of view, including the variational – i.e., functorial – interpretation of incompleteness.

[32] More detailed discussion of this conception would lead too far afield: see Awodey (2004a) for a fuller treatment.

But Carnap's own career and his forty-year quest for the concept of analyticity are good evidence that a definition of precisely the kind he sought, satisfying all of his constraints, is simply not available.

In order to see how we can now free Carnap's conception of logic and mathematics as empirically empty from its dependence on classical logicism, we can take a hint from Carnap himself (Carnap, 1939, 50): "if we regard interpreted mathematics as an instrument of deduction within the field of empirical knowledge rather than as a system of information, then many of the controversial problems are recognized as being questions not of truth but of technical expedience." Thus the very considerations which, according to the previous quotation, had led him to adopt logicism in the first place ("the use of mathematics in factual sentences"), here led him to recognize that all controversies about foundations of mathematics ultimately come down to questions of technical expedience – questions of (language) engineering.[33] Logicism is not so much a traditional foundational program for Carnap, but a way of implementing the regulatory ideal of understanding mathematics through its "application in empirical science." It is in this sense that Carnap wanted to dispense with "foundations,"[34] to *dissolve* foundational debates.[35]

Where then would the ghost of Carnap now turn, guided only by the priorities of empiricism and technical expedience? Perhaps, I think, to the descendants of Hilbert's axiomatic program, the mathematical structuralism of Bourbaki and its more recent "variational" extensions mentioned above.[36] This can be seen as a realization of the more "postulational" approach that Mac Lane suggested to Carnap back in the 1930s, and it is indeed a natural framework in which to exhibit mathematics as purely structural and *contentless*. For, on this view, axiomatic logic and mathematics provide the pure form

---

[33] In *Meaning and Necessity* the choice of a language structure is compared to "the choice of a suitable motor for a freight airplane . . . both are engineering problems, and I fail to see why metaphysics should enter into the first any more than into the second" (Carnap, 1956, §10, 43).

[34] Note that the word "foundations" is put in scare quotes in the title of the relevant §20 of Carnap (1939, 48).

[35] This is plainly the thrust of his best-known discussions of these issues, for example Carnap (1934, §§16–17, 84) and Carnap (1939, 1950a).

[36] As set out, for instance, by Mac Lane in *Mathematics, Form and Function* (New York, 1986). More recent treatments using Mac Lane's category theory explicitly include Awodey (1996, 2004).

of scientific theories, the content of which is then supplied empirically. During the writing of *Studies in Semantics*, as we have seen, some version of Frege's logicism had still seemed to Carnap to be the most natural and promising approach to realizing his goals for an empiricist understanding of logic and mathematics. Sixty years later, with the help of methods developed by Hilbertians like Mac Lane, it now seems possible to implement essentially the same empiricist program by other means.[37]

[37] I take this opportunity to record a personal anecdote. My interest in the topic of Mac Lane's early review of *Logical Syntax* stems from my conversations with him about this and his subsequent interactions with Carnap at the University of Chicago. Mac Lane was clearly disappointed that Carnap did not consult him concerning the defective definition of analyticity; on the other hand, he delighted in having lifted the word "functor" from *Logical Syntax* for his own purposes in category theory. The latter, in the end, might perhaps be Carnap's most far-reaching contribution to modern mathematics.

WILLIAM DEMOPOULOS*

11 Carnap on the rational reconstruction of scientific theories†

I. INTRODUCTION

Carnap's intellectual development is documented in his "Intellectual Autobiography" (Carnap, 1963a). For present purposes it is worth recalling that he studied with Frege at Jena in the years 1910–14, taking two courses on Frege's conceptual notation or Begriffsschrift and the course "Logic in Mathematics."[1] His early relationship to Russell also merits mention. Shortly after the First World War, Carnap wrote to Russell asking where he might purchase a second-hand copy of *Principia Mathematica*; Russell responded by copying out by hand 35 pages of its central definitions. From the intellectual autobiography we also learn that Carnap's interest in philosophy of physics emerged early in his career. As a doctoral student, he formulated the intention of writing a dissertation on the axiomatization of special relativity. The less than enthusiastic reception of this idea by Max Wien, the head of the Institute of Physics at Jena, led him to write on the foundations of geometry instead. The dissertation was completed in 1921 under the title "Der Raum," and it shows the central influence of Hilbert.

* This chapter was begun during my tenure as a visiting fellow of All Souls College. My thanks to the College for providing such an ideal environment for my work, and to Jeremy Butterfield for so graciously enduring the first formulations of these ideas. Comments by Dr. Gregory Lavers led to several improvements. I am much indebted to Robert DiSalle, Anil Gupta, and Michael Friedman for their careful reading of one or another earlier draft. Support from the Social Sciences and Humanities Research Council of Canada is gratefully acknowledged.
† Dedicated to the memory Herbert Feigl.
[1] See Frege (1979, 203–250) for the lecture text of the latter course. See Reck and Awodey (2004) for Carnap's notes from all three courses.

The core of Carnap's philosophy of science consists in his proposals for the rational reconstruction of the language of physics. The *Aufbau* (1928) was his first extended application of the method of reconstruction to the analysis of empirical knowledge; the approach taken there was gradually transformed and refined in later work. In *Logical Syntax* (1934c, §72) Carnap proposed that the logic of science is the proper replacement for traditional philosophy; in §82 he presented a "logical analysis" of the language of physics. The reconstruction that Carnap articulated in "Testability and Meaning" (1936–1937) – his first major publication in English – is the clearest anticipation of the mature view he developed in the 1950s and 1960s, which forms the focus of our study.

After briefly reviewing its historical context and philosophical motivation, my exposition begins with Carnap's final proposal for the rational reconstruction of the language of physics. This proposal has not received the attention it deserves; it is, for example, particularly relevant to the assessment of his long-standing debate with Quine over the possibility of drawing a non-arbitrary fact/convention dichotomy. Having presented Carnap's mature position on the nature of theoretical knowledge, I consider how various of his earlier views can be located within it. Although I defend Carnap against certain misconceptions, I am also concerned to expose a fundamental limitation in his account of theoretical knowledge.

II. LOGICISM, GEOMETRY, AND RELATIVITY

The principal influences on Carnap's approach to reconstruction are three. There is first and foremost the influence of modern logic and its deployment by Frege and Russell in their articulation of logicism. Secondly, there is Hilbert's work on the foundations of geometry, which developed a new account of the role of axioms for our understanding of the primitives of a mathematical theory. Finally, Einstein's theory of relativity was instrumental in Carnap's extension of Hilbert's analysis to a reconstruction of physics.

Logicism's attempt to represent mathematics as an extension of logic foundered, in Frege's case, on the inconsistency of his system, and, in the case of Russell, on the need to assume not obviously logical principles.[2] Its legacy was, therefore, mixed. The development of modern quantificational logic proved an indispensable tool for the logical analysis of the language of science. But logicism left unsolved the fundamental problem of responding to the Kantian claim that mathematics is not an extension of logic but is, in Kant's terms, *synthetic* a priori.

Hilbert's *Foundations of Geometry* (1899) articulated a view of geometrical axioms which provided the key to Carnap's emendation of logicism. Hilbert was widely interpreted (e.g. in Schlick, 1918, §7) as having shown that the role of intuition in geometrical knowledge can be wholly relegated to psychology. In particular, the classical view that spatial intuition provides the subject matter of geometry was decisively addressed by Hilbert's demonstration that axiomatic geometry need not have a fixed subject matter to which the axioms are responsible. The language of geometry is freely interpretable, subject only to the constraint that the interpretation must respect the logical category of its vocabulary. The subject matter of the axioms includes any system of objects that makes them true; the *truth* of the axioms thus consists in the existence of such a system of objects, and therefore amounts to nothing more than their *consistency*.

On this view, geometry is a priori in so far as its axioms are constitutive or definitive of their subject matter. Carnap perceived that this idea might plausibly be extended to arithmetic as well; the contribution of logicism to the philosophy of arithmetic would then be seen to lie not in its account of the axioms of arithmetic, but in its elucidation of mathematical reasoning as an elaboration of purely logical reasoning.[3] The philosophical interest of a successful extension of Hilbert's view of geometrical axioms to the rest of mathematics depends on whether the apriority of the axioms can be shown to derive from their analyticity. This requires both an explication of analyticity and a demonstration that the explication correctly characterizes the relevant cases.

For Carnap, the crucial notion on which the successful explication of analyticity relies is that of *factual content*. Carnap's solution to the problem of a priori knowledge is to argue that it lacks factual

---

[2] For further discussion, see Demopoulos and Clark (2005).
[3] By contrast with "Kant [who] thought that the actual *reasoning* of mathematics was different from logic" (Russell 1903, 458).

content and is, in this sense, analytic. So understood, analyticity can attach to a mathematical theory *independently* of whether or not it is recoverable from the basic laws of logic.[4]

Poincaré's contention that the geometry of physical space is indeterminate – so that the question which geometry is true of this space is not well formed – lies at the heart of the logical empiricists' theory of scientific theories. But it was Einstein's 1905 analysis of simultaneity that suggested a systematic means of addressing the question of factual content. For logical empiricism, the great success of the Special Theory established that the central task of scientific methodology is to provide a clear separation between factual and conventional components of scientific knowledge, especially in physics.[5]

Einstein had argued that the application of the relation of simultaneity depends on connecting distant events by some means of signaling. For the logical empiricists, this amounted to a demonstration that some principles appearing to be descriptive of physical events are in reality prescriptive statements controlling the empirical interpretation of the language of physics. Thus, although the equality of the to and fro velocities of light in any determination of distant simultaneity initially appears to be a simple descriptive claim, it is on Einstein's analysis a freely adopted convention giving empirical content to the relation of simultaneity. Indeed, many apparently descriptive statements – that asserting the isotropy of space, for example – turn out to have a non-factual and conventional character. By a natural extension, the traditional question of the correct geometry of space is one that is also relative to the adoption of conventions controlling the interpretation of the geometrical primitives; a central task of the philosophy of physical geometry is to uncover these conventions. Einstein's analysis of simultaneity thus provided a template for extending the method of rational reconstruction to empirical theories, one in which the fact/convention dichotomy is of central importance, and one that highlights the importance of principles of

---

4 The explication of "being without factual content" found in Carnap's later work – the focus of our study – gives precise expression to earlier formulations of Schlick and Hahn, whose views are recounted in Goldfarb (1996).
5 The canonical articulation of this view was given by Reichenbach (1928), a work Carnap always cited with admiration (see, for example, 1963a, 50) and for whose English translation Carnap supplied a preface.

epistemic interpretation for the basic concepts of an empirical theory. Later we will see in some detail how this template came to be reflected in Carnap's proposals.

III. THEORETICAL SENTENCES, OBSERVATION SENTENCES, AND CORRESPONDENCE RULES

For Carnap and the logical empiricists, factual content is expressed in terms of the observational vocabulary of a theory, where the notions of *observational term* and *observational sentence* are artifacts of the rational reconstruction. Putnam (1962) persuasively argued that *un*reconstructed scientific terms and sentences are not easily classified as observational or theoretical: they do not refer to *just* observable or unobservable events. But Putnam's observation, though correct, is largely irrelevant to the successful execution of a reconstructive program like Carnap's.

To make the distinction *in the language of the reconstruction*, it suffices that we can distinguish between observable and unobservable *events*, their properties and relations. Once we are given the distinction between observable and unobservable events, it is straightforward to force a correlative distinction in vocabulary, and it is then an easy matter to formulate the classification of sentences into theoretical, observational, and mixed that is essential to Carnap's reconstruction. Having the distinction available for the vocabulary of the reconstructed language of physics proves to be vital to the articulation, motivation, and philosophical significance of the logical empiricist view.

Specifically, given a division of the domain of a possible model for the language of physics into its observable and unobservable parts, we can introduce relation symbols whose interpretation is restricted to the observable part of the domain. The intended interpretation of the theoretical relation symbols is restricted to the unobservable part of the domain. We call the observation vocabulary of the reconstruction the *O-vocabulary*, its theoretical vocabulary the *T-vocabulary*.[6] An *O-sentence* is formed using only O-vocabulary, and

---

[6] A non-linguistic division of the domain into observable and unobservable parts is proposed in van Fraassen (1980); however, missing from van Fraassen's discussion is the recognition that a corresponding linguistic division of vocabulary can then be easily imposed.

a *T-sentence* is formed using only T-vocabulary. Primitive relation symbols are either wholly observational or wholly theoretical – i.e., there are no "mixed" relations, a point to which we will return. But there are, as we have noted, mixed *sentences*, and these are of great importance.

For logical empiricism, theoretical terms make no contribution to the factual content of a theory. They only acquire a content from the O-vocabulary in virtue of mixed sentences, called *correspondence rules*, which contain both T- and O-vocabulary. Correspondence rules (C-rules) establish a correspondence between theoretical relations in the domain of unobservable events and relations among observable events. They differ from the T-sentences by containing both O- and T-terms.

In the absence of C-rules, T-sentences are *true* provided they are *consistent*, and there is then no non-arbitrary answer to the question whether a theoretical claim is true. This contention would be entirely commonplace if, instead of C-rules, we were to speak of principles of *semantic* interpretation, thereby taking a specific semantic interpretation to be that which distinguishes truth from mere consistency. C-rules, however, are principles of empirical or *epistemic* interpretation, given in terms of the vocabulary belonging to the evidentiary basis of the theory. The logical empiricists rejected the view that merely giving a semantic interpretation can address the problem of interpreting theories belonging to an empirical science. From their perspective, the knowledge that the provision of such a semantic interpretation requires is precisely what is expressed by the C-rules; without them, we would have no reason to suppose that we could even *understand* a semantic interpretation of the T-vocabulary in the domain of actual events. This of course reflects the semantically privileged role the positivists assigned to the O-vocabulary in the interpretation of scientific theories.

Here Hilbert's *Geometry* and Einstein's analysis of simultaneity were decisive. Hilbert had proposed that the axioms of a mathematical theory define the theory's primitives. But, unlike a pure mathematical theory, a physical theory requires principles of empirical or *epistemic* interpretation. This was the lesson of Einstein. In contradistinction to principles of semantic interpretation, C-rules bridge the theoretical and observational vocabularies and secure the evidential basis for the theoretical claims of physics; they thereby elevate the theoretical statements to the status of genuinely synthetic claims about the world.

IV. RAMSEY AND CARNAP SENTENCES

As we noted earlier, Carnap's proposals for the rational reconstruction of the language of physics assume a division between T- and O-vocabulary that induces a corresponding division between T- and O-sentences. We will further assume that the division between T- and O-predicates is exhaustive: there are no *mixed* primitive predicates applying to both observable and unobservable events. Having the observation/theory distinction at the level of the vocabulary of the language of science is important to the theory of meaning that underlies the logical empiricist view of theories. According to this essentially concept-empiricist theory of meaning, our understanding of the meaning of primitive terms rests on our acquaintance with their referents. Notice, however, that a theory of this kind allows for the formation of expressions that are about items transcending our observation. In particular, a sentence built up exclusively from O-vocabulary may well be about unobservable events. This point is often missed in discussions of the logical empiricist conception of theories, but it is characteristic of both it and its classical antecedents.[7] What is vital to the epistemological point of the account is the sustainability of the dichotomy in primitive *vocabulary* on the basis of its reference. By contrast, *sentences* are O or T merely on the basis of the primitive vocabulary they contain.

If the restriction on mixed primitive predicates were relaxed, a correlative question would naturally arise at a later stage of our discussion, namely, whether mixed predicates, like T-predicates, pose a special difficulty. The reconstruction we are exploring requires that we exclude mixed primitive predicates from the language of the reconstruction or, if we allow them, that we classify them with T-predicates as requiring special consideration. We will proceed on the simpler assumption that there are no mixed primitive predicates. One may of course choose to weaken this assumption.

---

[7] The historical background is discussed in Demopoulos and Friedman (1985) and Demopoulos (2003a).

But to abandon the T- and O-vocabulary dichotomy altogether would be to engage in a completely different reconstructive project. For the present, our goal is to see where a sharp adherence to this dichotomy leads.

One difficulty the division between T- and O-vocabulary raises is that of explaining how, within this framework, it is possible to draw a non-arbitrary analytic/synthetic distinction. Since the O-vocabulary is completely understood, it can be argued that so also is the notion of truth in virtue of meaning for O-sentences. Hence the application of the analytic/synthetic distinction at the level of O-sentences is not problematic. By contrast, the whole point of this way of drawing the observation/theory distinction is to emphasize that the T-vocabulary is at best partially understood. It follows that every statement involving T-predicates is capable of playing two roles: it can be explanatory of the meaning of its constituent T-terms or it can express a substantive claim involving their use. But then it seems hopeless to suppose that we can have a non-arbitrary division of sentences containing T-predicates which separates those that are true in virtue of meaning from those that make factual claims. Under this conception of the meaning of the T-vocabulary, the two dichotomies, theory/observation and analytic/synthetic, appear to be in tension with one another – as Carnap himself points out (in Psillos, 2000, 162). We will soon see how this tension is resolved without rejecting either dichotomy.

The *first* phase of Carnap's reconstruction therefore introduces a distinction between T- and O-vocabulary which extends to a distinction in theoretical and observational sentences in the intended way. It must be stressed that the formulation of the language of physics this assumes is already heavily reconstruction-dependent. The conjunction of the correspondence rules and theoretical postulates comprising a theory is then given by

$$TC(O_1, \ldots, O_m; T_1, \ldots, T_n),$$

where $O_1, \ldots, O_m$ and $T_1, \ldots, T_n$ are the O- and T-predicates introduced at the first phase of the reconstruction.[8]

---

[8] A point of clarification about the notation: by a theory we mean the conjunction of its T- and C-sentences. The notation $TC(O_1, \ldots, O_m; T_1, \ldots, T_n)$ exhibits

The *second* phase of the reconstruction consists, in the first instance, in replacing a theory *TC* by the claim that there are theoretical relations satisfying the conditions imposed by the combination of theoretical and correspondence postulates. This is the content of the *Ramsey sentence* $R(TC)$ of *TC*, namely,

$$\exists X_1, \ldots, \exists X_n TC(O_1, \ldots, Om; X_1, \ldots, X_n),$$

which is the result of replacing the theoretical predicates $T_1, \ldots, T_n$ of *TC* with variables $X_1, \ldots, X_n$ of the appropriate logical category and type, and then existentially generalizing over the new variables. Such sentences were first discussed by Ramsey in his posthumously published "Theories" (Ramsey, 1929/1960), but the general idea of expressing what we would today call "satisfiability in a model" by a higher-order existentially quantified sentence was a common practice in the logical tradition of the 1930s.[9] From a model-theoretic perspective, the innovation of the Ramsey sentence consists in using a higher-order sentence to express satisfiability in a model relative to a fixed interpretation of a part of the language, namely, the O-vocabulary.

The Ramsey sentence of a theory is important for Carnap because it and the theory imply the same O-sentences,[10] and this motivates the proposal that the Ramsey sentence represents the factual content of the theory *TC*. Carnap's account of the *conventional* or *analytic* component of *TC* requires the notion of the *Carnap sentence* $C(TC)$ of *TC*, namely, the conditional whose consequent is *TC* and whose antecedent is $R(TC)$:

$$\textit{If } \exists X_1, \ldots, \exists X_n TC(O_1, \ldots, O_m; X_1, \ldots, X_n),$$
$$\textit{then } TC(O_1, \ldots, O_m; T_1, \ldots, T_n).$$

the non-logical constants of the vocabulary of the language in which the T- and C-sentences are expressed; it is to be understood as requiring that the non-logical vocabulary of any T- or C-sentence is contained in $\{O_1, \ldots, O_m; T_1, \ldots, T_n\}$. We are thus supposing the correspondence rules and theoretical postulates to be finite in number; this is an assumption that can always be met, though doing so may incur the cost of increasing the strength of the underlying logic of the theory. For an overview of relevant results, see van Bentham (1978).

[9] This is true even of Tarski's seminal papers: see Hodges (2004). For Carnap's own logical work of this period, see Reck's contribution to this volume.

[10] Here, and in what follows, see the Appendix for the justification of technical claims such as this one.

The Carnap sentence asserts that if *any* relations $X_1, \ldots, X_n$ satisfy $TC(O_1, \ldots, O_m; X_1, \ldots, X_n)$, then the relations $T_1, \ldots, T_n$ do. The conjunction $\mathbf{R}(TC) \wedge \mathbf{C}(TC)$ is obviously logically equivalent to TC.

In the presence of its Carnap sentence, a theory is equivalent to its Ramsey sentence. Thus if it could be shown that the Carnap sentence is plausibly regarded as analytic, we could conclude that a theory *is* its Ramsey sentence, since their equivalence would depend only on an analytic truth. Carnap argues that the Carnap sentence is analytic on the ground that all of its O-consequences – all the sentences in the O-vocabulary it implies – are logically true (L-true); the Carnap sentence is in this sense *observationally uninformative*. Thus, there is an obvious sense in which the Carnap sentence can be said to have no factual content and can, therefore, properly be regarded as analytic. Modulo an analytic truth, TC *is* $\mathbf{R}(TC)$. Carnap's reconstruction of the distinction between the factual and the conventional thus divides TC into two components, $\mathbf{R}(TC)$ and $\mathbf{C}(TC)$, the first expressing TC's factual content, the second merely a stipulation controlling the use of its theoretical vocabulary and expressing TC's analytic component. More generally, a sentence is *analytic* – or, more precisely, *analytic in TC* – if it is a consequence of just $\mathbf{C}(TC)$.

Carnap's enthusiasm for this proposal had many sources. Later we will see how it subsumes his earlier analysis of disposition terms by reduction sentences. But let us first consider in greater detail what is perhaps the chief virtue of the proposal: the simplicity with which it promises to draw a sharp and non-arbitrary division between the factual and analytic components of a theory. There are three desiderata Carnap imposes on a reconstruction seeking to incorporate such a division:

(i)   The conjunction of the factual and analytic components of TC is logically equivalent to TC.

(ii)   The factual component is O-equivalent to TC.

(iii)   The analytic component is observationally uninformative.

We have just seen how naturally these desiderata are fulfilled by Carnap's proposed rational reconstruction in terms of the Ramsey and Carnap sentences of a theory whose phase one reconstruction respects the division into T- and O-sentences.

V. A QUINEAN PROBLEM AND ITS SOLUTION

In a paper that is one of the most important secondary sources for our study, Winnie (1970) noted that Carnap's desiderata are not complete, and that this undermines the contention that the suggested division into analytic and factual components is non-arbitrary.[11] Suppose we take one of the T-postulates, T_i say, and propose the new and obviously equivalent reconstruction, $R(TC) \land [C(TC) \land T_i]$, which takes $[C(TC) \land T_i]$ as its analytic component. To satisfy Carnap's third desideratum, $[C(TC) \land T_i]$ must be shown to be observationally uninformative. This is the content of Winnie's observation:

Suppose TC is satisfiable and that T_i is a T-sentence logically implied by TC. Then $C(TC) \land T_i$ is O-uninformative.

Since this observation regarding T_i and $C(TC)$ can be iterated, there is nothing to exclude the acceptability of a reconstruction which takes the conjunction of *all* the T-postulates to be part of its analytic component.

It is an early objection of Quine (1951) that Carnap fails to characterize a non-arbitrary analytic/synthetic or fact/convention dichotomy. An initially plausible response (Maxwell, 1963) holds that the arbitrariness is harmless if it attaches only to the *un*reconstructed sentences of a science. But we have just seen that the objection applies even to the *second* phase of Carnap's proposed reconstruction, and this appears to be a complete vindication of Quine.

To address this difficulty, Winnie (1970, 150) adds a fourth desideratum:

1.   *(iv)* The analytic component of TC is observationally non-creative in TC,

where X *is observationally non-creative in TC* just in case TC logically implies X, and for any Y such that TC logically implies Y, every O-consequence of $X \land Y$ is an O-consequence of Y.[12] Observational

---

[11] That Carnap was not aware of this difficulty is evident from his remarks in (1963b, 915).

[12] Observational non-creativity is simply a special case of the non-creativity requirement that is standardly applied in the classical theory of definition: Let T be a set of axioms in the language L, and let T be a term not in L. Then a definition X(T)

creativity provides one way of understanding the contribution the T-postulates make to the factual content of a theory: without observationally creative T-sentences, some O-consequences would not be forthcoming, and to that extent, the factual content of the theory would be diminished.

It can be shown that desideratum *(iv)* is satisfied by Carnap's original proposal but not by any of the problematic extensions [C(*TC*) ∧ *T_i*] of the analytic component: every such extension is observationally creative in *TC* whenever *T_i* is a T-postulate not implied by C(*TC*). Indeed, the consequence class of the Carnap sentence characterizes exactly the sentences that are O-non-creative in *TC*: any sentence not implied by the Carnap sentence will, when added to C(*TC*), be O-creative in *TC*. The condition of O-non-creativity in *TC* thus rules out adding to the analytic component any sentence not implied by C(*TC*). Nevertheless, it tells us nothing specifically about the role of the T-sentences of a theory, since any sentence not implied by the Carnap sentence will be O-creative *whatever* its vocabulary.

VI. CONSIDERATIONS IN FAVOR OF CARNAP'S RECONSTRUCTION

There are many positive features of Carnap's reconstruction, understood in the manner just reviewed.

First, the division into factual and analytic components is independent of the formalization. Since the consequence class of the Carnap sentences of two distinct, but logically equivalent, formulations of a theory will be the same, so also will their characterizations of analytic and factual sentences. As Winnie (1970, 149) remarks, the relativity that attaches to the notion *postulate of T* does not attach to the notion *analytic in T*. We noted earlier that the ambiguous status of C-rules – they appear to be both law-like statements (factual) and interpretive (analytic) – makes the application of the analytic/synthetic distinction to the sentences of a *phase one* reconstruction highly problematic. With the incorporation of Winnie's emendation, these difficulties are completely avoided when the distinction is applied at the *second* reconstructive phase – when the

---

of *T* (in *T*) is *non-creative* if, whenever a sentence of *L* is a logical consequence of *T* ∧ X(*T*), it is a consequence of *T* alone.

analytic sentences are represented as the consequence class of $C(TC)$. There is no appeal to the difficult notion of the meaning of the T-terms, and the entire account of *analytic in T* proceeds using only logical consequence and the unproblematic notion of the meaning of the O-vocabulary.

Secondly, the approach locates precisely the factual component of a theory, and it does so without employing predicates that refer to unobservables. Hence, the account of factual content does not require a solution to the vexed problem of the meaning of the theoretical vocabulary. Carnap addresses this problem by replacing all the theoretical predicates with variables; hence, aside from the matter of their logical category, there is no need to appeal to the meanings of terms belonging to the theoretical vocabulary in order to provide for the factual content of a theory. This is perhaps the point at which Hilbert's influence is most evident.

Thirdly, the account subsumes Carnap's (1936–1937) analysis of theoretical terms in "Testability and Meaning." That analysis, which isolated the analytic and synthetic assumptions underlying the application of disposition predicates, can now be seen as an early anticipation of the present reconstruction in terms of Ramsey and Carnap sentences.

In "Testability and Meaning," Carnap presents criteria of application for a new "theoretical" predicate T, one whose intended interpretation is some *dispositional* property. The problem is to clarify when such a predicate applies by specifying a variety of conditions under which one might test for the presence or absence of the associated dispositional property; the characterization of test conditions and test results is to be given in terms of predicates for observable – i.e. *manifest* – properties. To this end, Carnap introduces the concept of a *reduction sentence* for T, i.e., sentences of the sort:

> For every x, if Ax, then if Bx, then Tx,
> For every x, if A' x, then if B' x, then Tx,
> For every x, if Cx, then if Dx, then $\neg$ Tx,
> For every x, if C' x, then if D' x, then $\neg$ Tx,

where $A, \ldots , D'$ are all primitive nondispositional O-predicates.

The theory C consisting of the conjunction of these four sentences is a mixed sentence. C is equivalent to the conjunction

For every x, if φ x, then Tx, and for every x, if ψ x, then ¬ Tx,

where φx is $(Ax \wedge Bx) \vee (A'x \wedge B'x)$ and ψx is $(Cx \wedge Dx) \vee (C'x \wedge D'x)$. *C* may therefore be written as

[*C*] *For every x, if φx, then Tx, and if ψx, then ¬Tx,*

from which we may infer the wholly observational sentence

[*S*] *For every x, if φx, then ¬ψx.*

Carnap (1963b, 967, and 1936–1937, §7) calls *S* the *representative sentence* of *C*; and he characterizes the conditional

If S, then C

as a meaning postulate for *C*. Thus, this conditional expresses the analytic component of *C*, while *S* expresses its factual component. But now the Ramsey sentence of *C*, namely

[*R*(*C*)] *There is an X such that for every x, if φx, then Xx, and if ψx, then ¬Xx,*

is logically equivalent to *S*, so that this approach to the reconstruction of a set of reduction sentences into analytic and factual components is just a special case of the general method employing Ramsey and Carnap sentences, as Carnap observes in (1963b, 966).

The motivation for reduction sentences is to capture the case of *term introduction by laws* (1936–1937, §5). By contrast with proper definitions, terms introduced in this way are not eliminable. Instead, the reduction sentences play a dual role: they partially determine the meaning of the new predicate *T* by specifying test conditions under which it holds (and fails to hold), while leaving open the possibility of a fuller specification; and they also have a factual content, expressed by *S*, which asserts that nothing falls in the class defined by the predicate $\varphi x \wedge \psi x$.

The reduction sentence analysis depends only on an observed/unobserved division among events. *C* is a theory that describes events all of which may be observable. The predicates *A*, . . . , *D′* have a privileged status within the reconstruction because they represent manifest or occurrent properties. *T* is distinguished from *A*, . . . , *D′* by its dispositional character, not because the events to which it applies are unobservable. *T* therefore has a lower degree of theoreticity than a predicate which applies only to unobservable events.

The conception of dispositional predicates captured by this account may be visualized as follows: Imagine that there are O-expressions which define regions F and K of a domain D, such that F is properly contained in K. We think of F and $D—K$ as, respectively, the domain and counterdomain of a predicate whose extension is defined on only part of D. Dispositional predicates, on this picture, represent conjectures regarding the location of the precise boundary of a totally defined region, one that is approximated "from below" by F and "from above" by K. Relative to the regions defined by the O-predicates K and F, the region which the dispositional predicate represents has the status of an "ideal" element which can only be approximated but never fully realized.

VII. IS A THEORY ITS RAMSEY SENTENCE?

We saw that Carnap's conception of what is factual can be defended against Quine's objection that the line between the factual and the analytic is necessarily arbitrary. But although this objection can be met, there is a more basic difficulty. Without calling into question the viability of a fact/convention dichotomy, the conception of the factuality of the theoretical postulates that emerges from Carnap's reconstruction is not sufficiently robust. The difficulty is that theoretical sentences, though factual, are *almost* logical truths and hence, in Carnap's reconstruction, *almost* analytic. This is a consequence of the reconstruction's conception of the theoretical vocabulary, since it is what justifies replacing theoretical terms by variables and identifying a theory with its Ramsey sentence. It is often suggested that the effect of Ramseyfication is to call into question the status of realism. But the more basic difficulty is whether, having come to a conception of the theoretical vocabulary that justifies identifying a theory with its Ramsey sentence, one can claim to have captured the sense in which our knowledge of the truth of theoretical statements is genuinely a posteriori and synthetic. This is arguably the fundamental methodological issue that a reconstruction of our theoretical knowledge must successfully address.

We can begin to see how the "quasi-analyticity" of theoretical claims arises by noting a peculiar feature of Carnap's own conception of the domain of the higher order variables of the Ramsey sentence. In his response to Hempel, Carnap says of the Ramsey sentence that while it

does indeed refer to theoretical entities by the use of abstract variables . . . it should be noted that these entities are . . . purely logico-mathematical enti- ties, e.g. natural numbers, classes of such, classes of classes, etc. Never- theless, R(*TC*) is obviously a factual sentence. It says that the observable events in the world are such that there are numbers, classes of such, etc. which are correlated with the events in a prescribed way and which have among themselves certain relations; and this assertion is clearly a factual statement about the world. (1963b, 963)

On this view, the existence claims peculiar to R(*TC*) concern only purely mathematical entities. Of course, identifying theoret- ical properties and relations with purely mathematical entities is at variance with the idea that the higher-order variables range over a domain built upon unobservable physical *events*. In his (1966, 255), Carnap offers a "clarification":

[. . . physicists may, if they so choose,] evade the question about [the exis- tence of electrons] by stating that there are certain observable events, in bubble chambers and so on, that can be described by certain mathematical functions, within the framework of a certain theoretical system . . . [T]o the extent that [the theoretical system] has been confirmed by tests, it is justi- fiable to say that there are instances of certain kinds of events that, in the theory, are called "electrons."

But it remains unclear whether this amounts to a concession.[13] I will not, however, pursue this issue further, since we can now formu- late the difficulty quite precisely, and in a way that is entirely inde- pendent of whether theoretical predicates are understood as purely mathematical properties and relations or as relations among actual events.

The crucial point is this. Suppose there is a model **M** in which the O-sentences hold. Then, provided only that the cardinality of **M** is not unduly restricted by the O-sentences, we can expand **M** to a model **M*** in which the T-sentences are also true. The sense of

---

[13] For a fuller discussion of the historical context and interpretation of these and related passages, including the important influence of Feigl and Maxwell on Car- nap's thought, see Psillos (1999, chapter 3).

"almost analytic" – and even "almost L-true" – that applies to the T-sentences is then the following:

> Modulo a logical assumption of consistency and an empirical assumption about cardinality, it follows that if the O-sentences are true, the T-sentences are also true.

The philosophical interest of this derives from the fact that the relations which, when assigned to the T-predicates occurring in a T-sentence T, make T true-in-M^*, also make T true. This follows from Carnap's reconstruction, because the content of T is reduced to the purely existential assertion that there are relations corresponding to the relational expressions of T that make it true. But, so long as T is satisfiable, this will hold as a matter of logic in any expansion of any model of the O-sentences provided only that the model is large enough.[14]

To see why this situation is unsatisfactory, consider again the elementary example we described earlier in connection with Carnap's analysis of dispositional predicates in "Testability and Meaning." Let T consist of the single sentence,

> T For every x, if Fx, then Rx, and if Rx, then Kx,

where F and K are O-terms and R is a T-term. Its Ramsey sentence is

> $R(T)$ There is an X such that for every x, if Fx, then Xx, and if Xx, then Kx.

The observational content of T is that every F is a K. Now T goes beyond this observational content by telling us that the theoretical property R weakly separates F and K in the sense that F is contained in R and R is contained in K. If true, this is a synthetic truth that we can only know a posteriori; it tells us something about the connection between the three properties F, K, and R, which may of course hold or not but in any case is not a logical consequence of the fact that F is contained in K. But this is not true of $R(T)$: we know a priori – as a matter of logic – that for any F and K, if F is contained in K, there

---

[14] Again, see the Appendix for the justification of these claims.

is an *X* weakly separating them. (If *K* − *F* is empty, let *F* = *X*; if it is not empty, and there is an *x* in *K* but not in *F*, put *X* = *F* ∪ {*x*}.)[15]

Notice, by the way, that contrary to an often-cited response to this line of objection, the difficulty we have raised need have nothing to do with the "reality" of the properties and relations which the Ramsey sentence quantifies over.[16] Even if our theory *T* were concerned with an "artificial" property *R*, it would still make perfect sense for us to distinguish the fact that *R* weakly separates *F* and *K*, both from the claim that *some property or other* separates them, and from the claim that a "real" property separates them. Our theory lacks the triviality of the former claim and the obscurity of the latter; neither claim is a faithful representation of what our theoretical knowledge aspires to tell us.[17]

VIII. EMPIRICISM AND RECONSTRUCTION

It is important to keep in perspective two interdependent but separate issues. There is first and foremost the task of reconstructing the purely theoretical statements of a physical theory in a way that preserves their status as a posteriori claims about the world. Then there is the very different issue of explaining how terms that purport to

---

[15] This simple example of a theory and its Ramsey sentence has been used by Zahar and Worrall (2001, 240–241) to argue that the proper explication of the "observational content" of *T* should not employ an unrestricted quantifier. So understood, the O-sentence

> *For every x, Fx only if Kx*

is strictly stronger than the observational content of *T*. It follows that on Zahar and Worrall's conception of observational content, **R**(*T*) is also strictly stronger than the observational content of *T*. Zahar and Worrall take this observation to undermine criticisms of Ramseyfication like the one raised in the text. But the central critical point does not depend on the exact explication of observational content, but on the difference, to which we have called attention, between *T* and **R**(*T*).

[16] See, for example, Lewis (1984, 227). Lewis's view has been highly influential. For example, Psillos (1999, 62f.), following Lewis, favors a solution along these lines – i.e., one that imposes constraints on the ranges of the variables introduced by Ramseyfication – as does Hochberg (1994), who elaborates Lewis's view in connection with a difficulty closely related to the one discussed in the text and expounded in Demopoulos and Friedman (1985).

[17] Compare, for example, Psillos (1999, 66–67), according to which the difficulty would not arise if we possessed a satisfactory notion of a "natural" relation. This, however, is no more to the point than the notion of a real relation: even non-natural relations can be the subject of non-trivial claims.

refer to unobservable entities can be meaningful. Carnap and the logical empiricist tradition emphasized the problem of the meaning of theoretical terms, arguing that its solution lies in replacing them by variables in the expression of the factual content of the theory; aside from the matter of their logical category, theoretical terms simply do not *have* a meaning that constrains their interpretation.

The difficulty, as we have seen, is that even the relatively liberal strictures of Carnap's mature execution of this program are too restrictive to allow it to capture the epistemic status we attach to our theoretical claims. In this sense, his attempt to extend Hilbert's conception of the meaning of the primitive terms of *pure* mathematics also to the case of *applied* mathematics does not succeed.

The notion that a term's meaningfulness is tied to the observability of its purported referent is a central tenet of classical empiricism, one which, with the notable exception of Feigl, the logical empiricists shared. In "Existential Hypotheses" (1950), Feigl argued persuasively, and in direct opposition to the prevailing current of opinion, for a clear separation of the role of the observation base in questions of *semantic interpretation* from its role in questions of *evidential support*. The question isolated by Feigl which forms the focus of his discussion is whether, because it is at best only indirectly connected with observation, the theoretical vocabulary has a merely formal significance. This, as we have seen, is precisely the assumption underlying Carnap's reconstruction of the language of physics. Our critical assessment of Carnap's account of theoretical claims as "almost analytic" is therefore a vindication of Feigl's reservations.

In view of his importance to Carnap's intellectual development and to the tradition of which logical empiricism is a continuation, it is interesting to observe that this classical empiricist tenet never formed a part of Frege's conception of meaning, neither in *Grundlagen* nor in the theory of sense and reference of his later writings.[18] This is in sharp contrast with Russell's theory of propositional understanding, with its emphasis on acquaintance. For the logical empiricists – here following Russell rather than Frege – it was

---

[18] Frege (1884/1980, §62) clearly shows Frege to have taken for granted the meaningfulness of terms whose reference is not given to us in experience. Feigl's was the first English translation of Frege's *Über Sinn und Bedeutung*; the discussion of "Existential Hypotheses" is clearly influenced by the realism Frege brought to the theory of meaning.

evident that theoretical terms must either be definable in terms of an observational vocabulary or, failing this, otherwise eliminated from the factual component of the reconstruction of the language of science. In light of our discussion, however, it seems that a perspective like Frege's – one that rejects the idea that the meaningfulness of a term is tied to the observability of its referent – is more suitable for formulating a satisfactory theory of theoretical knowledge.

Empiricism, from such a perspective, does not demand that we suspend judgment about whether the primitive terms of our theoretical vocabulary refer; but it does require that judgments regarding their referentiality be revisable in light of experience. We must be in possession of a set of principles controlling the application of our theoretical vocabulary, and we must be able to revise our criteria of application in a manner that is responsive to our experience of the world. But a successful empiricism must also yield the conclusion that our theoretical claims, when true, are at least sometimes significant extensions of their observational consequences. This second desideratum, as we have seen, is not satisfied by Carnap's reconstruction.

We may illustrate the basic idea for satisfying both desiderata by taking 'x is simultaneous with y' as the predicate whose criterion of application is to be explained, thus returning to Einstein's analysis of simultaneity.[19] Simultaneity is clearly of great theoretical significance in Special Relativity; but it is vital to a proper understanding of its role in our theorizing that it not be represented as a T-predicate in the sense of Carnap's reconstruction.

There is an extensive literature devoted to the factual status of the relation of simultaneity in Minkowski space-time.[20] For present purposes it suffices to assume that whether two events are simultaneous is as factual a question as whether they are causally connectible – where two events are *causally connectible* if they belong to the same world line of a massive or massless particle. The present discussion is therefore predicated on the *relative* factuality of simultaneity.

If simultaneity is a factual relation between events, then for an empiricist it is necessary to specify empirical criteria in accordance

---

[19] My remarks on simultaneity are indebted to DiSalle (2005).
[20] For a concise discussion of the principal issues surrounding this question, see Malament (forthcoming, section 3.1).

with which it can be said that pairs of events – including especially distant events – are or are not simultaneous. We therefore need criteria of application that enable us to extend our ordinary judgments involving simultaneity to cases which they may not originally have been designed to cover, and we wish to know whether, in the process, the criteria of application governing such judgments come to be subject to any new constraints.

Among the criteria of application we actually employ, it is clear that some implicitly assume a process of signaling – as, for example, when we count as simultaneous two distant events which are seen to coincide with some local event, such as the position of the hands of a clock. The use of signaling is prominent among our ordinary criteria of application for simultaneity and must be countenanced by the theoretical frameworks of both Special Relativity and Newtonian mechanics. But, because it admits infinitely fast signals, Newtonian mechanics allows for a velocity-*independent* criterion. Within the Newtonian framework, this criterion has the property of being in an appropriate sense, "absolute," since, being independent of any finitely transmitted signal, it is also independent of the relative velocity of the frame of reference. Since the Newtonian framework allows for the possibility of infinitely fast signals, the theoretically definable relation of simultaneity is also absolute – the same for all inertial frames.

There is, however, another criterion of application that uses finite signals, and is therefore velocity-*dependent*. Light signaling, according to Maxwell's theory of electro-magnetism, proceeds with a given (constant) finite velocity, and it is directly tied, as well, to our ordinary criterion of simultaneity, one based on the visual observation of distant events. Remarkably, however, when embedded in the context of Maxwell's theory, the discovery that the velocity of light is independent of the motion of the source shows light signaling to be as absolute a criterion of application as one which, like the Newtonian criterion, is based on the possibility of infinitely fast signals.

But adopting the light signaling criterion implicit in Maxwell's theory (which, in effect, is what Einstein does) has the striking consequence that the relation of simultaneity it governs is *relative*: "observers" in relative motion to one another – in different inertial frames – will disagree on which events are simultaneous. And this leads to the theoretical claim that the space-time generated by the relation of simultaneity is Minkowskian rather than Newtonian, a claim which, in the context of the present discussion, is correctly represented as a highly significant a posteriori discovery about the physical world.

By contrast, suppose that "x is simultaneous with y" is treated as a T-predicate, and the claim that space-time is Minkowskian is represented as a purely theoretical claim of a Carnapian reconstruction. The factual content the reconstruction assigns this theoretical claim is exactly similar to that of the toy theory of the property R considered in the previous section: the consistency of Minkowski geometry suffices to ensure its truth in any model of the O-sentences of a theory of space-time events of which it is a postulate. Such a view is not incoherent; but it does run deeply counter to the status we are inclined to assign theoretical claims of such importance.

IX. APPENDIX: PROOFS OF TECHNICAL CLAIMS

The Craig Interpolation Theorem is a fundamental theorem concerning the metatheory of first order logic. It tells us that if X_i $(i = 1, 2)$ are first order sentences in L_i such that $L = L_1 \cap L_2$ and $X_1 \wedge X_2$ has no model, then there is a sentence X of L such that X_1 implies X and X_2 implies $\neg$X. The basic meta-logical result for our analysis is a corollary to this theorem, one that figures importantly in the analysis of Carnap's notion of observational uninformativeness, since it implies that on a reconstruction like Carnap's a purely theoretical statement – one with no O-vocabulary items – has only L-true observational consequences. The proof of the corollary shows how the disjointness of the T- and O-vocabularies permits a type of model construction that plays a central role in our discussion.

> Let X and Y be sentences of a first order language without equality such that (i) X and Y share no nonlogical vocabulary, (ii) X logically implies Y, and (iii) X is satisfiable. Then Y is logically true.

Proof.[21] Arguing toward a contradiction, suppose that there is a model **M** in which Y fails so that $\neg$Y holds in **M**. Since X is satisfiable, it too has a model **N**, which we may assume is of the same

---

[21] Our proof-sketch is based on Robinson (1974, 5.1.8).

cardinality as $\mathbf{M}$. Let f be a one-one onto map from the domain N of $\mathbf{N}$ to the domain M of $\mathbf{M}$, and for each n-ary relation symbol R occurring in X define an n-ary relation R^M on M by the condition, $\langle a_1, \ldots, a_n \rangle$ is in R^M iff $\langle f^{-1}a_1, \ldots, f^{-1}a_n \rangle$ is in R^N. Since X holds in $\mathbf{N}$, this expands $\mathbf{M}$ to a model $\mathbf{M}^*$ for the vocabulary of X in which X holds when its relation symbols are interpreted by the relations R^M. Since X and Y have disjoint vocabularies, $\neg$Y is true in $\mathbf{M}^*$ iff $\neg$Y is true in $\mathbf{M}$. Thus X $\wedge$ $\neg$Y holds in M*, contrary to the hypothesis that X implies Y.

Notice that the language L for which the corollary holds is restricted: it is a language without equality. If L contained equality, $\neg$Y might hold only in a model of finite cardinality n; but if, for example, X holds only in infinite models, the argument will break down. Restricting the language prevents this, since satisfiability then implies satisfiability in a countably infinite model. This restricts the generality of the corollary, but it does not restrict its philosophical interest. The only effect of the restriction on L that we require is

(*) *The reconstruction applies to sentences which are true in countably infinite models if they are true at all.*

Taking L to be without equality is a simple way of ensuring (*), but it is not strictly necessary: we can simply impose the requirement (*) directly and proceed to avail ourselves of equality and the expressive resources it brings.[22]

To relate the corollary to the discussion in the body of the chapter and, in particular, to the claim that, modulo a logical assumption of consistency and an empirical assumption about cardinality, it follows that, if the O-sentences are true, the T-sentences are also true, notice that the proof of the corollary shows how any sufficiently large model of the O-sentences of a theory can be expanded to a model of the T-sentences, provided that the T-sentences are consistent. Since *any* such model of the O-sentences can be so expanded, any such model which is *also* a model of the C-rules can be so expanded.

Here are the justifications of the remaining technical claims of the paper.

---

[22] This addresses a question raised in Williams (1973, 303).

A theory and its Ramsey sentence have the same observational consequences.

In one direction the implication is immediate, and in the other it is only slightly less so. If there is an assignment to the variables $X_1, \ldots, X_n$ that satisfies $TC(O_1, \ldots, O_m; X_1, \ldots, X_n)$, then this assignment can form the basis of an interpretation of the non-logical constants $T_1, \ldots, T_n$ under which the theory is true. Hence if there is a model of $\mathbf{R}(TC) \wedge \neg X$, X an O-sentence, there is a model of $TC \wedge \neg X$.

All consequences of the Carnap sentence of a theory are O-uninformative.

It suffices to show that $\mathbf{C}(TC)$ is O-uninformative. If $\mathbf{C}(TC)$ implies X, then $\neg\mathbf{R}(TC)$ implies X and TC implies X. But since X is an O-sentence, $\mathbf{R}(TC)$ also implies X. Hence, $\mathbf{R}(TC) \vee \neg\mathbf{R}(TC)$ implies X, and X is L-true. Notice also that since for any T, $\mathbf{R}(T)$ is O-equivalent to T, the O-uninformativeness of $\mathbf{C}(TC)$ is equivalent to the claim that the Ramsey sentence of the Carnap sentence of TC is L-true.

Winnie's Observation: Suppose TC is satisfiable and that T_i is a T-sentence logically implied by TC. Then $\mathbf{C}(TC) \wedge T_i$ is O-uninformative.

We must show that if $\mathbf{C}(TC) \wedge T_i$ implies an observational X, then X is L-true. Since, by hypothesis, $\mathbf{C}(TC)$ implies $T_i \to X$, $\neg\mathbf{R}(TC)$ implies $T_i \to X$. Now TC implies $\mathbf{C}(TC)$, and by hypothesis TC implies T_i; hence, since TC implies X and X is an O-sentence, $\mathbf{R}(TC)$ *also* implies X, and therefore, $\mathbf{R}(TC)$ implies $T_i \to X$. Thus T_i implies X. Now T_i and X share no non-logical vocabulary and T_i is satisfiable. It therefore follows by the corollary to Craig's Interpolation Theorem that X is L-true. (Cf. section V of the appendix to Winnie (1970), and the discussion on pp. 149–150 of its reprinting in Hintikka (1975b). It should be noted that I have departed from Winnie's terminology.)

The Carnap sentence of a theory is O-noncreative.

Here is essentially Winnie's proof: Suppose that $\mathbf{C}(TC) \wedge X$ (X a consequence of TC) implies an O-sentence Y. By the definition of $\mathbf{C}(TC)$, it follows that $(\neg\mathbf{R}(TC) \vee TC) \wedge X$ implies Y; therefore $\neg\mathbf{R}(TC) \wedge X$ implies Y and $TC \wedge X$ implies Y. Since, by hypothesis TC implies X, TC implies Y; whence, since Y is observational, $\mathbf{R}(TC)$

implies Y, and therefore $\mathbf{R}(\mathbf{TC})$ implies X → Y. But we also have that ¬$\mathbf{R}(\mathbf{TC})$ implies X → Y. Thus, X implies Y.

> *Any sentence not implied by the Carnap sentence of a theory is O-creative in the theory.*

We are required to show that any X which is satisfiable and not a consequence of $\mathbf{C}(\mathbf{TC})$ is O-creative, where we may suppose, without loss of generality, that $\mathbf{TC}$ implies X. Thus by the definition of O-non-creativity, we must find a Y (Y a consequence of $\mathbf{TC}$) and a Z (Z an O-sentence) such that X ∧ Y implies Z, but Y by itself does not imply Z. To this end, put Y = X → $\mathbf{R}(\mathbf{TC})$ and Z = $\mathbf{R}(\mathbf{TC})$. Since $\mathbf{TC}$ implies $\mathbf{R}(\mathbf{TC})$, $\mathbf{TC}$ implies Y. Clearly, Z is an O-sentence, and X ∧ Y implies Z. To complete the proof, it remains to show that Y by itself does not imply $\mathbf{R}(\mathbf{TC})$, but this follows from properties of the relation of logical consequence which will be familiar from earlier proofs we have reviewed.

12 Carnap on probability and induction

I. INTRODUCTION

This chapter discusses Carnap's work on probability and induction, using the notation and terminology of modern mathematical probability, viewed from the perspective of the Bayesian or subjective school of probability. Carnap initially used a logical notation and terminology that made his work accessible and interesting to a generation of philosophers, but it also limited its impact in other areas such as statistics, mathematics, and the sciences. Using the notation of modern mathematical probability is not only more natural, but it also makes it far easier to place Carnap's work alongside the contributions of such other pioneers of epistemic probability as Frank Ramsey, Bruno de Finetti, I. J. Good, L. J. Savage, and Richard Jeffrey.

Carnap's interest in logical probability was primarily as a tool, a tool to be used in understanding the quantitative confirmation of a hypothesis based on evidence and, more generally, in rational decision-making. The resulting analysis of induction involved a two-step process: one first identified a broad class of possible confirmation functions (the *regular c-functions*), and then identified either a unique function in that class (early Carnap) or a parametric family (later Carnap) of specific confirmation functions. The first step in the process put Carnap in substantial agreement with subjectivists such as Ramsey and de Finetti; it is the second step, the attempt to limit the class of probabilities still further, that distinguishes Carnap from his subjectivist brethren.

So: precisely what are the limitations that Carnap saw as natural to impose? In order to discuss these, we must begin with his conceptS of probability.

II. PROBABILITY

The word probability has always had a multiplicity of meanings. In the beginning mathematical probability had a meaning that was largely *epistemic* (as opposed to *aleatory*); thus for Laplace probability relates in part to our knowledge and in part to our ignorance. During the nineteenth century, however, empirical alternatives arose. In the years 1842 and 1843, no fewer than four independent proposals for an objective or frequentist interpretation were first advanced: those of Jakob Friedrich Fries in Germany, Antoine Augustin Cournot in France, and John Stuart Mill and Robert Leslie Ellis in England. Less than a quarter of a century later, John Venn's *Logic of Chance* (Venn, 1866), the first book in English devoted exclusively to the philosophical foundations of probability, took a purely frequentist view of the subject.

Ramsey, in advancing his view of a quantitative subjective probability based on a consistent system of preferences (Ramsey, 1931), deftly side-stepped the debate by conceding that the frequency interpretation of probability was a perfectly reasonable one, one which might have considerable value in science, but argued that this did not preclude a subjective interpretation as well. During the twentieth century the debate became increasingly more complex, von Mises, Reichenbach, and Neyman advancing frequentist views, and Keynes, Ramsey, and Jeffreys competing logical or subjective theories.

Carnap sought to bring order into this chaos by introducing the concepts of *explicandum* and *explicatum*. Sometimes philosophical debates unnecessarily arise due to the use of ill-defined (or even undefined) concepts. For example, an argument about whether or not viruses constitute a form of life can only really arise from a failure to define just what one means by life; define the term and the status of viruses (whose structure and function are in many cases very well understood) will become clear one way or the other. This is essentially an operationalist or logical positivist perspective, a legacy of Carnap's days in the Vienna Circle. For Carnap the explicandum was the ill-defined concept; the explicatum the clarification of it that someone advanced.

But probability did not involve just a dispute over the explication of a term. The term itself did double duty, being used by some in an epistemic fashion (referring to the degree to which a hypothesis was credited), and by others in an aleatory fashion (to a frequency in a class or series). To unravel the Gordian knot of probability, one had to sever the two concepts and recognize that there are two distinct explicanda, each requiring separate exegesis.

II.1 Early views

In his paper "The Two Concepts of Probability" (1945b), Carnap introduced the terms *probability₁* and *probability₂*, the first referring to probability in its guise as a measure of confirmation, the second as a measure of frequency. This had twin advantages: putting the issue so clearly, debates about the one true meaning of probability became less credible; and the more neutral terminology helped shift the argument from issues of linguistic useage (which, after all, vary from one language to another), to conceptual explication. These ideas were developed at great length in Carnap's magisterial *Logical Foundations of Probability* (1950b), probabilities being assigned to sentences in a formal language. In his later work Carnap discarded sentences (which he viewed as insufficiently expressive for his purposes) in favor of events or propositions, which he regarded as essentially equivalent, and we shall adopt this viewpoint. (The main technical complication in working at the level of sentences is that more than one sentence can assert the same proposition; for example, $\alpha \wedge \beta$ and $\neg(\neg\alpha \vee \neg\beta)$.)

Carnap's approach was a direct descendant of Wittgenstein's relatively brief remarks on probability in the *Tractatus*, later developed at some length by Waismann (1930). Carnap, following Waismann, assumed the existence of a *regular measure function* $m(x)$ on sentences, defining these by first assuming a normalized non-negative function on molecular sentences and then extending these to all sentences. Carnap then defined in the usual way $c(h, e)$, the conditional probability of a proposition h given the proposition e, as the ratio $m(h \wedge e)/m(e)$.

Carnap interpreted the conditional probabilities $c(h, e)$ as a measure of the extent to which evidence e confirms hypothesis h. Such functions had already been studied by Janina Hosiasson-Lindenbaum (1940) a decade earlier. Unlike Carnap, Hosiasson-Lindenbaum took a purely axiomatic approach: she studied the general properties of confirmation functions $c(h, e)$, assuming only that they satisfied a basic set of axioms. There are several equivalent versions of this set appearing in the literature; here is one particularly natural formulation:

The axioms of confirmation

1. $0 \leq c(h, e) \leq 1$.
2. If $h \leftrightarrow h'$ and $e \leftrightarrow e'$, then $c(h, e) = c(h', e')$.
3. If $e \to h$, then $c(h, e) = 1$.
4. If $e \to \neg(h \wedge h')$, then $c(h \vee h', e) = c(h, e) + c(h', e)$.
5. $c(h \wedge h', e) = c(h, e) \cdot c(h', h \wedge e)$.

Carnap's conditional probabilities $c(h, e)$ satisfied these axioms (and so were plausible candidates for confirmation functions).

II.2 Betting odds and Dutch books

But just what do the numbers $m(e)$ or $c(h, e)$ represent? It was one of the great contributions of Ramsey and de Finetti to advance *operational definitions* of subjective probability; for Ramsey, primarily as arising from preferences, for de Finetti as fair odds in a bet. By then imposing rationality criteria on such quantities, both were able to derive the standard axioms for finitely additive probability. Ramsey, in a remarkable *tour de force*, was able to demonstrate the simultaneous existence of utility and probability functions $u(x)$ and $p(x)$. He did this by imposing natural consistency constraints on a (sufficiently rich) set of preferences, introducing the device of the *ethically neutral proposition* (the philosophical equivalent of tossing a fair coin) as a means of interpolating between competing alternatives. The functions $u(x)$ and $p(x)$ track one's preferences in the sense that one action is preferred to another if and only if its expected utility is greater than the other. (Jeffrey, 1983, discusses Ramsey's system and presents an extremely interesting variant of it.)

De Finetti, in contrast, initially gave primacy to probabilities interpreted as betting odds. (If p is a probability, then the corresponding odds are $p/(1 - p)$.) The odds represent a bet either side of which one is willing to take. (Thus, the odds of $2: 1$ in favor of an event means that one would accept either a bet of $2: 1$ for, or a bet of $1: 2$ against. This is somewhat akin to the algorithm for two children dividing a cake: one divides the cake into two pieces, the other chooses one of the two pieces.) De Finetti imposed as his rationality constraint the requirement that these odds be *coherent*; that is, that it be impossible to construct a *Dutch book* out of them. (In a Dutch book, an opponent can choose a portfolio of bets such that he is assured of winning money. The existence of a Dutch book is analogous to the existence of arbitrage opportunities in the derivatives market.) A conditional probability $P(A \mid B)$ in de Finetti's system is interpreted as a *conditional bet* on A, available only if B is determined to have happened. De Finetti was able to show that the probabilities corresponding to a coherent set of bettings odds must satisfy the standard axioms of finitely additive probability. For example, if one takes the axioms for confirmation listed in the previous sub-section, all are direct consequences of coherence.

John Kemeny, one of Carnap's collaborators in the 1950s, proved a beautiful converse to this result (Kemeny, 1955). He showed that the above five properties of a confirmation function are at once both necessary and sufficient for coherence. That is, although de Finetti had in effect shown that coherence implies the five axioms, in principle there might be other, incoherent confirmation functions also satisfying the five axioms. If one did not begin by accepting (coherent) betting odds as the operational interpretation of $c(h, e)$, this left open the possibility of other confirmation functions, ones not falling into the Ramsey and de Finetti framework. The power of Kemeny's result is that if one accepts the five axioms above as necessary desiderata for any confirmation function $c(h, e)$, then such functions necessarily assign coherent betting odds to the universe of events. This was a powerful argument in favor of the betting odds interpretation, and it appears to have persuaded Carnap, who adopted it. (Thus while in *Logical Foundations of Probability* Carnap had advanced no fewer than three possible interpretations for probability$_1$ – evidential support, fair betting quotients, and estimates of statistical frequencies – in his later work he explicitly abandoned the first of these, and wrote almost exclusively in terms of the second.)

The "normative" force of Dutch book arguments has itself been the subject of considerable debate. Armendt (1993) contains a balanced discussion of the issues and provides a useful entry into the literature.

II.3   Later views

The appearance of Carnap's book generated considerable discussion and debate in the philosophical community. A second volume was promised, but never appeared. Like many before him, who found themselves enmeshed in the intellectual quicksand of the problem of induction (such as Bernoulli and Bayes), Carnap continued to grapple with the problem, refining and extending his results, but found new advances and insights (both on the part of himself and others) coming so quickly, that he eventually abandoned as impractical the project of a definitive and systematic book-length treatment in favor of publishing from time to time compilations of progress reports. Two such installments eventually appeared (Carnap and Jeffrey 1971; Jeffrey, 1980), although even these were delayed far past their initially anticipated date of publication.

Because no true successor to his *Logical Foundations of Probability* ever appeared (the short technical monograph *The Continuum of Inductive Methods*, 1952, being of an entirely different nature), it is not always appreciated just how much of an evolution in Carnap's views about probability took place over the last two decades of his life. A decade later, for example, Carnap shifted his terminology, contrasting "*objective* (or statistical) *probability*" versus "*subjective* (or personal) *probability*" (Carnap, 1962, 304). This reflected in part a changing environment: the publication of the books by Good (1950) and Savage (1954), and the increasing appreciation of the pre-war contributions of Ramsey and de Finetti.

Indeed, Carnap's 1962 paper "The Aim of Inductive Logic" reflects views very similar to those of Ramsey and de Finetti: decision-making in the face of uncertainty involves utilities and probabilities (in their guise as degrees of belief). One distinguishes between *actual* degrees of belief, which are descriptive and psychological, versus *rational* degrees of belief, which are normative and ideal ("quasi-psychological"). Further distinctions are of course possible; see Good (1959 and 1965, chapter 1) for a detailed typology. (In a later note, Good, 1971, whimsically claims that one can distinguish at least $4^4 \cdot 3^6 \cdot 6 = 46,656$ possible varieties of Bayesians!)

Nevertheless, even accepting the subjective viewpoint, the issue remains: can the inductive confirmation of hypotheses be understood in quantitative terms? It was this later question that was of primary interest to Carnap, and the one to which he turned in a second paper "On Inductive Logic" (1945a).

III. CONFIRMATION

In order to better appreciate Carnap's analysis of the inductive process, let us briefly review the background against which he wrote.

First some basic mathematical probability. Suppose we have an uncertain event that can have one of two possible outcomes, arbitrarily termed "success" and "failure," and let S_n denote the number of successes in n instances ("trials"). If the trials are independent, and have a constant probability p of success, then the probability of k successes in the n trials is given by the *binomial distribution*:

$$P(S_n = k) = \binom{n}{k} p^k (1 - p)^{n-k}, \qquad 0 \le k \le n.$$

Here

$$\binom{n}{k} = \frac{n!}{k!(n-k)!}$$

is the *binomial coefficient*, and $n! = n \cdot (n-1) \cdot (n-2) \ldots 3 \cdot 2 \cdot 1$.

Suppose next that the probability p is itself random, with some probability distribution $d\mu(p)$ on the unit interval. For example, success and failure might correspond to getting a head or tail when tossing a ducat, and the ducat is chosen from a bag of ducats having variable probability p of coming up heads (reflecting the composition of coins in the bag). In this case the probability $P(S_n = k)$ is obtained by averaging the binomial probabilities over the different possible values of p. This average is standardly given by an integral, namely

$$P(S_n = k) = \int_0^1 \binom{n}{k} p^k (1 - p)^{n-k} d\mu(p), \qquad 0 \le k \le n,$$

but one of the attractions of the Carnap approach is that such an appeal to integration is unnecessary. (This is the first and last time an integral will appear in this chapter. Modern Bayesian statistics makes extensive use of such *integral representations*.)

In our example $d\mu(p)$ was aleatory in nature, tied to the composition of the bag. But it could just as well be taken to be epistemic, reflecting our degree of belief regarding the different possible values of p.

III.1 The rule of succession

In this analysis there are several important questions as yet unanswered. In particular, the nature of p (is it a physical probability or a degree of belief?) has not been specified, and no guidance has been given regarding the origin of the *initial* or *prior* distribution $d\mu(p)$. In particular, even if the nature of p is specificed, how does one determine the prior distribution $d\mu(p)$? For Laplace and his school, one had resort to the *principle of indifference*: lacking any reason to favor one value of p over another, the distribution was taken to be uniform over the unit interval: $d\mu(p) = dp$. In this case the integral simplifies to give:

$$P(S_n = k) = \frac{1}{n+1}, \qquad 0 \le k \le n.$$

Given this formula, it is a simple matter to derive the corresponding *predictive probabilities*. If, for example, X_j is a so-called indicator variable taking the values 1 or 0, depending on whether the outcome of the j-th trial is a success or failure, respectively (so that the number of successes S_n is $X_1 + \cdots + X_n$), then $P(X_{n+1} = 1 \mid S_n = k)$ is the conditional probability of a success on the next trial, based on the experience of the past n trials. Since the formula for conditional probability is $P(A \mid B) = P(A \text{ and } B)/P(B)$, it follows after a little algebra that

$$P(X_{n+1} \mid S_n = k) = \frac{k+1}{n+2}.$$

This is the celebrated (or infamous) *rule of succession*. Both it and the controversial principle of indifference on which it was based were the subject of harsh criticism beginning in the middle of the nineteenth century; see, for example, Zabell (1989). But in fact the Reverend Thomas Bayes, the eponymous founder of the subject of Bayesian statistics, employed a subtler argument that paralleled Carnap's later approach. Bayes (1764) reasoned that in a case of complete ignorance ("an event concerning the probability of which we absolutely know nothing antecedently to any trials made concerning it"), one has $P(S_n = k) = 1/(n+1)$ for all $n \ge 1$ and $0 \le k \le n$ (in effect Bayes takes the latter to be the definition of the former), and this in turn implies that the prior must be uniform. (The argument can be made rigorous by invoking the Hausdorff moment theorem; see Zabell, 1988. Stigler, 1982, argues that this does not entail the same paradoxes as the Principle of Indifference applied to the parameter p.)

This is how matters stood in 1921, the year John Maynard Keynes's *Treatise on Probability* appeared. Keynes's *Treatise* contains a useful summary of much of this debate; see also Zabell (1989). The next several decades saw increasing clarification of the foundations of probability and its use in inductive inference. But the particular thread we are interested in here involves a curious development that took place in two independent stages.

IV. EXCHANGEABILITY

In 1924 William Ernest Johnson, an English logician and philosopher at King's College, Cambridge, published the third volume of his *Logic*. In an appendix at the end, Johnson suggested an alternative analysis to the one just discussed, one which represented a giant step forward. But despite the respect accorded him in Cambridge, Johnson had only limited influence outside it, and after his death in 1931, his work was little noted. It is one of the ironies of this subject that Carnap later followed essentially the same route as Johnson, but to much greater effect, in part because his *Logical Foundations of Probability* embedded his analysis in a much more detailed setting, and in part because he continued to refine his treatment of the subject for nearly two decades (whereas Johnson died only a few years after the appearance of his book).

Johnson's analysis contained several elements of novelty. First he considered the case of $t \geq 2$ equipossible cases (instead of just two). The point of this was that in many of the most telling attacks on the Principle of Indifference, situations were considered where the outcome of interest could not naturally be considered as one of two equipossible competing alternatives. By encompassing the multinomial case (several possible categories rather than just two) Johnson's analysis applied to situations in which either the multiple competing outcomes can naturally be regarded as equipossible, or at least further analyzed into equipossible subcases.

IV.1 The permutation postulate

Second, Johnson presciently introduced the concept of *exchangeability*. Let us consider a sequence of random outcomes $X_1, \ldots, X_n$, each taking on one of t possible types $c_1, \ldots, c_t$. (For example, you are on the Starship Enterprise, and each time you encounter someone, they are either Klingon, Romulan, or Vulcan, so that $t = 3$.) Then a typical probability of interest is of the form

$$P(X_1 = e_1, X_2 = e_2, \ldots, X_n = e_n), \qquad e_i \in \{c_1, \ldots, c_t\}, \quad 1 \leq i \leq t.$$

In the classical inductive setting, the *order* of these is irrelevent, the only thing that matters being the counts or frequencies observed for each of the t categories. (More complex situtations will be discussed later.) Thus, if n_i is the number of X_j falling into the i-th category, it is natural to assume that all sequences $X_1 = e_1, X_2 = e_2, \ldots, X_n = e_n$ having the same frequency counts $n_1, n_2, \ldots, n_t$ have the same probability. Johnson termed this the *permutation* postulate. (Carnap called the sequences $e_1, \ldots, e_n$ *state descriptions*, the frequency counts $n_1, \ldots, n_t$ *structure descriptions*, and made the identical symmetry assumption.)

The permutation postulate (the assumption of *exchangeability* in modern parlance) was later independently introduced by the Italian Bruno de Finetti (see, for example, de Finetti, 1937), and became a centerpiece of his theory. For our purposes here, the important point is that if the sequence is assumed to be exchangeable, then an assignment of probabilities to sequences of outcomes $e_1, e_2, \ldots, e_n$ reduces to assigning probabilities $P(n_1, n_2, \ldots, n_t)$ to sequences of frequency counts $n_1, n_2, \ldots, n_t$. This is because there are (using the standard notation for the *multinomial coefficient*)

$$\binom{n}{n_1 \ n_2 \ \ldots \ n_t} = \frac{n!}{n_1! \, n_2! \ldots n_t!}$$

different possible sequences $e_1, e_2, \ldots, e_n$ giving rise to the same set of frequency counts $n_1, n_2, \ldots, n_t$, and each of these is assumed to be equally likely, so by exchangeability and the additivity of probability

$$P(n_1, n_2, \ldots, n_t) = \left(\frac{n!}{n_1! \, n_2! \ldots n_t!} \right) P(e_1, e_2, \ldots, e_n).$$

(That is, the probability of a state description $e_1, \ldots, e_n$, times the number of state descriptions having the same corresponding structure description $n_1, \ldots, n_t$, gives the probability of that structure description.)

It is a simple but nevertheless instructive exercise to verify that the predictive probabilities in this case take on a simple form:

$$P(X_{n+1} = c_i \mid X_1 = e_1, X_2 = e_2, \ldots, X_n = e_n)$$
$$= P(X_{n+1} = c_i \mid n_1, n_2, \ldots, n_t).$$

(That is, although the conditional probability apparently depends on the entire state description $e_1, \ldots, e_n$, in fact it only depends on the corresponding structure description $n_1, \ldots, n_t$.) In statistical parlance this is summarized by saying that the frequencies $n_1, \ldots, n_t$ are *sufficient statistics*: no information is lost in summarizing the sequence $e_1, \ldots, e_n$ by the counts $n_1, \ldots, n_t$.

IV.2 *The combination postulate*

But what do we choose for $P(n_1, n_2, \ldots, n_t)$? In the case $t = 2$, this reduces to assigning probabilities to the pairs (n_1, n_2). A little thought will show that Bayes's postulate (that the different possible frequencies k are equally likely) is equivalent to assuming that the different pairs (n_1, n_2) are equally likely (since $n_1 = k, n_2 = n - n_1$ and n is fixed). This in turn suggests the probability assignment that takes each of the possible structure descriptions to be equally likely, and this is in fact the path that both Johnson and Carnap initially took (Johnson termed this the *combination postulate*). Since there are

$$\binom{n+t-1}{t}$$

possible structure descriptions (aka "ordered t-partitions of n," a well-known combinatorial fact), and each of these is assumed equally likely, one has

$$P(n_1, n_2, \ldots, n_t) = \frac{1}{\binom{n+t-1}{t}}.$$

It then follows from the assumption of exchangeability that any state description $e_1, e_2, \ldots, e_n$ having the structure description $n_1, n_2, \ldots, n_t$ has probability

$$P(e_1, e_2, \ldots, e_n) = \frac{1}{\binom{n+t-1}{t}\binom{n}{n_1 \, n_2 \ldots n_t}}.$$

This is Carnap's m^* function. Having thus specified the probabilities of the "atomic" sequences, all other probabilities, including the rules of succession, are completely determined. Some simple algebra in fact yields

$$P(X_{n+1} = c_i \mid n_1, n_2, \ldots, n_t) = \frac{n_i + 1}{n + t}.$$

This is Carnap's c^* function.

V. THE CONTINUUM OF INDUCTIVE METHODS

Although the mathematics of the derivation of the c^* system is certainly attractive, its assumption that all structure descriptions are equally likely is hardly compelling, and Carnap soon turned to more general systems. It is ironic that here too his line of attack very closely paralleled that of Johnson. After criticisms from C. D. Broad (1924) and others, Johnson devised a more general postulate, later termed by I. J. Good (1965) the *sufficientness postulate*. This assumes that the predictive probabilities for a particular type i are a function of how many observations of the type have been seen already (n_i), and the total sample size n. It is a remarkable fact that this characterizes the predictive probabilities aka rules of succession (and therefore the probability of any sequence).

V.1 The Johnson–Carnap continuum

Suppose $X_1, X_2, \ldots, X_n, \ldots$ represent an infinite sequence of observations, and that at each stage there are t possible outcomes. Assume the following three conditions are satisfied:

1. There are at least three types of species; $t \geq 3$.
2. Any state description $e_1, \ldots, e_n$ is a priori possible: $P(e_1, \ldots, e_n) > 0$.
3. The "sufficientness postulate" is satisfied:

$$P(X_{n+1} = e_i \mid n_1, \ldots, n_t) = f_i(n_i, n).$$

Then (unless the outcomes are independent of each other, so that observing one or more provides no predictive power regarding the others) the predictive probabilities have a very special form: there exist positive constants $\alpha_1, \ldots, \alpha_t$ such that for all $n \geq 1$, states e_i, and structure descriptions $n_1, \ldots, n_t$,

$$P(X_{n+1} = e_i \mid n_1, \ldots, n_t) = \frac{n_i + \alpha_i}{n + \alpha_1 + \cdots + \alpha_t}.$$

This truly beautiful result characterizes the predictive probabilities up to a finite sequence of positive constants $\alpha_1, \alpha_2, \ldots, \alpha_t$. Note the c^* measure of confirmation is a very special case of the continuum, with $\alpha_i = 1$ for all i.

Technical note: The assumption that sequences of arbitrary length satisfy the permutation postulate implies that their probabilities have an integral representation of the type mentioned earlier in section III; this is the content of the celebrated *de Finetti representation theorem*. Many results in the literature of inductive inference are often easier to state, prove, or interpret in terms of such representations. For example, Johnson's theorem can be interpreted as asserting that the averaging measure in the appropriate integral representation is a member of the classical *Dirichlet family* of prior distributions. Happily, our ability to characterize the predictive probabilities in the above concrete manner means that in principle we can entirely pass over this interesting but more mathematically complex fact.

V.2 History

The result itself has an interesting history. Johnson considered the special case when the function $f_i(n_i, n) = f(n_i, n)$; that is, it does not depend on the category or type i. In this case there is just one parameter, α, since $\alpha_i = \alpha/t$ for all i. Johnson did not publish his result in his own lifetime (shades of Bernoulli and Bayes!); he had planned a fourth volume of his *Logic*, but only completed drafts of three chapters of it at the time of his death. A (then very young) R. B. Braithwaite edited the chapters for publication, and they appeared as three separate articles in *Mind* in 1932 (Johnson, 1932). (It is ironic that G. E. Moore, the editor of *Mind*, questioned the desirability of including a mathematical appendix giving the details of the proof in such a journal, but Braithwaite – fortunately – insisted.) Due to its posthumous character, the proof as published contained a few lacunae, and a desire to fill these led to Zabell (1982). Although Johnson did not consider the asymmetric case, the just cited paper shows that not only can the above-mentioned lacunae be filled, but that Johnson's method very naturally generalizes to cover the asymmetric case (when the predictive function $f_i(n_i, n)$ depends on i), the case $t = \infty$, and the case of finite exchangeable sequences that are not infinitely extendible.

Carnap followed much the same path, except that initially he considered only the symmetric, category independent case, and *assumed* both the sufficientness postulate and the form of the predictive probabilities given in the theorem. It was only later that his collaborator John G. Kemeny was able to prove the equivalence of the two (assuming $t > 2$). Carnap subsequently extended these results, first to cover the case $t = 2$ (Carnap and Stegmüller, 1959); and finally in Jeffrey (1980, chapter 6) abandoned the assumption of symmetry between categories and derived the full result given above (see also Kuiper, 1978). The historical evolution is traced in Schilpp (1963, 74–75 and 979–980), Carnap and Jeffrey (1971, 1–4 and 223), and Jeffrey (1980, 1–5 and 103–104).

VI. INTERPRETATION OF THE CONTINUUM

Let us consider a specific method in the continuum, say with parameters $\alpha_1, \ldots, \alpha_t$. Then one can write the rule of succession as

$$P(X_{n+1} = c_i \mid n_i) = \frac{n_i + \alpha}{n + \alpha} = \left(\frac{n}{n+\alpha}\right)\left[\frac{n_i}{n}\right] + \left(\frac{\alpha}{n+\alpha}\right)\left[\frac{\alpha_i}{\alpha}\right].$$

The two expressions in square brackets have obvious interpretations: the first, n_i/n is the *empirical frequency*, and represents the input of our experience; the second, $\frac{\alpha_i}{\alpha}$, is our initial or prior probability concerning the likelihood of seeing c_i (set $n_i = n = 0$ in the formula). The two terms in rounded brackets, $n/(n+\alpha)$ and $\alpha/(n+\alpha)$, sum to one and express the relative weight accorded to our observations versus our prior information. If α is small, then $n/(n+\alpha)$ is close to one, and the empirical frequencies n_i/n are accorded primacy; if α is large, then $n/(n+\alpha)$ is small, and the initial probabilties are accorded primacy. The joint probability of a sequence of events can be built up from a sequence of conditional probabilities. For example: the joint probability

$$P(X_1 = e_1, X_2 = e_2, X_3 = e_3)$$

can be expressed as

$$P(X_1 = e_1) \bullet P(X_2 = e_2 \mid X_1 = e_1) \bullet P(X_3 = e_3 \mid X_1 = e_1, X_2 = e_2)$$

This has the important consequence that one can express joint probabilities in terms of initial probabilities and rules of succession (which is why the latter are so important).

VII. CONFIRMATION OF UNIVERSAL GENERALIZATIONS

Suppose all n observations are of the same type; for example, that we are observing crows and that thus far all have been black. In such situtations, it is natural to view our experience as indicating not merely that most crows are black, but as confirming the "universal generalization" that *all* crows are black. This apparently natural expectation, however, leads to apparently considerable complexities.

VII.1 Paradox feigned

This is because it is an interesting (and sometimes thought paradoxical) property of the Johnson–Carnap continuum that universal generalizations have zero probability of occurring. Given n black crows, for example, it follows from the formula at the end of the last section that the probabiity that the next k crows are also black is

$$\left(\frac{n+\alpha_i}{n+\alpha}\right) \cdot \left(\frac{n+1+\alpha_i}{n+1+\alpha}\right) \cdot \ldots \cdot \left(\frac{n+k-1+\alpha_i}{n+k-1+\alpha}\right).$$

It is not hard to see that this product tends to zero as k tends to infinity (see, for example Knopp, 1947, 218–221, for the necessary technical tools).

This was viewed as a defect of Carnap's system by a number of critics, for example Barker (1957, 87–88) and Ayer (1972, 37–38, 80–81). The property had in fact been noted much earlier in the special case of the rule of succession for dichotomous outcomes; see Zabell (1989, 306–308) for a number of examples.

VII.2 Paradox lost

It is possible to see what is going wrong in terms of the sufficientness postulate. Suppose there are three categories, 1, 2, and 3, and that none of the observations to date are of the first type. What can one say about

$$P(X_{2n+1} = c_1 \mid n_1, n_2, n_3)?$$

According to the sufficientness postulate, there is no difference between the cases (a) $n_2 = 2n, n_3 = 0$, (b) $n_2 = 0, n_3 = 2n$, and (c) $n_2 = n_3 = n$. But from the point of universal generalizations there is an obvious difference: the first and second cases confirm different universal generalizations (which may have different initial probabilities), while the third case disconfirms both generalizations. Any continuum of inductive methods that confirms universal generalizations must treat these cases differently.

Thus it is necessary to relax the sufficientness postulate, at least in the case when $n_i = n$ for some i. This diagnosis suggests a simple remedy. Suppose we weaken the sufficientness postulate so that the "representative functions" $f_i(n_1, \ldots, n_t)$ (to use yet another terminology that is sometimes employed) are assumed to be functions of n_i and n unless $n_i = 0$ and $n_j = n$ for some $j \neq i$. Then it can be shown (see, for example, Zabell, 1996) that as long as the observations are exclusively of one type, the representative functions consist of two parts: a term corresponding to the posterior probability that all future observations will also be of this type (the "universal generalization"), and a term corresponding to a classical Johnson–Carnap continuum; and this continues to be the case as long as all observations are of a single type. If, however, at any stage a second type is observed, then the representative functions revert to those of the pure Johnson–Carnap form.

Thus the criticisms of the Johnson–Carnap continuum were easily answered even at the time they were made: in hindsight the diagnosis of the problem in terms of the sufficientness postulate is apparent, the minimal modification of the postulate necessary to remove the difficulty results in an expanded continuum that adds precisely the desired universal generalizations (and no more), and this can be proved via a straightfoward modification of the classical proof of Johnson (for further discussion and references, see Zabell, 1996).

This extension of the original Carnap continuum is a special case of a richer class of extensions due earlier to Hintikka, Niiniluoto, and Kuipers.

VII.3 Hintikka–Niiniluoto systems

In order to appreciate Hintikka's contribution, consider first the category symmetric case. Let $T_n(X_1, X_2, \ldots, X_n)$ denote the number of distinct types or species observed in the sample. In the continuum discussed in the previous sub-section the predictive probabilities now depend not just on n_i and n, but also on T_n, the number of instantiated categories. Specifically: is $T_n = 1$ or is $T_n > 1$? Thus put, this suggests a natural generalization: let the predictive probabilities be *any* function of n_i, n, and T_n. The result is a very attractive extension of the Carnap continuum.

In brief, if the predictive probabilities depend on T_n, then in general they arise from mixtures of Johnson–Carnap continua concentrated on sub-sets of the possible types. Thus, given three categories a, b, c, the probabilities can be concentrated on a or b or c (universal generalizations), or Johnson–Carnap continua corresponding to the three pairs (a, b), (a, c), (b, c), or a Johnson–Carnap continuum on all three. In retrospect, this is of course quite natural. If only two of the three possibilities are observed in a long sequence of observations (say a and b), then (in addition to giving us information about the relative frequency of a and b) this tentatively confirms the initial hypothesis that *only* a's and b's will occur. In the more general category asymmetric case, the initial probabilities for the six different generalizations (a, b, c, ab, ac, and bc) can differ, and the predictive probabilities are postulated to be functions of n_i, n, and the observed *constituent*: that is, the specific set of categories observed. (Thus in our example it is not enough to tell one that $T_n = 2$, but *which* two categories or species have been observed.)

This beautiful circle of results originates with Hintikka (1966), and was later extended by Hintikka and Niiniluoto (1980). The monograph by Kuipers (1978) gives an outstanding survey and synthesis of this work, including discussion of Kuipers's own contributions.

VII.4 The Popper–Carnap controversy

Karl Popper was a lifelong and dogged opponent of Carnap's inductivist views. In appendix 7 of his *Logic of Scientific Discovery* (Popper, 1968) he makes the claim that the logical probability of a universal generalization must be zero! Given the existence of the very simple examples discussed above, this can only be regarded today as a curiosity, akin to "are viruses alive?" debates. (That is, it is only possible if one does not give a precise definition of logical probability. For two deconstructions of Popper's claim, see Howson, 1973 and 1987.)

For those interested in the more general debate between Popper and Carnap, their exchange in the Schilpp volume on Carnap (Schilpp, 1963) is a natural place to start. One important thread in the debate was *Miller's paradox*; Jeffrey (1975) is at once a useful reprise of the initial debate, and a spirited rebuttal. For a more sympathetic view of Popper, see Miller (1997).

Both the original Johnson–Carnap continuum and its Hintikka–Niiniluoto–Kuipers generalizations are of great interest, but share a common weakness. *If* what one is trying to do is to capture precisely the notion of a category-symmetric state of knowledge – *no more and no less* – then the one and only constraint is that the resulting probabilities be invariant under permutation of the categories. (The recognition that even in such cases the complete list of frequencies may contain relevant information regarding individual categories appears to go back to Turing; see Good, 1965, chapter 8.) This does not mean, however, that nothing of interest can be said; the mere presence of exchangeability enables a number of interesting qualitative conclusions to be made. The next section illustrates one of these (see also the remarks in the last section).

VIII. INSTANTIAL RELEVANCE

One important desideratum of a candidate for confirmation is *instantial relevance*: if a particular type is observed, then it is more likely that such a type will be observed in the future. In its simplest form, this is the requirement that if $i < j$, then

$$P(X_j = 1 \mid X_i = 1) \geq P(X_j = 1)$$

(the X_k, denoting as before indicators that take on the values 0 or 1).

It is not hard to see that exchangeability, by itself, does not ensure instantial relevance. Suppose, for example, that one is selecting balls at random from an urn containing three red and two black balls. If the sampling is *without replacement* (that is, after observing the color of a ball, you do not put it back), then the probability of selecting a red ball is initially 3/5, but the probability of selecting a second red ball, *given the first was red*, has decreased to 1/2.

In the past there was a small cottage industry devoted to investigating the precise circumstances under which the principle of instantial relevance does or does not hold for a sequence of observations. If the observations in question can be imbedded in an *infinitely* exchangeable sequence (that is, into an infinite sequence $X_1, X_2, \ldots,$ any finite segment $X_1, \ldots, X_n$ of which is exchangeable), then instantial relevance does hold. After the power of the de Finetti representation theorem was appreciated, very simple proofs of this were discovered (see, for example, Carnap and Jeffrey, 1971, chapters 4 and 5).

Technical note: There are also simple ways of demonstrating this that do not appeal to the representation theorem. The principle of (positive) instantial relevance is equivalent to the assertion that the observations are *positively correlated*. And if $X_1, X_2, \ldots, X_n$ is an exchangeable sequence of random variables, then an elementary argument shows that the correlation coefficient $\rho = \rho(X_i, X_j)$ satisfies the simple inequality

$$\rho \geq -\frac{1}{n-1}.$$

This is because (using both the formula for the variance of a sum and the exchangeability of the sequence) if $\sigma^2 = Var[X_i]$, one has

$$0 \leq Var[X_1 + \cdots + X_n] = n\sigma^2 + n(n-1)\rho\sigma^2.$$

Thus, if the sequence can be indefinitely extended (so that one can pass to the limit $n \to \infty$), it follows that $\rho \geq 0$. The case $\rho = 0$ then corresponds to that of independent observations (the past conveys no information about the future and inductive inference is impossible); and the case $\rho > 0$ corresponds to inductive inference and positive instantial relevance.

IX. LATER DEVELOPMENTS

The publication of *Logical Foundations of Probability* and *The Continuum of Inductive Methods* more than half a century ago led to a renaissance in the use of probability theory to model the inductive process. The Schilpp volume gives a good sense of the first decade of the resulting debate. Carnap himself continued to work on the technical development of the subject for the rest of his life; indeed, the analysis of inductive inference represents the greater portion of his work during this period. Carnap's book with Stegmüller (Carnap and Stegmüller, 1959) and his long articles in Carnap and Jeffrey (1971) and Jeffrey (1980) were the principal progress reports.

IX.1 Partial exchangeability

One important aspect of inductive inference is its appeal to *analogy* in its various forms: outcomes are proximate to each other in time, or are of similar type. Carnap obtained only partial results in this case (see Carnap and Jeffrey, 1971; Jeffrey, 1980). De Finetti was more successful, at least conceptually. He formulated a concept of *partial exchangeability*, differing forms of partial exchangeability corresponding to differing forms of analogy. Outstanding discussions include those of Diaconis and Freedman (Jeffrey, 1980, chapter 11) and Jeffrey (1988); de Finetti's orginal paper appears in translation in Jeffrey (1980, chapter 9).

One of the problems in formulating a concept of partial exchangeability is deciding on an appropriate generalization of exchangeability. One approach would be to require invariance for some subgroup of permutations of the time index; another – and very fruitful one – is via the use of *sufficient statistics*. In the original case of exchangeability, the sufficient statistics were the frequencies $n_1, \ldots, n_t$, in the sense that all sequences having the same frequencies had the same probability. Then assigning probabilities to sequences $e_1, \ldots, e_n$ reduces to assigning probabilities $P(n_1, \ldots, n_t)$ to their frequencies. This suggests considering alternative sufficient statistics corresponding to other forms of exchangeability.

One example is *Markov exchangeability* (describing a form of analogy in time). Suppose $X_0, X_1, \ldots$ is an infinite sequence of random outcomes, each taking values in the set $S = \{c_1, \ldots, c_t\}$. For each $n \geq 1$, consider the statistics X_0 (the initial state of the chain) and the *transition counts* n_{ij} recording the number of transitions from c_i to c_j in the sequence up to X_n. (That is, the number of times $k, 0 \leq k \leq n - 1$, such that $X_k = c_i$ and $X_{k+1} = c_j$.) If for all $n \geq 1$, all sequences $X_0, \ldots, X_n$ starting out in the same initial state x_0 and having the same transition counts n_{ij} have the same probability, then the sequence is said to be *Markov exchangeable*.

Of course one might ask why Markov exchangeability is a natural assumption to make. Diaconis and Freedman (1980, 248) put it well: "If someone . . . had never heard of Markov chains it seems unlikely that they would hit on the appropriate notion of partial exchangeability. The notion of symmetry seems strange at first . . . A feeling of naturalness only appears after experience and reflection."

IX.2 *The sampling of species problem*

Another important problem concerns the nature of inductive inference when the possible types or species are initially unknown (this is sometimes referred to in the statistical literature as the *sampling of species problem*). Carnap thought this could be done using the equivalence relation R: *belongs to the same species as*. (That is, one has a notion of equivalence or common membership in a species, without prior knowledge of that species.) Carnap did not pursue this idea further, however, because he thought that it would introduce further complexities into the analysis, the attempt to deal with which would have been premature given the relatively primitive state of the subject at that time.

Carnap's intuition was entirely on the mark here. Although it is in fact possible to develop a theory for the sampling of species scenario that is entirely parallel to the classical continuum of inductive methods, the technical difficulties arising are much greater; exchangeable random *sequences* being replaced by exchangeable random *partitions*. Fortunately, the English mathematician J. H. C. Kingman did the necessary technical spadework in a brilliant series of papers a quarter of a century ago. For a description of how Kingman's beautiful results enable one to establish a parallel inductive theory for this case, including a Johnson-type characterization of an analogous continuum of inductive methods, see Zabell (1992 and 1997).

X. CONCLUSIONS

The subjective view of the nature of probability is the dominant one in philosophy today. Probabilities represent consistent numerical degrees of belief, consistency meaning either consistency of preferences, or the inability to make a Dutch book. These impose certain constraints on numerical measures of belief – the axioms of finitely additive probability – and any numerical set function consistent with these axioms represents a consistent set of degrees of belief. Absent further information, however, the personal or subjective theory in its pure form imposes no further conditions on such numerical quantities. This is a far cry from the unique probabilities derived from principles of indifference by Bayes, Laplace, and their successors, including the early Johnson and the Carnap of the *Logical Foundations of Probability*. Can one say then that Ramsey and de Finetti have won out over Carnap?

Not entirely. Carnap was always a conciliator, inclined to identify commonalities and points of agreement. Indeed, Carnap himself tells us (in his last, posthumously published work on inductive inference):

I think there need not be a controversy between the objectivist point of view and the subjectivist or personalist point of view. Both have a legitimate place in the context of our work, that is, the construction of a set of rules for determining probability values with respect to possible evidence. At each step in the construction, a choice is to be made; the choice is not completely free but is restricted by certain boundaries. Basically, there is merely a difference in attitude or emphasis between the subjectivist tendency to emphasize the existing freedom of choice, and the objectivist tendency to stress the existence of limitations. (Jeffrey, 1980, 119)

There is little difference between this and I. J. Good's view (1952, 107), for example, that symmetry arguments are "suggestions for using the theory . . . [belonging] to the technique rather than the theory itself."

Like his distinguished predecessors Bernoulli and Bayes, Carnap continued to grapple with the elusive riddle of induction for the rest of his life. Throughout he was an effective spokesman for his point of view. But although the technical contributions of Carnap and his school remain of considerable interest even today, Carnap's most lasting influence was more subtle but also more important: he largely shaped the way current philosophy views the nature and role of probability, in particular its widespread acceptance of the Bayesian paradigm (as, for example, in Earman, 1992; Howson and Urbach, 1993; and Jeffrey, 2004).

13 Carnapian pragmatism

Rudolf Carnap is a curious figure in twentieth-century philosophy. His principal reputation is as a leading exponent of logical positivism (or logical empiricism), a school of thought that, according to lore, is notably rigid and technical as well as dismissive of other ways of doing philosophy. One of Carnap's most-read essays (Carnap, 1932d/ 1959) argues, for example, for the elimination or overcoming of metaphysics based on strict adherence to syntactic and verificationist strictures on meaningfulness. W. V. Quine's most famous essay – arguably, the single most famous essay in analytic philosophy – "Two Dogmas of Empiricism" (1951/1980) singles out Carnap as its most important target and uses the notion of "dogma" to characterize the key commitments of his version of empiricism. Quine's essay begins with the bold claim that "modern empiricism has been conditioned in large part by two dogmas" – dogmas his readers would at the time closely associate with Carnap – and then argues that embracing an empiricism without these dogmas has two principal effects:

One effect of abandoning [the dogmas] is, as we shall see, a blurring of the supposed boundary between speculative metaphysics and natural science. Another effect is a shift toward pragmatism. (Quine, 1951/1980, 20)

Quine's rejection of Carnapian dogmas has been highly influential in the subsequent development of analytic philosophy; Carnap's rejection of Heideggerian "metaphysics" has been widely rejected by those who advocate philosophies influenced by continental philosophy. These facts have led to a view within philosophy of Carnap as a dogmatic thinker, a philosophical hard-liner.[1]

---

[1] For more recent and subtle accounts of Carnap's relations to Heidegger and Quine, see, for example, Friedman (2000) and Creath (this volume), respectively.

This standard view of Carnap is difficult to square with aspects of Carnap's espoused philosophy, however. Indeed, the more one engages with Carnap's thought, the more one finds a sort of open-mindedness and pragmatism right at its very core. Carnap rejected radical verificationism by the mid-1930s, for example. At that time he also placed at the center of his project in "the logical syntax of scientific language" a principle that he dubbed "the Principle of Tolerance." He expresses this principle as a principle of proper method in logic: "it is not our business to set up prohibitions, but to arrive at conventions" (Carnap, 1934c/1937, 51). He expands upon this idea a page later, writing that "in logic there are no morals. Everyone is at liberty to build up his own logic, i.e. his own form of language, as he wishes" (Carnap, 1934c/1937, 2). Similarly, in the debate with Quine, Carnap was the first to wield the term "dogma" in characterizing his opponent's position:

To decree dogmatic prohibitions of certain linguistic forms instead of testing them by their success or failure in practical use, is worse than futile; it is positively harmful because it may obstruct scientific progress . . . *Let us be cautious in making assertions and critical in examining them, but tolerant in permitting linguistic forms.* (Carnap, 1950a/1956, 221)

In the same article he takes Quine's then recent suggestion that in adjudicating ontological disputes "the obvious counsel is tolerance and an experimental spirit" (Quine, 1948/1980, 19; quoted in Carnap, 1950a/1956, 215, n. 5) to indicate both a convergence in their attitudes and a concession to Carnap's by-then long-held Principle of Tolerance.

From within Carnap's thought, then, we have a view that stresses open-mindedness, tolerance, plurality, and an experimental spirit – all well-known hallmarks of philosophical pragmatism. Indeed, Carnap himself stresses again and again that in questions of choice of a logic or linguistic framework, practical or pragmatic considerations are the only considerations that can be raised; on this matter, his views converge importantly (if not wholly) with a version of pragmatism about logic offered up in the American context by the pragmatist C. I. Lewis, one of Quine's teachers, back in the 1920s. Carnap also adopts the term "pragmatics" as the empirical study of the relations of languages to their users – a term he adopts from the work of the young pragmatist philosopher Charles Morris, who himself was elaborating on George Herbert Mead's account of language and meaning. Thus, Carnap not only thought his own philosophy had considerable pragmatic elements but these elements actually connected his thought to the work of philosophers in the tradition of American pragmatism.[2]

The business of this chapter will be to untangle this interpretive knot: how is it that Carnap can have passed into philosophical lore as a rigid dogmatic thinker while himself stressing tolerance and pragmatism as central elements of his own philosophy? The best way to approach this issue is through a consideration of what terms such as "tolerant," "practical," and "pragmatic" meant in Carnap's own philosophical parlance and what philosophical roles they played. Along the way, we can acquire a bit of insight into the larger historico-philosophical issue of the relations in general between logical empiricism and American pragmatism.

I. THE THEORETICAL AND THE PRACTICAL: CARNAP'S FUNDAMENTAL PHILOSOPHICAL COMMITMENT

Quine's Carnap is fundamentally an empiricist who accepts certain positions and commitments as a consequence of his understanding of the project of empiricism. Thus, for example, because Carnap, on Quine's view, was attempting to justify our claim to know the physical world in our best scientific theories, and because empiricism requires a foundation for knowledge in experience, Carnap comes to adopt a reductionist thesis that seeks to explain the meaning of scientific terms within a language that makes reference only to experience. Indeed, this reductionism is the second dogma – and the more fundamental one – discussed in "Two Dogmas."

Several more recent commentators have argued that Quine has misplaced the most fundamental philosophical commitments of Carnap. I have argued (Richardson, 1998, 2003b), in particular, that Carnap's most fundamental commitment is not to empiricism but to scientific philosophy. That is to say, whereas Quine reads Carnap as wishing to bolster the scientific enterprise by providing an epistemology that shows how scientific knowledge is grounded in

---

[2] On Lewis's pragmatic theory of the a priori, see Richardson (2003b). On Morris, see Reisch (2003, 2005).

experience, I read Carnap as most fundamentally committed to bringing scientific standards of knowledge production into philosophy itself. The task is not philosophically to ground or justify science but to reconstruct philosophy on a strictly scientific basis. This requires bringing the tools used by science in its modes of understanding the world into philosophy itself. This is why, in Carnap's hands, philosophy becomes a technical discipline that looks to mathematized natural science for its proper tools and methods.

Scientific philosophy is a large arena and comes in many versions. So, the move to scientific philosophy only aids the interpretation of Carnap's philosophy if the sort of scientific philosophy that it is can be further specified. For the issue of Carnap's pragmatism, it is important to notice a way in which Carnap's version of scientific philosophy descends from the Kantian and neo-Kantian traditions in German philosophy.[3] For this issue, the relation of Carnap's philosophy to Kant's is not really a question of what is epistemologically of interest or even of what a proper epistemological question is; it is rather a matter of the relations between properly scientific questions and questions of other sorts.[4] Within Kant's own philosophy, there is a strict distinction between what he calls the "theoretical" and the "practical" uses of reason. The former is the role of reason in constructing systems of representations of the world – the use of reason in constructing theories of how the world works. The latter is the role of reason in explaining, justifying, and motivating action – the use of reason in the decision of what to do. This division undergirds Kant's distinction between a transcendental account of theoretical knowledge in science, which deals with the a priori use of theoretical reason, and a transcendental account of morality, which deals with the a priori use of practical reason. Practical reason is not, however, excised from Kant's account of science: often in scientific work an agent wishes not simply to represent the world but to undertake an action; in such circumstances practical reason plays a role in science

---

[3] Pragmatism was named after the pragmatic as it appeared in Kant's philosophy, as was stressed by Dewey (1931, chapter 1), following Peirce. Peirce wished to stress the distinction between the transcendental elements of Kant's account of freedom (the practical) and the empirical elements (the pragmatic) and to endorse only the latter. Carnap's practical element in knowledge is a priori but he has no pure practical reason upon which to ground morality.

[4] Carnap's debts to Kantian and neo-Kantian traditions on these matters have been stressed by, for example, Sauer (1985, 1989), Friedman (1987, 1992a), and Richardson (1998).

itself. Thus, for example, it is not a demand of reason that a geometer construct an equilateral triangle, but if the geometer wishes to construct one, practical reason guides her choice of operations. The difference between the practical use of reason in geometry and morality is, for Kant, that in the latter case reason gives itself its own ends: the unique role of the categorical imperative is that it is an end that reason sets for itself.

A strict and principled distinction between the theoretical and the practical finds expression in Carnap throughout his career. Carnap is far more chary than Kant in using the terminology of faculties of the mind, and, for this reason, he does not usually express the distinction in terms of two uses of reason. The theoretical, however, is the realm of representation and belief, whereas the practical, for Carnap, is the realm of decision and the will. Thus, in an essay from 1934, Carnap insists on a strict distinction between theoretical questions and practical decisions. The former is a matter for scientific investigation of nature; the latter is a matter of the need, within the realm of action, for decision. While theoretical knowledge might help one make a proper decision, the insistence upon the practical is, for Carnap, an insistence upon the need for decision in the realm of activity and an insistence that no amount of knowledge is the very same thing as the decision to act upon it. Carnap puts the point this way:

If I want to be clear about whether or not I should eat the apple that is lying before me, then that is a matter of resolution, of practical, not theoretical, decision. One tends, however, to express the uncertainty of resolution in the same linguistic form as the uncertainty of knowledge, that is, in the form of a question: Should I eat this apple? This verbal form simulates for us a question where there is no question. Neither my own thought nor all the theories of science are capable of answering that apparent question, not as if there were a limit to human understanding, but simply because there is here no question. Theoretically, from every day or scientific knowledge, all that can be said is: "if you eat the apple, your hunger will disappear (or: you will poison yourself; or: you will be sent to jail; or . . .")". These theoretical assertions regarding the expectable results can of course be very important for me; however, the resolution cannot be taken away from me by them. It is a mater of practical resolution whether I want to satisfy myself or remain hungry; whether I want to be poisoned or stay healthful; the concepts "true" and "false" cannot be used here.[5] (Carnap, 1934e, 258)

---

[5] All translations from previously untranslated work are my own.

The distinction between the theoretical and the practical becomes crucial to Carnap in the mid-1930s, exactly when he wishes to enunciate clearly his Principle of Tolerance. This principle pertains to the foundations of logic: it says that there are no conditions to be placed on the choice of a logic beyond a certain level of clarity about which logic is actually being chosen. One can present any properly constructed set of linguistic forms and then announce that one has chosen to use it. The choice of a logic is beholden to no other constraints. This is due to a crucial epistemic role played by logic on Carnap's account: logic provides the formal conditions of sense-making. Suppose we wish to know the reason the sky is blue. The object for which we want the reason is the sentence "the sky is blue"; a theoretical reason is then another sentence within the same language from which our target sentence logically follows. The very notion of a theoretical reason, therefore, makes sense only internal to a logical framework. Thus, there is no realm of theoretical reasons that can be appealed to in advance of the adoption of a logical system. Similarly, since theoretical reasons are formed within but are not about the logical framework, no theoretical reasons for altering a framework can be given internal to that very framework.

There are two aspects of Carnap's meta-logical stance. The first is the construction of a logical system as an engineering task. This is the role of syntax – if everything is syntactically well-constructed, we have a candidate logical framework.[6] Since there are alternative such logical systems, we now have different possible systems of theoretical reason and the choice between them is wholly practical.

This logical pluralism leads Carnap to alter somewhat the scheme for theoretical and practical reasons as expounded in 1934 when he takes it up again his later work. He no longer denies that there are practical questions. Instead, he introduces a distinction between internal or theoretical questions that can be answered once a framework is in place and external or practical questions regarding choice of framework. He uses the distinction, for example, to discuss the unclarity in the philosophical issue of the reality of the world of spatio-temporal things. Given the language of physics, the question

---

[6] It is at this point that the logician or philosopher is enjoined to offer "syntactical rules instead of philosophical arguments" (Carnap, 1934c/1937, 52).

is trivial – of course, there are spatio-temporal things. Carnap now denies that there is a further metaphysical and theoretical question that the realism question can be addressing. Rather, all that is left is the practical question of whether we wish to adopt the language of physics in the first place:

> Those who raise the question of the reality of the thing world itself have perhaps in mind not a theoretical question as their formulation seems to suggest, but rather a practical question, a matter of practical decision concerning the structure of our language. We have to make the choice whether or not to accept and use the forms of expression in the framework in question. (Carnap, 1950a/1956, 207)

And once the question has been formulated this way, the relevant considerations of a practical nature are questions of the expediency of the language on offer given our cognitive purposes. These considerations will incline us to accept the language or not, but the acceptance or rejection is itself an act of volition, a practical decision.

Carnap's views, it must be noted, commit him to a form of practical freedom that is explicitly appealed to in the Principle of Tolerance. In the absence of this kind of freedom, the principle, as a principle of permission, simply makes no sense. Moreover, as we have seen, this sort of practical freedom is necessary for theoretical knowledge to be possible at all. The adoption of some logical system is necessary for there to be a notion of evidence or theoretical reason in the first place.

This view is a generalization and radicalization in Carnap's hands of the lessons he found in the methods of modern physical science. Einstein's Special Theory of Relativity, in particular, led Carnap to a sort of physical conventionalism that he early on expressed in robustly Kantian language: Physical theory requires choices determining the physical meanings of terms that are not uniquely determined by experiences – notions such as simultaneity for events at a distance from one another, for example – choices which then allow the coordination of mathematical systems to the world of experience. Such mathematized physics allows the prediction and explanation of physical occurrences and, thus, the achievement of objective knowledge of the world. Conventions thereby serve as conditions of the possibility of objective knowledge, playing the key methodological role within the realm of theoretical reason of Kant's synthetic a priori. Substantially this same view is still in place regarding the choice of a logical system in Carnap's later work, but Carnap no longer finds it helpful to use Kantian language in explaining the view. Since the choice is of an analytic, logical framework, Carnap comes to view his philosophy as a form of empiricism. Carnap's empiricism depends for its structure upon the presumption of practical freedom, however. In Carnap's hands, the epistemological role played by the analytic sentences of a language, far from depending upon a prior empiricism, depends on the practical freedom of the epistemic agents and first gives sense and meaning to empiricism itself.[7]

What, then, is the source of Carnap's conviction that such practical freedom exists? The key clue is contained in the passage from "Empiricism, Semantics, and Ontology," a portion of which we have already cited:

To decree dogmatic prohibitions of certain linguistic forms instead of testing them by their success or failure in practical use, is worse than futile; it is positively harmful because it may obstruct scientific progress. The history of science shows examples of such prohibitions based on the prejudices deriving from religious, mythological, metaphysical, or other irrational sources, which slowed up the developments for shorter or longer periods of time. Let us learn from the lessons of history. Let us grant to those who work in any special field of investigation the freedom to use any form of expression which seems useful to them; the work in the field will sooner or later lead to the elimination of those forms which have no useful function. *Let us be cautious in making assertions and critical in examining them, but tolerant in permitting linguistic forms.* (Carnap, 1950a/1956, 221)

The general line here is as obvious as it is surprising, given the reputation of logical empiricist philosophy of science as having no "role for history." Carnap thinks that the history of science is unintelligible to anyone who does not grant the sort of practical freedom that his philosophy put in center stage. For example, one could not begin to understand the development of physical science in the twentieth century without an appreciation that the development of the Special Theory of Relativity depended upon emerging scientific awareness of the role of definitions in theory construction and upon a commitment to a particular set of conventional definitions. Since a properly

---

[7] Of course, there is in Carnap's account no notion of practical reason setting its own ends – there is no categorical imperative and no grounding of morals in Carnap.

scientific philosophy is intended to foster scientific progress, it has to grant that epistemic agents in fact have the sort of epistemic freedom that finds expression in science and secures scientific progress. Practical freedom of thought is a lesson of the history of science.[8]

II. PHILOSOPHICAL TECHNOLOGY AND PRACTICAL FREEDOM: A NEW TASK FOR PHILOSOPHY

The passage from "Empiricism, Semantics, and Ontology" recently quoted contains another feature that needs to be remarked upon. Carnap there expresses the view that traditional philosophy has not played the role of fostering the freedom of thought necessary for scientific progress. Indeed, for Carnap, quite the opposite is true: traditional philosophy has sought to set limits of thought. This inherent conservatism that he saw in traditional philosophy is a large part of the reason Carnap sought to eliminate or overcome metaphysics and to replace traditional philosophy with a philosophy that offers new tools for science. These tools both express the practical freedom of thought in science and offer new conceptual resources for the clarification of hitherto unclear aspects of scientific thought.

The social conservatism served by traditional metaphysics is well expressed in the following passage from Carnap's 1934 paper on the difference between practical decisions and theoretical questions:

Since metaphysical philosophy and metaphysical (in contrast to mythological) theology have no content, but are only expressions of feeling, there is here no theoretical refutation in the proper sense. The sequences of words in these theories are just as far beyond true and false as are lyric poems. But of course one can take these theories in another sense as objects of theoretical investigation, and indeed from many different points of view. One can show the lack of sense of these theories in a logical and epistemological investigation. Beyond this, the conditions and effects of these illusions can be

---

[8] Carnap did not often discuss free will in his philosophy. When he did discuss it, his view interestingly provides him exactly the practical freedom we have been discussing (Carnap, 1966/1974, 221): "Free choice is a decision made by someone capable of foreseeing the consequences of alternative courses of action and choosing that which he prefers. From my point of view there is no contradiction between free choice, understood this way, and determinism, even of a strong classical type." Since free will is not contradicted in any physically possible world, it can be presumed in philosophy.

studied through investigations of a sociologist and a psychologist; one can determine, for example, that it is here a matter of wish fulfillment and similar things, whose systematic advancement and diffusion in social struggle serves as a diversion and a smoke screen. In order to avoid misunderstanding, it should here be remarked that we are not speaking here of a conscious goal but rather of the factual social function, which in the main does not come into the consciousness of the practitioners but is rather hidden by a justifying ideology. (Carnap, 1934c, 259)

Whereas traditional metaphysics impedes scientific advancement, scientific philosophy aids that advancement. It does this by offering an indefinitely large array of tools for the future progress of science in the form of artificial languages that can serve as a sort of conceptual technology for the clarification of science. It has not been stressed enough how central to Carnap's self-understanding is the idea that his philosophy offers tools to science. His favored accounts of logic stress its instrumental nature. The two important aspects of philosophical technology are clearly expressed in this passage from his *Formalization of Logic*:

[Semantics] is rather to be regarded as a tool, as one among the logical instruments needed for the task of getting and systematizing knowledge. As a hammer helps a man do better and more efficiently what he did before with his unaided hand, so a logical tool helps a man do better and more efficiently what he did with his unaided brain . . . [The development of modern logic has made it] possible not only to increase the safety and precision of the deductive method in realms already known, but also to reach results which could not have been obtained at all without the new tools. (Carnap, 1943, viii)

The tools the philosopher offers to science are available should the scientist so choose – again expressing the practical freedom at the base of scientific work. Also, these tools share two features of all technologies: they can aid in the efficiency of what we already do and can allow us to achieve things beyond our unaided means.

Such talk is, I believe, at the core of the question regarding the point and success of scientific philosophy for Carnap – it is ultimately a form of conceptual engineering to be adjudged wholly on its ability to offer useful frameworks for doing science. As he writes in "Empiricism, Semantics, and Onotology":

The acceptance or rejection of abstract linguistic forms, just as the acceptance or rejection of any other linguistic forms in any branch of science, will
finally be decided by their efficiency as instruments, the ratio of the results
achieved to the amount and complexity of the efforts required. (Carnap,
1950a/1956, 21)

There are certain structural requirements on tools (screwdrivers cannot be made of liquid or gas at normal pressures, for example), but
beyond these a tool is justified only in so far as it aids in a task. The
proof of the pudding is in the eating, but the proof of the technologies
of cooking are in the making of such provable puddings. Constraints
such as truth make no sense for hammers or for copper-clad cookware
and make, for Carnap, just as little sense for the formal technologies
of logic.

Carnap's enthusiasm for a technological understanding of logical
systems elucidates his invocation of the principle of tolerance in
Logical Syntax:

The range of possible language-forms and, consequently, of the various possible logical systems, is incomparably greater than the narrow circle to which
earlier investigations in modern logic have been limited . . . The fact that no
attempts have been made to venture still further from the classical forms
is perhaps due to the widely held opinion that any such deviations must be
justified – that is, that the new language-form must be proved to be "correct"
and to constitute a faithful rendering of "the true logic" . . . To eliminate
this standpoint, together with the pseudo-problems and wearisome controversies which arise as a result of it, is one of the chief tasks of this book.
In it, the view will be maintained that we have in every respect complete
liberty with regard to the forms of language . . . Before us lies the boundless
ocean of unlimited possibilities. (Carnap, 1934c/1937, xiv–xv)

This is not the instrumentalism with regard to theories that sometimes, it is suggested, follows from logical empiricism. Carnap does
not argue that scientific theories are only instruments of prediction or control, without semantic content and devoid of the possibility of being true or false. No, scientific theories are formulated
within linguistic frameworks and can be evaluated for semantic
content, including, of course, empirical content. Instrumentalism
rather applies to the choice of linguistic framework itself, which
lacks empirical content and serves only to clarify and make precise the semantic content of the theories framed within it. A logical

framework, for Carnap, is neither a body of doctrine nor a mirror-image of the world. It is an instrument for scientific understanding of the world and is justified to the extent that it aids in that endeavor.

It is little wonder, then, that Carnap found some of Quine's objections to his own work dogmatic. In "Empricism, Semantics, and Ontology," Carnap was responding to objections Quine made to his work in semantics. Quine, in essence, argued that Carnap's semantic vocabulary – which employed terms such as "analytic," "meaning," "intension," and "proposition" – requires a metaphysical commitment to the existence of suspect entities. Quine argued, for example, that there are no clear identity conditions for propositions and that, therefore, it is important to exclude them from one's ontology. Carnap recognizes no standards for admitting or rejecting a semantical language that employs such terms, however, beyond the ability of a semantical language to aid in the clarification of heretofore confused issues. Thus, his response to Quine's nominalism is this:

> For those who want to develop or use semantical methods, the decisive question is not the alleged ontological question of the existence of abstract entities but rather the question whether the use of abstract linguistic forms or, in technical terms, the use of variables beyond those for things (or phenomenal data), is expedient and fruitful for the purposes for which semantical analyses are made, viz. the analysis, interpretation, clarification, or construction of languages of communication, especially languages of science . . . The critics will have to show that it is possible to construct a semantical method which avoids all references to abstract entities and achieves by simpler means essentially the same results as the other methods. (Carnap, 1950a/1956, 220–221)

Carnap was never convinced that Quine could achieve such results, and the limiting results of Quine's naturalistic semantics – the indeterminacy of translation, the inscrutability of reference – might be taken as evidence that Quine's technological means ill-serve the task.[9]

---

[9] This Carnapian objection to Quine might miss Quine's point, which may not have been to construct nominalist semantical methods that achive the results that he, Carnap, achieved by other means. Quine's point may well have been eliminativist – to show how science can continue without a semantical system at all. My aim is to exhibit, not defend, the engineering point of view that underpins Carnap's understanding of Quine.

III. CARNAP AND AMERICAN PRAGMATISM

The question whether Carnap is a pragmatist is obscured by continuing questions regarding what pragmatism is or what "pragmatism" means. Pragmatism has often been understood to be a theory of truth or a theory of enquiry. Those who wished to endorse pragmatism in the early twentieth century, however, often espoused a more expansive view. It was not meant to be a *theory* of anything, really, but rather a certain philosophical attitude or habit of mind. For example, James's answer to the question of what pragmatism means is this:

No particular results then, so far, but only an attitude of orientation, is what the pragmatic method means. *The attitude of looking away from first things, principles, "categories," supposed necessities; and of looking towards last things, fruits, consequences, facts.* (James, 1907/1948, 146)

By the time Carnap arrived in the United States in 1936, pragmatism had become in essence what John Dewey's philosophy said it was. It was an account and an endorsement of "creative intelligence" or a "scientific habit of mind" in human affairs.

Little wonder, then, that Carnap thought his philosophy had something in common with American pragmatism. He endorsed a scientific habit of mind and sought, as did Dewey, both to instill that habit of mind in philosophy itself and philosophically to understand and promote it. In this assessment, several younger scholars trained in the pragmatic tradition, especially Charles Morris and Sidney Hook, shared Carnap's sense of an important kinship between logical empiricism and American pragmatism. Moreover, as previously noted, Carnap's account of the practical adoption of a logical system agreed in overall structure with C. I. Lewis's account of a "pragmatic a priori": both views held that logic is not confirmed by experience but is necessary for the conceptualization of experience needed for knowledge; both claimed, therefore, that only pragmatic criteria such as fruitfulness or simplicity can guide the choice of a logic. In line with this view, both Lewis and Carnap took their logical work to be the elaboration of multiple systems of logic, systems that could be presented as options to scientists or philosophers with certain sorts of epistemological work to do.[10]

---

[10] It is for this reason that Quine identifies Carnap's views and Lewis's on linguistic frameworks at the end of "Two Dogmas." The terms of Quine's objections seem

Carnap's commitment to the practical/theoretical distinction and his view of logical systems as instruments for philosophical and scientific progress, we have argued, undergird Carnap's own version of pragmatism. Precisely these commitments, however, provide points of departure from the pragmatism espoused by the two leading American pragmatists of the 1930s and 1940s, C. I. Lewis and John Dewey. In an essay written in 1941 but first published much later, Lewis discusses four differences he sees between logical positivism and pragmatism – and takes Carnap as his exemplary logical positivist. The first three differences revolve around issues of empiricism, scientism, and metaphysics, wherein Lewis finds pragmatism a more fluid and, therefore, more nuanced and correct position; the fourth point of difference is over the status of valuational judgments in logical empiricism.

Lewis's discussion is highly perceptive and points to fundamental differences between the pragmatism of Dewey and himself, on the one hand, and Carnap's view, on the other. Interestingly, the two differences of most importance are exactly regarding the question of logic as a metaphysically neutral tool for doing philosophy and the practical/theoretical distinction. We cannot discuss Lewis's essay in great detail, but we can give a sense of it, thereby indicating the division between pragmatism and logical positivism circa 1940. The first issue concerns Lewis's sense that Carnap's logicizing of all philosophical problems misses the philosophical significance of pragmatism's own commitment to empiricism, endorsement of science, and rejection of at least parts of metaphysics. Lewis is at pains to indicate a way in which stress on the logical relations among sentences cannot capture, for example, empirical meaning in the sense needed for his own pragmatism:

Such empirical meaning consists precisely in what Carnap here excludes, the associated imagery or the criterion in terms of sense by which what is meant is recognized when presented in experience. Words and sentences without associated imagery are marks or noises without significance. Without associated imagery, strings of marks or of noises are not even words or sentences – are not even nonsense. (Lewis, 1970, 96)

Lewis here adopts an account of the relation of language to experience that Carnap had already by the mid-1930s rejected as

more natural for rejecting Lewis's rather than Carnap's version of logical pluralism, however.

a fundamental confusion of two different questions: an empirical question of the thoughts associated with words in natural language and a logical question of the relations of sentences in a suitable rigorized language of science. Carnap's own rejection of this view depends on his prior commitment to formal languages of logic as the proper tools for doing philosophy. In endorsing the view above, Lewis fundamentally distances himself from this view of logic and its place in philosophy:

This difference between the logical-positivistic and the pragmatic mode of approach to questions of meaning runs very deep, eventually, because this attempt to logicize all problems, and to regard them as correctly and unambiguously statable only in "the formal mode" – in terms of the syntax of language – is connected with the logical-positivistic conception that philosophy has no legitimate business except that of logical analysis, and that philosophical questions which are characteristically stated in "the material mode," and which, e.g., concern the relation between something stated and given in experience, or between experience and real objects are "pseudoproblems." (Lewis, 1970, 96)

Lewis seeks here to insist that questions rendered moot for Carnap by adoption of a proper technology for scientific philosophy are the key questions for pragmatism, ones that cannot disappear without pragmatism itself disappearing.

This is a significant difference between Lewis and Carnap, but there is one even more important to Lewis's account: Pragmatism, for Lewis, cannot accept a principled fact/value distinction. In the language of this essay, the key difference is that Lewis rejects Carnap's theoretical/practical distinction. This is a fundamental point of departure between the Lewis–Dewey wing of pragmatism and Carnap's philosophy: Lewis and Dewey both wish to establish a proper science of value and do not wish to follow Carnap in his view that value and preference are practical matters which, for precisely this reason, stand wholly outside of science. In order to fix the topic of the controversy, it is useful to see how Carnap discusses value within the context of the rejection of metaphysics. Here is a characteristic example:

Theoretically it can only be shown that philosophical and religious metaphysics are in certain circumstances a narcotic, dangerous and harmful to reason. We reject this narcotic. If others enjoy partaking in it, we cannot refute them theoretically. That in no way means that it has to be a matter

of indifference to us how people decide on this point. We can provide theoretical illumination regarding the origin and effects of the narcotic. Beyond
this, we can influence the practical decision that people make on this point
through appeals, education, and example. Only we want to be clear that this
influence lies outside the theoretical realm of science. (Carnap, 1934e, 260)

By contrast, Lewis wishes to have the philosophical ability to say,
if we may take up Carnap's metaphor, that philosophical narcotics
are harmful to human nature, in the way that heroin or opium are.
And this requires that Lewis can appeal to a realm of proper human
flourishing within philosophy itself.

Lewis's basic idea – and this is an idea found quite explicitly also
in Dewey – is that an objective realm of values based on a proper
philosophical understanding of human nature will ground the natural value of epistemic life and show why certain aspects of traditional metaphysics and religion are harmful to human flourishing.
Indeed, Lewis believed that if epistemic life were based simply on
personal preference (a preference for accurate prediction, for example) and did not foster the proper ends of human life, then knowledge
itself would be importantly arbitrary. His essay on pragmatism and
logical empiricism ends on this point:

The validity of cognition itself is inseparable from that final test of it which
consists in some valuable result of the action which it serves to guide.
Knowledge – so the pragmatist conceives – is for the sake of action; and
action is directed to the realization of what is valuable. If there should be
no valid judgments of value, then action would be pointless or merely capri-
cious, and cognition would be altogether lacking in significance. (Lewis,
1970, 112)

As mentioned above, similar views can be found in Dewey's work.
Dewey's pragmatism is grounded in a biological and social naturalism that makes enquiry the primary activity of human beings. Creating the social conditions within which properly run enquiry can
obtain in all aspects of life becomes for Dewey the political and social
project of philosophical pragmatism; creating these social conditions
depends on an adequate science of values. This project has two salient
consequences for the topic of this essay: first, Dewey argues that the
theoretical/practical distinction is a large part of the social problem
of his age, and, second, that a science of values will increase human
freedom by exposing the empirical conditions of valuation. On the

first point, Dewey stresses that a principled distinction between the practical attitude and the theoretical attitude is expressive of a fundamental split in modern life in the 1930s and 1940s between what is intellectually sound and what is emotionally gratifying. Dewey's work seeks to heal this division of loyalties in the life of modern man:

The hard-and-fast impassible line which is supposed by some to exist between "emotive" and "scientific" language is a reflex of the gap which now exists between the intellectual and the emotional in human relations and activities. The split which exists in present social life between ideas and emotions, especially between ideas that have *scientific* warrant and uncontrolled emotions that dominate practice, the split between the affective and the cognitive, is probably one of the chief sources of the maladjustments and unendurable strains from which the world is suffering . . . We are living in a period in which emotional loyalties and attachments are centered on objects that no longer command that intellectual loyalty which has the sanction of the methods which attain valid conclusions in scientific inquiry, while ideas that have their origin in the rationale of inquiry have not as yet succeeded in acquiring the force that only emotional ardor provides. The *practical* problem that has to be faced is the establishment of cultural conditions that will support the kinds of behavior in which emotions and ideas, desires and appraisals, are integrated. (Dewey, 1944/1970, 444–445)

Regarding the freedom-enhancing prospects of an empirical theory of valuation, Dewey runs an argument by analogy. Increased knowledge of, for example, electricity or heat has increased, not decreased, the power we have to bend those things to our desires, to use them to further our ends. Similarly, an empirical theory of values and desires themselves will allow us to control our values and desires, bringing them more into line with what we would like them to be. Without such a theory, emotions remain, as Dewey said in the previous paragraph, "uncontrolled" – we would continue to have no adequate knowledge that can be used for emotional and affective engineering; with such a theory, we can bring intelligent planning and control into affect and desire themselves:

That growth of knowledge of the physical – in the sense of the nonpersonal – has limited the range of freedom of human action in relation to such things as light, heat, electricity, etc., is so absurd in view of what has actually taken place that no one holds it. The operation of desire in producing the valuations that influence human action will also be liberated when they, too, are ordered by verifiable propositions regarding matters-of-fact. (Dewey, 1944/1970, 445–446)

Thus, the key features of Carnap's version of pragmatism are not features his pragmatism shared with the leading American pragmatists of his era. In particular, both Dewey and Lewis wanted to ground their pragmatism in an account of human nature, thereby gaining the ground to combat misguided intellectual pursuits in a different way than does Carnap: Carnap has a preference that we not engage in such pursuits and would like to persuade others not to do so on practical grounds; Lewis and Dewey wish to show that these pursuits are counter to the proper values and goals of human life. In Dewey's view, the practical/theoretical split as conceived by Carnap is itself a symptom of the modern era's division between the intellectually secured and the emotionally motivating, a split his own work sought to overcome. For his part, Carnap would have to view Dewey's pragmatism as a confusion of distinct endeavors, the empirical understanding of humanity, on the hand, and the logical understanding of the possibility of knowledge, on the other. Indeed, Carnap would have to find Dewey guilty of conflating the logical distinction between assertion or judgment and decision.

Thus, at the end of the day, it is the difference over methodological naturalism that undergirds the difference between Carnapian pragmatism and the pragmatism of Lewis and Dewey: Lewis and Dewey both need and think they can have a place in philosophy to speak of the proper nature and interests of humanity; Carnap has no such need and no such place. While Quine is famous for a return to naturalism as well as pragmatism in his rejection of Carnap's philosophy, his views do not substantially return American philosophy to the point of view of Dewey. For Dewey's philosophy takes as given that intelligent activity is goal-directed and, thus, intentional, and his naturalism is aimed at revealing such intentional structures; "desire, having ends-in-view, and hence involving valuations is the characteristic that marks off human from nonhuman behavior" (Dewey, 1944/1970, 446). Quine's naturalism is a version of physicalism that denies that much sense can be made of intentional idioms such as the goal towards which an enquiry aims. The active point of view encoded in and central to Lewis's and Dewey's pragmatism – and that finds expression in Carnap in the practical decisions that underpin scientific theorizing – is almost wholly absent from Quine's naturalistic conception of the human subject of epistemology.

More important, from the current point of view, is the distinction between the Lewis–Dewey vision of freedom and Carnap's own view. Lewis and Dewey wish to provide an empirically grounded vision of the actively striving human individual and society and to bind the human good to the progress of knowledge. From Carnap's point of view, this conflates the logical and the empirical and reinstitutes exactly the confusion of the logical and the psychological of his own earliest work. In essence, interestingly, from Carnap's point of view, the Lewis–Dewey version of pragmatism exactly robs them of being able to view a logical system as an instrument that can be chosen or left aside. The locus of dispute becomes two visions of human agency: the Lewis–Dewey vision of the empirical human agent and the Carnapian vision of the practically free conceptual engineer.

IV. CARNAP, DOGMATIST?

One question remains: if Carnap's philosophy stresses tolerance, open-mindedness, and "an experimental spirit," how is it that he has acquired the reputation as a hard-liner and dogmatist? There is a sense in which that question is easy to answer. Most younger philosophers meet Carnap first and foremost as Quine's vanquished interlocutor and, thus, as the leading purveyor of empiricist dogma in the twentieth century. Despite his own respect and affection for Carnap, Quine's account of him as a dogmatist has stuck. Similarly, in A. J. Ayer's anthology, *Logical Positivism* (Ayer, 1959), which has served for almost fifty years as an introduction to logical positivism in the English-speaking world, Carnap is represented by certain transitional papers from the early 1930s in which he takes argumentative lines that are easy to interpret as closed-minded. In "Overcoming of Metaphysics," Carnap does not notably espouse the Principle of Tolerance in how he wields logic to argue against metaphysics – indeed, the Principle of Tolerance was just then coalescing in his mind. Moreover, he does not clearly indicate in that essay just how unpersuasive his case would of necessity be to a Heideggerian. Finally, Carnap was a leader of a movement – logical empiricism – that in the hands of its expositors often looked less tolerant than Carnap's approach was; Ayer's work, especially his youthful scorched-earth logical positivism as presented in *Language, Truth and Logic* (Ayer, 1936), is important in this context also.

In the main, Carnap took his own advice and pursued technical work aimed at offering tools for philosophical and scientific progress. His work requires a level of technical sophistication to understand. Readers will often want to have an argument at the start that such work will lead to fundamental illumination on philosophical and scientific issues. But there is, in Carnap's work, typically no such argument; in Carnap's hands, the technologies of logic are introduced in response to his sense that all other roads to philosophical progress have been blocked and that this route should now be tried. Those who have not been convinced to follow Carnap in this will not find an argument that they cannot pursue non-technical means in their philosophy or that the particular technical means Carnap is pursuing must work for any given issue. Such a priori guarantees and refutations are exactly what Carnap's pragmatism precludes.

For Carnap philosophically pernicious dogmatism had always been of the form "unless you are guaranteed in advance that this line of philosophical argument will resolve the issue, you should not pursue it." Pragmatism, for him, is the experimental desire to use new philosophical tools as you construct them in order to see if they can help with some bit of philosophical puzzlement. His use of logical tools stems from his appreciation that none of the traditionally important questions of epistemology can be asked in advance of a logical structure being in place; his sense of liberation came from the idea that there is a "boundless ocean of unlimited possibilities" (Carnap, 1934c/197, xv) in modern logic that had not yet been exploited in philosophy.

Carnap's work has been very important for the development of philosophy of science, logic, and analytic philosophy generally in the twentieth century. The recent flowering of historical interest in his work has led to a deeper understanding among historians of analytic philosophy of the nature and subtlety of Carnap's work and its historical contexts. Attention to Carnap's pragmatism holds promise of bringing the experimental spirit of Carnap's scientific philosophy back into the contemporary analytic philosopher's self-understanding. Since the self-understanding of the philosopher as a co-worker in the promotion of a scientific and progressive world conception was central to Carnap's philosophical vision, recovery of this experimental spirit might be the ultimate recovery of Carnap's work in philosophy.

14 Quine's challenge to Carnap

There are two routes by which Rudolf Carnap arrived at his mature philosophy and the central concept of analyticity within it. Both have the same starting point, Kant's conception of the a priori. But the paths themselves were different. One progressed from Kant's theory of space through the development of non-Euclidian geometries, the methodological and metamathematical researches into geometry of Poincaré and Hilbert, and Einstein's theory of relativity on to Carnap's own reworking of his philosophy of empirical science in the light of these developments. The other path, which will be emphasized here, traces the history of logic, or perhaps more precisely the history of the philosophy of logic. Even that story is too long to recount here, so I will confine myself to its last step, the point in the 1930s when the basic features of Carnap's philosophy crystallized.

Carnap's mature philosophy was prompted most immediately by his recognition that there are alternative logical systems. That is, there is more than one body of doctrine that purports to give the general structure of legitimate deductive reasoning, and these alternatives cannot be translated into one common system in any satisfactory way. Carnap's response in the mid-1930s was to develop a broad philosophic view according to which what we take to be logical truths (and the rest of those commitments traditionally thought to be a priori) do not describe the world in substantive ways but rather jointly constitute or structure the language used to describe that world. There are many such languages, and the choice among them is a question of convenience rather than correctness.

Carnap's idea here is enormously interesting, and it deserves to be more widely understood and explored. Part of the reason why it has not been fully investigated in recent decades is that from the early 1950s W. V. Quine mounted a sustained challenge to some of Carnap's central concepts. The purpose of this chapter is to investigate this challenge, at least in a preliminary way. In the first section I lay out the fundamentals of Carnap's mature philosophy as a response to the multiplicity of logics. In the second, I briefly explore Carnap's second path according to which Carnap's central distinctions are a response to certain problems in the confirmation of scientific theories. Third, I try to determine just what Quine's complaint is. This is worth doing because Quine's central papers have been understood in such different ways that at least some of those interpretations must be wrong or misleading. Finally, I assess the prospects for meeting Quine's challenge and reflect briefly on subsequent developments.

I. LOGICS AND LANGUAGES

If there is only one system of logic, no question as to which is correct would arise. But if there is more than one, this question is neither easily dismissed nor readily answered. Logic is too general to be a matter of direct observation. Moreover, the actual practice of logicians (and mathematicians too for that matter) treats their enquiries as effectively a priori, that is, as not to be justified by an appeal to observation. But the most traditional account of a priori knowledge is one that supposes that we have some sort of direct metaphysical insight into the nature of reality.[1] Such accounts are hopeless. There are philosophers, of course, who do harbor hopes for such revealed truths, but neither Carnap nor Quine would have been even slightly tempted. So if we are denied methods that would directly establish one system of logic as correct, what else can we do? Well, we can try to justify a choice of system indirectly via argument. But that argument will presuppose some system of logic, and our efforts will be circular. Of course, we have no choice but to use the logic we accept to reflect on the logic we accept. Such a procedure might undermine our assumptions. If we are lucky, however, our various beliefs will not be self-undermining but can instead be brought into

---

[1] This supposed metaphysical insight is sometimes called intuition. It should not, however, be confused with Kantian intuition or that involved in intuitionist logic.

"reflective equilibrium."[2] Whatever our success in achieving equilibrium, however, it would do nothing to show that other sets of
belief (in this case other systems of logic) are not also fully stable,
and it would do nothing to show that our system is right and the
others wrong.

By the 1930s these were not idle speculative possibilities. In addition to the system of *Principia Mathematica* (Whitehead and Russell,
1910–1913), that by this time could already be called classical, there
was an array of constructivist and intuitionist alternatives. These
challenged classical concepts of disjunction, negation, quantification (both universal and existential), and even the idea that there are
exactly two truth values. The alternatives looked and were taken to
be dramatically different from one another. And there was no reason to hope that all but one would prove self-defeating. Indeed, the
deviant systems were, if anything, less likely than classical logic to
be shown to be inconsistent.

Perhaps it is natural to view logic as a theory like other theories,
to think that it has a subject matter and makes claims about that
domain of objects, in short, to think that it has content. If this is the
right way to think about logic, then there ought to be some fact of
the matter as to which of the various systems of logic is correct. As
our recent reflections indicate, however, the sad cost of thinking that
there is a straightforward fact of the matter about logic is a profound
skepticism; the truth may be out there, but even if we stumble onto
it, we shall never have good reason to believe that we have done
so.

And there is a traditional alternative to viewing systems of logic as
theories about which there is a fact of the matter. Kant held that logic,
along with other a priori domains such as geometry and arithmetic,
structured or constituted our other representings, those that do make
genuine empirical claims about the world. Moreover, one does not
have to be explicitly Kantian or uses phrases such as "the constitutive a priori" (cf. De Pierris, 1992) in order to deny that there is a
fact of the matter about logic. Wittgenstein's *Tractatus* (1922) shows
us a view of logic that is Kantian in this very respect. Of course,
for Wittgenstein what logic structures is not the human mind, as

---

[2] The phrase "reflective equilibrium" is due to John Rawls (1971). The same idea
specifically applied to logic is discussed in Nelson Goodman (1955, 65–68).

in Kant, but language. Indeed, for Wittgenstein logic and language are not separable. It is after all the deep logical grammar of language that governs how its elements combine to form propositions and also which propositions follow from which others. Perhaps more than any other book, the *Tractatus* marks what is called the linguistic turn in philosophy.

Carnap started his career as a neo-Kantian, and absorbed much from the *Tractatus*.[3] So even before confronting the problem of a multiplicity of logics, Carnap was inclined to see logic as constitutive rather than as substantive. And there is a significant auxiliary motive for such an inclination. The idea that there is no fact of the matter about logic, or alternatively the idea that it has no content, would allow one to reconcile the evident a prioricity of logicians' practice with a wholesome empiricism. Such an empiricism would address all questions about which there was a fact of the matter and would need no appeal to direct metaphysical insight.

To say that logic is without content is by itself to say nothing about alternative logics. For Kant logic was a finished subject, Aristotle having finished it. So if logic structures the way humans represent the world, it structures everyone's mind in the same way. Correspondingly for Wittgenstein, while the outward forms of French and German may differ, the logical structure of language, its deep structure, is everywhere the same. For both Kant and the Wittgenstein of the *Tractatus* there was logic but not logics. Carnap probably held some such view when he started writing *The Logical Syntax of Language* (1934c/1937). Once one concedes, however, that logic is without content it is easier to consider alternative logics and to say that they are without content as well. If they have no content there can hardly be a question of correctness in the choice among them. This choice could be at most a question of convenience or pragmatic utility. This is precisely the perspective, enshrined in the Principle of Tolerance, that was central to Carnap's philosophy for the rest of his life.

In *Logical Syntax* Carnap not only confronts the idea that there is more than one logic, he presents two of them. But he retains

---

[3] Kant and Wittgenstein are cited here as predecessors that held a constitutive view of logic. They are far from the only important influences on Carnap. A fuller account would, of course, discuss Frege, Hilbert, Poincaré, Einstein, Russell, Neurath, and Gödel.

the Wittgensteinian idea that the core of a language is the ways its elements can be connected into sentences and the connections among sentences such that one or more can be said to logically imply another. The system of connections is primary and says everything there is to say about a given language and its parts. If there are different logics, then, it will be best to treat them as different languages and to keep constant track of what language a given sentence is in. Carnap presents the logics much as logicians standardly present their systems. He lists various grammatical categories and the symbols falling under them and then uses this to define (in what he calls formation rules) the sentences of the two languages. Thereafter, this grammatical information is used (in what he calls transformation rules) to define for each language which of its sentences follow directly from which (sets of) other sentences of that same language. The word "language" here is perfectly appropriate, but it must be remembered that what is at issue are formal structures of the sort usually presented by logicians. They are, thus, more specifically artificial languages as objects of study or as proposals for the replacement of our usual languages. Carnap later used the phrase "linguistic framework" to capture this idea of a formal structure construed as a language or as a proposal for a part thereof.

Of the two languages that Carnap exhibits, the first, **L I**, is more nearly in accordance with the systems advanced by intuitionist logicians and constructivist mathematicians. It is logically weaker and hence less likely to be inconsistent. Moreover, every sentence in it is either completely verifiable or completely refutable on the basis of a finite number of elementary (atomic) sentences, and it has the interesting virtue of being able to describe its own syntax. But it would not seem to be able to express all of classical mathematics. The second language, **L II**, is powerful enough to express classical mathematics, which is convenient in the formulation of mathematically rich scientific theories. This increases the risk of contradiction, of course, but no actual contradiction is known. Gödel had shown that no such language, i.e., no language sufficiently rich to express classical mathematics, could be complete in the following sense: A language would be complete if there were a consistent (recursive) axiomatization such that for each mathematical sentence either it or its negation would be derivable from those axioms. Without diminishing the importance of Gödel's results and without contradicting them, Carnap distinguishes between derivability and a new, highly semantical notion that he calls logical consequence, or consequence for short. He is then able to show that **L II** not only can express classical mathematics; it is also complete in this different sense, namely that every mathematical sentence is such that either it or its negation is a consequence of the null set of axioms. Tarski was later to identify Carnap's notion here as the first viable concept of logical consequence (Tarski, 1936b/1956).[4] So both **L I** and **L II** are languages worth investigating.

Logical consequence is, just as derivability has always been, relative to the system or language at hand. It will simplify matters (and save a great deal of ink), however, if we take this relativity for granted and let the context indicate what language is at issue. Sentences that are the consequences of the null set are in effect guaranteed to be true in that language. And since what does the guaranteeing are the constitutive rules that give the expressions of the language their meaning, it is not unreasonable to say that those sentences guaranteed to be true are true in virtue of their meaning. These are the sentences that Carnap calls *analytic*. This would include logic and mathematics and much else besides. Thus, in saying that there is no uniquely correct logic or equivalently that there is no fact of the matter as to which language is correct, Carnap would not be denying that the sentences of our favorite logic are true. Quite to the contrary, he holds that what he takes to be the truths of logic are analytically true in his language. And if your logic differs from his, then it can be analytically true as well, but in a different language.

The move from viewing logic as a body of doctrine to viewing it as rules collectively constituting a particular language is significant. A language is not the sort of thing to be correct or incorrect. It might be convenient for certain purposes or risky in certain ways, and what is sayable in one language may not be sayable at all in another. But to ask whether a given language is correct is just wrongheaded. Carnap puts this by proposing a Principle of Tolerance: "It is not our business

---

4 Tarski's acknowledgement of Carnap is far from straightforward. More precisely Tarski initially credits Carnap with the "first attempt to formulate a precise definition of the proper concept of consequence" (1936b/1956, 413). Tarski then complains that Carnap's definitions are too complex to discuss. Then he discusses them – disparagingly. Then he gives what he takes to be the correct definition. Then he argues that this definition is equivalent to Carnap's.

to set up prohibitions, but to arrive at conventions" (1934c/1937, 51, italics omitted). On the next page he expresses it a bit more fully:

In logic there are no morals. Everyone is at liberty to build up his own logic, i.e., his own form of language, as he wishes. All that is required of him is that if he wishes to discuss it, he must state his methods clearly, and give syntactical rules instead of philosophical arguments. (1934c/1937, 52)

Note that Carnap calls Tolerance a principle. It is not a claim that needs to be proved or even confirmed. It is rather a stance or practical strategy of resisting the urge to find the one and only correct logic. Because some logic or other will be presupposed in such a quest, even if we settle on some candidate, we will not be in a position to say that this is the right one and the others are wrong. Adopting the strategy that is the Principle of Tolerance, thus, will allow us to sidestep a lot of fruitless philosophic wrangling. So Carnap urges us to treat the choice of language forms as conventional. He views the choice as a practical one for which there is and could be no evidence that we have made the uniquely correct one. This is not to say all choices are equally good. They differ in practical ways: one could be more convenient to use or allow a simpler description of the world or help us reach more efficiently some outcomes that we value. Classical logic, for example, is more suitable for physics but is more likely to be inconsistent than intuitionist logic. So the latter is safer at the cost of considerable inconvenience in physics.

Just so there is no mistake, in saying "In logic there are no morals," Carnap is not rejecting what is usually called moral theory. Carnap's views on moral philosophy are too complex to be discussed here, but as just suggested, practical values do have a role in the pragmatic assessment and comparison of linguistic frameworks. Some languages are better than others. Carnap's use of the word "morals" here is intended to convey only that he rejects the idea that any notion of absolute correctness is appropriate in this context.

If logic is in this sense conventional, then so are its limits. Indeed, any sentence (not any proposition) can be adopted conventionally. That sentence (and any sentences for that matter) will have a precise meaning only after the totality of constitutive principles has been chosen. And the meaning of the sentence will be relative to whatever constitutive rules are chosen. This is why it is a mistake to interpret Carnap as claiming that anything can be made true by convention where the "things" in "anything" are claims that have some prior meaning. In adding new constitutive rules one changes the meaning of the *sentences*.

Not only do we have the freedom to lay down constitutive rules out beyond the first-order predicate calculus and even beyond set theory, it is frequently convenient to do so. In the history of science, for example, it has been frequently useful to introduce novel vocabulary that has not and probably cannot be explicitly defined in the terms of our prior vocabulary. If reasonable inferences are to be made from one claim in this vocabulary to another such claim, it might be advisable to introduce for this purpose new inference rules specifically involving, indeed partly defining, the novel concepts. Similarly it may prove advantageous to introduce other new inference rules that link the new claims with observational judgments framed in the antecedent terminology. In changing the inference rules, we can, of course, keep an old word spelled in a familiar way as long as we remember that the meaning of the word has changed. The point in all this is not that scientific theories must be set up in a certain way, but rather that scientists should have the freedom to develop their theories in whatever way is useful to their science, to the efficient and suggestive formulation of theories, to their employment in useful prediction, and to effective choices among alternative claims via judicious testing. As we shall see, it is here that the two paths to Carnap's mature philosophy join.

The notion of logic embodied in all this is extraordinarily broad. It covers not only the traditional domain of logic but also philosophy of science and the non-psychological parts of epistemology. In fact, Carnap thinks of himself as providing a new conception of philosophy. Philosophers will make proposals for the logic of science, that is, for the structure of reasoning within science, and cooperatively explore the technical consequences of adopting them. The standard of appraisal for the proposals is their utility within science. Thus, philosophy is considered as a kind of conceptual engineering that serves science rather than a mysterious enterprise that somehow locates its own domain of facts that are deeper than those that science can reveal.

II. THE SECOND PATH: EMPIRICAL SCIENCE

We have been discussing domains such as logic that have traditionally been viewed as a priori and noted that the special way of viewing their claims that Carnap envisions here could be extended, if convenient, into other domains. Suppose that our primary focus had been empirical science instead and our aim was to understand reasoning therein and in particular how we could sometimes have good reasons for accepting one theory over another. Then the same distinction we have been talking about might have emerged as a feature of our best account. That is, it might emerge as a feature of our best account that some claims within an empirical science genuinely describe the world and other claims are better understood as partly constituting the genuinely descriptive ones. In fact, Carnap was as much concerned with empirical science, and specifically with relativity theory, as he was with pure logic. There is no room here to trace the history of accounts of scientific testing or even of Carnap's own path. But at least a word is in order about what advantages he saw within empirical science for taking some claims there as having the special constitutive status that we discussed for pure logic. As often for Carnap it is the example of relativity theory and especially of geometry that he has most clearly in mind.

Relativity theory raises questions about the geometrical structure of physical space. Such a geometry claims that physical space has some specific Euclidian or non-Euclidian structure, and this structure summarizes a vast array of claims about distance relations. But any talk of physical distance seems to presuppose some empirical method of measuring it, whether that method is direct or indirect. These methods link up observationally determinable claims, say about the behavior of meter sticks or light rays, with the claims about distance. As Poincaré showed, however, one and the same physical space could be described as Euclidian or as non-Euclidian if different methods of measurement were employed for the two descriptions. This is a predicament that would later be called underdetermination. There seems to be no way for the empirical evidence alone to favor one such description-cum-method-of-measurement over another. This breeds skepticism. Moreover, there is the very real danger that this underdetermination is quite general, and if so, it breeds a corrosive skepticism. Perhaps, as some have thought, simplicity in one of its many senses could give one of the alternatives an edge. That makes simplicity attractive, but it has proved extraordinarily difficult to articulate the required sense of simplicity as a substantive principle or to show that it is an objective indicator of truth.

Happily, there is at least one way out of this morass. We might take some of the presupposed linkages, not as claims genuinely describing features of the world, but as constitutive principles that give meaning to a concept of length. If we do, then Poincaré's two apparently conflicting descriptions of geometrical structure are not in fact rival hypotheses, for their central terms are different in meaning. Both can be true, and if borne out by the evidence, both can be confirmed as much as any general empirical claim. The prospect of a pervasive skepticism about the theoretical domain is thus avoided.

There is even a place for simplicity in Carnap's account. If there were a clear articulation of the notion, there is no reason why it could not be one of the constitutive principles for confirmation. As a constitutive principle there would be no need to show that the simpler theory is more likely to be true or even that choosing the simpler theory gets us to the truth, as independently understood, more efficiently. Apart from this role, simplicity can also be a ground for making a practical choice among linguistic frameworks, that is, among alternative proposals for structuring the language of science. Here there is no question of achieving a uniquely correct result. So if the notion of simplicity remains vague or subjectively applied, there is no difficulty so long as all parties are clear about what language is chosen by each.

Thus even apart from pure logic there is within our emerging understanding of empirical reasoning a motive for us to take our various claims to be of importantly different kinds: Some directly represent the world, and others are best understood as endowing those descriptive, empirical claims with structure and meaning. This strategy of interpretation has a number of advantages. First, it allows for a natural representation of the reasoning that we actually do in science and of the asymmetric presuppositions of our various claims (as when Newtonian science presupposes the calculus). Second, because the various sciences will have their own concepts and these concepts will have their own structure (as when Darwinian biology rejected the sort of natural kinds that Mill thought was required for reasoning in physics), it does some justice to fact that the texture of reasoning may vary from one discipline to another. Finally and most importantly from Carnap's perspective, it allows for a helpful criterion of identity and conflict among claims generally. This deflates and defuses many theoretical conflicts (as in the Poincaré case), an outcome that is particularly welcome because many of these are not readily resolved by appeal to empirical evidence alone. That it also defuses philosophic debates over scientific methods is an added bonus. Of course, these advantages, even if taken collectively and at face value, do not prove that Carnap's strategy of interpretation is the correct one. Carnap is not concerned to show that there even is a correct one. What he does want is to propose structures of reasoning that will be helpful to science. It is certainly evidence in favor of the utility of his proposals both that they are able to reflect the structure and texture of scientific reasoning that, in so far as we can tell, scientists themselves have chosen and also that the proposals can also show us how to avoid fruitless conflicts.

Carnap had progressed along this second path before his groundbreaking work in *Logical Syntax*, but his attention had been focused largely on theoretical concepts and their links to observation in the form of measurement procedures. In this he was already a pluralist. As noted earlier, however, in logic he had not been. Moreover, prior to the early 1930s, while Carnap was prepared to say that our concepts overall could be built up in various ways, he took it for granted that a phenomenal observation base more correctly represents our epistemic situation. Shortly before he met Quine, Carnap began systematically to take up the idea that we have genuine options both in what we take as evidence and in what we take as logic. As a result of this reconsideration of evidence and logic the two paths fused into his mature philosophy, that is, into a general account of the logic of science. This gives an understanding of logic and mathematics pursued as independent sciences and also of their integration into empirical science. As a more or less seamless part of this integration Carnap's account assigns to methods of testing and measurement the same kind of constitutive role that he saw in logic generally. Finally, his account gives an understanding of philosophy as part of the overall scientific enterprise.

III. QUINE'S CHALLENGE

We have been discussing Carnap's mature philosophy and of the place of a certain distinction within it, namely, a distinction between claims that genuinely represent the world (the substantive claims) and others (the constitutive ones) that instead of representing give form, structure, and meaning to all the sentences of the language. In this I have barely mentioned analyticity, but it has never been far off-stage. The analytic sentences, remember, are the ones whose accept-ability is guaranteed by the constitutive principles. In turn the con-tradictory sentences are those whose unacceptability is guaranteed by the constitutive principles, and the synthetic sentences are all the rest. So in effect, the question of whether one can draw an analytic/synthetic distinction is exactly the same question as whether one can distinguish between the constitutive and the substantive. If the answer to both is no, then Carnap's mature philosophy fails, and the avenue it offers for avoiding skepticism and sidestepping many conflicts in both science and philosophy is foreclosed as well.

Notoriously, Quine rejects the analytic/synthetic distinction, and his "Two Dogmas of Empiricism" (1951) is generally taken as the primary text. The distinction we are told is unclear or even unintel-ligible. But Quine's argument here must itself be counted as at least a bit unclear given that its defenders have interpreted it in strikingly different ways. Some have thought that Quine argued that the dis-tinction to be vague or imprecise,[5] others that it was circular.[6] Still others claimed that Quine held it was not general enough.[7] Some would have it that according to Quine the distinction can be under-stood perfectly well but there are no analytic claims.[8] And there is a large contingent of interpreters who hold that Quine charged the distinction with lacking explanatory value (Burge, 1992, 6 and 10). A different group maintains that the target was really incorrigibility (Passmore, 1966).

As in the story of the blind men and the elephant, these vari-ous authors are not merely making things up. Each can cite textual evidence, and each has some claim to be part of the story. Part of the problem lies with the text of "Two Dogmas." It hints at a great many things, but it is not very explicit. We are told at the outset that analyticity is unclear but not what makes it so. Perhaps with Potter

---

[5] This seems to be the suggestion of Carl Hempel's (1958, 54) where he says that the notions of analyticity and synonymy "are by no means as clear as they were long considered to be" and cites Quine's "Two Dogmas." It also seems to have been Carnap's initial understanding of Quine, expressed in Carnap and Quine (1990).

[6] See, for example, Soames (2003, vol. I, 355–360).

[7] Ernest Lepore takes the argument to be that the notion is not general enough, that is, not "transcendent" (1995, esp. 471f.).

[8] This seems to be Jerry Fodor's position in Fodor and Lepore (1992, 25).

Stewart he knows it when he sees it. "Analytic" could be clarified by defining it, perhaps in terms of logical truth and synonymy. But, he says, "synonymy" is unclear in just the same way. Perhaps that term could be clarified in turn by defining that by appeal to necessity. But again that is said to have the very same unclarity. When defining necessity in terms of analyticity is considered, that is ruled out on grounds of circularity. Plainly, however, the problem is not the circularity itself. Any sequence of definitions if carried far enough has nowhere to turn except back on itself. And Quine is perfectly happy with circularity in both confirmation and semantics; that is what his holism is. The real problem is this unspecified unclarity that infects each of the terms in the circle.

So what does Quine want? In "Two Dogmas" there is at most a hint that we might not even notice but for the rest of Quine's writings. Both before "Two Dogmas" and repeatedly after it Quine insists that he must be provided "behavioral criteria" for all intelligible terms and for "analytic" in particular. What Quine is demanding for analyticity, then, is essentially what Carnap demanded for physical length and other notions that were suitable for empirical science, namely, an indication in observational terms as to when the use of these notions was appropriate. This might fall short of a complete definition and the link to the observable might be indirect, but that link had to be there. What Quine takes as observable, in the case of language, is behavior, hence the expression "behavioral criteria." Carnap might have called them "empirical criteria," and in the literature they were variously called correspondence rules, or bridge principles. The point of the demand is to make the term useable in a proper empirical theory, in this case in empirical linguistics.

Note that Quine is imposing a demand that our terms meet an empiricist criterion of significance in the tradition of Ayer, Hempel, and Carnap himself. These three would have exempted logical and mathematical terms.[9] Quine is not endorsing any specific version of these criteria, except to extend it to all terms whatever. Ironically, many of Quine's interpreters who have taken him to give a

---

[9] This is because each of the three accepted an analytic/synthetic distinction, at least at the time that he was advancing an empiricist criterion of meaning. Hempel's case is special only in that he seems to have given up the search for an empiricist criterion and to have done so about the same time he began to have doubts about the analytic/synthetic distinction, that is, about 1950.

convincing argument against the tenability of the analytic/synthetic distinction themselves utterly reject the idea that our terms must meet an empiricist criterion of significance.[10] Even more of his interpreters reject the idea that when it comes to language all evidence is behavioral evidence.[11] No doubt the conflict between what Quine does say and what these writers are willing to have him say is part of why he has been so inventively interpreted.

IV. IS QUINE'S DEMAND REASONABLE AND CAN IT BE MET?

Having identified the core of Quine's argument against analyticity, it is only fair to determine, if we can, the legitimacy of his demand for behavioral criteria and the prospects for meeting that demand should it be found acceptable. The first of these issues is bound to be controversial, and Carnap in particular would reject the idea that he needs to provide behavioral criteria and hence to satisfy empiricist criteria of significance for analyticity. He is not, he thinks, doing something for which questions of confirmation even arise. If Carnap were doing empirical linguistics and making claims to the effect, say, that a certain English sentence were analytic, then perhaps Quine's demands would be reasonable. But Carnap is not. He is engaged not in empirical linguistics but in a form of metamathematics. Carnap's whole mature philosophy centers on the idea that logic (broadly understood so as to include standard logic, mathematics, and his own metamathematical or meta-logical investigations of formal systems) is best seen as having a structuring, meaning-giving role rather than a describing one. Given that Carnap explicitly denies that his own attributions of analyticity are intended to have empirical content, it is illegitimate for Quine to demand that Carnap produce behavioral or other empirical criteria that will show that these attributions do have such content.

---

[10] Thus, for example, Scott Soames makes it plain in chapter 13 of (2003, vol. I, 271–299) that he regards such empiricist criteria, or as he calls them, verificationist criteria, as unacceptable. Tyler Burge is only marginally less explicit (Burge, 1992, 5).

[11] The number of authors here is again large, but as examples see Soames (2003, vol. II, 244) and Burge (1992, 29f.).

That Quine does demand to be shown that Carnap's logical investigations have empirical content says a great deal about how different
Quine's starting assumptions are. Contrary to Carnap, he begins it
seems with the assumption that logic has content. He takes it for
granted as well that an empiricism of some sort is correct. Thus,
an empiricist account of logic must be found, that is, one that treats
logic as contentful. Then, and perhaps only then, it is perfectly legitimate to demand of logic, including Carnap's metalinguistic account,
what an empiricist like Carnap would demand of physics, namely
that one shows it to have empirical content by providing the criteria
that link the account with empirical evidence. Obviously Quine's
assumption that logic has content is squarely at odds with Carnap's
standpoint that logic is constitutive rather than substantive (contentful).[12]

Perhaps this difference will appear more graphically if we recall
that at bottom Carnap is not describing natural languages but *proposing* alternatives. Proposals may be wise or unwise but not true or
false. In turn, we cannot empirically confirm or disconfirm that they
are true or false.

Carnap could go further and point out that mathematical geometers do not concern themselves with the apparatus of measurement
and surveys. And he could mention as well that logicians, including Quine, do not in their logic textbooks give empirical directions
for telling one object from another or for reidentifying them. Carnap
would not imagine that he has thereby proved that one must draw
an analytic/synthetic distinction or that Quine's view is defective.
Carnap does not conceive of his strategy of drawing the distinction
as the sort of thing that can be proved at all.

Is this defense of Carnap's position successful? Well, it does tend
to blunt the force of Quine's demand. And I think it is legitimate for
Carnap in his own work to follow the example of most geometers and
set aside questions of empirical criteria. It does not follow, however,
that there is absolutely no sense in which Quine's demands must be
met, or at least must be meetable. It is all very well to say that Carnap
is making proposals rather than describing natural languages, but he

---

[12] For a discussion of the fundamental differences between Quine's and Carnap's initial philosophic assumptions, especially with respect to the meaning of empiricism,
see Richardson (1997).

is not even making proposals unless we know what it would be for someone to accept and act on them. Nor could we evaluate them for utility unless we know what it is to adopt the proposals.

Perhaps continuing the analogy with geometry will make this clearer. As Quine pointed out many years before "Two Dogmas," a pure mathematical geometry completely divorced from methods of linear measurement can be thought of as a mathematical rather than an empirical theory (Quine, 1936). But the cost of this is that it ceases to be a theory specifically about space; it would no more be about spatial points than it would be about ordered n-tuples of real numbers or for that matter about any sufficiently numerous domain whatsoever. Only when some methods of measurement are supposed as waiting in the wings does the abstract formalism earn its claim to be a geometry at all. So it is with Carnap's metamathematics of language. Without appropriate linkages to behavior even proposals are no more than abstract formalisms that forfeit their claims to be about language at all.

This concession to Quine on my part is rather un-Carnapian, but it is also extremely narrow. I have conceded that there must be behavioral criteria of some sort, at least in principle, but when we apply those criteria to English it need not turn out that the sentences that Carnap proposed that we take as analytic turn out to be analytic sentences of English. Carnap's whole point was that we could set up the language of science in rather different ways. So, for example, if it should be discovered that some specific set theory is not analytic in English, that is no reason why we should not propose that it be so in the language we adopt.

My concession is also narrow in another way. I agreed that there must in principle be behavioral criteria, but it does not follow that those criteria need to be particularly sophisticated or that Carnap need worry very much. Once again our analogy with geometry can help. Linear distance can be measured in a variety of ways from crudely pacing out a stretch of road to the sophisticated deployment of a laser-assisted transit and level. But even if such methods were confined to pacing, the geometer could legitimately claim to be giving a theory of space and not merely of numbers. The mathematical geometer could even proceed to ignore the details of measurement methods altogether. In general mathematical geometers know little of surveying and for good reason – they have other things to worry about. In Carnap's case, as long as there are behavioral criteria for some terms on the basis of which analyticity can be defined, he need not worry if those criteria are very crude. Indeed, as long as there are some he need not even know what they are, at least not if the features of language that interest him are themselves rather abstract and mathematical.

So what are the prospects for providing behavioral criteria and thus saving Carnap's program from the narrow but legitimate part of Quine's attack? Quite good. Here, however, my discussion must be preliminary and truncated. Still, there are several points worth noting. First, finding criteria for, and to that extent reforming, useful scientific concepts is an ongoing project – always. No one should suppose that we have the final methods of measuring length any more than we have the final theory in physics.

Second, finding simple preliminary behavioral criteria that will turn terms from the theory of meaning into empirical concepts is actually rather easy. Quine himself does it – twice – almost without noticing that he has done so. Shortly after Carnap died Quine developed an account of analyticity, and he published it in *Roots of Reference* (1974). On this account, a sentence is analytic just in case everyone in the community learned the truth of the sentence in the process of learning its component words, and these words are learned if they allow for fluent discourse and effective coordinated action. This does seem to be behavioral, and Quine's most serious objection is that on this criterion set theory would not be analytic, chiefly because there is no unanimity on which set theory to adopt. Because Quine thinks of mathematics as just logic plus set theory, Quine concludes that mathematics would not be analytic by his criterion either.

It is worth a moment to see the inadequacy of this objection. First, sentences can be analytic according to the criterion even if they are reducible to a body of doctrine that as a whole is not analytic. Reducibility depends on the truths of one doctrine lining up with the truths of another and not on any facts about how those truths are learned. For example, "Two is even," and "Seven is a prime number," would both be analytic according to the criterion regardless of what truths they are reduced to. Indeed, all the familiar parts of mathematics would count as analytic by Quine's criterion regardless of whether they are reducible at all or to what. This would tend to vindicate Carnap's assumption that mathematics is analytic even in English. For that matter, much of set theory would be analytic on the criterion even if set theory as a whole is not. Second, and more important, whatever may the case with English, Quine has provided enough of a criterion for analyticity for Carnap to meet the rather narrow legitimate part of Quine's demand as conceded a few paragraphs back. Carnap is best thought of as making proposals or perhaps as considering alternative proposals rather than as doing empirical linguistics. So he thinks he has no need of empirical criteria at all. I, however, conceded what Carnap did not, namely that making proposals requires that it be possible, at least in principle, to tell whether the proposal has been adopted. This narrow sense is the only sense in which Quine's demand for empirical criteria is legitimate. Here the question of how the criterion would play out in English is irrelevant. What was wanted was a criterion that would apply to proposals. Quine has provided that.

In *Pursuit of Truth* (1990, 1992) Quine also provided an account of synonymy within a language. Roughly the idea is that two expressions from the same language are synonymous just in case they are interchangeable in any critical semantic mass without changing the test conditions thereof. "Critical semantic mass" is just Quine's fancy name for any body of doctrine sufficiently large to have observational consequences. Another way of putting the idea is that synonymy is interchangeability *salva confirmatione*. Quine's immediate complaint is that it doesn't apply across languages and hence does not directly solve his worries about translation. Had he looked more closely he would have seen that it could address the issue of translation, but that does not matter here. Even within a language this criterion is sufficient to allow an account of analyticity, and that is enough for now.

Is this as well as we can do in providing behavioral criteria? It is all that we need to do. But much more sophisticated criteria are available. I have tried to provide those elsewhere (Creath, 1994, esp. 298f.) and so will not do so here. Thus, it does seem that, contra Carnap, Quine's demands for behavioral criteria are reasonable but only in a very narrow sense and that, contra the very clear suggestion of "Two Dogmas," these restricted demands can be met – even Quine has done so. Having assured ourselves that behavioral criteria can in principle be provided, we can now say that Carnap is free to ignore them. In so far as the task he adopts is the metamathematical examination of alternative linguistic structures, he is indeed in the position of the mathematical geometer. For once that geometer is satisfied that there are methods of surveying, he or she can ignore them and say with a clear conscience "Surveying is no doubt an important task, but it is not mine."

V. CONCLUSION

We have seen that Carnap's mature philosophy revolves around a central distinction between those claims that genuinely have content and describe the world and those others that serve instead to structure or constitute the language in which we describe that world. The former are substantive claims, and Carnap calls them synthetic. The sentences that are guaranteed to be true by the constituting part can be said to be true in virtue of meaning, in virtue of the language thus constituted. These Carnap calls analytic. His analytic/synthetic distinction, therefore, is an emblem of this whole way of looking at human reason and at the knowledge we might achieve by using that reason. It is a striking view and one that has the exciting potential to release us from fruitless conflicts both in philosophy and in science. Carnap reached this new view from two directions. On one path he confronted unflinchingly the idea that there are genuinely different logics available to us, and in response he adopted the Principle of Tolerance. This is basically the strategy of so conceiving of the issue that it does not even make sense to ask which logic is the uniquely correct one. The other path, and it ultimately joins with the first, arises from a deep reconsideration of our prospects in choosing among apparently rival physical theories, especially theories of physical space. Carnap's response once again was to urge that what had seemed to be a theoretical question of how the world really is would be understood better and more fruitfully as a practical question of how to structure the language of science. In effect, this is the question of how to structure human reason in this important context.

The opportunity that Carnap put before us in the 1930s is tantalizing, but for the most part it has been promise as yet unfulfilled. The causes of this are complex and involve the interruptions of war and Carnap's move from the context of Europe to that of America. But another major cause has to be reckoned to be an argument developed by Quine and expressed most famously in "Two Dogmas of Empiricism." This argument seems to have persuaded many prominent philosophers for a full generation that there was something defective in Carnap's central distinction between the analytic and the synthetic and therefore in his whole philosophic enterprise. On close inspection, however, that argument is not as compelling as it must have seemed. Quine's demand for behavioral criteria for the distinction is legitimate only in an extremely narrow sense, and in that sense the demand can be met; even Quine has done so.

Carnap has offered us a strategy. The task ahead is to explore it and to explore as well any alternative strategy that we can devise and articulate. Quine himself has fascinating suggestions at the end of "Two Dogmas." Surely both can be investigated in a spirit of cooperation. In this way the controversy between Carnap and Quine can be seen not as a resting place but as a new beginning.

BIBLIOGRAPHY

Editors' note:

Archives: Two archival collections are cited giving the date of composition, where known, as follows:

(ASP) Archives for Scientific Philosophy, Special Collections, University of Pittsburgh Libraries. Catalog number starting with RC given in citation. All ASP items are quoted by permission of the University of Pittsburgh. All rights reserved.

(UCLA) Charles E. Young Research Library, Department of Special Collections, University of California at Los Angeles, manuscript collection 1029 (Rudolf Carnap Papers), Box 2, Folder CM3. All items quoted by permission. All rights reserved.

Published sources: Entries are arranged by author and date of publication. Where more than one edition appears in an entry, all the relevant dates are given separated by slashes. The corresponding publication information is given in order, separated by semicolons. Thus, in "Carnap, 1934c/1937" the "1934c" picks out a unique bibliographic entry, in this case the original publication date, and the "1937" gives the date for the English translation described in the second part of the entry.

Anderson, Anthony, 1989. "Russell on Order in Time," in Savage and Anderson (eds.), 1989, pp. 249–263.

Angelelli, Ignacio, 1982. "Frege's Notion of *Bedeutung*," in L. J. Cohen *et al.* (eds.), *Logic, Methodology and Philosophy of Science*, Vol. VI. Amsterdam: North-Holland, pp. 735–753.

Armendt, Brad, 1993. "Dutch Books, Additivity, and Utility Theory," *Philosophical Topics* 21: 1–20.

Ash, Mitchell G., 1998. *Gestalt Psychology in German Culture 1890–1967: Holism and the Quest for Objectivity*. Cambridge: Cambridge University Press.

Awodey, Steve, 1996. "Structure in Mathematics and Logic: A Categorical Perspective," *Philosophia Mathematica* 4: 209–237.

2004. "An Answer to G. Hellman's Question 'Does Category Theory Provide a Framework for Mathematical Structuralism?'," *Philosophia Mathematica* 12: 54–64.

Awodey, Steve and Carus, A. W., 2001. "Carnap, Completeness, and Categoricity: The *Gabelbarkeitssatz* of 1928," *Erkenntnis* 54: 145–172.

2004. "How Carnap Could Have Replied to Gödel," in S. Awodey and C. Klein (eds.), 2004, pp. 203–223.

2007. "Carnap's Dream: Gödel, Wittgenstein and the *Logical Syntax*," *Synthese*.

Awodey, Steve and Klein, Carsten (eds.), 2004. *Carnap Brought Home: The View from Jena*. Chicago and La Salle: Open Court.

Awodey, Steve and Reck, Erich H., 2002a. "Completeness and Categoricity, part 1: Nineteenth-century Axiomatics to Twentieth-century Metalogic," *History and Philosophy of Logic* 23 (1): 1–30.

2002b. "Completeness and Categoricity, part 2: Twentieth-century Metalogic to Twenty-first-century Semantics," *History and Philosophy of Logic* 23 (2): 77–94.

Ayer, Alfred Jules, 1936. *Language, Truth and Logic*. London: Gollancz.

(ed.), 1959. *Logical Positivism*. New York: Free Press.

1972. *Probability and Evidence*. London: Macmillan.

Bar-Hillel, Yehoshua, 1956. "Husserl's Conception of a Purely Logical Grammar," *Philosophy and Phenomenological Research* 17: 362–369.

Barker, Stephen F., 1957. *Induction and Hypothesis*. Ithaca, NY: Cornell University Press.

Bayes, Thomas, 1764. "An Essay towards Solving a Problem in the Doctrine of Chances," *Philosophical Transactions of the Royal Society of London* 53: 370–418.

Beaney, Michael, 2004. "Carnap's Conception of Explication: From Frege to Husserl?," in S. Awodey and C. Klein (eds.), 2004, pp. 117–150.

Belnap, Nuel and Massey, Gerald, 1990. "Semantic Holism," *Studia Logica* 49: 67–82.

Beth, Evert W., 1963. "Carnap's Views on the Advantages of Constructed Systems over Natural Languages in the Philosophy of Science," in P. A. Schilpp (ed.), 1963, pp. 469–502.

Bohnert, Herbert G., 1975. "Carnap's Logicism," in Hintikka (ed.), 1975b, pp. 183–216.

Bonk, Thomas (ed.), 2003. *Language, Truth and Knowledge: Contributions to the Philosophy of Rudolf Carnap*. Vienna Circle Institute Library, Vol. II. Dordrecht: Kluwer.

Bonk, Thomas and Mosterín, Jesus, 2000. "Editors' Introduction," in Carnap 2000, pp. 1–54.

Braithwaite, Richard B., 1973. "Editorial Foreword," in J. M. Keynes, *A Treatise on Probability* (*Collected Works*, Vol. VIII). London: Macmillan, pp. xv–xxii.

Broad, Charlie Dunbar, 1924. "Mr. Johnson on the Logical Foundations of Science," *Mind* 33: 242–261, 369–384.

Burge, Tyler, 1992. "Philosophy of Language and Mind: 1950–1990," *Philosophical Review* (January) 101: 3–51.

Carnap, Rudolf, 1922. "Der Raum. Ein Beitrag zur Wissenschaftslehre," *Kant-Studien*, Ergänzungsheft 56. Berlin: Reuther & Reichard.

1923. "Über die Aufgabe der Physik," *Kant-Studien* 28: 90–107.

1924. "Dreidimensionalität des Raumes und Kausalität," *Annalen der Philosophie* 4: 105–130.

1925. "Über die Abhängigkeit der Eigenschaften des Raumes von denen der Zeit," *Kant-Studien* 30: 331–345.

1926. *Physikalische Begriffsbildung*. Karlsruhe: Braun.

1927. "Eigentliche und uneigentliche Begriffe," *Symposion* 1: 355–374.

1928a/1967. *Der logische Aufbau der Welt*. Berlin-Schlachtensee: Weltkreis-Verlag; translated as *The Logical Structure of the World* by R. A. George. Berkeley and Los Angeles: University of California Press.

1928b/1967. *Scheinprobleme in der Philosophie: Das Fremdlpsychische und der Realismusstreit*. Berlin-Schlachtensee: Weltkreis-Verlag; translated as *Pseudoproblems in Philosophy* by R. A. George. Berkeley and Los Angeles: University of California Press.

1929. *Abriss der Logistik*. Vienna: Springer Verlag.

1930a/1959. "Die alte und die neue Logik," *Erkenntnis* 1: 12–26; translated as "The Old and the New Logic," in A. J. Ayer (ed.), 1959, pp. 133–147.

1930b. "Die Mathematik als Zweig der Logik," *Blätter für deutsche Philosophie* 4: 298–310.

1930c. "Bericht über Untersuchungen zur allgemeinen Axiomatik," *Erkenntnis* 1: 303–310.

1931. "Die logizistische Grundlegung der Mathematik," *Erkenntnis* 2: 91–105.

1932a/1934. "Die physikalische Sprache als Universalsprache der Wissenschaft," *Erkenntnis* 2: 432–465; translated as *The Unity of Science*, by M. Black. London: Kegan Paul, Trench, Trubner & Co.

1932b/1959. "Psychologie in physikalischer Sprache," *Erkenntnis* 3: 107–42; translated as "Psychology in Physicalistic Language," in A. J. Ayer (ed.), 1959, pp. 165–198.

1932c/1987. "Über Protokollsätze," *Erkenntnis* 3: 215–28; translated as "On Protocol Sentences," by R. Creath and R. Nollan, *Noûs* 21: 457–470.

1932d/1959. "Überwindung der Metaphysik durch logische Analyse der Sprache," *Erkenntnis* 2: 219–41; translated as "The Elimination of Metaphysics through Logical Analysis of Language," by A. Pap in A. J. Ayer (ed.), 1959, pp. 60–81.

1934a. "Die Antinomien und die Unvollständigkeit der Mathematik," *Monatshefte für Mathematik und Physik* 41: 263–284.

1934b. *Die Aufgabe der Wissenschaftslogik.* Vienna: Verlag Gerold und Co.

1934c/1937. *Logische Syntax der Sprache.* Vienna: Springer; translated by Amethe Smeaton, Countess von Zeppelin as *The Logical Syntax of Language.* London: Kegan Paul, Trench, Trubner & Co.

1934d/1984. "On the Character of Philosophical Problems," *Philosophy of Science* 1: 5–19; Reprinted in *Philosophy of Science* 51: 5–19.

1934e. "Theoretische Fragen und praktische Entscheidungen," *Natur und Geist* 2: 257–260.

1935a. "Ein Gültigkeitskriterium für die Sätze der klassischen Mathematik," *Monatshefte für Mathematik und Physik* 42: 163–190.

1935b/1953. "Formalwissenschaft und Realwissenschaft," *Erkenntnis* 5: 30–37; translated as "Formal Science and Factual Science," in *Readings in the Philosophy of Science*, ed. H. Feigl and M. Brodbeck. New York: Appleton-Century-Crofts, pp. 123–128.

1936a. "Über die Einheitssprache der Wissenschaft: Logische Bemerkungen zum Projekt einer Enzyklopädie," *Actes du Congrès Internationale de Philosophie Scientifique, Sorbonne, Paris 1935*, Facs. 2, *Unité de la science*. Paris: Herman and Cie, pp. 60–70.

1936b. "Von der Erkenntnistheorie zur Wissenschaftslogik," *Actes du Congrès Internationale de Philosophie Scientifique, Paris 1935*, Facs. 1, *Philosophie scientifique et empiricisme logique*. Paris: Herman and Cie, pp. 36–41.

1936c/1949. "Wahrheit und Bewährung," *Actes du Congrès Internationale de Philosophie Scientifique, Paris 1935*, Facs. 4, *Induction et probabilité*. Paris: Hermann & Cie, pp. 18–23; translated as "Truth and Confirmation," in *Readings in Philosophical Analysis*, ed. H. Feigl and W. Sellars. New York: Appleton-Century-Crofts, pp. 119–127.

1936–1937. "Testability and Meaning," *Philosophy of Science* 3: 419–471; and *Philosophy of Science* 4: 1–40.

1939. *Foundations of Logic and Mathematics.* International Encyclopedia of Unified Science, Vol. I, no. 3. Chicago: University of Chicago Press.

1942. *Introduction to Semantics.* Cambridge, MA: Harvard University Press.

1943. *Formalization of Logic.* Cambridge, MA: Harvard University Press.

1945a. "On Inductive Logic," *Philosophy of Science* 12: 72–97.

1945b. "The Two Concepts of Probability," *Philosophy and Phenomeno-logical Research* 5: 513–532.

1946. "Modalities and Quantification," *Journal of Symbolic Logic* 11: 33–64.

1947/1956. *Meaning and Necessity: A Study in Semantics and Modal Logic.* 1st and 2nd editions. Chicago: University of Chicago Press.

1950a/1956. "Empiricism, Semantics, and Ontology," *Revue Interna-tionale de Philosophie* 4: 20–40; reprinted with revisions in Carnap 1947/1956, pp. 205–221.

1950b/1962. *Logical Foundations of Probability.* 1st and 2nd editions. Chicago: University of Chicago Press.

1952. *The Continuum of Inductive Methods.* Chicago: University of Chicago Press.

1954/1958/1968. *Einführung in die symbolische Logik, mit besonderer Berücksichtigung ihrer Anwendungen.* Vienna: Springer; translated and enlarged as *Introduction to Symbolic Logic and its Applications*, by W. Meyer and J. Wilkinson. New York: Dover; 3rd edition (German). Vienna and New York: Springer-Verlag.

1955/1956. "Meaning and Synonymy in Natural Languages," *Philosophi-cal Studies* 6: 33–47; reprinted in Carnap 1947/1956, pp. 233–247.

1956. "The Methodological Character of Theoretical Concepts," in H. Feigl and M. Scriven (eds.), *The Foundations of Science and the Con-cepts of Psychology and Psychoanalysis.* Minneapolis: University of Minnesota Press, pp. 38–76.

1962. "The Aim of Inductive Logic," in E. Nagel, P. Suppes, and A. Tarski (eds.), *Logic, Methodology and Philosophy of Science.* Stanford: Stanford University Press, pp. 303–318.

1963a. "Carnap's Intellectual Autobiography," in P. A. Schilpp (ed.), 1963, pp. 3–84.

1963b. "E. W. Beth on Constructed Language Systems," in P. A. Schilpp (ed.), 1963, pp. 927–933.

1963c. "My Views on Ontological Problems of Existence," in P. A. Schilpp (ed.), 1963, pp. 868–873.

1963d. "Replies and Systematic Expositions," in P. A. Schilpp (ed.), 1963, pp. 859–1013.

1963e. "Reply to Grünbaum," in P. A. Schilpp (ed.), 1963, pp. 952–958.

1963f. "Value Judgements," in P. A. Schilpp (ed.), 1963, pp. 999–1013.

1966/1974. *Philosophical Foundations of Physics: An Introduction to the Philosophy of Science*, ed. Martin Gardner. New York: Basic Books; reprinted with minor revisions as *An Introduction to the Philosophy of Science.* New York: Basic Books.

1993. "Interview mit Rudolf Carnap (1964)," in W. Hochkeppel (ed.), *Mein Weg in die Philosophie*. Stuttgart: Reclam, pp. 133–147.

2000. *Untersuchungen zur allgemeinen Axiomatik*, ed. Thomas Bonk and Jesus Mosterin. Darmstadt: Wissenschaftliche Buchgesellschaft.

2005. "Von Gott und Seele; Scheinfragen in Metaphysik und Theologie," in R. Carnap, *Scheinprobleme in der Philosophie und andere metaphysikkritische Schriften*, ed. T. Mormann. Hamburg: Meiner, pp. 49–62.

Carnap, Rudolf and Bachmann, Friedrich, 1936. "Über Extremalaxiome," *Erkenntnis* 6: 166–88.

Carnap, Rudolf, Hahn, Hans, and Neurath, Otto, 1929/1973. *Wissenschaftliche Weltauffassung: Der Wiener Kreis*. Vienna: Artur Wolf Verlag; translated as "Scientific Conception of the World: The Vienna Circle," in Neurath, 1973, pp. 299–318.

Carnap, Rudolf and Jeffrey, Richard C. (eds.), 1971. *Studies in Inductive Logic and Probability*, Vol. I. Berkeley and Los Angeles: University of California Press.

Carnap, Rudolf and Quine, Willard Van Orman, 1990. *Dear Carnap, Dear Van: The Quine–Carnap Correspondence and Related Work*, ed. Richard Creath. Los Angeles: University of California Press.

Carnap, Rudolf and Stegmüller, Wolfgang, 1959. *Inductive Logik und Wahrscheinlichkeit*. Vienna: Springer-Verlag.

Carus, A. W., 1999. "Carnap, Syntax, and Truth," in *Truth and its Nature (if any)*, ed. J. Peregrin. Dordrecht: Kluwer, pp. 15–35.

2007. *Carnap in Twentieth-Century Thought: Explication as Enlightenment*. Cambridge: Cambridge University Press.

Cassirer, Ernst, 1910/1953. *Substanzbegriff und Funktionsbegriff*. Berlin: Bruno Cassirer; reprinted in *Substance and Function and Einstein's Theory of Relativity*. New York: Dover Publications, pp. 1–346.

Ceynowa, Klaus, 1993. *Zwischen Pragmatismus und Fiktionalismus: Hans Vaihinger's "Philosophie des Als Ob."* Würzburg: Königshausen & Neumann.

Coffa, Alberto, 1991. *The Semantic Tradition from Kant to Carnap: To the Vienna Station*, ed. L. Wessels. Cambridge: Cambridge University Press.

Creath, Richard, 1991. "The Unimportance of Semantics," *PSA 1990: Proceedings of the Philosophy of Science Association*, Vol. II. East Lansing, MI: Philosophy of Science Association, pp. 405–416.

1994. "Functionalist Theories of Meaning and the Defense of Analyticity," in *Logic, Language, and the Structure of Scientific Theories*, ed. Wesley Salmon and Gereon Wolters. Pittsburgh and Konstanz: University of Pittsburgh Press and Universitätverlag Konstanz, pp. 287–304.

1996. "Languages Without Logic," in Ronald N. Giere and Alan W. Richardson (eds.), 1996, pp. 251–265.

de Finetti, Bruno, 1937/1964. "La prévision: ses lois logiques, ses sources subjectives," *Annales de l'Institut Henri Poincaré* 7: 1–68; translated and edited by H. E. Kyburg, Jr. and H. E. Smokler as "Foresight: Its Logical Laws, Its Subjective Source," in *Studies in Subjective Probability*. New York: Wiley, pp. 93–158.

Demopoulos, William, 2003a. "On the Rational Reconstruction of Our Theoretical Knowledge," *British Journal for the Philosophy of Science* 54: 371–403.

2003b. "Russell's Structuralism and the Absolute Description of the World," in Griffin (ed.), 2003, pp. 392–419.

Demopoulos, William and Clark, Peter, 2005. "The Logicism of Frege, Dedekind and Russell," in *The Oxford Handbook of the Philosophy of Mathematics and Logic*, ed. Stewart Shapiro. Oxford: Oxford University Press, pp. 129–165.

Demopoulos, William and Friedman, Michael, 1985/1989. "Bertrand Russell's *Analysis of Matter*: Its Historical Context and Contemporary Interest," *Philosophy of Science* 52: 621–639; reprinted as "The Concept of Structure in *The Analysis of Matter*," in W. Savage and A. Anderson (eds.), 1989, pp. 183–99.

De Pierris, Graciela, 1992. "The Constitutive A Priori," in Philip Hanson and Bruce Hunter (eds.), "Return of the A Priori," *Canadian Journal of Philosophy*, supplementary Vol. 18: 179–214.

Dewey, John, 1931. *Philosophy and Civilization*. New York: Minton, Balch, and Co.

1944/1970. *Theory of Valuation*. Chicago: University of Chicago Press; reprinted in *Foundations of the Unity of Science*, Vol. II. ed. O. Neurath, R. Carnap, and C. Morris. Chicago: University of Chicago Press, pp. 381–447.

Diaconis, Persi and Freedman, David, 1980. "De Finetti's Generalizations of Exchangeability," in Jeffrey (ed.), 1980, pp. 233–249.

DiSalle, Robert, 2006. *Understanding Space-Time: The Philosophical Development of Physics from Newton to Einstein*. Cambridge: Cambridge University Press.

Dreyfus, Hubert (ed.), 1982. *Husserl, Intentionality and Cognitive Science*. Cambridge, MA: MIT Press.

Dummett, Michael, 1981. *The Interpretation of Frege's Philosophy*. Cambridge, MA: Harvard University Press.

1993. *Origins of Analytic Philosophy*. Cambridge, MA: Harvard University Press.

Earman, John, 1992. *Bayes or Bust? A Critical Examination of Bayesian Confirmation Theory*. Cambridge, MA: MIT Press.

Einstein, Albert, 1905/1952. "Zur Elektrodynamik bewegter Körper," *Annalen der Physik* 17: 891–921; translated in H. A. Lorentz, *et al.* (eds.) as "On the Electrodynamics of Moving Bodies," in *The Principle of Relativity*. New York: Dover, pp. 37–65.

1921. *Geometrie und Erfahrung*. Berlin: Springer.

Farber, Martin, 1943. *The Foundations of Phenomenology: Edmund Husserl and the Quest for a Rigorous Science of Philosophy*. Cambridge, MA: Harvard University Press.

Feigl, Herbert, 1950. "Existential Hypotheses: Realistic versus Phenomenalistic Interpretations," *Philosophy of Science* 17: 35–62.

Feigl, Herbert and Sellars, Wilfrid (eds.), 1949. *Readings in Philosophical Analysis*. New York: Appleton-Century-Crofts.

Fodor, Jerry and Lepore, Ernest, 1992. *Holism: A Shopper's Guide*. Oxford: Blackwell.

Føllesdal, Dagfinn, 1958/1994. *Husserl und Frege: Ein Beitrag zur Beleuchtung der Entstehung der phänomenologischen Philosophie*. Oslo: Aschehoug; translated as "Husserl and Frege: A Contribution to Elucidating the Origins of Phenomenological Philosophy," in L. Haaparanta (ed.), *Mind, Meaning and Mathematics: Essays on the Philosophical Views of Husserl and Frege*. Dordrecht: Kluwer, pp. 3–47.

1969. "Husserl's Notion of Noema," *Journal of Philosophy* 66: 680–387.

1974. "Phenomenology," chapter 19 in E. C. Carterette and M. P. Friedman (eds.), *The Handbook of Perception*, Vol. I. New York: Academic Press, pp. 377–386.

1982. "Response (to Mohanty)," in Dreyfus (ed.), 1982, pp. 52–56.

1990. "Noema and Meaning in Husserl," *Philosophy and Phenomenological Research* 50 (supplement): 263–71.

1998. "Husserl, Edmund (1859–1938)," *Routledge Encyclopedia of Philosophy*, Vol. IV. London: Routledge, pp. 574–588.

Fraenkel, Adolf, 1919/1923/1928. *Einleitung in die Mengenlehre*. Revised 2nd and 3rd editions. Berlin: Springer.

Fraenkel, Abraham and Bar-Hillel, Yehoshua, 1956. *Foundations of Set Theory*. Amsterdam: North-Holland.

Frege, Gottlob, 1879/1997. *Begriffsschrift: Eine der arithmetischen nachgebildete Formelsprache des reinen Denkens*. Halle a/S: Louis Nebert; reprinted in Frege 1997a, pp. 47–78.

1884/1950/1980/1997. *Die Grundlagen der Arithmetik, eine logisch mathematische Untersuchung über den Begriff der Zahl*. Breslau: W. Koeber; translated by J. L. Austin as *The Foundations of Arithmetic*.

Oxford: Blackwell; revised 2nd edition translated by J. L. Austin as *The Foundations of Arithmetic: A Logico-Mathematical Enquiry into the Concept of Number*. Evanston, IL: Northwestern University Press; reprinted in Frege 1997a, pp. 84–129.

1891/1997. *Funktion und Begriff*. Jena: Hermann Pohle; translated as "Function and Concept," in Frege, 1997a, pp. 130–148.

1892b/1984/1997. "Über Sinn und Bedeutung," *Zeitschrift für Philosophie und philosophische Kritik* 100: 25–50; translated by M. Black as "On Sense and Meaning," in Frege 1984, pp. 157–177; translated as "On Sinn and Bedeutung," in Frege 1997a, pp. 151–171.

1893/1903/1967. *Die Grundgesetze der Arithmetik*. Vols. I (1893) and II (1903). Jena: Pohle; translated in part as *The Basic Laws of Arithmetic: Exposition of the System*. Los Angeles: University of California Press.

1894/1984. "Besprechung der E. Husserl, Philosophie der Arithmetik, I," *Zeitschrift für Philosophie und philosophische Kritik* 103: 313–332; translated by H. Kaal in Frege 1984, pp. 195–209.

1900/1980. "Letter to Hilbert, 6.1.1900," in *Philosophical and Mathematical Correspondence*, ed. G. Gabriel *et al.* Oxford: Blackwell.

1903. "Über die Grundlagen der Geometrie," *Jahresbericht der Deutschen Mathematiker-Vereinigung* 12: 319–324, 368–375.

1918/1984/1997. "Der Gedanke: Eine logische Untersuchung," *Beiträge zur Philosophie des deutschen Idealismus*, Bd. 1: 58–77; translated by P. Geach and R. Stoothoff as "Thought," in Frege 1984, pp. 351–372; reprinted in Frege 1997a, pp. 325–345.

1969/1997. "Ausführungen über Sinn und Bedeutungen," in *Nachgelassene Schriften*, H. Hermes *et al.* eds. Hamburg: Meiner, pp. 128–136; translated as "Comments on *Sinn* and *Bedeutung*," in Frege, 1997a, pp. 172–180.

1979. *Posthumous Writings of Gottlob Frege*, ed. H. Hermes *et al.* Chicago: University of Chicago Press.

1984. *Gottlob Frege: Collected Papers on Mathematics, Logic, and Philosophy*, ed. B. McGuiness. Oxford: Blackwell.

1997a. *The Frege Reader*, ed. M. Beaney. Oxford: Basil Blackwell.

1997b. *Posthumous Writings of Gottlob Frege*, ed. H. Hermes *et al.* Oxford: Basil Blackwell.

Freudenthal, Hans, 1962. "The Main Trends in the Foundations of Geometry in the 19th Century," in *Logic, Methodology and Philosophy of Science*, ed. E. Nagel, P. Suppes, and A. Tarski. Amsterdam: North-Holland, pp. 613–621.

Friedman, Michael, 1987/1999. "Carnap's *Aufbau* Reconsidered," *Noûs* 21: 521–45; reprinted in Friedman 1999a, pp. 89–113.

1988/1999. "Logical Truth and Analyticity in Carnap's *Logical Syntax of Language*," in *History and Philosophy of Modern Mathematics*, ed. William Asprey and Philip Kitcher. Minneapolis: University of Minnesota Press, pp. 82–94; reprinted in Friedman 1999a, pp. 198–233.

1992a/1999. "Epistemology in the *Aufbau*," *Synthese* 93: 15–57; reprinted in Friedman 1999a, pp. 114–162.

1992b. *Kant and the Exact Sciences*. Cambridge, MA: Harvard University Press.

1999a. *Reconsidering Logical Positivism*. Cambridge: Cambridge University Press.

1999b. "Tolerance and Analyticity in Carnap's Philosophy of Mathematics", in Friedman, 1999a, pp. 198–233.

2000. *A Parting of the Ways: Carnap, Cassirer, and Heidegger*. Chicago: Open Court.

2003. "Kuhn and Logical Empiricism," in *Thomas Kuhn*, ed. T. Nickels. Cambridge: Cambridge University Press, pp. 19–44.

Gabriel, Gottfried, 2002. "Frege, Lotze, and the Continental Roots of Early Analytic Philosophy," in *From Frege to Wittgenstein*, ed. E. Reck. New York: Oxford University Press, pp. 39–51.

2003. "Carnap's *Elimination of Metaphysics through Logical Analysis of Language*: A Retrospective Consideration of the Relationship between Continental and Analytic Philosophy," in *Logical Empiricism: Historical and Contemporary Perspectives*, ed. P. Parrini, W. C. Salmon, and M. H. Salmon. Pittsburgh: University of Pittsburgh Press, pp. 30–42.

2004. "Introduction: Carnap Brought Home," in S. Awodey and C. Klein (eds.), 2004, pp. 3–23.

Galison, Peter, 1996. "Constructing Modernism: The Cultural Location of *Aufbau*," in R. N. Giere and A. W. Richardson (eds.), 1996, pp. 17–44.

Giere, Ronald N. and Richardson, Alan W. (eds.), 1996. *Origins of Logical Empiricism*. Minnesota Studies in the Philosophy of Science, Vol. XVI. Minneapolis: University of Minnesota Press.

Gödel, Kurt, 1929/1986. "Über die Vollständigkeit des Logikkalküls," Ph.D. thesis, University of Vienna; translated as "On the Completeness of the Calculus of Logic," in Gödel, 1986, pp. 60–100.

1930/1986. "Die Vollständigkeit der Axiome des logischen Funktionenkalküls," *Monatshefte für Mathematik und Physik* 37: 349–360; translated as "The Completeness of the Axioms of the Functional Calculus of Logic," in Gödel, 1986, pp. 102–123.

1931/1986. "Über formal unentscheidbare Sätze der *Principia Mathematica* und verwandter Systeme I," *Monatshefte für Mathematik und Physik* 38: 173–198; translated as "On Formally Undecidable

Propositions of *Principia Mathematica* and Related Systems I," in Gödel, 1986, pp. 144–195.

1986. *Collected Works: Publications 1929–1936*. Vol. I, ed. Solomon Feferman *et al.* Oxford: Oxford University Press.

1995. "Is Mathematics Syntax of Language?," (versions III and V) in *Collected Works: Unpublished Essays and Lectures*, Vol. III, ed. Solomon Feferman *et al.* Oxford: Oxford University Press, pp. 334–362.

2003. *Collected Works: Correspondence A–G*. Vol. IV, ed. Solomon Feferman *et al.* Oxford: Oxford University Press.

Goldfarb, Warren, 1996. "The Philosophy of Mathematics in Early Positivism," in R. N. Giere and A. W. Richardson (eds.), 1996, pp. 213–230.

2003. "Rudolf Carnap" (editorial introduction), in S. Feferman *et al.* (eds.), 2003, Oxford: Clarendon Press, pp. 335–341.

2005. "On Gödel's Way In: The Influence of Rudolf Carnap," *Bulletin of Symbolic Logic* 11: 185–193.

Goldfarb, Warren and Ricketts, Thomas, 1992. "Carnap and the Philosophy of Mathematics," in *Wissenschaft und Subjektivität*, ed. D. Bell and W. Vossenkuhl. Berlin: Academie Verlag, pp. 61–78.

Good, Irving John, 1950. *Probability and the Weighing of Evidence*. New York: Hafner Press.

1952. "Rational Decisions," *Journal of the Royal Statistical Society B* 14: 107–114.

1959. "Kinds of Probability," *Science* 129: 443–447.

1965. *The Estimation of Probabilities: An Essay on Modern Bayesian Methods*. Cambridge, MA: MIT Press.

1971. "46656 varieties of Bayesians," *American Statistician* 25: 62–63.

Goodman, Nelson, 1951/1977. *The Structure of Appearance*. Cambridge, MA: Harvard University Press; 3rd edition. Dordrecht: Reidel.

1955. *Fact, Fiction, and Forecast*. Cambridge, MA: Harvard University Press.

1963a. "Faulty Formalization," *Journal of Philosophy* 60: 578–579.

1963b. "The Significance of *Der Logische Aufbau der Welt*," in P. A. Schilpp (ed.), 1963, pp. 545–558.

Griffin, Nicholas (ed.), 2003. *The Cambridge Companion to Bertrand Russell*. Cambridge: Cambridge University Press.

Hahn, Hans, 1933/1987. *Logik, Mathematik, und Naturerkennen*. Vienna: Verlag Gerold; translated as "Logic, Mathematics, and Knowledge of Nature," in *Unified Science*, ed. B. McGuinness. Dordrecht: Reidel, pp. 24–45.

Haller, Rudolf, 1982/1991. "Das Neurath-Prinzip – Grundlagen und Folgerungen," in *Arbeiterbildung in der Zwischenkriegzeit*. Vienna:

Österreichisches Gesellschafts- und Wirtschaftsmuseum, pp. 79–87; translated as "The Neurath Principle: Its Grounds and Consequences," in Uebel (ed.), 1991, pp. 117–130.

1985/1991. "Der erste Wiener Kreis," in *Erkenntnis* 22: 341–358; translated as "The First Vienna Circle," in Uebel (ed.), 1991, pp. 95–108.

Hardcastle, Gary L. and Richardson, Alan W. (eds.), 2003. *Logical Empiricism in North America*. Minnesota Studies in the Philosophy of Science. Vol. XVIII. Minneapolis: University of Minnesota Press.

Hart, W. D., 1971. "The Real Sense of the *Tractatus*," *Journal of Philosophy* 68: 273–288.

Hempel, Carl G., 1935a/2000. "On the Logical Positivists' Theory of Truth," *Analysis* 2: 49–59; reprinted in Hempel 2000, pp. 9–21.

1935b/2000. "Some Remarks on Facts and Propositions," *Analysis* 2: 93–96; reprinted in Hempel 2000, pp. 21–25.

1958/1965. "The Theoretician's Dilemma: A Study in the Logic of Theory Construction," in Herbert Feigl *et al.* (eds.), *Minnesota Studies in the Philosophy of Science*. Vol. II. Minneapolis: University of Minnesota Press, pp. 37–98; reprinted in Hempel's *Aspects of Scientific Explanation*. New York: Free Press, pp. 173–226.

1963. "Implications of Carnap's Work for the Philosophy of Science," in P. A. Schilpp (ed.), 1963, pp. 685–710.

2000. *Selected Philosophical Essays*, ed. R. Jeffrey. Cambridge: Cambridge University Press.

Hilbert, David, 1899/1971. *Grundlagen der Geometrie*. 1st edition. Leipzig and Stuttgart: Teubner; translated by Leollnger from the revised 10th edition as *Foundations of Geometry*, enlarged by Paul Bernays. La Salle: Open Court.

1918. "Axiomatisches Denken," *Mathematische Annalen* 78: 405–456; reprinted in *Gesammelte Abhandlungen*. Vol. III. Berlin: Springer, pp. 146–56.

Hilbert, David and Ackermann, Wilhelm, 1928. *Grundzüge der theoretischen Logik*. Berlin: Springer.

Hill, Claire Ortiz, 1995/2000. "Husserl and Hilbert on Completeness," in J. Hintikka (ed.), *From Dedekind to Gödel*. Dordrecht: Kluwer, pp. 143–163; reprinted in C. O. Hill and G. E. Rossado Haddock (eds.), *Husserl or Frege?: Meaning, Objectivity and Mathematics*. Chicago and LaSalle, IL: Open Court, pp. 179–198.

Hintikka, Jaakko, 1966. "A Two-Dimensional Continuum of Inductive Methods," in J. Hintikka and P. Suppes (eds.), *Aspects of Inductive Logic*. Amsterdam: North-Holland, pp. 113–132.

1975a. "Carnap's Heritage in Logical Semantics," in J. Hintikka, 1975b, pp. 217–242.

(ed.), 1975b. *Rudolf Carnap, Logical Empiricist.* Dordrecht and Boston: Reidel.

Hintikka, Jaakko and Niinuluoto, Ilkka, 1980. "An Axiomatic Foundation for the Logic of Inductive Generalization," in R. Jeffrey (ed.), *Studies in Inductive Logic and Probability.* Vol. II. Berkeley: University of California Press, pp. 157–181.

Hochberg, Herbert, 1994. "Causal Connections, Universals, and Russell's Hypothetico-Scientific Realism," *Monist* 77: 71–92.

Hodges, Wilfrid, 1986. "Truth in a Structure," *Proceedings of the Aristotelian Society* 86: 135–151.

2004. "What Languages Have Tarski Truth Definitions?," *Annals of Pure and Applied Logic* 126: 93–113.

Hosiasson-Lindenbaum, Janina, 1940. "On Confirmation," *Journal of Symbolic Logic* 5: 133–148.

Howard, Don, 1996. "Relativity, *Eindeutigkeit*, and Monomorphism: Rudolf Carnap and the Development of the Categoricity Concept in Formal Semantics," in R. N. Giere and A. W. Richardson (eds.), 1996, pp. 115–164.

Howson, Colin, 1973. "Must the Logical Probability of Laws be Zero?," *British Journal for Philosophy of Science* 24: 153–163.

1987. "Popper, Prior Probabilities and Inductive Inference," *British Journal for Philosophy of Science* 38: 207–224.

Howson, Colin and Urbach, Peter, 1993. *Scientific Reasoning: The Bayesian Approach.* 2nd ed. La Salle, IL: Open Court.

Hudson, Robert, 1994. "Empirical Constraints in the *Aufbau*," *History of Philosophy Quarterly* 11: 237–251.

Hume, David, 1748. *Enquiry Concerning Human Understanding.* London: A. Millar.

Husserl, Edmund, 1891/1970. *Philosophie der Arithmetik: Psychologische und Logische Untersuchungen*, Bd. I. Halle: C. E. M. Pfeffer; reprinted in L. Eley (hrsg.), *Husserliana*, Bd. XI, 1970. The Hague: M. Nijhoff.

1900–1901/1970. *Logische Untersuchungen.* Bd. I-II. Halle: Max Niemeyer; translation of 2nd German edition, Bd. I and Bd. II, Teil 1, 1913, and Bd. II, Teil 2, 1921, by J. N. Findlay as *Logical Investigations*, 2 vols., 1970. London: Routledge & Kegan Paul.

1903/1981. *Rezension von Palágyi, Zeitschrift für Psychologie und Physiologie der Sinnesorgane* 31: 287–94; translated by D. Willard as "A Reply to a Critic of my Refutation of Logical Psychologism," in P. McCormick and F. Elliston (eds.), *Husserl: Shorter Works*, 1981. Notre Dame, IN: University of Notre Dame Press, pp. 152–158.

1911/1965. "Philosophie als strenge Wissenschaft," *Logos* 1: 289–341; reprint edition by W. Szilasi (ed.). Frankfurt am Main: V. Klostermann;

translated by Q. Lauer as "Philosophy as Rigorous Science," in *Phenomenology and the Crisis of Philosophy*. New York: Harper and Row, pp. 71–147.

1913/1950/1983. *Ideen zu einer reinen Phänomenologie und phänomenologischen Philosophie. Erstes Buch. Jahrbuch für Philosophie und phänomenologische Forschung.* Bd. I; augmented text with later insertions edited by W. Biemel, in *Husserliana* Vol. III, The Hague: M. Nijhoff; translated by F. Kersten as *Ideas Pertaining to a Pure Phenomenology and to Phenomenological Philosophy: First Book.* The Hague: M. Nijhoff.

1921/1970. *Logische Untersuchungen*, Bd. II, Teil 2. *Zweite Auflage.* Halle: M. Niemeyer; translated by J. Findlay as *Logical Investigations*, Vol. II, pt. 2. London: Routledge & Kegan Paul.

1929/1970/1974. *Formale und transzendentale Logik: Versuch einer Kritik der logischen Vernunft.* Halle: M. Niemeyer; Sonderdruck aus *Jahrbuch für Philosophie und phänomenologische Forschung*, Bd. X; reprinted in P. Janssen, *Husserliana.* Vol. XVII, 1974. The Hague: M. Nijhoff; translated by D. Cairns as *Formal and Transcendental Logic*, 1970. The Hague: M. Nijhoff.

1939a/1975. "Entwurf einer 'Vorrede' zu den Logischen Untersuchungen," published by E. Fink in *Tijdschrift voor Philosophie I*, pp. 106–133, 319–335; translated by P. Bossert and C. Peters as *Introduction to the Logical Investigations: A Draft of a Preface to the Logical Investigations, 1913.* The Hague: M. Nijhoff.

1939b/1973. *Erfahrung und Urteil: Untersuchungen zur Genealogie der Logik.* Edited by Ludwig Landgrebe. Prague: Academia Verlagsbuchhandlung; translation by J. Churchill and K. Ameriks as *Experience and Judgment: Investigations in a Genealogy of Logic.* Evanston, IL: Northwestern University Press.

1952. *Ideen zu einer reinen Phänomenologie und phänomenologischen Philosophie. Zweites Buch. Phänomenologische Untersuchungen zur Konstitution*, ed. M. Biemel. The Hague: M. Nijhoff.

1954/1970. *Die Krisis der europäischen Wissenschaften und die transzendentale Phänomenologie: Eine Einleitung in die phänomenologische Philosophie.* Parts published in *Philosophia* 1 (1936): 77–176; text first published in W. Biemel (ed.), *Husserliana.* Vol. V, 1954; translated by D. Carr as *The Crisis of European Sciences and Transcendental Phenomenology: an Introduction to Phenomenological Philosophy*, 1970. Evanston, IL: Northwestern University Press.

1956. "Zur Auseinandersetzung meiner transzendentalen Phänomenologie mit Kants Transzendentalphilosophie," in R. Boehm (ed.), *Erster*

Philosophie, I, Husserliana. Vol. VII. The Hague: M. Nijhoff, pp. 381–395.

1960/1973. *Cartesian Meditations: An Introduction to Phenomenology.* Translated by D. Cairns. The Hague: M. Nijhoff; original language printed in S. Strasser (ed.), *Cartesianische Meditationen und Pariser Vorträge. Husserliana.* Vol. I, 2nd edition, 1973. Haag: M. Nijhoff.

1961. "Aufgabe und Bedeutung der 'Logische Untersuchungen'," in W. Biemel (ed.), *Phänomenologische Psychologie, Vorlesungen Sommersemester 1925, Husserliana.* Vol. IX. The Hague: M. Nijhoff, pp. 20–46.

1966/2001. *Analysen zur passiven Synthesis. Aus Vorlesungs- und Forschungsmanuskripten 1918–1926.* Edited by M. Fleischer. *Husserliana.* Vol. XI; translated by A. Steinbock, with additional materials, as *Analyses Concerning Passive and Active Synthesis: Lectures on Transcendental Logic.* Dordrecht: Kluwer.

Hylton, Peter, 1990. *Russell, Idealism and the Emergence of Analytic Philosophy.* Oxford: Clarendon Press.

James, William, 1907/1948. "What Pragmatism Means," in *Pragmatism: A New Name for some old Ways of Thinking.* New York: Longmans, Green & Co., pp. 43–81; reprinted in *Essays in Pragmatism,* ed. Alburey Castell. New York: Hafner, pp. 141–158.

Jeffrey, Richard C., 1975. "Probability and Falsification: Critique of the Popper Program," *Synthese* 30: 95–117.

(ed.), 1980. *Studies in Inductive Logic and Probability.* Vol. II. Berkeley and Los Angeles: University of California Press.

1983. *The Logic of Decision.* 2nd edition. Chicago: University of Chicago Press.

1988. "Conditioning, Kinematics, and Exchangeability," in W. L. Harper and B. Skyrms (eds.), *Causation, Chance, and Credence.* Vol. I. Dordrecht: Kluwer, pp. 221–255.

1994. "Carnap's Voluntarism," in D. Prawitz, B. Skyrms, and D. Westerståhl (eds.), *Logic, Methodology, and Philosophy of Science.* Vol. IX, pp. 847–866.

2004. *Subjective Probability: The Real Thing.* Cambridge: Cambridge University Press.

Johnson, William Ernest, 1924. *Logic, Part III: The Logical Foundations of Science.* Cambridge: Cambridge University Press.

1932. "Probability: The Deductive and Inductive Problems," *Mind* 41: 409–423.

Kambartel, Friedrich, 1968. *Erfahrung und Struktur: Bausteine zu einer Kritik des Empirismus und Formalismus.* Frankfurt am Main: Suhrkamp Verlag, pp. 155–170.

Kant, Immanuel, 1781/1976. *Kritik der reinen Vernunft*, Riga: J. F. Hartknoch; Hamburg: Meiner.

1783/1950. *Prolegomena zu einer jeden küftigen Metaphysik die als Wissenschaft wird auftretten können.* Riga: J. F. Hartknoch; translated by Lewis White Beck as *Prolegomena to Any Future Metaphysics*. Paramus, NJ: Prentice Hall/Library of Liberal Arts.

Kemeny, John, 1948. "Models of Logical Systems," *Journal of Symbolic Logic* 13: 16–30.

1955. "Fair Bets and Inductive Probabilities," *Journal of Symbolic Logic* 20: 263–273.

1956. "A New Approach to Semantics: Part I," and "A New Approach to Semantics: Part II," *Journal of Symbolic Logic* 21: 1–27 and 149–161.

Ketland, J., 2004. "Empirical Adequacy and Ramsification," *British Journal for the Philosophy of Science* 55: 287–300.

Keynes, John Maynard, 1921. *A Treatise on Probability*. London: Macmillan.

Klein, Carsten, 2004. "Carnap on Categorical Concepts," in S. Awodey and C. Klein (eds.), 2004, pp. 295–316.

Knopp, Konrad, 1947. *Theory and Application of Infinite Series*. New York: Hafner Press.

Kraft, Viktor, 1950. *Der Wiener Kreis: Der Ursprung des Neopositivismus.* Vienna and New York: Springer.

Kripke, Saul, 1963. "Semantical Considerations on Modal Logics," *Acta Philosophica Fennica* 16: 83–94.

Kuhn, Thomas, 1962. *The Structure of Scientific Revolutions*. Chicago, University of Chicago Press.

Kuipers, Theo A. F., 1978. *Studies in Inductive Probability and Rational Expectation*. Dordrecht: D. Reidel.

Laqueur, W. Z., 1962. *Young Germany: A History of the German Youth Movement*. New York: Basic Books.

Lepore, Ernest, 1995. "Quine, Analyticity, and Transcendence," *Nous* 29: 468–480.

Lewis, Clarence Irving, 1970. "Logical Positivism and Pragmatism," in J. D. Goheen and J. L. Mothershead, Jr. (eds.), *Collected Papers of Clarence Irving Lewis*. Stanford, CA: Stanford University Press, pp. 92–112.

Lewis, David, 1984. "Putnam's Paradox," *Australasian Journal of Philosophy* 6: 221–236.

Lindenbaum, Adolf and Tarski, Alfred, 1935. "Über die Beschränktheit der Ausdrucksmittel deduktiver Theorien," *Ergebnisse eines mathematischen Kolloquiums* 7: 15–23.

Lotze, Rudolf H., 1874/1884. *Logik: Drei Bücher vom Denken, vom Untersuchungen und vom Erkennen. System der Philosophie*, Erster Teil. Leipzig: S. Hirzel; translated by B. Bosanquet as *Logic: In Three Books, of Thought, of Investigation, and of Knowledge*. Oxford: Clarendon Press.

1880/1888. *Logik: Drei Bücher vom Denken, vom Untersuchungen und vom Erkennen*. Zweite Auflage. Leipzig: S. Hirzel; translated by B. Bosanquet as *Logic: In Three Books, of Thought, of Investigation, and of Knowledge*. 2nd edition, 1888. Oxford: Clarendon Press.

Mac Lane, Saunders, 1938. "Carnap on Logical Syntax," *Bulletin of the American Mathematical Society*, pp. 171–176.

1986. *Mathematics, Form, and Function*. New York: Springer.

Mahnke, Dietrich, 1923/1977. "Von Hilbert zu Husserl: Erste Einführung in die Phänomenologie, besonders der formalen Mathematik," *Unterrichtsblätter* XXIX (3/4) *Abteilung Forschung und Schule*, pp. 34–37; translated by D. Boyer as "From Hilbert to Husserl: First Introduction to Phenomenology, Especially that of Formal Mathematics," in *Studies in History and Philosophy of Science* 8: 71–84.

Majer, Ulrich, 1997. "Husserl and Hilbert on Completeness," *Synthese* 110: 37–56.

Malament, David, forthcoming. "Classical Relativity Theory," in J. Butterfield and J. Earman (eds.), *Handbook of the Philosophy of Physics*. Amsterdam: Elsevier.

Mancosu, Paolo, 1999. "Between Russell and Hilbert: Behmann on the Foundations of Mathematics," *Bulletin of Symbolic Logic* 5: 303–330.

Maxwell, Grover, 1963. "The Necessary and the Contingent," in H. Feigl and G. Maxwell (eds.), *Minnesota Studies in the Philosophy of Science*. Vol. III. Minneapolis: University of Minnesota Press, pp. 398–404.

Mayer, Verena, 1992. "Carnap und Husserl," in D. Bell and W. Vossenkuhl (eds.), *Wissenschaft und Subjectivität*. Berlin: Akademie Verlag, pp. 185–201.

Mill, John Stuart, 1865/1979. *An Examination of Sir William Hamilton's Philosophy and of the Principal Questions Discussed in his Writings*. London: Longman, Green, Longman, Roberts, and Green; reprinted in J. M. Robson (ed.), *The Collected Works of John Stuart Mill*. Vol. IX. London and Toronto: Routledge & Kegan Paul and University of Toronto Press.

Miller, David, 1997. "Sir Karl Raimund Popper, CH, FBA," *Biographical Memoirs of Fellows of the Royal Society of London* 43: 367–409.

Mohanty, Jitendranath N., 1982. "Husserl and Frege: A New Look at Their Relationship," in Dreyfus (ed.), 1982 pp. 43–52.

Mormann, Thomas, 1999. "Neurath's Opposition to Tarskian Semantics," in J. Wolenski and E. Köhler (eds.), 1999, pp. 165–178.

2000. *Rudolf Carnap*. Munich: Beck.

2003. "Synthetic Geometry and the *Aufbau*," in T. Bonk (ed.), 2003, pp. 45–64.

2006a. "Carnap's Conventionalism and Differential Geometry," *PSA 2004: Proceedings of the Philosophy of Science Association*. East Lansing, MI: Philosophy of Science Association.

2006b. "Werte bei Carnap," in *Zeitschrift für philosophische Forschung*.

Nagel, Ernest, 1961. *The Structure of Science*. London: Routledge & Kegan Paul.

Neurath, Otto, 1931a/1973. *Empirische Soziologie*. Vienna: Springer; translated as "Empirical Sociology," in Neurath, 1973, pp. 319–421.

1931b/1983. "Physikalismus," *Scientia* 50: 297–303; translated as "Physicalism," in Neurath, 1983, pp. 52–57.

1932a/1983. "Protokollsätze," *Erkenntnis* 3: 204–214; translated as "Protocol Statements," in Neurath, 1983, pp. 91–99.

1932b. "Soziologie in physikalischer Sprache," *Erkenntnis* 2: 312.

1932c/1983. "Soziologie im Physikalismus," *Erkenntnis* 2: 393–431; translated as "Sociology in the Framework of Physicalism," in Neurath, 1983, pp. 58–90.

1934/1983. "Radikaler Physikalismus im 'Wirkliche Welt'," *Erkenntnis* 4: 346–362; translated as "Radical Physicalism and 'the Real World'," in Neurath, 1983, pp. 100–114.

1935/1983. "Physikalismus und Erkenntnisforschung," *Theoria* 2: 97–105, 234–236; translated as "Physicalism and the Investigation of Knowledge," in Neurath, 1983, pp.159–171.

1973. *Empiricism and Sociology*, ed. M. Neurath and R. S. Cohen. Dordrecht: Reidel.

1983. *Philosophical Papers*, ed. R. S. Cohen and M. Neurath. Dordrecht: Reidel.

Niiniluoto, Ilkka, 1999. "Theories of Truth: Vienna, Berlin, and Warsaw," in J. Wolenski and E. Köhler (eds.), 1999, pp. 17–26.

2003. "Carnap on Truth," in T. Bonk (ed.), 2003, Dordrecht: Kluwer, pp. 1–25.

Oberdan, Thomas, 1993. *Protocols, Truth and Convention*. Amsterdam: Rodopi.

Parsons, Charles D., 2001. "Husserl and the Linguistic Turn," in J. Floyd and S. Shieh (eds.), *Future Pasts: The Analytic Tradition in 20th Century Philosophy*. New York: Oxford University Press, pp. 123–141.

Passmore, John, 1966. *One Hundred Years of Philosophy*. 2nd edition. Harmondsworth, UK: Penguin Books.

Pincock, Christopher, 2002. "Russell's Influence on Carnap's *Aufbau*," *Synthese* 131: 1–37.

2005. "A Reserved Reading of Carnap's *Aufbau*," *Pacific Philosophical Quarterly* 86: 518–543.

Poincaré, Henri, 1902/1952. *La science et l'hypothèse*, Paris: E. Flammarion; translated as *Science and Hypothesis*. New York: Dover.

La valeur de Science. Paris: E. Flammarion; translated by G. B. Halstead as *The Value of Science*, in *The Foundations of Science*. New York: Harper and Row, pp. 199–355.

Popper, Karl, 1959/1968. *The Logic of Scientific Discovery*. New York: Basic Books; 2nd edition, New York: Harper and Row.

1963. "Truth, Rationality and the Growth of Knowledge," in *Conjectures and Refutations*. London: Routledge & Keagan Paul, pp. 239–260.

Post, Emil, 1921. "Introduction to a General Theory of Elementary Propositions," *American Journal of Mathematics* 43: 163–185.

Psillos, Stathis, 1999. *Scientific Realism: How Science Tracks the Truth*. London: Routledge.

2000. "Rudolf Carnap's 'Theoretical Concepts in Science'," *Studies in History and Philosophy of Science* 31: 151–172.

Putnam, Hillary, 1962. "What Theories are Not," in E. Nagel, P. Suppes, and A. Tarski (eds.), *Logic, Methodology and Philosophy of Science*. Stanford, CA: Stanford University Press, pp. 215–227.

Quine, Willard Van Orman, 1936/1976. "Truth by Convention," in *Philosophical Essays for Alfred North Whitehead*, ed. O. H. Lee. London: Longman, Green and Co., pp. 90–124; reprinted in Quine 1976, pp. 77–106.

1948/1980. "On What There Is," *Review of Metaphysics* 2: 21–38; reprinted in Quine, 1980, pp. 1–19.

1951/1963/1980. "Two Dogmas of Empiricism," *Philosophical Review* 60: 20–43; reprinted in Quine, *From a Logical Point of View*. 2nd edition, revised. New York: Harper, pp. 20–46; reprinted in Quine, *From a Logical Point of View*, 2nd edition, revised. Cambridge, MA: Harvard University Press, pp. 20–46.

1963/1976. "Carnap and Logical Truth," in Schilpp 1963, pp. 385–406; reprinted in Quine, 1976, pp. 107–132.

1974. *Roots of Reference*. LaSalle, IL: Open Court.

1976. *Ways of Paradox*. Revised and enlarged. Cambridge, MA: Harvard University Press.

1980. *From a Logical Point of View*. 2nd edition. Cambridge, MA: Harvard University Press.

1990/1992. *Pursuit of Truth*. Cambridge, MA: Harvard University Press.

Ramsey, Frank Plumpton, 1931a/1960. "Theories," in R. B. Braithwaite (ed.), *The Foundations of Mathematics and Other Logical Essays*. London:

Kegan Paul, Trench, Trubner & Co., pp. 212–236; later printing: Patterson, NJ: Littlefield-Adams.

1931b. "Truth and Probability," in R. B. Braithwaite (ed.), *The Foundations of Mathematics and Other Logical Essays*. London: Kegan Paul, Trench Trubner & Co., pp. 156–198.

Rawls, John, 1971. *A Theory of Justice*. Cambridge, MA: Harvard University Press.

Reck, Erich H., 2004. "From Frege and Russell to Carnap: Logic and Logicism in the 1920s," in S. Awodey and C. Klein (eds.), 2004, pp. 151–180.

Reck, Erich and Awodey, Steve (ed. and trans.), 2004. *Frege's Lectures on Logic: Carnap's Student Notes, 1910–1914*. Chicago: Open Court.

Reichenbach, Hans, 1928/1958. *Philosophie der Raum-Zeit-Lehre*. Berlin: W. de Gruyter; translated by Maria Reichenbach as *Philosophy of Space and Time*. New York: Dover.

1938. *Experience and Prediction*. Chicago: University of Chicago Press.

Reisch, George, 1991. "Did Kuhn Kill Logical Empiricism?" *Philosophy of Science* 58: 264–277.

2003. "Disunity in the *International Encyclopedia of Unified Science*," in G. L. Hardcastle and A. W. Richardson (eds.), 2003, pp. 197–215.

2005. *How the Cold War Transformed Philosophy of Science*. Cambridge: Cambridge University Press.

Rescher, Nicholas (ed.), 1985. *The Heritage of Logical Positivism*. Lanham and New York: University Press of America.

Richardson, Alan W., 1994. "Carnap's Principle of Tolerance," *Aristotelian Society*, Supplementary Volume 68: 67–82.

1997. "Two Dogmas about Logical Empiricism: Carnap and Quine on Logic, Epistemology, and Empiricism," *Philosophical Topics* 25: 145–168.

1998. *Carnap's Construction of the World: The* Aufbau *and the Emergence of Logical Empiricism*. Cambridge: Cambridge University Press.

2003a. "The Geometry of Knowledge: Lewis, Becker, Carnap and the Formalization of Philosophy in the 1920s," *Studies in the History and Philosophy of Science* 34: 165–182.

2003b. "Logical Empiricism, American Pragmatism, and the Fate of Scientific Philosophy in North America," in G. L. Hardcastle and A. W. Richardson (eds.), 2003, pp. 1–24.

Rickert, Heinrich, 1892. *Der Gegenstand der Erkenntnis*. Freiburg: Mohn.

Ricketts, Thomas, 1994. "Carnap's Principle of Tolerance, Empiricism and Conventionalism," in P. Clark and B. Hale (eds.), *Reading Putnam*. Oxford: Blackwell, pp. 176–200.

1996. "Carnap: From Logical Syntax to Semantics," in R. N. Giere and A. W. Richardson (eds.), 1996, pp. 231–250.

2003. "Languages and Calculi," in G. Hardcastle and A. Richardson (eds.), 2003, pp. 257–280.

2004. "Frege, Carnap, and Quine: Continuities and Discontinuities," in S. Awodey and C. Klein (eds.), 2004, pp. 181–202.

Robb, A. A., 1914. *A Theory of Space and Time*. Cambridge: Cambridge University Press.

Robinson, Abraham, 1963/1974. *Introduction to Model Theory and the Metamathematics of Algebra*. Amsterdam: North-Holland and New York: American Elsevier; 2nd revised edition.

Rollinger, Robin D., 2004. "Brentano and Husserl," in Dale Jacquette (ed.), *The Cambridge Companion to Brentano*. New York: Cambridge University Press, pp. 255–276.

Roy, Jean-Michel, 2004. "Carnap's Husserlian Reading of the *Aufbau*," in S. Awodey and C. Klein (eds.), 2004, pp. 41–62.

Russell, Bertrand, 1903. *The Principles of Mathematics*. London: George Allen & Unwin.

1912/1967. *The Problems of Philosophy*. London: William and Norgate; later printing. Oxford: Oxford University Press.

1914a/1926. *Our Knowledge of the External World as a Field for Scientific Method in Philosophy*. La Salle and Chicago: Open Court; revised edition, 1926. London: Allen & Unwin.

1914b/1986. "The Relation of Sense-Data to Physics," reprinted in J. Slater (ed.), 1986, pp. 3–26.

1914c/1986. "On Scientific Method in Philosophy," Oxford: Clarendon Press; reprinted in J. Slater (ed.), 1986, pp. 55–73.

1919. *Introduction to Mathematical Philosophy*. London: Allen & Unwin.

1921. *The Analysis of Mind*. London: Allen & Unwin.

1927. *The Analysis of Matter*. New York: Harcourt, Brace and Co.

1940. *Inquiry into Meaning and Truth*. London: Allen & Unwin.

1948. *Human Knowledge: Its Scope and Limits*. New York: Simon and Schuster.

1967–1969/1998. *Autobiography*. London: Routledge.

1986. "Letter on Sense Data," in J. Slater (ed.), 1986, pp. 88–89.

Ryckman, Thomas A., 1996. "Einstein Agonists: Weyl and Reichenbach on Geometry and the General Theory of Relativity," in R. N. Giere and A. W. Richardson (eds.), 1996, pp. 165–209.

2005. *The Reign of Relativity: Philosophy in Physics 1915–1925*. Oxford Studies in Philosophy of Science Series. New York: Oxford University Press.

Sarkar, Sahotra, 2003. "Husserl's Role in Carnap's *Der Raum*," in T. Bonk (ed.), 2003, pp. 179–190.

Sauer, Werner, 1985. "Carnap's *Aufbau* in Kantianischer Sicht," *Grazer Philosophische Studien* 23: 19–35.

1989. "On the Kantian Background of Neopositivism," *Topoi* 8: 111–119.

Savage, Leonard J., 1954. *The Foundations of Statistics*. New York: John Wiley. Reprinted 1972, New York: Dover.

Savage, Wade and Anderson, Anthony (eds.), 1989. *Rereading Russell*. Minnesota Studies in the Philosophy of Science. Vol. XII. Minneapolis: University of Minnesota Press.

Scanlan, Michael, 1991. "Who Were the American Postulate Theorists?," *Journal of Symbolic Logic* 56: 981–1002.

Schilpp, Paul Arthur (ed.), 1963. *The Philosophy of Rudolf Carnap*. The Library of Living Philosophers. Vol. XI. LaSalle: Open Court.

Schlick, Moritz, 1918/1974. *Allgemeine Erkenntnislehre*, Berlin: Springer; translated from 2nd edition by A. E. Blumberg as *General Theory of Knowledge* with an Introduction by H. Feigl and A. E. Blumberg. New York: Springer.

1926/1979. "Erleben, Erkennen, Metaphysik," *Kant-Studien* 31: 146–158; translated as "Experience, Cognition, and Metaphysics," in Schlick, 1979, pp. 99–111.

1930/1979. "Die Wende der Philosophie," *Erkenntnis* 1: 4–11; translated as "The Turning Point in Philosophy," in Schlick, 1979, pp. 154–160.

1934a/1979. "Über das Fundament der Erkenntnis," *Erkenntnis* 4: 79–99; translated as "On the Foundation of Knowledge," in Schlick, 1979, pp. 370–387.

1934b/1979. "Philosophie und Naturwissenschaft," *Erkenntnis* 4: 379–396; translated as "Philosophy and Natural Science," in Schlick, 1979, pp. 139–153.

1935a/1979. "Facts and Propositions," *Analysis* 2: 65–70; reprinted in Schlick, 1979, pp. 400–404.

1935b/1979. "Sur les 'Constatations'," Part C of *Sur le Fondement de la Connaissance* (French translation of German original by Charles E. Vouillemin), Actualités scientifique et industrielles 289. Paris: Hermann & Cie.; translated as "On 'Affirmations'," in Schlick, 1979, pp. 407–413.

1936/1979. "Sind die Naturgesetze Conventionen?," in *Induction et Probabilité*, *Actes du Congrès International de Philosophie Scientifique*, Paris 1935, IV, *Actualités scientifique et industrielles* 391. Paris: Hermann & Cie., pp. 8–17; translated as "Are the Laws of Nature Conventions?," in Schlick, 1979, pp. 437–445.

1937/1979. "L'École de Vienne et la Philosophie Traditionnelle," in *L'Unité de la Science: la Méthode et les Méthodes*, Travaux de IXe

Congrès International de Philosophie IV, Actualités scientifique et industrielles 533. Paris: Hermann & Cie., pp. 99–107; translated as "The Vienna School and Traditional Philosophy," in Schlick, 1979, pp. 491–498.

1979. *Philosophical Papers.* Vol. II. Ed. H. Mulder and B. van de Velde-Schlick. Dordrecht: Reidel.

Schlotter, S., 2004. *Die Totalität der Kultur: Philosophisches Denken und politisches Handeln bei Bruno Bauch.* Würzburg: Königshausen and Neumann.

Sellars, Wilfrid, 1956/1997. "Empiricism and the Philosophy of Mind," in *Minnesota Studies in the Philosophy of Science, Vol. I: The Foundations of Science and the Concepts of Psychology and Psychoanalysis,* H. Feigl and M. Scriven, eds. Minneapolis: The University of Minnesota Press, pp. 253–329; reprinted as *Empiricism and the Philosophy of Mind.* Cambridge, MA: Harvard University Press.

Sher, Gila, 1991. *The Bounds of Logic: A Generalized Viewpoint.* Cambridge, MA: MIT Press.

Sieg, Wilfried, 1999. "Hilbert's Program: 1917–1922," *Bulletin of Symbolic Logic* 5: 1–44.

Skorupski, John, 1989. *John Stuart Mill.* London and New York: Routledge.

Slater, John (ed.), 1986. *The Collected Papers of Bertrand Russell.* Vol. VIII. London: Allen & Unwin.

Sluga, Hans, 1980. *Gottlob Frege.* The Arguments of the Philosophers Series. London: Routledge & Kegan Paul.

1999. "Truth before Tarski," in *Alfred Tarski and the Vienna Circle,* ed. J. Wolenski and E. Köhler, pp. 27–41.

Soames, Scott, 2003. *Philosophical Analysis in the Twentieth Century.* Princeton, NJ: Princeton University Press.

Spiegelberg, Herbert, 1981. *The Context of the Phenomenological Movement.* The Hague: M. Nijhoff.

Stadler, Friedrich, 2001. *The Vienna Circle: Studies in the Origins, Development, and Influence of Logical Empiricism.* Translated by C. Nielsen et al. Vienna and New York: Springer.

Stein, Howard, 1992. "Was Carnap Entirely Wrong, After All?," *Synthese* 93: 275–295.

Stigler, Stephen M., 1982. "Thomas Bayes's Bayesian Inference," *Journal of the Royal Statistical Society Series A,* 145: 250–258.

Tarski, Alfred, 1932. "Der Wahrheitsbegriff in den Sprachen der deduktiven Disziplinen," *Akademischer Anzeiger der Akademie der Wissenschaften in Wien, Mathematisch-naturwissenschaftliche Klasse* 69: 23–25.

1936a/1956. "Der Wahrheitsbegriff in den formalisierten Sprachen," in *Studia Philosophica* 1: 261–405; translated as "The Concept of Truth in Formalized Languages," in Tarski 1956, pp. 152–278.

1936b/1956. "Über den Begriff der logischen Folgerung," in *Actes du Congrès International de Philosophie Scientifique III*. Paris: Hermann, pp. 1–8; translated by J. H. Woodger as "On the Concept of Logical Consequence," in Tarski, 1956, pp. 409–420.

1956/1983. *Logic, Semantics, and Metamathematics*. Oxford: Oxford University Press; 2nd edition, Indianapolis: Hackett.

Tsou, Jonathan Y., 2003. "The Justification of Concepts in Carnap's *Aufbau*," *Philosophy of Science* 70: 671–689.

Uebel, Thomas E. (ed.), 1991. *Rediscovering the Forgotten Vienna Circle: Austrian Studies of Otto Neurath and the Vienna Circle*. Dordrecht: Kluwer.

1992a. *Overcoming Logical Positivism from Within*. Amsterdam: Rodopi.

1992b. "Rational Reconstruction as Elucidation? Carnap in the Early Protocol Sentence Debate," *Synthese* 93: 107–144.

1995. "Physicalism in Wittgenstein and the Vienna Circle," in *Physics, Philosophy and the Scientific Community: Festschrift for Robert S. Cohen*, ed. K. Gavroglu, S. Schweber, and M. Wartofsky. Dordrecht: Kluwer, pp. 327–356.

2001. "Neurath and Carnap in Exile: Can their Disputes Be Resolved?," *International Studies in the Philosophy of Science* 15: 211–220.

2003 "On the Austrian Roots of Logical Empiricism: The Case of the First Vienna Circle," in *Logical Empiricism: Historical and Contemporary Perspectives*, ed. P. Parrini, W. Salmon, and M. Salmon. Pittsburgh: University of Pittsburgh Press, pp. 67–93.

2004. "Carnap, the Left Vienna Circle and Neopositivist Antimetaphysics," in S. Awodey and C. Klein (eds.), 2004, pp. 247–278.

2005a. "Learning Logical Tolerance: Hans Hahn on the Foundations of Mathematics," *History and Philosophy of Logic* 26: 175–209.

2005b. "Political Philosophy of Science in Logical Empiricism: The Left Vienna Circle," *Studies in History and Philosophy of Science* 36: 754–773.

2007. "Philosophy of Social Science in Early Logical Empiricism," in A. W. Richardson and T. E. Uebel (eds.), *The Cambridge Companion to Logical Empiricism*. Cambridge: Cambridge University Press.

van Bentham, Johan, 1978. "Ramsey Eliminability," *Studia Logica* 37: 321–336.

van Fraassen Bas C., 1980. *The Scientific Image*. Oxford: Oxford University Press.

Venn, John, 1866. *The Logic of Chance*. London: Macmillan.

Waismann, Friedrich, 1930. "Logische Analyse des Wahrscheinlichkeitsbe-
griffs," *Erkentniss* 1: 228–248.

Wedberg, Anders, 1973. "How Carnap Built the World in 1928," *Synthese*
25: 337–371.

Werner, Meike, 2003. *Moderne in der Provinz: Kulturelle Experimente im
Fin de Siècle Jena*. Göttingen: Wallstein.

Weyl, Hermann, 1927. "Philosophie der Mathematik und Naturwissenschaft," in *Handbuch der Philosophie*, ed. Alfred Bäumler and Man-
fred Schröter. Munich: R. Oldenbourg.

Whitehead, Alfred North and Russell, Bertrand, 1910–1913. *Principia Mathematica*. Vols. I–III. Cambridge: Cambridge University Press.

Willard, Dallas, 1984. *Logic and the Objectivity of Knowledge: A Study in
Husserl's Early Philosophy*. Athens, OH: Ohio University Press.

Williams, P. M., 1973. "Review of R. Cohen and M. Wartofsky (eds.), *Boston
Studies in the Philosophy of Science Vol. 8*," *British Journal for the
Philosophy of Science* 24: 299–307.

Windelband, Wilhelm, 1884. "Beiträge zur Lehre vom negativen Urtheil,"
in *Strassburger Abhandlungen zur Philosophie: Eduard Zeller zu
seinen siebzigsten Geburtstage*. Tübingen: C. B. Mohr (P. Siebeck),
pp. 167–195.

Winnie, John, 1970/1975. "Theoretical Analyticity," in R. Cohen and M.
Wartofsky (eds.), *Boston Studies in the Philosophy of Science*. Vol. VIII.
Dordrecht and Boston: Reidel, pp. 289–305; reprinted in Hintikka (ed.),
1975, pp. 143–159.

Wittgenstein, Ludwig, 1921/1922/1998. *Logisch-philosophische Abhandlung*, in *Annalen der Naturphilosophie* 14: 185–262; also (in 1922)
as *Tractatus Logico-Philosophicus*. London: Routledge & Kegan Paul;
reprinted in *Logisch-philosophische Abhandlung*, ed. B. McGuinness
and J. Schulte. Frankfurt am Main: Suhrkamp, pp. 1–178.

Wolenski, Jan and Köhler, Eckehart (eds.), 1999. *Alfred Tarski and the Vienna
Circle*. Dordrecht: Kluwer.

Wolters, Gereon, 1985. "'The First Man Who Almost Wholly Understands
Me': Carnap, Dingler, and Conventionalism," in N. Rescher (ed.), 1985,
pp. 93–107.

Zabell, S. L,. 1982. "W. E. Johnson's 'Sufficientness Postulate'," *Annals of
Statistics* 10: 1091–1099.

1988. "Symmetry and its Discontents," in *Causation, Chance, and Credence*. Vol. I., ed. W. L. Harper and B. Skyrms. Dordrecht: Kluwer,
pp. 155–190.

1989. "The Rule of Succession," *Erkentniss* 31: 283–321.

1992. "Predicting the Unpredictable," *Synthese* 90: 205–232.

1996. "Confirming Universal Generalizations," *Erkentniss* 45: 267–283.

1997. "The Continuum of Inductive Methods Revisited," in *The Cosmos of Science: Essays of Exploration*, ed. John Earman and John D. Norton. Pitttsburg-Konstanz Series in the Philosophy and History of Science. University of Pittburgh Press/Universitätsverlag Konstanz, pp. 351–385.

Zach, Richard, 1999. "Completeness before Post: Bernays, Hilbert, and the Development of Propositional Logic," *Bulletin of Symbolic Logic* 5: 331–366.

Zahar, Elie, 2001. *Poincaré's Philosophy: From Conventionalism to Phenomenology*. Chicago: Open Court.

Zahar, Elie and Worrall, John, 2001. "Ramseyfication and Structural Realism," in E. Zahar, *Poincaré's Philosophy: From Conventionalism to Phenomenology*, appendix IV. Chicago: Open Court, pp. 236–251.

Zilsel, Edgar, 1941. "Phenomenology and Natural Science," *Philosophy of Science* 8: 26–32.

INDEX